AT-RISK STUDENTS

SUNY Series, Youth Social Services, Schooling and Public Policy
Barry M. Franklin and José R. Rosario, Series Editors

AT-RISK STUDENTS

Portraits, Policies, Programs, and Practices

edited by

ROBERT DONMOYER

AND

RAYLENE KOS

State University
of New York
Press

Published by
State University of New York Press, Albany

Production by Susan Geraghty
Marketing by Lynne Lekakis

Printed in the United States of America

For information, address State University of New York
Press, State University Plaza, Albany, N.Y., 12246

Library of Congress Cataloging-in-Publication Data

At-risk students : portraits, policies, programs, and practices /
    edited by Robert Donmoyer and Raylene Kos.
        p. cm. — (SUNY series youth social services, schooling, and
    public policy)
    Includes bibliographical references and index.
    ISBN 0-7914-1393-4
    1. Socially handicapped children—Education—United States.
    2. Socially handicapped children—Education—United States—Case
    studies. I. Donmoyer, Robert. II. Kos, Raylene. III. Series.
    LC4091.A925 1993
371.96′7—dc20   92-5481
                                                                CIP

10 9 8 7 6 5 4 3 2 1

CONTENTS

INTRODUCTION

This book is about students who are at risk of either not completing high school or of completing school without the necessary knowledge, skills, and attitudes to function in adult life. The basic premise of the book is that at-risk students are highly idiosyncratic, far more idiosyncratic than our common-sense stereotypes and even researchers' ideal types would lead us to believe.

The assumption about idiosyncracy is supported in the first part of the book by a series of case studies or verbal portraits of particular at-risk students. Some of the students portrayed here fit our traditional notions of students at risk, but their portraits reveal idiosyncratic features which are at least as significant as their stereotypical ones. There are also portraits of students who are clearly at risk but who would not normally be labeled as such.

The second half of the book focuses on programs, policies, and practices designed to help at-risk students. Some of the chapters demonstrate what happens when our attempts to help are insensitive to the sort of idiosyncracy illuminated in the book's first section. Other chapters explore new ways of approaching and thinking about educational programs, policies, and practices—ways which might better accommodate the complexity of the students we wish to serve.

The idea for this book grew out of our own experiences as educators. Both of us began our careers in education teaching students who now would be labeled at risk. In the early 1970s, for example, Robert Donmoyer taught "disadvantaged" students (the label of choice at the time) in a Harlem elementary school. He quickly learned that although all of his students displayed the characteristics then associated with the term "disadvantaged" and now associated with the term "at risk," they were also as different from each other as they were similar. Maritza and Ricardo, for instance, responded positively to teacher praise, as researchers predicted they would, but Danny seemed indifferent to the positive comments of his teacher and Marvin reacted with outright hostility.

1

Later, as he sat in the kitchen of one of his students' homes and listened as his student translated his question to a parent into Spanish and the parent's answer into English, he could not help but wonder who was the disadvantaged one. He also realized that his student got little credit for his bilingual abilities in the school setting. If anything, his bilingualism was regarded as a liability; at best it was ignored.

The definition of *disadvantaged* seemed even more problematic when the prospect of budget cuts and unemployment caused Donmoyer to retreat to a school in an affluent suburb. There he encountered students who economically wanted for nothing, but they often seemed disadvantaged in other ways. Sometimes the advantages they had even put them at a disadvantage. Many of the suburban students, for instance, spent their days going from violin lessons to soccer clinics to dance classes to a multitude of other well-planned, professionally organized activities. They spent their days, in other words, with teachers and coaches who structured their time and told them what to do. Donmoyer could not help but wonder what would happen to these students when they entered the adult world where there would not always be a coach or a teacher to structure their time and organize their experiences. Oddly, while many of Donmoyer's inner-city students seemed disadvantaged by an absence of structure in their lives, his suburban students seemed disadvantaged by too much structure. While scholars had written extensively about the former problem, they had been virtually silent about the latter.

Raylene Kos's early experiences in education were strikingly similar. During an interview for her first job, she was asked by a superintendent whether she thought she could work with "inner-city students." The superintendent worded it as a warning—"Are you sure you want to work with such students?" Feeling a bit apprehensive after such an introduction to this particular teaching position, she interviewed with the principal of the school and blurted out, "I think you should know that I've never had any experience with inner-city children." He responded coolly, saying, "And what is the difference between my students and other students?" Raylene got the job and embarked upon a critical learning experience. Many of her students had overwhelming problems in their lives, but their problems were not all the same, the way they

handled their problems were not the same, and they themselves were not the same. It soon became apparent that the term "inner-city students" was so general as to be meaningless. It did not help her understand her students' difficulties, it did not inform her as to how to best help them learn, and it did not help students to have hope for their futures. As one fifteen-year-old, self-proclaimed prostitute told her, "We the bad ones, Miz Kos, and you can't fuckin' teach us."

Later in her career, Raylene taught students in a somewhat rural district. These learning-disabled students, who had been through nine years of programs especially designed for their learning needs, were hostile and disengaged from school. The repetitive programs, the separation from their peers so that they could receive individualized instruction, the years of bearing the label of being dumb had taken their toll. Yet these were not students without talents. One young man had a knack for drafting. A shy girl wrote poetry which her mother rewrote to correct the spelling. Another boy could tear down a motorcycle engine and put it back together in working condition without ever having received instruction in engines. Another young man who had the gift of gab was considered virtually unteachable because of his "visual/auditory processing deficits." But, he had a burning desire to be a car salesman, and he seemingly had the talent to be successful at the job.

After entering the lives of these very diverse students, Raylene came to realize that school structures, set programs, and teacher expectations had as much, if not more, to do with student achievement as any characteristic ascribed to a particular student. Indeed, many of her students only felt "disadvantaged" or "disabled" in the school setting.

When we left the world of practice and entered academia, we carried with us these experiences and the insights and sensitivities they generated. Both of us, for instance, have thought and written about the limitations of traditional social science research methods. Both have been involved with the development of alternative research procedures, procedures which are intended to serve very different functions than the ones served by traditional social science methodology. Both of us also have supplemented our focus on the impact of research on educators' cognitive structures with stud-

ies of the impact of organizational structures on learning. This book is a manifestation of all these concerns.

PART 1

Portraits

CHAPTER 1

At-Risk Students: Insights from/about Research

Robert Donmoyer, The Ohio State University
Raylene Kos, Westerville City Schools

This chapter reviews the research on at-risk students. The chapter also looks critically at the research and considers how research can and cannot contribute to our efforts to help at-risk youth.

The statistics reported by the popular press are startling:

- Each year 700,000 students drop out of high school, costing the nation more than $240 billion in lost earnings and foregone taxes.
- Dropout rates for black and Hispanic youth are two times greater than the white student dropout rate.
- A third of high school graduates cannot order two items from a lunch menu and then calculate how much change they are owed after paying a cashier three dollars.
- By the year 2000, the bulk of the labor force will come from minority-group students; nearly 40 percent of those students are now considered functionally illiterate.
- In many urban areas 40 to 50 percent of black teenagers are unemployed; at times the amount has risen to 70 percent.

- Every year nearly half a million teenagers give birth; half of these teenagers never complete high school; many end up on welfare.

- Ninety percent of black teenage mothers are unmarried at the time of their child's birth; only 33 percent eventually marry.[1]

Statistics such as these have created widespread concern about students who are at risk of either not graduating from school or of graduating without the necessary academic, social, and emotional skills to function as productive citizens and workers. Concern has been expressed not only by humanitarians and educators; members of the business community and other hardheaded pragmatists have also been forced to recognize the problem. Levin (1989a), for instance, has made the case for increased funding for educational programs for at-risk students on decidedly pragmatic grounds. He presents a series of cost-benefit analyses which clearly demonstrate that the cost of paying for added educational programs today is significantly less than the cost associated with public assistance, unemployment benefits, adult education, job training, and judicial system expenses in the future. It is not surprising that those concerned about who will pay their pensions in the future have joined the large cadre of individuals who recognize both the magnitude of the problem of at-risk students and the need to translate concern into action.

Increased funding, of course, is a necessary but not a sufficient condition for ameliorating the problem. We need also to be concerned with the substance of the policies, programs, and practices we fund. Educational interventions always have the potential to make matters worse rather than better, to contribute to the problem rather than be part of the solution. The War on Poverty during the 1960s, for instance, demonstrated the limits of merely throwing money at problems: Great Society programs designed to help the poor often became mired in bureaucratic rules and procedures that hindered rather than helped educators and others attempting to solve problems associated with poverty.

Before taking action, therefore, it makes sense to consult research so that our actions will be intelligent. It also makes sense to examine research findings critically. We now know that no research is totally objective and that research "findings" frequently tell as much about who did the studying as they do about what was being studied. Great Society programs, it should be remembered, were developed with the assistance of some of the most astute social scientists and policy analysts around and were based on some of the most sophisticated social science research available. Yet this expertise could not guarantee programs that could meet the needs of *particular* people in *particular* sites. Indeed, we will argue that if the linkage between research, policy, and practice is too tight, one can guarantee there will be problems.

The points made thus far can be stated succinctly: Before we attempt to resolve the problem of at-risk students, it makes sense to ask both what research reveals and what it conceals about the problem. This chapter addresses both of these questions. In the process it also articulates the rationale which has guided the development of this book.

INSIGHTS FROM RESEARCH

Here we will review literature related to two questions: (1) What characteristics and conditions place students at risk? and (2) What types of programs and practices can best meet the needs of at-risk students? For both questions, the literature provides less than definitive answers.

Characteristics and Conditions

Traditionally, at-risk students have been defined in terms of their personal and familial characteristics. Sometimes school performance variables such as absenteeism and below-grade-level academic performance are also cited as indicators of at-riskness, but these generally are seen as intervening variables caused by out-of-school factors (Richardson et al. 1989). Specific factors associated with being at risk generally include membership in a racial or ethnic minority, low socioeconomic status, a single parent in the home, and low educational attainment by one or both parent(s) (Pallas, Natriello, and McDill 1989).

It is difficult, however, to establish causal relationships between any of these factors and students' at-risk status. One problem is that variables cannot normally be isolated. In our society, minorities are more likely to be poor; women who are heads of households often earn less money than male heads of households; minority families are more likely to be headed by a single parent, usually female; and the poor are more likely to leave school early (Fernandez and Shu 1988).

An even more significant problem is suggested by Trueba (1988): Many studies provide examples of students who may be categorized by all of the previously mentioned conditions yet still be quite successful in school. Hahn (1987) makes the same point with negative evidence; he notes that statistics released by the Chicago Board of Education revealed that the dropout rate even among white students was 38 percent.

Richardson et al. (1989) have argued that the problems associated with identifying characteristics and conditions which put students at risk are not merely technical; rather talk of at-risk students is rooted in an epidemiological metaphor of school success and failure and this metaphor limits the characteristics and conditions we consider. Richardson and her colleagues note that the purpose of epidemiological research in the field of medicine is to identify categories of people who are prone to certain diseases or illnesses and then to find methods for lessening the likelihood that disease and illness will occur within the identified groups. "It is this identification-and-prevention/treatment sequence," Richardson and her colleagues write, "which the term at risk seems to carry when used in non-medical areas of education, such as study of school failure and dropping out" (1989, p. 4). Later they add:

> Unfortunately, the decision to employ an epidemiological mode for the study of these problems limits educators' ways of thinking about these phenomena. Since the problem is believed to be inherent in the student, then the search for the cause is limited to the characteristics of the students themselves. Characteristics of our society and school are left unexamined. (p. 6)

The research of Richardson et al. in fact suggests that at riskness involves much more than the characteristics students bring with them to school and the conditions from which students have come. Indeed, the data Richardson and her colleagues report demonstrate that the defining properties of at riskness vary from classroom to classroom and even within a classroom as the classroom changes over time. For example, when new students who display more dramatic adjustment problems enter the classroom, students who once were labeled at risk by the classroom teacher may no longer be defined as such. Similarly a student may be labeled at risk by one teacher but not by another, either because the student responds differently to the teachers' different teaching styles or because each teacher defines at risk differently.

Findings such as these have led Richardson and her colleagues to propose a social constructivist model rather than an epidemiological one to explain at riskness in schools. They describe the model as follows:

> It is an interactive view in which the perception of at-riskness is constructed within a particular social or cultural context. The child brings to the classroom a certain number of characteristics that have been shaped by background and personal factors and past experiences in school. This child interacts with a classroom context that includes other children, teacher(s), and materials. In addition, what happens in the classroom is shaped, in part, by school level factors that are often influenced by district level factors. The focus in this approach is not on the child alone, but on the interaction between the child and these nested contexts. (1989, p. 7)

Richardson et al. conclude that there are sufficient commonalities in American culture and enough similarities among classrooms, schools, and districts within that culture so that some students will more than likely be categorized as at risk in any educational setting. These students display either clearly identifiable physical, cognitive, or emotional conditions or have background and family circumstances which make it extremely unlikely that they can learn in any of this culture's classrooms and schools. Special assistance will be required to help these students as well as other students whose problems are masked by their ability to play the school's social game even while they are failing to master essential academic material. Richardson and her colleagues, however, also suggest that large numbers of students who are classified as being at risk in certain educational situations can be quite successful when classroom and school characteristics change. This fact encourages us to move beyond an epidemiological perspective and its attempts to identify personal characteristics and conditions which predict at-riskness. Instead, we can focus on the properties of schools and classrooms which encourage success and failure (see, for example, Kos 1991). As various scholars have noted (see, for example, Wehlage and Rutter 1986), educators can more easily control school and classroom variables than they can the personal, socioeconomically based variables traditionally associated with the term "at risk."

School Programs and Classroom Practices

The conclusion that school programs and classroom practices may be influential in either placing or not placing students at risk suggests a second question: What programs and practices should be employed to maximize the likelihood of school success for students who, under some circumstances, might be at risk? The answer from the literature is less than definitive. The literature, in fact, endorses a rich array of approaches. Not all of the approaches are contradictory, of course, but they often suggest quite different variables to which we should attend in planning and funding programs.

Implicit in the programmatic literature, in fact, are five ideal types of school programs and practices:

1. supplemental programs;
2. whole-school restructuring programs;
3. therapy programs;
4. intervention team approaches; and
5. community/home/school partnership programs.

Supplemental Programs   This is the most common response discussed in the literature. The response is consistent with the epidemiological orientation discussed above.

Supplemental programs can take many different forms. Jones, Pollock, and Marockie (1988), for instance, describe an all-day kindergarten program which their data indicate helped children overcome behaviors that led to failure." Mikulecky (1990) describes a supplemental summer program which, the data suggest, reduced summer learning loss among at-risk students. Cahoon (1989) describes a special volunteer tutor program which paired university students with at-risk elementary school students; self-report data indicate this program was perceived as being very beneficial by participants.

The sort of pull-out programs commonly used to deliver services in Chapter 1 reading programs (Birman et al. 1987) represent another form of supplementary program. Research suggests such programs generally produce very limited effects which do not hold over time (Carter 1984). This conclusion holds even when students are not literally pulled out of the classroom but instruction is delivered to a small group by a Chapter 1 teacher in the student's regular classroom environment (Archambault 1989). Slavin's (1989) review of the literature, in fact, suggests that only one-to-one tutorial programs and individually adapted computer-assisted instruction is effective with at-risk students.

Alternative schools and schools within schools are also types of supplemental programs commonly discussed in the literature. Wehlage and his colleagues (1986, 1987, 1989), for instance, have studied a sample of highly successful programs of this type and compiled a list of common characteristics: Small enough school populations (twenty-five to one hundred students) to allow for personalized, face-to-face relations between staff and students; a sense among students of ownership of the school program and responsibility for their own education; a sense among students of membership in a community, a sense which translates into commitment to learning; voluntary participation in the alternative program by both students and staff; applications for admission and dismissal for inappropriate behavior; individualized approaches to instruction geared toward mastery of clearly defined objectives and prompt feedback about whether mastery has been achieved; active participation by students within the classroom and experiential learning opportunities outside of school; and joint decision making and cooperation on the part of teachers.

Whole-School Restructuring Programs Sometimes educators have attempted to respond to the needs of at-risk students not by creating special supplemental programs but by altering the regular school's structure. Support for viewing the school as a whole as a significant factor in promoting achievement comes from the effective-schools research (see for example Mackenzie [1983] and Rutter et al. [1979]).

School restructuring efforts can take a wide variety of forms. Most, for instance, include some form of site-based management—the argument being that those closest to the problem are best equipped to respond to the particular problems of particular at-risk students—but site-based management can look quite different in different contexts. Sometimes, for instance, shared decision making is seen as synonymous with site-based management (Conley and Bacharach 1990). This is not the case, however, in the effective-schools literature. This literature endorses a principal-directed version of site-based decision making.

Scholars have also begun to differentiate between formally structured shared decision making at the building level and the sort of informal cooperative decision making about instruction which Wehlage and his colleagues observed in successful alternative programs. Cuban (1989), for example, argues that what happens at the level of school governance is often irrelevant to the educational process; data presented by Gitlin, Margonis, and Brunjes in a later chapter in this book support this conclusion.

Other aspects of whole-school restructuring efforts may be more appropriate analogs at the school-building level for characteristics which Wehlage et al. observed in successful alternative programs. Dawson (1987), for instance, describes an Oregon middle school in which whole-school restructuring had taken place. One component of the restructured program was the homeroom class which stayed together with the same teacher for three years. The goal was to insure that at least some personal face-to-face relationships, the sort of relationships which Wehlage and his colleagues observed in successful alternative programs—developed even in a large school setting.

Therapy Programs   Sometimes the concern for teacher/student relationships and student affect evidenced in the last example becomes the central focus of programmatic reform. Such initiatives can be labeled therapy programs. Theoretical support for such programs comes from humanistic psychology (Glaser 1978; Maslow 1954; Rogers 1983) and from the affective education movement which applies humanistic psychology principles to educational practice.

Greene and Uroff (1989) provide an example of a therapy program. In the program they describe, teachers receive three hundred hours of training in learning styles, group process and communication skills, class management techniques, effective discipline methods, and problem-solving skills. At the onset of the school year, students work with teachers to establish the school rules. Punishment is minimized; instead, help in solving problems is offered. This particular school, like other schools which could be placed under the therapy program's umbrella, strives for a warm, accepting environment; the assumption is that such an environment will develop students' self-esteem and that increased self-esteem will lead to greater motivation to learn.

Intervention-Team Programs   A fourth type of program discussed in the literature involves the formation of within-school teams of staff members (normally classroom teachers, an administrator, and support personnel such as guidance counselors, school psychologists, and disability specialists) charged with analyzing specific students' difficulties and generating specific solutions to their problems. Intervention-team approaches generally have developed out of the special education field. At times programs were developed to decrease the number of inappropriate referrals for special education screening, but the approach is also consistent with the ideals (if not always the reality) associated with the Individualized Educational Program (IEP) meeting.

Technically, intervention-team programs could be categorized as yet another type of supplemental program. However, because the focus in intervention-team programs is on a process to generate solutions appropriate for specific students in specific situations rather than on any substantive strategies and solutions defined a priori, we believe it is justifiable to treat the intervention-team approach as a separate ideal type.

Baker and Sansone (1990) provide a descriptive study of one intervention team formed to respond to referrals from grades nine to twelve who were thought to be potential dropouts. Over a two-and-a-half-month period, the team focused on seventy students and recommended thirty-seven different interventions. These included interventions that required alterations of existing schools structures (e.g., modifying a schedule for a chronically tardy student); special groupings of students (e.g., homerooms with extra teacher support); district-level interventions (transfer to alternative schools); and community-level interventions (e.g., liaisons with community drug and alcohol programs). Baker and Sansone report that successful interventions must be individualized and respond to the idiosyncratic characteristics of particular students and particular circumstances. They could discern no pattern linking certain kinds of interventions with certain kinds of students. This point about the idiosyncratic nature of students and their problems is important, we believe. We will return to this point and explore it more fully in the second half of this chapter.

School/Community Linkage Programs   Baker and Sansone's (1990) mention of interventions which link the school with the community suggests a fifth and final ideal type of programmatic response: a model in which linkages among community, home, and school play the central role. Intellectual support for this model can be found in anthropologically oriented work which suggests that at-risk students' school and out-of-school environments are often radically different cultures (Au 1980; Au and Jordan 1981; Vogt, Jordan, and Tharp 1987). Some studies even suggest that poor school performance is a mechanism for maintaining cultural identity and, hence, from an anthropological perspective, is a highly functional achievement (Willis 1977). If these anthropological analyses are correct, it would seem that building bridges between school and community and finding ways to learn about and accommodate the culture of the home are prerequisites to helping students be successful in school.

Linking home and school is a central goal of James Comer's (1980) School Development Model, which was developed in several New Haven, Connecticut, schools over the past twenty years and is now implemented in seventy schools in eight different states. Comer's model, however, was influenced less by anthropological research than by the personal experiences of its developer, a professor of child psychiatry at Yale University. Chenoweth (1991) attempts to capture Comer's own school experience by quoting from a document published by the Prince George County Public Schools, one of the implementation sites for the School Development Program:

> There was never a time at the A&P store that . . . they [Comer's parents] didn't meet somebody from their school . . . teacher, clerk, custodian or principal. And there was always an exchange about how they [Comer] were doing in school and what was expected from them [Comer]. And in these and many other ways their motivation for both academic learning and appropriate social behavior was established and reinforced. His [Comer's] friends, from families under more stress, didn't have the same support. (p. 5)

Comer's model attempts to recreate the types of relationships he experienced as a child and those which theory suggests are necessary for normal development by involving parents and community members in school life.

Eclectic Approaches The diversity of programmatic strategies just reviewed, along with evaluation data about the positive impact of many of these strategies, gives credence to Cuban's (1989) conclusion that we have a pretty good idea of strategies that are effective with at-risk students but we do not know how to put the pieces together into a comprehensive program. An absence of research knowledge, however, has not kept some individuals from constructing more comprehensive programmatic responses.

Comer's School Development Model, for instance, is not only an example of the fifth ideal type described above; there are other components to the model than the central focus on school/home relationships. Like two other well-known comprehensive models, Slavin's (1989a) Success for All program and Levin's (1989b) Accelerated Schools approach, the School Development Model draws eclectically from a number of the ideal types discussed above.

Table 1.1, which was taken from a paper by Chenoweth (1991), summarizes the major components of these three models. The table demonstrates the similarities among the models. It also highlights some significant differences. The most glaring differences can be found in the area of curriculum and instruction. Comer designates no specific pedagogical or curricular approaches; he assumes that existing approaches will be adequate once the school climate has been changed, parents have been integrated into the life of the school, and students have become motivated.

By contrast, Levin's Accelerated Schools model prescribes that teaching methods normally used with gifted and talented students should be employed in educating students who are at risk. Levin does not provide a precise picture of what these methods look like, but, given his emphasis on enrichment and his use of gifted and talented programs as models, it is likely that teaching methods in Accelerated Schools will differ significantly from those currently in use. We would certainly expect them to differ from the methods which are quite precisely specified in Slavin's (1989a) Success for All approach.

TABLE 1.1.
EMERGING MODELS OF SCHOOLING FOR AT-RISK STUDENTS

	School Development	Success for All	Accelerated
Founder	James Comer, M.D. Yale University	Robert Slavin Johns Hopkins University	Henry Levin Stanford University
Key Goal	To build consensus between the home and school by attending to unfulfilled child development and relationship needs.	To bring all students up to grade level in basic academic skills by the end of third grade.	To bring all students up to grade level by the end of elementary school.
Guiding Principles	1) School climate is improved through an applied understanding of child development and through a process of participatory management. 2) A consensus of direction and support is promoted by increased parental presence in the school.	1) All students must have a decent grounding in the basic academic skills of reading, writing, and math by the end of third grade. 2) Most students should not be diverted from the regular classroom.	1) Unity of purpose in which all school activities are examined in light of the school vision. 2) Decision making with responsibility for people who know the school best and are closest to the classroom 3) Building on strengths rather than deficiencies or faults of students, staff, and parents.

Concept of Child	Virtually all students can be successful. Low-achieving students are viewed as "underdeveloped."	Virtually all students can be successful. Well-designed school programs can prevent school failure.	Virtually all students can be successful. The situation or the school rather than the student is at risk.
Organization and Governance	—School planning and management team —Mental health team	—Use of teachers as reading tutors —Preschool and kindergarten program —Family support team —program coordinator	—Cadres/task forces —Steering committee —Site as a whole
Curriculum and Instruction	No specific focus. Builds on existing school program. A supportive and understanding climate will insure that students are ready and motivated to learn.	Based on best available research on what works with at-risk students. Prescribed curriculum and instructional approaches.	Approaches used to educate gifted and talented students are even more meaningful and relevant for at-risk students. General enrichment approaches and principles are encouraged.

Source: Chenoweth 1991.

The Success for All model, in fact, emphasizes direct instruction geared toward student mastery of discretely defined objectives. Even the version of cooperative learning incorporated by Slavin and his colleagues (1990a) is quite controlled and teacher directed. Slavin's model also incorporates a highly prescriptive curriculum, one which Chenoweth (1991) characterizes as being virtually "teacher proof." This aspect of Success for All stands in direct opposition to Levin's emphasis on site-based decision making.

Justification Through Research   Slavin (1989b, 1990b) justifies his specificity on curriculum and instruction matters by claiming the procedures he has incorporated into his model have been legitimated by research. The claim is not totally unfounded. Slavin, in fact, has adopted a rather rigorous and quite public set of criteria for assessing whether or not research establishes the success of any particular program. To be judged successful by Slavin, a program had to produce effect sizes in mathematics and/or reading of at least +.25. Also, either control groups or the assessment of year-to-year rather than fall-to-spring gains had to be used in the evaluation for the intervention to be considered successful.

Despite these clearly stated, rather rigorous criteria, Slavin's attempt to legitimate the methods he employs in his model by referring to research conceals more that it reveals. His criteria, for instance, do not address the adequacy of the dependent variables employed in the evaluation studies he examines. He makes no mention of the fact that successful methods and strategies, when combined, will not necessarily add up to programmatic success. He ignores the fact that even if the combination of programmatic elements is successful in one setting—and a later chapter in this volume by Allington and McGill-Franzen suggests Slavin's program has been successful in one school—programs often do not travel well to new sites. Finally, Slavin makes no mention of the fact that even the most statistically significant findings he reports are still *probablistic* findings. They tell us that the interventions were helpful with some students, possibly even a majority of students. Probabilistic findings, however, also tell us that not all students were helped. If we really want "success for *all*," therefore, we will have to develop programs which allow and even encourage teachers to break the rules suggested by research, rather than endorse programs which border on being "teacher proof."

The research literature on curriculum and instruction effects on at-risk students, in fact, is much more complex than Slavin suggests. One can find reputable studies within this literature to justify quite different, even contradictory approaches to teaching and curriculum organization. Carnine and Kameenui (1990), for instance, present a research-based argument for the sort of teacher-directed, skill-oriented approach which characterizes much of Slavin's Success for All program. Hansen (1989) and Allen and Carr (1989) on the other hand, present a research-based case for more indirect process orientations, orientations which Carnine and Kameenui's research suggests are ineffective. Matters get even more complicated when we examine research cited by Means and Knapp (1991) and Haberman (1991). The cognitive-oriented approach they espouse is, in a sense, a kind of direct instruction model but the model is more different from Carnine and Kameenui's version of direct instruction than it is similar. In several significant respects the cognitive-oriented approach endorsed by Means, Knapp, and Haberman is closer to the process-oriented teaching supported by Allen and Carr and Hansen, yet there are also significant differences.

Given the confusion that exists within the literature on curriculum and instruction effects on at-risk students, it is not surprising that Cuban (1989), after reviewing that literature, concluded that teachers of at-risk students should have the flexibility to choose from a wide range of instructional strategies (Cuban endorses everything from whole language to direct instruction) and to match methods with particular student needs.

INSIGHTS ABOUT RESEARCH

Cuban's response, we believe, is understandable but needlessly glib. We agree that teachers will need to have tremendous freedom if the often idiosyncratic needs of their students are to be accommodated. This is a basic assumption which has guided the development of this book. Teachers' ability to appropriately match teaching methods with students' needs should not be romanticized, however. It should be remembered that empowered teachers who are today's heroes were often yesterday's villains (Kozol 1967; Rist 1970) and that the rules and regulations which today are perceived as solutions were often enacted to protect students from teachers' quite negative self-fulfilling prophesies.

Thus, although we agree that we must inevitably rely on the skill and artistry of classroom teachers to match teaching methods with the needs of individual students, we also believe that teachers will need assistance in doing this. One source of assistance is research.

Research can help assist teachers and also administrators, program developers, and policy makers to make more intelligent decisions. Research, however, if used inappropriately, can also reinforce ignorance and legitimate stereotypes. Given the confusion and apparent contradictions evident in the research literature, for instance, one could read that literature selectively and uncritically and legitimate a wide range of educational approaches. The field of education is filled with true believers in everything from mastery learning to whole language and each true believer will claim that "research shows" the superiority of his or her particular educational "religion."

In the remainder of this chapter, therefore, we want to critically examine the research literature on at-risk students. Our tack will be to sort out and account for the confusion in the literature on program and practice effects on at-risk students. In the process we will also develop the fundamental assumptions which undergird this text.

Some Simple Explanations and Simple Solutions

Some of the confusion outlined above can be accounted for fairly easily and resolved by either specifying more precisely what we are talking about or by adhering more closely to standard operating research procedures long endorsed (though not necessarily followed) by the social science research community.

One reason researchers reach different conclusions, for instance, is that they often use quite different dependent variables and indicators of success. Some studies use a school's dropout rate as a dependent variable, for instance, while other studies use measures of student achievement. A study by Miller, Leinhardt, and Zigmond (1988) suggests a potential problem here. They report that, in the school they studied, school staff kept at-risk students from dropping out by informally negotiating with them lower academic requirements and expectations. If this situation generalizes to other schools, it is easy to understand why researchers who measure a school's success by calculating the dropout rate will reach different conclusions than researchers who use academic performance as their dependent variable.

Disagreement about indicators of success certainly helps explain why Hansen (1989) and Means and Knapp (1991) reach different conclusions than Carnine and Kameenui (1990) about the merits of Carnine and Kameenui's version of direct instruction. The following comments by Hansen, for instance, indicate that the very process of direct instruction is seen as problematic by her:

> For decades, we have been the ones who decided whether students were doing well, and we thought it was our responsibility, within daily lessons, to motivate children. This, however, may hurt rather than help children.
>
> They may come to rely on us too much, and learned helplessness may set in. We know this often happens because we lament the lack of initiative in at-risk children. The task is to figure out how to move the initiative from our court into theirs. (Hansen 1989, p. 27)

Similarly, Means and Knapp (1991) reject using student mastery of discrete, hierarchically ordered skills to indicate program success as Carnine and Kameenui do. The studies that inform Means and Knapp's thinking focus on very different dependent variables. They write:

> A fundamental assumption underlying much of the curriculum in America's schools is that certain skills are "basic" and so must be mastered before students are given instruction in more "advanced" skills, such as reading comprehension, written composition, and mathematical reasoning. For many students, particularly those most at risk of school failure, one consequence of adherence to this assumption is that instruction focuses on these so-called basics (such as phonetic decoding and arithmetic operations) to the exclusion of reasoning activities, of reading for meaning, or of communicating in written form. Demonstrated success on basic skills measures becomes a hurdle that must be overcome before the student receives instruction in comprehension, reasoning, or composition.
>
> The findings of research in cognitive science question this assumption and lead to quite a different view of the way children

learn. By discarding assumptions about skill hierarchies and by attempting to understand children's competencies as constructed and evolving both within and outside of school, researchers are developing models of intervention that start with what children know and expose them to explicit applications of what has traditionally been thought of as higher-order thinking.

The research on which these models are based has provided a critical mass of evidence that students regarded as educationally disadvantaged can profit from instruction in comprehension, composition, and mathematical reasoning from the very beginning of their education. (1991, p. 285)

The problem here can be stated succinctly: Educational issues are at least partially conceptual and, until conceptual problems are resolved—until we define what we mean by fundamental terms such as "learning" and "teaching" and agree on how to operationalize our agreements in our research—educational issues cannot be resolved empirically (Donmoyer 1985).

One can also attribute some of the confusion found in the literature to the sort of traditional design errors outlined by Campbell and Stanley (1963) years ago. A frequent problem, for instance, involves what Campbell and Stanley refer to as external validity. Stated colloquially, results get overgeneralized. Fernandez and Shu (1988) have noted this problem in their review of data from the High School and Beyond study of Hispanic students. They found that many dropout prevention programs were not effective because many at-risk Hispanic students quite simply did not fit researchers' and program developers' ideal type of at-risk students; hence, the educational interventions prescribed had either a neutral or a negative effect.

Problems such as the two just mentioned are not only identifiable; they are also correctable. We can, for example, more clearly articulate and develop procedures to debate disagreements about the dependent variables and indicators of success we employ in our studies (Donmoyer 1990, 1991a, 1991b). Similarly we can specify more precisely the subset of at-risk students we have studied and indicate more specifically the populations to which findings can be generalized. If we do these things, research will undoubtedly provide a clearer, less-confusing picture of what works with at-risk students. "Clearer" and "less confusing," however, are still relative terms.

The Inevitable Limits of Educational Research

The basic premise of this book, in fact, is that research can never tell us what to do with particular students who are potentially at risk and, that if we use research findings too prescriptively in deciding what we should do, we will inevitably make matters worse rather than better for some. Our argument is a simple one.

Part of the argument involves the nature of students who are potentially at risk: They are complex, idiosyncratic individuals. There are commonalities among potentially at-risk students, of course, and subpopulations can be identified whose members have even more in common with each other. We noted above, for instance, Fernandez and Shu's (1988) observation that at-risk Hispanic students may be more different than similar to other students who potentially are at risk. Anyone who has worked with Hispanic students, however, will also understand the anthropologist's dictum: There is often as much variation within a cultural group as between cultural groups. Even within subgroups of Hispanics (e.g., Cuban Americans, Mexican Americans, Puerto Ricans) idiosyncracy will appear alongside cultural commonalities, and this idiosyncracy may quite often be educationally significant.

This conclusion leads to the second part of our argument: Educational research (and social science research in general), at least as it has been practiced in the past, does not even attempt to accommodate the idiosyncracy of at-risk students because social science research is about ideal types. Social science research, in other words, is about groups and categories of people, not individuals. It is about at-risk *students* not *an* at-risk student.

The work of Fernandez and Shu cited above demonstrates this. They are concerned with Hispanic students who are potentially at risk, not with Carlos or Maria or Gilberto. To the extent that social scientists are interested in Carlos, Maria, or Gilberto at all, it is as exemplars of ideal types. What they have in common with others in their group is what is important. Everything else is noise.

The matter can be stated even more baldly: Ideal types are, at base, stereotypes. They may not emerge from malicious intent as many other stereotypes do, but the effect can be the same: Researcher ideal types greatly simplify our perceptions of at-risk students; they focus our attention on a relatively small number of variables; they obscure idiosyncracy.

The ideal typical nature of social research is the primary reason why social science has only been able to tell us what will probably occur rather than what will definitely happen, and it is why social scientists will never be able to produce anything but conclusions that are probabilistic. The problem is not that social science research is relatively young and that research methods are not yet adequate. Even if we employ the most sophisticated procedures imaginable and avoid every potential pitfall detailed by Campbell and Stanley (1963), social science findings will never apply to everyone they ostensibly describe because social science research is not designed to do this. It is designed to tell us about groups of people and their characteristics, not about an individual's particular idiosyncrasies.

The Utility of Traditional Social Science Research

Of course, none of this means that social science inspired educational research is useless in confronting the problems of at-risk students. Social science may not be able to provide precise prescriptions for practice, but it certainly can be used heuristically.

Weiss (1981), for example, suggests one heuristic function for social science research in her study of policy makers' utilization of research in formulating health policy. She indicates that research was of little use in problem solving but very important in problem framing. Social science research helped structure policy makers' thinking by supplying language with which to conceptualize policy questions. In the process, research directed policy makers' attention to possibilities and options which probably would not have been considered in the absence of research. Social science research can certainly serve a similar role in the decision making of educational policy makers as well as teachers, administrators, and program developers concerned with educating students at risk.

Traditional social science research can also tell us what is typical and give us some sense of what will typically occur if we employ different types of educational strategies. This sort of information will be especially useful to educational policy makers. Unlike teachers, who must be concerned with educating idiosyncratic individuals, policy makers are primarily concerned with aggregates. Like social scientists, it is functional for policy makers to think in terms of *types* of people.

Of course, policy makers must realize that if educators are to meet the needs of students, they must design policies and programs which allow for considerable discretion at the school and classroom levels. After all, a probabilistic generalization which tells us what will typically occur also informs us that the atypical will occur with some individuals in some settings. Therefore even relatively definitive research findings do not automatically translate into policies and programs.

For instance, we noted earlier that there is clear evidence about the ineffectiveness of pull-out programs for at-risk students. This evidence should not automatically lead to the conclusion that policies should be adopted which ban such programs. Because the findings about pull-out programs are probabilistic, there are undoubtedly some places where pull-out programs work; they may even be the most functional way to accommodate the needs of at-risk students in certain settings. Policy makers may, in the end, conclude that the benefits of banning pull-out programs still outweigh the costs, but such a conclusion cannot be drawn automatically from the social science data. Indeed, given the probabilistic nature of social science data, bans and nonnegotiable requirements should probably be options of last resort.

The Significance of the Argument

The views just presented may seem so commonsensical and self-evident that some readers may wonder why we have taken the space to state them, much less develop a whole book around them. For most of this century, however, the "obvious" views presented above have gone unrecognized by many researchers, policy makers, and educators. Even today, many who acknowledge the significance of idiosyncracy and the ideal typical nature of social science have not always adjusted their thinking about research, policy, and practice to adequately accommodate these insights.

An Historical Perspective   During the first half of this century, for instance, progressive educators had two interrelated items on their reform agenda: (1) taking the schools out of politics and (2) establishing a cadre of professionals who they assumed would make educational decisions on the basis of research rather than political considerations. Implicit in the early progressives' view of both professionalism and educational research was a social engineering metaphor which emphasized establishing research-based standard operating procedures for practice and hierarchical control to insure the procedures got implemented (Callahan 1964; Tyack 1972).

Often the social engineering metaphor was even made explicit. Franklin Bobbitt (1924), the father of the curriculum field, began his classic text *How to Make a Curriculum,* by likening the work of curriculum developers to the work of engineers. Similarly, the father of the educational administration field, Ellwood P. Cubberly, wrote in 1909:

> Our schools are, in a sense, factories in which the raw products (children) are to be shaped and fashioned into products to meet the various demands of life. The specifications for manufacturing come from the demands for the twentieth-century civilization, and it is the business of the school to build its pupils according to the specifications laid down. This demands good tools, specialized machinery, continuous measurement of production to see if it is according to specifications, the elimination of waste in manufacture, and a large variety in the output. (p. 338)

Raymond Callahan's (1964) historical account of the influence of the efficiency movement on school administration and historian David Tyack's (1972) description of school administrators' search for a "one best system" demonstrate that Cubberly and Bobbitt's social engineering orientation was shared by the field in general.

Researchers encouraged educators' social engineering view of professionalism and suggested that research could provide the necessary knowledge base to make social engineering possible. In 1910, for instance, Thorndike wrote in the lead article of the inaugural issue of *The Journal of Educational Psychology* that:

> [a] complete science of psychology would tell every fact about everyone's intellect and character and behavior, would tell the cause of every change in human nature, would tell the result which every educational force—every act of every person that changed any other or the agent himself—would have. It would aid us to use human beings for the world's welfare with the same surety of the result that we now have when we use falling bodies or chemical elements. In proportion as we get such a science we shall become masters of our own souls as we are now masters of heat and light. Progress toward such a science is being made. (p. 6)

Social engineering images did not leave public consciousness after early progressives such as Thorndike, Cubberly, and Bobbitt were no longer players in the public arena. As late as the 1970s federal policy makers funded elaborate planned variation studies which policy analysts assured them would tell which policies and programs were most effective and consequently which should be mandated or funded. Within education, Project Follow Through (Abt Associates 1977; Haney and Villaume 1977) is the best-known example of a planned variation study. The goal of this program was to determine the relative effectiveness of different early childhood education models in educating disadvantaged (the adjective of choice at the time) students.

Other indicators that social engineering imagery influenced thought and practice well into the second half of this century include the use of discrepancy models of program evaluation that assessed particular programs by comparing them to a model program which research established as successful in another site; the majority of the research conducted in educational psychology including process-product studies of teaching, virtually the only research on teaching conducted prior to the 1970s (Good, Biddle, and Brophy 1975); and a host of programs and practices such as competency-based teacher education and competency-based teacher evaluation which were legitimated by either explicit or implicit references to process-product studies of teacher effectiveness.

Increased Skepticism   Over time, members of the research community, at least, have become increasingly skeptical about researchers' ability to deliver the sort of knowledge base which would make social engineering possible. The inability of the Project Follow Through education to provide definitive results, for instance, generated skepticism in the minds of many who previously had espoused the virtues of planned variation studies (Rivlin and Timpane 1975). One group of scholars, after reviewing Project Follow Through data, took note of the probabilistic nature of the findings of the study and indicated that this aspect of the findings

> . . . should be honored widely and serve as a basis of educational policy. Local schools do seem to make a difference. The peculiarities of individual teachers, schools, neighborhoods, and homes influence pupils' achievement far more than whatever is

captured by labels such as basic skills or affective education. (House et al. 1978, p. 462)

Discrepancy evaluation models also have begun to be criticized. Spindler, for example, wrote these comments about a discrepancy-oriented evaluation of programs established by the Youth Employment Demonstration Act:

> My first reaction was, "Why would anyone expect different programs in different urban sites to replicate a model program in another site?" This expectation is against the first law of sociocultural systems in that all such systems (and a program of any kind is a sociocultural system) are adaptations to their environment. We should expect each program to show significant deviation from the initiating model, and from each of the other programs. The question should not be, "Do they deviate?" or even "How do they deviate?", but rather, "Are they adapting well (functionally) to their respective environments?" (Spindler, as cited in Fetterman 1981, p. 70)

Furthermore, even Thorndike's field of education psychology has undergone some rather dramatic changes over the past several decades. By the mid 1970s for instance, a new line of research on teaching—one which focused on the complex process of teacher thinking rather than discrete teaching behaviors (e.g., Clark and Yinger 1977; Shulman and Lanier 1977) had begun to be established. Even Gage, a die-hard supporter of process-product models of research on teaching, was forced to acknowledge in 1978 that such research could, at best, only provide a general knowledge base for teaching and that teacher artistry would always be required to adjust and shape that knowledge base to the needs of particular students and particular situations.

Today process-product studies are difficult to find within research on teaching literature. That literature is dominated by studies of teacher thinking, a subject which is normally investigated with methods more associated with the largely descriptive discipline of anthropology than with Thorndike's social engineering oriented field of study.

Educational psychology's shift in perspective about social science's ability to provide a knowledge base to support social engineering, however, probably can be seen most clearly in the career of the eminent educational psychologist Lee Cronbach. By the mid 1950s, Cronbach had already established himself as a skilled player of Thorndike's research game. In 1956, however, Cronbach told the American Psychological Association that the complexity of human phenomena requires a minor alteration in the traditional game plan. Rather than searching for laws which were universal and context free, Cronbach argued, researchers should attempt to identify cause-effect relationships between certain educational treatments on the one hand and certain types of individuals (in Cronbach's terms, individuals with certain aptitudes) on the other. In colloquial terms, he made the case for researchers attending to learning styles.

In the mid 1970s, however, after nearly twenty years of searching for aptitude/treatment interactions and nearly twenty years of frustration brought on by "inconsistent findings coming from roughly similar inquiries," Cronbach (1975) told the American Psychological Association:

> Once we attend to interactions, we enter a hall of mirrors that extends to infinity. However far we carry our analysis—to third order or fifth order or any other—untested interactions of still higher order can be envisioned. (p. 119)

Compounding the problem of complexity is the problem of culture. Cronbach cited Bronfenbrenner's historical look at child-rearing practices of middle- and lower-class parents. Class differences documented in the 1950s were often just the reverse of practices that had been observed in the 1930s. Cronbach concluded:

> The trouble, as I see it, is that we cannot store up generalizations and constructs for ultimate assembly into a network. It is as if we needed a gross of dry cells to power an engine and could only make one a month. The energy would leak out of the first cells before we had half the battery completed. So it is with the potency of our generalizations. (p. 123)

In his 1975 article, Cronbach emphasized that the social world was no less lawful than the physical world. The problem was that social laws were too complex and the social world too changeable to identify them. By the early 1980s, however, Cronbach had rejected even the notion of social laws. He began suggesting that the entire cause-effect way of thinking which undergirds the social engineering view of professionalism and the traditional view of research is an inappropriate way to characterize social phenomena. By 1982, in fact, Cronbach had arrived at a position similar to that of symbolic interactionists (Blumer 1969) and ethnomethodologists (Garfinkle 1967): Human action is constructed not caused, Cronbach concluded; those who expect research to produce the sort of definitive cause-effect generalizations promised by Thorndike and by himself in earlier days are simply, in Cronbach's words, "waiting for Godot."

Vestiges of Earlier Ways of Thinking Among Researchers   Not everyone has arrived at as radical a position as Cronbach's, of course. Even those who acknowledge the ideal typical nature of social science often do not alter their fundamental thinking about the nature and purpose of research. No better example of this exists than N. L. Gage. In his 1978 book, *The Scientific Basis for the Art of Teaching,* after acknowledging the need for teacher artistry in applying research findings, Gage proceeds to declare that research has definitively established the superiority of direct instruction over more informal or child-centered approaches. In making his case, Gage not only lumps together a wide variety of informal approaches (studies of everything from informal modes of teaching to schools which have open architecture) and ignores the indicators of success problem discussed earlier in this chapter. He also ignores the probabilistic nature of the findings he uses to reach his questionable conclusions.

Even more contemporary and seemingly more enlightened critics of traditional social science research often seem imprisoned by traditional conceptions of the form and function of empirical inquiry. Cuban, for instance, has written:

> [N]o pat formulas to grow effective schools yet exist. Knowing how to put together the right combination of people, things, and ideas to create a productive setting that supports at-risk students and the adults that work with them remains just out of our reach so far. (1989, p. 30)

Whether he intends to or not, Cuban's comments suggest that with a bit more time and effort, research will be able to determine formulas for successful programs. If we take this suggestion seriously we should embark on a new round of planned variation studies. If past is prologue and our analysis is correct, however, such studies will net little.

There are more promising signs within the research community, of course. For instance, as we noted in the above discussion of research on teaching, educational researchers now have a broad array of methodological options from which to choose. Some of the most revealing research cited in this chapter, for instance, was qualitative in nature. Still, most of the qualitative studies about at-risk students employ relatively conservative versions of qualitative research (Miles and Huberman 1984) rather than more radical versions which shift the focus of the research enterprise from the typical and general to the idiosyncratic. (See for example, Eisner 1985; Lincoln and Guba 1985; Lawrence-Lightfoot 1983.) The research of Richardson and her colleagues (1989) which we discussed at length above demonstrates this point. Although the research was built around twelve case studies, the book by Richardson and her colleagues focuses on results of a cross-case analysis and the four ideal types of at-risk students which the cross-case analysis generated. The individual case study data are, for the most part, buried in the book's appendices.

Now we do not want to imply that Richardson's analysis or the analyses found in other more- or less-traditional qualitative stories in the literature are not helpful. The literature review presented in the first part of this chapter demonstrates quite clearly their utility. We believe, however, that studies which focus on the idiosyncracies of particular at-risk students are also useful. They can add depth and dimension to our thinking. Among other things, such studies can function as antidotes to the labels and ideal types provided by more traditional social science research and to the stereotypical thinking which labels and ideal types encourage. To date, however, this sort of work has been grossly underrepresented in the literature on at-risk students.

Program, Policy, and Practice Responses   Thus, the research community's response to the recognition of the limits of research has been relatively conservative and a bit confused. In the realms of policy, program development, and practice the situation is even more confused, though not at all conservative. One can, in fact, discern two rather extreme and quite antithetical responses.

One response is to basically ignore the ideal typical, probabilistic nature of social science and to continue to attempt to socially engineer school success for at-risk students. Teacher-proof curricula such as DISTAR, for instance, are still being used in schools across the nation, especially in special education programs (Kuder

1990). Also states such as Florida, Tennessee, and Texas have used the probabilistic findings of teacher effectiveness research to design checklist type instruments to assess teachers' competence and make certification and merit-pay decisions. Florida did abolish its merit-pay system recently when some of the state's most dedicated and gifted teachers failed to score high enough on the state's effectiveness instrument to qualify for extra compensation, but elsewhere the practice of using foolproof, research-based systems to assess and reward teacher performance is alive and well.

At the opposite end of the continuum are certain teacher empowerment advocates who would do away with most policies and programmatic prescriptions and maximize the authority of classroom teachers. The teacher empowerment movement, of course, is fueled by multiple motives, but clearly one important motive comes from the recognition of the limits of what Wise (1982) has called "legislated learning."

We believe neither extreme is defensible if we want to help at-risk students. The traditional social engineering response is not defensible because, as we have noted, researchers will never be able to provide a knowledge base to make social engineering possible. If we want to assist individual at-risk students we will always have to rely on the artistry of classroom teachers. As even Gage (1978) has noted, teacher artistry can be informed by social science knowledge, but can never be reduced to the findings of social science research.

Teachers, however, do not teach in a vacuum. Policy makers will not stop legislating, particularly now when there is a perception of crisis in American education; nor should they. Research on the self-fulfilling prophesy phenomenon demonstrates that the cognitive structures a teacher brings to a classroom can be as damaging to students as the bureaucratic structures policy makers impose upon it. Limited teacher knowledge and limited planning time can be as damaging as restrictive rules and regulations. The idea that most teachers or groups of teachers have the necessary knowledge and time to construct their classroom curricula from scratch is just not realistic.

Rather than resorting to social engineering or romanticizing empowered teachers, we should ask a somewhat paradoxical question: How can we structure the educational environment in such a way as to honor and accommodate idiosyncracy?

CONCLUSION AND INTRODUCTION

The question about structuring for idiosyncracy is addressed in the second half of this book. Through a series of cases, we consider how policy makers and program developers can provide teachers "direction with discretion," to use a phrase coined by two of our contributors. Certain contributors to the book's second section also consider how teachers can structure their classrooms to accommodate the idiosyncracies of their students.

In the first part of the book, various writers present in-depth verbal portraits of particular at-risk students. These verbal portraits represent the sort of research which has been underrepresented in the literature on at-risk students to date. The next chapter introduces and provides a brief rationale for the portraits which will follow.

NOTE

1. These statistics were taken from the following sources: *Wall Street Journal,* February 9, 1990; *Newsweek* 95 (27), Special Issue, June, 1990; *U.S. News & World Report* 106 (25), June 26, 1989, 45–53.

CHAPTER 2

The Purpose of Portraits: Rethinking the Form and Function of Research on At-Risk Students

Robert Donmoyer, The Ohio State University

This chapter introduces and provides a rationale for the case material which is presented in subsequent chapters. Specifically the chapter describes the characteristics of the work presented here and discusses what the reader can expect to receive by reading it. The issue of generalizability of case studies receives particular attention.

Several years ago two of my colleagues at The Ohio State University received a research grant to study young children's development. The two professors made a rather odd couple. One was an accomplished social scientist by training and temperament, and a person well schooled in statistical analysis and research design. His coinvestigator was equally bright, but she had spent most of her career working as a teacher. Their different backgrounds created creative tensions and many disagreements.

One ongoing problem revolved around the teacher's complaint that none of the statistical descriptions they were generating described any of the actual students they had studied. The social scientist acknowledged this fact but could not see why his coinvestigator considered this a problem. Social science research, he

37

explained patiently (and eventually somewhat impatiently) focused on commonalities and generalities; it described types or categories of people not actual people. To this the teacher/teacher educator's response was always the same: Teachers do not teach categories or types; they teach children.

The problem the teacher/teacher educator raised was the same problem that was discussed at some length in chapter 1. In chapter 1 we noted that one way to resolve the problem raised by my Ohio State colleague was for everyone to be clear about what research can and cannot do. Social science research, we noted, can never provide prescriptions for practice. In an enterprise such as teaching—an enterprise in which the goal is ultimately to help individuals—research can never tell us what to do. It can only help us think about a problem and suggest possible solutions. In short, it can only serve a heuristic function. Teacher artistry will always be required to adjust and shape researcher's findings about ideal types to fit the idiosyncratic students in a particular classroom. Sometimes the teacher-as-artist will even have to ignore social scientists' conclusions entirely, for social science findings never really apply to everyone they ostensibly describe.

Recognizing that research can only serve a heuristic function also opens the door to new forms of research which may serve somewhat different heuristic roles. When we realize that research is no longer a pathway to truth or a source of prescription for practice, we are freer to develop new approaches to research and even break the traditional rules of research codified in such books as Campbell and Stanley's (1963) *Experimental and Quasi-experimental Designs for Research.*

Subsequent chapters in this section of the book present such tradition-breaking research. Each chapter presents a description—verbal portraits we call them—of one or more at-risk students. The creators of these verbal portraits, which often read more like literature than conventional social science, were as interested in capturing students' unique qualities as they were in describing how the students they studied are similar to other students at risk.

This particular chapter is designed to introduce and provide a brief rationale for the verbal portraits which follow. Two questions are addressed: (1) How can this work be characterized and what are its characteristics? and (2) What heuristic function do verbal portraits serve? In other words, what can a reader expect to get from studies about the idiosyncracies of students they will un-doubtedly never meet?

LABELS AND CHARACTERISTICS

Different scholars have characterized the alternative approach to research being presented in this section of the book in different ways. Cronbach (1975), for example, has talked of research which is "more historical than scientific" (p. 125). What Cronbach may have been attempting to capture by using history as a metaphor for a new form of educational research is suggested by the philosopher of history, William Dray (1957). Dray discusses the fundamentally different ways in which scientists and historians use theoretical constructs such as the construct of revolution. When the historian sets out to explain the French Revolution, Dray writes, he/she

> is just *not interested* in explaining it as a revolution—as an as-tronomer might be interested in explaining a certain eclipse as an instance of eclipses; he is almost invariably concerned with it as different from other members of its class. Indeed, he might even say that his main concern will be to explain the French Revolu-tion's taking a course unlike any other; that is to say, he will explain it as unique. . . (p. 47)

A similar point is made by the anthropologist Clifford Geertz (1973), although Geertz uses the term "thick description" to char-acterize the kind of research we are talking about. When a re-searcher is providing thick description, according to Geertz, he or she is explicating the layers of meaning which exist in a particular situation. The focus once again is on the idiosyncratic, on "local knowledge" (Geertz, 1983) rather than abstract universal catego-ries which, in traditional social science, subsume the local. Geertz emphasizes that this does not mean that a thick-description—oriented researcher does not use more general theoretical con-structs. Like Dray, however, he indicates that theory in the kind of research we are talking about is used largely as a rhetorical device. The goal of thick description, in other words, is not the develop-ment of theory, even the sort of grounded theory (Glaser, 1978) associated with qualitative research; rather theory helps to struc-ture discussions of the idiosyncratic.

While Cronbach looks to history and Geertz's reference point is cultural anthropology, Elliot Eisner (1985, 1991) employs art and literary criticism models to conceptualize the kind of work presented in the remaining chapters of part 1. Among other things, Eisner's discussions of educational criticism emphasize the narrative modes of reporting used in the kind of research we are talking about. Eisner, in fact, recommends that modes of reporting be unabashedly literary.

I do not want to leave the impression that Eisner's educational criticism, Geertz's thick description, and Cronbach's "historical more than scientific" research are completely identical to each other. There are many subtle and, for certain purposes, significant differences. Some of these differences are reflected in the different chapters presented in this book. The chapter by Barone, for instance, is clearly an educational criticism, while the chapter by Gleason would probably be categorized by most people as a micro version of Geertz's thick description.

For our purposes, however, the differences are less important than the similarities: All the chapters presented here tell stories, and the stories focus on individuals rather than on ideal types; all the authors are at least as interested in explicating how their subjects are different from other at-risk students as in indicating how they are similar.

We have chosen the term "portraits" to label the work that is being presented here. The term, which was used by Sara Lawrence-Lightfoot (1983) in her book *The Good High School,* seems appropriate for several reasons. It is not associated with any existing academic discipline or field of study as are the terms "historical," "thick description," and "art criticism." Indeed, when employed in the context of research, the term is obviously to be taken metaphorically rather than literally. The term, therefore, can subsume the other discipline-based terms listed above.

Also, the portrait metaphor communicates, at a relatively intuitive, unconscious level, important characteristics of the kind of research which will be presented here. I will conclude this section of the chapter by articulating three of these characteristics.

First, modern portrait painters generally do not paint generic people; rather they attempt to capture on canvas the unique quirks and idiosyncracies of their subjects. They expect people who know their subject to recognize their subject in their painting. The researchers who have contributed verbal portraits to this volume have a similar goal. They use pseudonyms, of course, to protect their subjects' privacy, but if they have done their job well, the subject will certainly see himself or herself in the verbal portraits that have been created, and others, undoubtedly, will also. (There are some interesting ethical and political dilemmas here, of course. For a discussion of these see Lincoln and Guba 1985; Eisner and Peshkin 1990.)

Second, no one expects a portrait to function like a mirror. No portrait painter can capture all that is unique and special about an individual. A portrait will always be an abstraction no matter how lifelike it may appear. The same thing can be said about the work that appears here. The adjective "holistic" has often been used to describe the sort of work we are presenting in part 1. The adjective, however, should not be taken too literally, and it should probably be used primarily to characterize the intentions of the researcher rather than to describe the product the researcher produced.

Finally we expect different painters to paint quite different portraits of the same individual. We expect to be able to recognize the portrait's subject in each painting, of course, but we would also expect to see the artist's particular style, technique, training, and point of view in each. Once again, the same statements apply to the verbal portraits which appear here (and, indeed, given the analysis presented in chapter 1, to any other form of research as well).

UTILITY QUESTIONS

But why are verbal portraits useful? What can someone expect to get from reading the chapters that follow? What is their heuristic value? How will reading about the idiosyncracies of a few students the reader almost certainly never will meet help the reader when confronting other students who will undoubtedly have their own idiosyncracies? In the words of the traditional social scientist: What is the generalizability of the work reported in the chapters that follow?

An adequate answer to the generalizability question requires what some would call a paradigm shift, or at least a shift in perspective and language. Traditional social scientists think of generalizability in terms of sampling and statistical theory. This is consistent with social scientists' focus on the typical. A search for typicality requires not only that we study large numbers of people or situations, but also that the people and situations in the study are reasonably representative of the population being described. Sampling procedures can give us a representative sample, and statistical analysis can tell us how representative our sample really is.

Given this concern with the typical and the way of thinking about generalizability which logically follows from it, it is not surprising that traditional social scientists have been skeptical about the utility of the sort of case study work presented in this book. Campbell and Stanley (1963), for instance, have declared that: "[S]uch studies have such a total absence of control as to be of almost no scientific value" (p. 6). The emphasis on the typical made n of 1 studies useless by definition (except, of course, for hypothesis-generation purposes). By definition, a finding could only be considered generalizable if we had a large and reasonably representative sample.

Social scientists' definition of generalizability in no way exhausts the common-sense meanings associated with the term. In real life, in fact, we generalize from individual cases all the time. There are problems with this sort of generalizing, of course, but, as chapter 1 pointed out, there are also some serious problems associated with social scientists' approach to generalization. Furthermore, our case-by-case, commonsense approach to generalizability could not be so laden with problems that it is useless. If it were, we could not pay people on the basis of experience.

The importance of experience—including experience in very different sorts of settings—was alluded to in the introduction of this book. Raylene Kos and I noted there that I had taught in three very different school environments—inner city, affluent suburbia, and rural island—in the course of my public school career. Despite these differences—and I would argue because of them—I increasingly became a better teacher. Each year, even when I moved to a radically different environment, teaching became easier. I could more easily anticipate the consequences of my actions. Increasingly, I could even control events. Generalization, in a psychological sense, occurred.

The language of schema theory—in particular, schema theorists' notions of assimilation, accommodation, integration, and differentiation—can help us conceptualize and describe this more psychological series of generalizations. According to schema theorists, all knowledge of the empirical world must be filtered through cognitive structures which inevitably shape what we know. Some schema theorists call this process *assimilation*. Schema theorists, however, also describe a complimentary process called *accommodation*. This process involves the reshaping of cognitive structures to accommodate novel aspects of what is being perceived. After the complimentary processes of assimilation and accommodation have occurred, a cognitive structure will be both more *integrated* (a particular structure will be able to accommodate more things) and more *differentiated* (a particular structure will be divided into substructures).[1]

Schema theorists' language can easily be applied to my experiences as a teacher who moved from an inner-city school to a suburban one, and eventually to a school in a rural island community. In the introduction of this book, for instance, I mentioned my changing perspective on the whole issue of disadvantaged. I noted, for instance, that each new situation forced me not only to assimilate new people, places, and things to pre-existing cognitive structures; I also had to accommodate differences. As a consequence my cognitive structures expanded and became more refined. For instance, before I taught in the ghetto, I had been socialized to think of my students as disadvantaged (the synonym for at risk at the time). When I began teaching, initially, I assimilated my students and their behavior into that category. Quickly, however, there were some pieces that did not fit. For example, when I visited my Hispanic students' parents and needed my bilingual students to serve as my translator, it was I who felt disadvantaged. Such experiences had to be accommodated. I was forced to rethink my notion of disadvantagedness and to define disadvantage in more than economic terms. In schema theory terms, my cognitive structures associated with the term "disadvantaged" became more integrated (the term was now applied to more things) and more differentiated (I could now distinguish between economic and other sources of disadvantagedness).

My enriched schema was helpful when I had to work with a very different population of students in affluent suburbia. Here I found children who economically wanted for nothing and who at a very early age had a wealth of mainstream cultural knowledge and skills. Yet some of these same children, these children whose lives were a constant journey from soccer practices to ceramic classes to violin lessons to special math-tutoring sessions to library programs to who knows where, often had been emotionally neglected by professional parents who assumed other professionals (i.e., the soccer coach, the ceramics teacher, etc.) would do their parenting for them. I wondered what it was like to spend so much time with paid professionals rather than parents, and I also wondered how successful my students would be outside of class without an instructor controlling and directing them. Life, after all, is not a series of classes, at least not for most people. These children, at times, seemed much less able to know their own minds, to direct themselves toward things they wanted, and to function together as a group without the benefit of an adult's direction than many of the children I had worked with in the ghetto.

My experience in suburbia, in other words, expanded my cognitive structures associated with the term disadvantaged. The structures, in schema theory terms, became both more integrated and more differentiated. I now had a richer sense, for instance, of the types of noneconomic factors which could disadvantage people. This enriched understanding came in handy when I moved to a rural island community and taught students, some of whom were disadvantaged by the same economic-related factors which disadvantaged many of my inner-city students and some of whom were disadvantaged by many of the same factors I had encountered earlier in suburbia. Because of my earlier experiences, I could recognize my students' quite different needs and even knew a bit about what I might do to help meet their needs.

Of course, I did not only assimilate my island students into my existing cognitive structures. There was also idiosyncracy to be accommodated—the geographic isolation associated with living on an island brought its own unique problems and its own sort of disadvantages—so the cognitive structures also became enriched. In schema theory terms, they became even more integrated and differentiated.

In summary to this point: schema theorists give us an entirely different way of viewing generalization. According to this view, generalization is a psychological phenomenon. It occurs through experience in the world with different individuals and different situations. In fact, difference is an asset from this perspective. The more our experiences in the world differ, the more opportunity there is for accommodation to occur and, consequently, the more opportunity for more integrated and differentiated cognitive structures to develop.[2]

Experience, of course, can be vicarious as well as direct. Anyone who has sat around a campfire and been taken away to other times and places by a skilled storyteller will know what is meant by the term vicarious experience. Similarly, anyone who has lost himself or herself in the pages of a well-written novel will be able to attest to the power of vicarious experience not only to influence our emotions and motivation, but also to shape and reshape our thinking.

It is vicarious experience that the verbal portraits in the subsequent chapters will provide. But why rely on vicarious experience, one might ask. Why is vicarious experience needed to supplement direct experience? What can vicarious experience give us that direct experience cannot?

There are multiple answers that could be given to these questions. Here let me focus on two rather obvious ones. First, case study writers can take us to places we might never go and introduce us to people we might never meet in the course of our everyday lives. The other chapters in the first section of this book make this point nicely. Many of us will not have an opportunity to work in a reading clinic as has Raylene Kos, the author of chapters 3 and 7, and consequently, we may not have an opportunity to get to know students like Ben and Karen, at least in the way Kos has. Few of us will travel to Appalachia as the author of chapter 4 does and meet a student like Billy Charles Barnett. We may not ever be able to meet a truly gifted student like Andrew, or at least we may not be able to get to know him and his family as intimately as the author of chapter 9 has. We may not have an opportunity to meet a pregnant teenager like Victoria, or, if we do, it is unlikely we will have the time to get to know her and her culture to the extent that the author of chapter 8 does, and to come to understand, as the author has come to understand, why an apparently foolish, irrational act might, to the teenager in a particular cultural context, seem sensible and desirable. If we work in schools as teachers and guidance counselors we will undoubtedly encounter students like Alston and Everetta, but, like Alston and Everetta, it is unlikely they will be willing to share their stories with us, at least not as openly as they have shared their stories with the author of chapter 10.

The case of Paul in chapter 11 makes the point most dramatically. Paul is clearly an outlier. He is so mentally handicapped that he must live out his life behind the walls of an institution. No one is worried about whether Paul will graduate from high school or develop the necessary skills to function in the adult world. Neither of these options is within the realm of possibility.

In conventional social science research, with its emphasis on typicality, Paul would more than likely not even be included in a sample of at-risk students, or, if he were, data would undoubtedly be thrown out before analysis. When we view generalization from a psychological/schema theory perspective, however, the outlier is prized; outliers offer us more to accommodate and, hence, more opportunity to develop more integrated and more differentiated cognitive structures.

The story of Paul, for instance, is not just a story of an exceedingly mentally handicapped youth. It is also a story of professionals who exacerbate Paul's problems by misinterpreting Paul's actions, in large part because they failed to look for the person behind their professional categories. After reading the account of Paul in chapter 11, I, at least, was forced to rethink my relationship with Jeffrey, a mildly learning-disabled elementary school student I taught for two years many years ago. I had to ask myself whether many of Jeffrey's problems were, in fact, created by me and my misinterpretations of his actions just as many of Paul's problems were created by the misinterpretations of his institution's staff. Had I never encountered Paul in the pages of this book or had he been less of an outlier and had his story, as a consequence, been less dramatic, I may have never asked this question and never seen my professional activity in this new light.

There is a second reason why the vicarious experience generated by case studies is an important supplement to direct experience: In case studies we have an opportunity to see through the eyes of the researcher, to take advantage of what Eisner (1985, 1991) would call the case study writer's connoisseurship. Traditional views of research, of course, would see this reliance on the researcher's connoisseurship as threatening objectivity and, hence, as problematic. We now know, however, that the most rudimentary acts of perceptions are influenced by a priori assumptions (Neisser 1976) and that subjectivity can never be completely banished from the research process. We noted in chapter 1, for instance, that even in traditional social science studies we learn as much about the researcher and the research tradition he or she has been socialized into as we do about the phenomenon the researcher studied. When we think of the utility of research from the perspective of schema theory, the researcher's influence becomes a potential asset.

Indeed, the case study writers who present verbal portraits in the first section of this book bring a wealth of experience and knowledge to their studies and therefore they see—and can help us see—things which we might not notice if we encountered the students they describe directly. In chapter 6, for example, we benefit from the author's years of experience as a classroom teacher and many months as a participant observer in the classroom in which Andy and Libby are students. In chapter 9, we benefit from the author's sensitivity to factors which put gay and lesbian students at risk. (Indeed, until Raylene Kos and I talked informally with the author of chapter 9 about other matters, we did not even associate the notion of at-riskness with being lesbian or gay, and we had not recognized the desirability of including a chapter like the one the author of chapter 9 eventually wrote for us.)

In chapter 11 we benefit from the author's training as an anthropologist. This training has provided him not only with methods of observation and theories to guide and make sense of the observation process; the training has also inculcated a nonjudgmental attitude which encourages seeing from others' perspectives and assuming that others are behaving rationally and sensibly from their point of view. This attitude helped the author of chapter 11 see—and, in turn, made it possible for him to help us see—things which the other professionals on the scene failed to notice.

CONCLUSION

Now it is time to turn to the verbal portraits which have been prepared for this book. If our contributors have done their job well—and we believe they have—the vicarious experiences their work provides should both expand and explode our conceptions of at-risk students. In the language of schema theory, the verbal portraits which follow should force us to accommodate new attributes and characteristics under our at-risk conceptual umbrellas. In the process, our notions of at-riskness should become both more integrated and more differentiated.

NOTES

1.   These notions are particularly prominent in the work of Piaget (1971). I want to articulate two caveats with respect to my use of Piagetian theory. First, Piaget's theory is actually two theories: a stage theory of child development and a more general theory of cognitive functioning. Piaget's stage theory is probably better known; it is also the least defensible part of Piaget's work. In employing Piaget's concepts, I in no way endorse his stage theory. Rather, it is his more general descriptions of cognitive processing that I am utilizing here.

Second, Piaget developed his terminology in the process of trying to explain the origin of what he termed "logico-mathematical knowledge." Piaget's way of characterizing cognitive functioning need not be limited to this narrow sphere of understanding, however (Turner, 1973). Here I will employ the notions of assimilation, accommodation, integration, and differentiation far more liberally and relate schema theory to various sorts of social knowledge, including the sort of visceral, affect-laden knowledge discussed by Berlin (1966).

2.   For a more complete discussion of a psychological view of generalizability see Donmoyer (1990).

CHAPTER 3

"Nobody Knows My Life But Me!" The Story of Ben, A Reading Disabled Adolescent

Raylene Kos, The Ohio State University at Lima

This chapter provides a verbal portrait of Ben. Ben is in many respects the classic at-risk student: He is poor, black, male, a bit hyperactive, the victim of a troubled home life, a problem reader. He is also, as portrayed by the author of this chapter, an idiosyncratic individual. Ben's declamation, "Nobody knows my life but me!," serves as a plaintive rejoinder both to common-sense stereotypes and to social scientists' ideal types.

Adolescent disabled readers create a difficult challenge for our schools. Some of these students, perceiving school as an increasingly futile experience, drop out of school, while others express their futility through inappropriate behaviors. Teachers of these students often feel a sense of frustration at their seeming inability to do something positive for the student. Recent studies into the problem of reading disability have begun to acknowledge that perhaps we need to look at the problems of these failing students from a different perspective, particularly the perspective of the students themselves.

This case study is an attempt to look through the eyes of one fifteen-year-old disabled reader and consider his perspective when

49

interpreting events, environments, behaviors, and interactions which appear to affect his ability to read. Perhaps this perspective will allow us to reinterpret what we think we have seen before. Bruner (1986) states that "it is far more important, for appreciating the human condition, to understand the ways human beings construct their worlds than it is to establish the ontological status of the products of these processes" (p. 46). This is very thought provoking for those working with so-called "disabled" students, since the basis of the disability model has been to label children based on prescribed sets of observed behaviors that determine their status. It is doubtful that anyone asked the students whether they deserved or wanted these labels. Their responses might have been quite revealing.

I would like to make a few explanatory remarks about the content of this chapter. My intention in doing this study was to explore reading disability from the perspective of a reading-disabled adolescent. I had vague expectations of what I would find based on my experiences as a teacher of adolescents in a learning-disabilities classroom. I must admit that I thought I would find that this student was hindering his own learning through his own behaviors. In my classroom experience, it had frequently occurred to me that such students did not understand the importance of reading in their lives. Understanding, of course, assumed that the students should accept my view of why reading was important. After all, I was the teacher and I knew about these things. However, my expectations were overwhelmed by the barrage of information and emotion uncovered in this study, and I ended up studying myself as well as my student, Ben. This became, in a sense, not just the story of a struggling young man, but also the story of a struggling teacher, who I now feel may give voice to many other teachers' struggles.

This study also increased my empathy for the teachers dealing with students such as Ben. As an old slang phrase puts it, he can be a "real piece of work." The wonder of it is that teachers facing so much uncertainty and frustration every day stick with the task. Only a true commitment to kids could account for such perserverance.

As the young man in the study expresses so aptly, no one can know another person's life entirely, so it might appear that a study which intends to uncover the basis of a student's reading disability is quite broad in scope. However, the intent of this chapter is not necessarily to present the whole picture, because one researcher could never assume all the perspectives necessary to do that. The purpose is to share one part of a whole with the hope that others will see this portrait and notice resemblances to a disabled reader they know.

BEN'S STORY

"You gonna make me read this whole thing by myself? That's cruel!" he said, sneaking a glance to see if this tactic would work. A direct appeal for sympathy was an attempt to avoid reading, but it was no more effective than his other ploys—sleepiness, fatigue, changing the subject, or pains someplace in his body. Legs were particularly bothersome appendages for him. I arched a brow at him and said, "Define cruel." He gave in with a grin and a shrug, and I grinned back in acknowledgment of a good try. He haltingly began to read.

I first met Ben when his father brought him to a reading clinic where I was supervising tutors. Ben was slouching and disheveled, and his eyes slid past mine when I spoke to him. He had an air of defensiveness about him and a slight touch of slyness which I took as a challenge even while being a bit charmed by it. When he awkwardly shook my hand and gave me a lopsided grin, I was hooked.

He received tutoring for two quarters from a different tutor each quarter; both tutors were in my office frequently with such complaints as, "He falls asleep in the middle of the book!," "He doesn't want to do anything," or "He's not trying!" And when I observed their sessions, he was exactly as they described him. Finally, increasing absences forced us to discontinue him as a tutee for our student tutors. However, I wasn't quite ready to give up on him, especially since he had started dropping by my office just to pass the time before and after tutoring, and I was developing a picture of a young man who was confused about himself, worried that he couldn't read well, and desperately wanted people to like him. He was also a manipulator, as most kids are, and I've always enjoyed watching kids put together a good scam.

Ben was a real problem when he began to be tutored, because

he appeared completely disinterested. The tutors would plan sessions with a variety of activities designed to hold Ben's attention and get him involved in reading. He would participate in games that enabled him to practice needed skills, revealing a very competitive nature, but the minute a book was placed in front of him, he started to fade. After about four sentences, his eyes began to droop, his voice became slurred, and pretty soon he looked almost asleep. Of course this either made the tutors confused or angry. Either way, Ben had taken control of the session. One tutor discovered he would read Garfield cartoons, so for the last few weeks of the quarter she was able to maintain his attention by increasing the game activities and focusing on Garfield. In actuality, Ben did little reading. This tutor's reaction was to feel guilty that she wasn't accomplishing more. It appeared that Ben had her right where he wanted her, feeling sorry for him and blaming herself.

The second tutor was less willing to take the blame, and her disappointment turned to anger. Ben's absences steadily increased. The last thing he needed was another teacher yelling at him or laying a guilt trip on him. The situation seemed like a power play which I watched with great interest. The tutor wanted him to follow her plan of instruction, and Ben wanted to advance his own plan. I guess you could say he won, because he did get himself out of tutoring for good.

In between explaining how Ben was manipulating them, and counseling the tutors on ways to improve their relationship with Ben, I also began to talk with Ben. He was happy to sit in my office and chat, but he didn't want to talk about tutoring. "It's boring" was his most frequent response. However, he always showed an interest in the books on the reading rack and any children's books in my office. He also began bringing in books to show me, either personal books or schoolbooks. He would tell me, "This is what I'm reading now," establishing himself as a reader who really didn't need to be tutored like the little kids. By the end of his second quarter, when he showed up, his first stop was my office. He'd slump down in a chair, give me a tentative grin, and test the waters.

B: Somethin' came up.
R: Oh, what was that?"
B: Well, like, . . .

and he was off into his newest invention for why he had been absent or late. He always watched me carefully out of the corner of his eye to see how I would take these excuses. This was a mannerism of his, which at first appeared somewhat challenging, but was to become a game between us. The trick was not to react to the challenge, because he would go into an automatic patterned response at the first sign of adult disapproval. His face went blank, his chin set, his shoulders hunched, and he refused eye contact. However, a nonjudgmental response, such as, "That sounds interesting," or "Well, I can see where that would keep you busy," earned a half-shamed smile. He knew I didn't buy the excuse, but I was also acknowledging his power to decide not to come to tutoring. At that point, the doors were opened to talk about the situation. He would then sometimes suggest he had made a poor choice, saying "I know, I know. I should have been here." And I would respond, "Well, that's your choice." The important thing that we established was that I had no power to make him appear for tutoring, although I could cause him discomfort by calling his dad. I also acknowledged that if I chose that route, he still had the power to sabotage the tutoring session. That didn't seem a logical move, since the goal was to improve his reading. However, I explained, and he understood, that I also had a responsibility to his father. The building of a relationship between us began at this point, when he realized that I accepted his power and was asking him to use it responsibly. My major request was that he call if he wasn't coming. He found this reasonable, but unfortunately, his propensity for losing everything given to him, including phone numbers, made things very difficult. I did suggest tatooing the clinic number on his forehead, but as Ben cleverly pointed out, unless there was a mirror by the phone, it wouldn't do any good.

This type of understated sense of humor slowly began to emerge and it was a delight to discover the witty, sassy young man he usually kept hidden under a bored exterior. I was totally enchanted when, after catching him in a big fib, I asked him why he made up stories.

B: Cause, cause that's what little kids do [accompanied by his lopsided grin and sly look]. . . You know how it was, when you was a kid you did somethin' like that too. [Shakes his finger at me] Now don't say you didn't cause I know you did! [Laughs heartily]

R: Well, I probably did. I'll give that to you.
B: Everybody do that. It's not lyin'—it's exaggeratin'.
R: Uh, you're drawing a real thin line here Ben. [Laugh]

His face lit up in situations like this, I think because he truly enjoyed creating links of common behaviors between us. He behaved as though very few adults have accepted this sort of bond-making effort from him. It was almost a discovery process. It was a revelation for me to see the yearning for acceptance in this sullen-looking kid whose body language yelled, "Get off my case!"

Many of our conversations involved comparing notes about being a teacher and being a student. This began when he was expressing his displeasure over a teacher's comments to him. As an afterthought he said, "Why would he act that way?" Instead of defending or attacking the teacher's actions, I told Ben of a similar situation I had experienced and how I felt toward the student at that time. I discovered that he was very interested in this new perspective, and after that he frequently asked for an explanation of events in his life from a different perspective. Sometimes he would make up events just to hear my interpretation. For instance, he once told me that, while he was washing the car, a white man drove up in his driveway and purposely hit Ben's dog. He used this narrative to stimulate my views on prejudice. This was on his mind, because he told me several other stories, some more likely to be true than others, about mild confrontations he had with whites.

These conversations may seem unrelated to reading, and at first they did to me too. Then it slowly dawned on me what had developed between us. Regardless of our totally different life experiences, we could talk to each other. Looking back, I can see that Ben was a very unsure and somewhat distrustful young man when I met him, with good reason, and reading was probably a low priority compared to his need to maintain some control over the events in his life. Before we could deal with his reading problem, we had to establish a safe environment where he could freely display his weaknesses in that area, secure in knowing there was no chance of ridicule and at least a reduced chance of failure. He had to know I valued him, his opinions, his feelings, before he could trust me enough to choose what I could offer him. This relationship built slowly over the sixteen weeks he was being tutored in the clinic so that once we began the study we had a foundation upon which to build. It was also important to Ben that he was approached separately from his father about participation in the study. I made it clear that he had the power to discontinue his participation at any time, and he could go over anything I wrote or taped. He signed the consent forms after I explained fully what both of us might gain from this cooperative project.

To begin my study, I wanted to find out from Ben how he perceived the task of reading, what part he might be playing in maintaining his reading disability, and why the educational system hadn't worked for him. We began meeting twice a week for open-ended interviews which were audiotaped and sometimes videotaped and for reading tutoring sessions. Ben enjoyed seeing himself on tape and we shared the embarrassment of seeing ourselves as others see us. I decided I looked like a prissy teacher, which delighted him, and he decided he didn't look half bad. He always wanted to watch playbacks so he could check out his look and laugh at our mannerisms. It was nice to notice that he laughed more at himself rather than at me. As we watched playbacks, he often added or clarified information. I frequently read back portions of transcriptions or played back portions of audiotapes to get his second reaction, asking him, "Is this what you meant?" or prompting him with, "That's interesting. Tell me more." He seemed to gain in maturity and confidence as he realized that what he said was important to me and as he perceived himself as a partner in this learning experience.

We began by exploring his thoughts on reading.

R: What do you think reading is?
B: [immediate response] Hard! Hard and fun in some ways. When you're reading you get the expression [*sic* "impression"] of . . . like when girls write you notes, you read it and then that will tell you what's in there.

Ben had found an excellent reason to read because his girlfriend wrote him notes frequently. He read one to me, missing several words, but he got enough to understand the gist of her message. If he had been able to read all the words by himself, I probably never would have seen it, because it was a bit personal. He was a little embarrassed, but really more proud that a girl would say such things to him. This was a powerful literacy event in his life as it gave him status and proof of his attractiveness to girls. Unfortunately the possibility of expanding this literacy experience did not work out for Ben.

> R: Do you get lots of notes?
> B: Uh huh.
> R: Do you write her back?
> B: No [disparaging tone] cause I can't spell that good.
> R: Oh, I see. Does she know why you don't write her back?
> B: Naw. I just tell her I don't write notes [macho type gestures].
> R: Oh, okay.
> B: And, uh, I ain't lyin'. I just don't.
> R: But if you could spell better . . . ?
> B: Yeah, I would.
> R: What would you call that . . . [gesture indicating the note situation]
> B: A little . . . protective.
> R: Of yourself.
> B: Yeah.

This was only one of the strategies Ben used to protect himself from ridicule. It often seemed that he was deluding himself into thinking his problem wasn't that bad.

Later in the study, I observed Ben in a social studies class going through the motions of copying notes from the board, even though he told me later that he couldn't get the notes copied.

> R: Were you able to get the notes down?
> B: No, you see, I'm a slow writer, cause I can't spell that good and you know all these other kids are just lookin' up and they can spell the words. And I gotta keep lookin' up.

He was only able to copy about half the notes that day and they were not very legible. Yet he kept going through the motions, and when the other kids appeared to be getting done, he also acted as though he was finished for the day. It was worth his while to keep pretending because, as he said, "If you read, you're considered smart." His uncertain self-esteem could not afford exposure. In his words:

> B: When you get in the real world you can't be stutterin' when you read . . . cause they'll make fun of you.

Stuttering was Ben's way of describing disfluency.

There also appeared to be more subtle ways of maintaining a reading facade, even to himself. During the course of our association, Ben never openly admitted to the severity of his reading problem. Instead he would hedge a bit.

> R: What is your opinion about your reading?
> B: It's good, but not the best.

He told me a boy named Sean could read better than him.

> R: Why aren't you reading as well as Sean?
> B: Cause, he, he got a higher reading level.
> R: Are you born with those?
> B: Uh huh.
> R: You mean, he was born and God said he's going to read better than him. Is that the way it happens?
> B: Well, sorta. God says whether you're going to be learning disabled.

Another way of hedging was expressed frequently.

> R: Why do you think you can't read as well as them?
> B: Cause I'm lazy.
> R: You can't read well because you're lazy?
> B: Yeah, cause I can do it if I put my mind to it.

I thought this was an interesting contradiction in his thinking. On one hand being learning disabled could provide an easy excuse, but he was obviously not convinced of that. His assertion that he could do it if he tried was a hint that he was still trying to maintain some control over a confusing situation. I interpreted this as a very good sign for Ben, because to me it meant that Ben had not completely given up.

I thought that one of the things that may have kept Ben hanging on was his curiosity and his realization that books have words in them that could give him information and enjoyment. He really liked books and carried them around with him even when he didn't have to. When I asked Ben about the books, he told me that he read on his own. He would read when his dad grounded him, forcing him to stay in the house, and also before going to bed.

> B: When like I go to bed a bit earlier than I'm supposed to . . . and there's nothin' on TV, I just pick up my book and start reading.

His favorite book was one of the Garfield anthologies given to him by his first tutor. He kept it on a shelf by his bed. Ben shared other books with me that he carried around in his bookbag and read when he was on the school bus or in homeroom. Sometimes the books were rather difficult, like a paperback about military airplanes, but he could look at the photographs, make out some words, and most importantly, give the appearance of reading. So this reading served a social purpose, but I believe the real attraction was what was in the books. Once I presented Ben with twenty beautifully illustrated nonfiction books and asked him to choose three or four which he might like to read over the course of two weeks. I left the room for a few minutes and when I returned there was a stack of three books pushed off to the side. Ben was deeply involved in the first chapter of a book on killer bees. I picked up the three books and said, "I see you've chosen some books." He answered, "No, not those. I want to keep these," pointing to the large pile. He held up the book in his hand and asked, "Can we start with this one?" The books he had chosen included *Mars, Uranus, Mummies Made in Egypt, Fossils, The Gray Squirrel,* and *Earthquakes.*

Whenever I brought in new books he was always anxious to look through them and see what they were about. He would make comments about what he already knew about various topics, usually prefaced by, "Wow, I know about this stuff!" It pleased him to be able to share the knowledge he had. I capitalized on this enthusiasm by encouraging him to teach me about things he knew. For instance he read a book about the Harlem Globetrotters, and the knowledge he had greatly enhanced the book for me. I've learned a lot about basketball from Ben.

I used nothing but good children's literature with Ben, both fiction and nonfiction. Most of the time he seemed to enjoy the nonfiction the most. Only once did he question my use of a children's book and that was when we began to read the wonderful book *Mars* by Seymour Simon, which is filled with large photographs taken by the Viking and Mariner spacecraft. The page opposite each photograph contained text written in letters nearly one-half-inch high. He asked why they had to make the letters so big. Was it because it was for little kids? I showed him the difficult words and he realized that little kids certainly couldn't read it. Then we tried to figure out why the publisher had made the text so large. We finally decided it was so it balanced with the photo on the adjoining page. This made sense to him and he said it probably would look dumb if there was just this little section of words on a big piece of paper.

During the initial part of this study, I attempted to form a clear picture of the extent of Ben's reading skills. I was able to access the records from Ben's clinic experience and found that a reading grade-equivalent-level of primer level was obtained from the Gates-MacGinitie Reading Test, Form A, Level 1. Both tutors reported that Ben made little effort during testing, and refused to complete the comprehension section. In order to check these results, I administered an informal reading inventory and found that Ben could read with ease and understanding at the second-grade level. At the third-grade level his competence fell, mostly due to lack of knowledge of some content words which affected his comprehension. I observed Ben's reading and analyzed his miscues to determine what strategies Ben used when reading. I found that he used the following strategies in roughly the sequence shown.

1. Sound out the word using initial then final consonants
2. Guess
3. Break the word into parts
4. Skip the word
5. Ask for help

His strengths were a fairly good basic sight-word vocabulary and the ability to blend sounds together. His greatest weaknesses were an extremely deficient meaning vocabulary and the lack of self-monitoring skills. He would frequently try to figure out a word and then either guess or skip it, without seeming at all concerned about the loss of meaning. It is possible that this approach to hard words was also part of his good reader facade, because good readers don't have to ask for help very often.

Next I explored how Ben himself described his approach to reading. The following excerpt gave a glimpse into his ideas.

R: When you have a book in front of you how hard do you try?
B: I try hard.
R: Tell me what you do that someone else would be able to observe that shows you try hard.

B; When I get stuck, I don't ask for help. I try to do it myself.
R: What do you try to do?
B: Try to pronounce them out.
R: How would you—Let's just say I gave you this word right here, . . . [Writes word "Propositional."] How would you go about trying to figure out what that word was?
B: Split it between that.
R: Where would you split it?
B: [points to space between prop/o]
R: What does that say right there?
B: Prop-o. . .
R: Okay, go on. Now what else would you do?
B: Proposition. Uh, I don't know that word.
R: You just said all but the last two letters.
B: Personal?
R: Proposition . . . ?
B: Propositional! Still don't know it.

This was Ben at his best, and it pointed out a sequence of strategies. Ben first looked at the initial letters, clustering them into a pronounceable segment. He attempted to work through to the end of the word. If the word didn't make sense, he made a guess based on initial and sometimes final word features. If the guess was incorrect he simply continued to read, regardless of loss of meaning. But obviously he had some skills at blending letter clusters together to make a sound that seemed like a word. The problem was that he didn't recognize many of the words he sounded out. Ben had an extremely limited meaning vocabulary, so while he could read adequately at about the second-grade level, above that level, where more and more vocabulary or interest words begin to appear, his reading broke down.

As an example, Ben chose to read a book about squirrels which was a bit above his level. I agreed since we had recently spent a morning looking at, feeding, and talking about squirrels. However, he missed quite a number of words including *incisor, kernel,* and *fungus.* He pronounced them correctly, and if I hadn't noticed a puzzled look on his face I would have assumed he knew the words. For instance, for the word *incisors,* the sentence read, "The squirrel uses his incisors to open the nuts." The accompanying picture showed a squirrel holding a nut up to his mouth. I asked Ben, "What does that mean?" He answered, "It means he has hands that can open nuts." I asked him, "Do you know what *incisor* means?" When he answered no his tone of voice said I should have known he didn't know that word. And he was right. After all, how often do we go around talking about incisors? Examples of other words he could pronounce but did not know were *reveal, conceal, badger,* and *rural.*

Feeding the squirrels was very enjoyable with Ben along to prod me to look at them anew. I had first noticed his interest when we were sitting at a picnic table at the university after visiting a science lab. He kept saying, "Look at the squirrel!" I told him that we would have to bring some food and he became very excited. So the next week we both brought peanuts and spent an hour in a little bower where squirrels like to play. There were three squirrels that day, a mother and two babies. Ben was fascinated. "Look how they hold their food! Just like me eatin' a sandwich!" "He's hangin' upside down in that tree. How does he do that?" He was able to entice one squirrel very close by holding a peanut out. He said, "What are they diggin' around for?" and "How come they got such big eyes?" When I didn't know for sure, we worked out possible answers together. He also had interesting insights. "They must like livin' here. There's nothin' to bother them." "Like what?" I asked. "You know—predators." We later took a trip to a natural history museum where he noticed similarities between the squirrel and other rodents on display. He also saw a mummy which made him anxious to read Aliki's *Mummies Made in Egypt.* To me this was exhilarating and also a bit sad, as it clearly showed the types of experiences and concepts he had missed somewhere along the line.

It had become obvious that Ben did want to read. I had seen no signs of laziness, no falling asleep over books, no "bad attitude." Actually, my confusion was growing. If he could learn so well, was so motivated, then what was the problem? By working so closely with him, it was no longer possible for me to hold to my expectation that disabled readers like Ben did something that kept them disabled. It couldn't be the time I spent with him, because he was in some learning-disability classes and those teachers would be able to spend considerably more time with him. It couldn't be his intelligence, because he seemed pretty normal to me. As a matter of fact, my most pressing question became, why does anyone think this kid is LD? I spent several sessions virtually peering at everything Ben did, trying to find some sign of a learning disability. Finally, I knew I had to look at his school records and see why he was placed in special education. With some help from friends, I was able to get permission to look at the records in just a few days. This was what I found.

Ben was a product of special education placements beginning in the first grade. He was referred to the school psychologist within the first weeks of first grade. The referring teacher reported:

> He is dispruptive, hyperactive, and craves attention. . . He stays in trouble constantly . . . and is always picking fights with peers. His school work is poor due to his inability to sit still and to follow directions.

He was about seven years old at this time, living in one of a series of foster homes. Ben was placed in a classroom for the educable mentally retarded for "therapeutic" reasons, although the testing psychologist noted that scores were most likely depressed due to Ben's short attention span during testing. Interestingly, eight months later in the same school year, Ben was retested and found to have an IQ score of 90, making him ineligible for EMR. The school had established a program for children with severe behavior handicaps during this year and the evaluation team considered this as a placement. However, Ben was placed in a learning disability classroom, presumably because his behavior was not severe enough for SBH. Ben remained in LD classes until fifth grade, when "severe problems with peer interaction" led to his placement in SBH. He stayed there for one year, was reported to do very well, and then was placed back in LD where he has remained.

Records showed that Ben's reading ability had wavered between second- and third-grade levels since the fourth grade. His most recent school records indicated he was reading below the third-grade level and his teacher said he would receive an F for the year in reading due to lack of effort.

A psychologist who tested Ben at the middle of his seventh-grade year, due to a change in school districts, noted skills so deficient that he is reported to have said, "Where has this kid been all these years?" I would extend that to say, "And what has the special educational system been doing with him?" His latest LD placement was done on an override, which meant he either did not qualify or only marginally qualified according to state standards, but the evaluation team did not wish to place him in regular classes where his deficient skills would ensure his failure. At this point, it was probably the only possible choice.

I was shocked after reading these reports. They were so sterile. Hadn't anyone considered the emotional stress Ben must have been under in first grade, not having a real family, craving attention? And the teacher even said that—"He . . . craves attention." So he got a label instead of understanding. My anger began to grow. What kind of system was this that could call a child special and treat him so poorly that by the time he reached seventh grade he could barely write? My indignation ran rampant and my curiosity grew. What was happening in school now?

I asked Ben what sort of things he did in his LD reading class that taught him about reading.

B: Read dull cards.
R: Cards? What kind of cards?
B: NFL cards and stuff like that. [Reading kit cards]
R: Do you read for the teacher individually or in groups.
B: By myself.
R: So if you come up against a word you don't know, what happens?
B: Nothin'.
R: Nothing? Do you ask?
B: Yeah, but it ain't worth it.
R: Why, what happens when you ask?
B: Cause she tells me to figure it out, and I'm like, "I can't figure it out."

Sticking to my illusions, I at first thought this was just Ben being difficult, but then in another conversation he told me more about his view of teacher help.

R: What do the teachers do to help you.
B: They put [point out] the *i, u,* stuff like that. Vowels, short *i,* long *i,* and I don't get that stuff.
R: When you come to that word, you can't make any sense. What would you do at that point?
B: I'd ask her for help then I can tell you what they do. They go, "Put the two dots here," and they put a line and I'm like, "What's this?" cause I don't understand this. [He showed me an example of diacritical marks.]
R: And then do they tell you what the word is?

B: No, they tell you to sound it out.

R: Okay, so you're sitting there trying to sound it out. What if you still don't get it?

B: Then they finally give in and tell me the word.

R: How does that appear to you—when they—Is that helpful?

B: No, it makes it harder for me.

R: It makes it harder?

B: Yeah.

R: If you could describe how your teachers are feeling at that moment, how would you describe—if you were the teacher how do you think they are feeling right now?

B: PO'd. They'd be mad, cause they think that's a word I should know or somethin' like that.

R: How do you feel right then?

B: I feel mad! Cause all I want them to do is tell me the word instead of sittin' there trying to help me when I already tried it!

Both voice and body language made his frustration very clear. And after working with him, I knew that this was the wrong approach. He knew how to sound words out, he just didn't always know what they meant when he did so.

After thinking about this information, I decided it was necessary to interview Ben's teachers and observe in his classrooms. This was not only a way to further my understanding of Ben, but also a way of confirming or disconfirming the information I had obtained from Ben. I asked Ben what he thought about this and he seemed a bit hesitant. I explained that I really needed to see what was going on in the school, and he told me that his teachers yelled at him a lot. I suggested that he might like to structure my visit in such a way that he was more comfortable. As a result, I agreed to pretend I didn't know him and would only speak to him if he spoke to me first.

My observations in Ben's classrooms were prefaced by a telephone conversation with one of his teachers who told me:

Z: You won't see anything. He just sits there. He's already failed for the year, but they won't retain him because he's too old. He hasn't done enough to pass.

R: I'm also interested in observing his interactions with his peers.

Z: He's been in SBH, you know, and he's got some real behavior problems. For example, today he wiped snot all over a kid's book.

That's the sort of thing he does all the time. The other kids get pretty fed up.

R: I imagine so.

Later in the conversation she told me that Ben was more like a developmentally handicapped student than an LD student. I was astounded, and I remained astounded for weeks after my visit to the school. Two such disparate views of one young man were hard to believe.

I first observed in the social studies classroom mentioned previously, in which Ben was unable to copy the notes from the board. In a brief conversation with the teacher following the class, he expressed his feelings about having Ben in his class in a voice edged with sadness and puzzlement: "He just doesn't do anything. . . . He really doesn't belong in here." I had to agree, there didn't seem to be any place for Ben in the class, but it wasn't due to his not doing anything. It was my perception that he worked very hard to look busy, to look like it all made sense to him.

I then went to Ben's LD language arts class. This observation lent credence to much of what Ben had told me about reading instruction in school. After a few minutes of socializing with another boy named Rick, Ben settled down to work on a ditto sheet concerning letter writing. He sighed a lot as he worked on this. The teacher was situated at her desk in the front of the room working with another student. What follows is an excerpt from the field notes taken during that observation.

> Ben gets up and gets a dictionary from the shelf. He is trying to find a word in it so he can check the spelling or the meaning. His lips move a bit, saying the sounds of the first letter of the word, which appears to be a *p*. His forehead is wrinkled in concentration. Rick is not working at all, but is rolling his jeans above his knees. This is eighth grade shorts day. Ben suddenly slouches back in his chair and sticks his legs out in the aisle with a loud sigh. With a look of disgust, Ben puts his paper in the dictionary and closes the book rather loudly. He pulls himself out of his chair as if it is an effort, and shuffles up to the teacher's desk, his body language expressing apathy or perhaps reluctance. Rick grabs his paper and follows. Allen gets up from the chair by the teacher and brushes past Ben. Ben says, "Don't be hittin' me," with a challenging stance, shoulders forward and chin down. Allen says he didn't, he was just getting by. He speaks in a

monotone. Rick has walked to the front of the teacher's desk and she tells Rick to sit down by her. Ben has to move so that Rick can sit in the chair. Rick gives Ben a little grin of triumph, and Ben responds by murmuring something, but smiles. He stands to the side until the teacher is done with Rick. Then Ben takes the chair and puts the dictionary on the desk, opening it to his paper. The teacher turns her chair slightly back from the desk. He says he can't find the word. She asks him how it sounds. He says he knows he is in the right section, but he can't find it. He sits back in his chair, away from the book. She tells him something, and he flips a couple of pages. It appears as though he has sounded out the word and matched the vowel sound with the wrong letter, therefore not being able to find the word. The teacher tells him the vowel. He flips the pages, and begins to run his finger down a page. She points to a word and tells him to find out what it means. He gives her a small look of disgust, turning his face away quickly. She looks at him expressionlessly, then pulls her chair closer to the desk and picks up a paper. Ben goes back to his desk and mumbles some uncomplimentary comment about school. After he sits down, he looks at the dictionary for a few minutes. Then he says to the teacher, "Which one do I put down?" She answers, "Which one do you think would be closest?" He responds with a grunt and concentrates on this. Then with a loud sigh, he writes something on his sheet. The room becomes very quiet.

This interaction further suggested the mismatch of instruction with student need. The teacher encouraged use of consonant and vowel sounds and the use of the dictionary. It seemed apparent from Ben's last comment that what he really wanted was to know what the word meant.

As the class progressed, Ben went to the next assignment which was one of the reading kit cards he had described to me. He concentrated on a story about a young pilot and then answered the multiple-choice questions. The assignments were placed on the teacher's desk when done. She made no comment on them at that time, except to ask if he had checked his work. At one point, when Ben and Rick were talking, the teacher ask if he needed her to read with him, but he refused. The offer appeared to be intended as a means of behavior control.

Ben interacted with Rick several times during the class. They spoke quickly and with enthusiasm in strong black dialect, making it difficult for me to follow the conversation. However, it was apparent that the boys understood each other well. Ben also interrupted his work to get out all of his money and count it, take things in and out of his book bag, and comb his hair. It was apparent that Ben initiated most of the interactions in the class and drew the most teacher comments. It was also apparent that he didn't have enough work to keep him occupied the entire period.

Following this class, I conducted a forty-minute open-ended interview with both LD teachers, designated in this paper as X and Z. I had not really anticipated them being together, but that was the way they structured the situation. It was their lunch hour, and they took turns going to get their lunches during the interview, bringing their food back with them. The interview was very illuminating in that it raised the possibility that teacher expectations could be having a great effect on Ben's ability or motivation to learn.

The teachers both felt that Ben made very little effort in school and their talk was frequently punctuated with statements such as the following:

X: He just sits and does nothing.
Z: It's just simple, he won't figure out or take that time at home.
X: It depends on whether or not he wants to.

Another teacher concern was Ben's poor behavior and lack of social skills, much of which they attributed to hyperactivity.

X: He's so disruptive and his attention deficit syndrome is just real handicapping. . . . And, uh, being hyper, which he is, uh, it was difficult. He would, he'd leave his seat to go do his, uh, sharpen a pencil, pick up a piece of paper or any excuse at all to get out of his seat. And he would bump into people and disturb everyone else. And then they would yell, "Ben!" and that's the way it went.

I found this very interesting as I had never once seen Ben act in a hyperactive manner. If anything, he was a bit sluggish sometimes. I kept track for a few tutoring sessions after this to see how much time he did spend working and how much time he wasted. One day he worked for forty-five out of fifty-five minutes, and on another occasion he worked for fifty-two out of sixty minutes. It seemed to me that all of our sessions had been like that. That doesn't seem like a hyperactive kid to me, but I think the word hyperactive is frequently misused to describe kids that are bored and want to have some fun to alleviate the boredom.

Nevertheless, the teachers thought he was hyperactive. Furthermore, the teachers' understanding of hyperactivity or attention deficit disorder has left them feeling somewhat powerless to deal with Ben's behaviors.

> X: You know, I went to this workshop a couple of years ago, and this attention deficit syndrome, no matter how much you train them, they don't improve that. It just doesn't improve.

The teachers described Ben's incredible lack of skills when Ben first entered their classroom in seventh grade, suggesting a very impoverished elementary education, regardless of special education.

> X: He couldn't write, he couldn't—uh, no cursive at all. He could print his name. . . He was almost a total nonreader when he got here.

In view of this, what was interesting to me was what they attributed to be the causes of his reading and learning difficulties.

> Z: His speech is very bad. And he even said something that you [R], we both didn't even understand and I said [gesturing to R], "What is he talking about?"

This occurred during my classroom observation when Ben and Rick were engaged in conversation using black dialect. It was interesting that once Ben told me, when I was explaining a bit about a sociolinguistics class I was taking, that he knew what I was talking about. He said that sometimes white teachers—

> B: [excitedly] It's like, if she don't know how we talk, then she don't know what we be sayin'!

Ben was very proud of his understanding and implied that it was the teacher's job to learn how the kids talked. But to continue with the teachers' comments:

> X: There's no feed-in to his brain through his ears, so to speak. He doesn't recall, um, things. That's why I always figured he needed so

much visual support in everything he does and that's why he doesn't
understand what he's reading. He doesn't retain reading concepts
and ideas and has a difficult time with it—sequencing of stories and
things cause he just doesn't take the comprehension of the whole
story in. It just doesn't feed into his brain.
R: Do you have any theories on that? Why it's happening?
X: Well, I think auditory disabilities are a severe handicap to intelligence, I really do. . .
Z: [speaking about Ben's lack of success in the social studies class]
Evidently he has no auditory abilities. He just can't listen.

Teacher X later said that Ben not only had attention deficit disorder and poor auditory perception, but also he had visual perception problems and a perceptual processing difficulty.

As I said, I was astounded. He doesn't recall things? Ask him
about Michael Jordan's basketball career. He doesn't retain concepts? Ask him about the theories of the canals on Mars. He
doesn't understand what he's reading? Ask him about killer bees.
And if nothing gets through his ears to his brain, how is it he has
memorized dozens of rap lyrics from the tapes he plays? It seemed
the teachers didn't address instructional issues, but talked around
them using vague, abstract labels. Not once could I get a clear
positive statement about Ben. It seemed to me they had him pegged
in a corner marked failure, shaking their heads in sympathy, and
denying any personal role in the problem.

I shared some of the teachers' responses with Ben, trying very
hard to be noncommittal about my reactions, to see how he reacted. Unfortunately the tape recorder was not plugged in properly,
so much of this conversation was lost. However, as soon as he left I
wrote down as much as I could remember. One particular exchange stuck in my mind very well. I told him that his teacher said
he really didn't try very hard. He said she was on his case again
that day.

R: What happened.
B: Aw, she don't like me [flatly and with conviction].
R: What does she do to make you think that?
B: [angrily] Man! She don't know. She thinks she know all about my
life. Nobody knows my life but me!

The more I thought about it, the more this made sense to me.
These teachers appeared to be assuming that they knew what Ben

was doing and not doing, but they actually were making judgments based on their beliefs about how a good student behaves. I continued to try to see the situation from Ben's perspective.

R: Are you in trouble a lot?
B: Yeah.
R: In school or at home?
B: In school, at home.
R: Tell me about trouble at school.
B: Arguments with teachers and stuff like that. [Very strong non-verbals being expressed here, as though it made him angry to think about it.]
R: Let's talk about arguments with teachers for a minute so I can get kind of a picture. I'm a teacher, so I know how these things go. How about your English teacher. You go in your class and sit down in your chair.
B: No.
R: That's not what happens. What happens?
B: The bell rings, you get your work, then sit down in your chair.
R: What else?
B: That's it.
R: So how do you fight with your teacher? What do you do, or what does she do—it could be both ways—that causes a fight?
B: Walkin' around.
R: So you get out of your chair.
B: [Nods]
R: Does she think you're not supposed to get out of your chair?
B: You gotta like raise your hand before you get out of your seat.
R: Does everybody in class do that except you?
B: [Nods]
R: Why don't you raise your hand?
B: I just don't feel that—if you do your work, you don't need to raise your hand.
R: So you're not in agreement with the rule.
B: Right.

I set up a situation which is typical in classrooms to see how Ben interpreted the interaction.

R: So like, if a teacher says, "Ben get out your book," and you say, "What book?", and the teacher says, "Ben, you know which book it is!", she takes that and she thinks, "I gave a direct order, Ben did not comply with the order," and the teacher gets frustrated with Ben.

B: [very animated] Yeah, but, askin' them is tryin' to be nice to them and makin' sure I got the right book. An' she only hear [gesture of confusion] and stuff. That don't make no sense! She act like she know we would know that. . . [Waves his hand in frustration, dismissing the subject.]

Who do you suppose was really more frustrated, Ben or the teachers? It seemed to me that Ben was not only frustrated but also totally confused. For some reason he was still holding on to the idea that school wasn't really supposed to be like this and maybe it would change.

I carried my righteous indignation around with me for several weeks, and tried to get it down on paper so I could share this educational travesty with others, but the story wouldn't come. I tried again. Everything I wrote seemed shallow and petty. Ben was there in the story and that should have been enough. After all, it was his story. But when I thought about that, it slowly began to occur to me, that this wasn't just Ben's story. It couldn't be just Ben's story, because I had been wrong from the start. He didn't do much of anything to become reading disabled, a failure in school. Most of it had been done to him by an impersonal, ineffective system. The reason I couldn't write it was that I had to acknowledge my part in the system. It made no sense for me to be so angry at Ben's teachers after such a long period of time, because they were doing the best they knew how, and they personally didn't do this to Ben. After all they didn't see him until he was thirteen. My anger had another source. When I listened to the words of Ben's teachers, I was hearing a faint echo of my own words about that occasional kid in my classes who wasn't worth my effort because he just wouldn't try. And I had to face the fact that maybe that kid was just as super as Ben, but I hadn't taken the time to find out then, and now it was too late. It was a humbling realization that forced me to give up some of the anger and expand my empathy for the teachers, while at the same time fueling what had become my advocacy of Ben.

As I said before, Ben sometimes made up stories to test my reaction, but there was usually a bit of truth in them. It was as if the stories were his way of expressing something he wished were true. One of the things he wished was that he had a strong peer group where he belonged and in which he could just be one of the crowd.

He told me a fascinating story, not quite true, embellished certainly, but with a strand of truth running through it. At this point in his life, Ben had developed an image which he felt he must maintain, if only for himself. This following story gave me a glimpse into his perception of the image he wanted to project.

R: You told me the other day when we were talking about—that reading makes you look smarter in front of your friends. Tell me a little about that.

B: Well, see like, everybody from my school don't read. I mean, if you read you're considered smart. [Pause]

R: Okay, so if you read, you're considered smart. Does that make you more popular?

B: No. Beatin' up people makes you popular.

R: Oh really. Are you popular?

B: Yeah.

R: Do you beat up a lot of people?

B: I'm, I'm like in a gang.

R: Uh huh.

B: And to get in the gang you got to beat up the other leader or at least tie.

R: What's the name of your gang?

B: Uh, Uptown. You probably heard of us.

R: No, I don't know much about the gangs here. Is this a big gang?

B: No, we don't go around terrorizing'. . .

R: You just. . .

B: We just a bunch of people who hang together, call each other up and tell 'em where we want 'em to be, an' all that.

R: Mmm.

B: Or what the plan is for the day.

R: Okay, um, so if you read you're considered smart and that gets you. . .

B: Eligible to fight their leader.

R: Oh, so if you want to be a leader of your own gang kinda you have to be considered smart?

B: [Nods]

R: Mmm. Smart in what ways? Just reading smart or are there other ways of being smart?

B: Just reading smart.

R: If you beat [the leader] then you would become the leader of your gang.

B: And that gang.

R: Does that mean that everyone would want to fight you?

B: No.

R: Why not?

B: Cause, you see, what the leader is doin' is sit around and have their people go out and fight.

R: [Laugh]

B: Like "Frankie, go fight this dude. Sammy, go fight that dude. You go fight him, and I'll fight. . ." [His voice changes to a type of street dialect that I have only heard on TV gangster movies. He makes expansive gestures with his hands as though he really is talking to these people.]

R: So the leader is the brains?

B: The Boss.

R: He's the boss, he's the brains, he's the lazy guy. Everyone else gets in trouble and he sits there and laughs. Is that what happens?

B: [Grins, nods]

R: Ahh, and you want that job?

B: [Nods vigorously]

R: Is it good to be in a gang?

B: You get recognition.

R: All right. From . . . who?

B: Girls. That's why I like to be in a gang.

R: Well, sure, I can see that.

B: Have you ever heard the term when . . . if you're a football player all the girls want to get close to you?

R: Um hm.

B: Cause they think you're big and tough?

R: Um hm.

B: That's a gang.

R: That's interesting. What do the teachers think about gangs?

B: They crack on us.

R: Uh, explain that to me.

B: Make jokes.

R: Oh, does that bother you?

B: Umm . . . no. I tell, I tell my people just stay cool.

Fantasy? Perhaps. His best friend told me there wasn't a gang, just a bunch of kids who played basketball together. However, more than fantasy, there appeared to be a need to present himself as someone with power, someone who was important and respected. Perhaps that's the appeal of gangs. The other interesting story he told me, which may actually have happened at one time, was a story which highlighted his belief that reading is important.

R: You said that most of the kids in your school couldn't read.

B: Well, you know . . . not . . . well, uh. They, they can read . . . uh . . . aw! [Gestures with hands imply confusion]

R: No, go ahead.

B: I can't explain it.

B: Could they read this book?

B: Yeah.

R: Easy book, huh?

B: Yeah.

R: Are you saying. . .

B: They can read any kind of book. But they give you like a certain kind of book that they thought was hard and you gotta read it. See, so it might be like a dictionary. . .

R: Your friends do this?

B: Yeah.

R: Is this something you have to do to prove that you're smart?

B: Yeah.

R: Describe to me how you. . .

B: Whew! Like, "I bet you can't finish that paragraph in 15 minutes and if you miss a word, it don't count."

R: Okay, so what happens if he says, "So?" and doesn't do it?

B: [Snaps fingers] Frankie! [Points as though directing somebody, implies there will be a fight.]

So to Ben, reading was part of the fantasy of how one proved oneself smart, powerful and respected, at least to one's peers.

Ben has now moved on to high school. We took a two-month break from tutoring, not because we wanted to, but because with his volunteer basketball-coaching schedule and my class schedule, it was impossible to meet. I have recently heard from him and he continues to fail subjects in his LD classes. So we're going to begin tutoring again at whatever odd hour we can find. Our main goal is to get him reading at least at the seventh-grade level, but we are also going to have to work on ways he can present himself in a better light to the teachers who have the power over grades. I know he can do it, but we are really racing the clock and his tolerance level. It's hard to say how long Ben can be expected to put up with the frustration and failure in school before he just decides to quit.

What I have learned from Ben has convinced me that my original belief was correct. Reading improvement is essential for Ben to progress any further in school or to have any chance of graduating. However, reading improvement is, for Ben, complexly interwoven with social, psychological, and educational factors. I think at times we all want to be valued and respected for the knowledge we have about ourselves—what we can do, what is hard for us, what helps us, what hinders us—and have that knowledge taken seriously by those we look to for help. This is what Ben has told me he needs to become "smart," to become a reader.

REFLECTIONS

When doing a case study such as this one, perhaps there is always an element of emotional involvement which subtly skews the researcher's interpretations in one direction or another. I felt this was a positive aspect of this study as my involvement made me feel emotions Ben was feeling, distance myself from the teacher role, and see school in a way I had never viewed it before, through the eyes of a student for whom school made little sense. As a result, I think I really captured one small part of Ben's experience. It has also allowed me to more critically analyze my responses to other students, and to more critically consider the role of student-teacher interactions in student performance.

One has to wonder, considering the obvious emotional upheavals in his life, whether Ben was properly placed in special classes. Several instances of retesting before the times required by state regulations (every three years), and psychologists' hedging comments in their reports, along with the changes from program to program, seem to indicate an uncertainty about what to do with Ben. But as McDermott (1987) states, "Once a child is tracked it is almost impossible for him to break loose" (p. 198). The teachers indicated that his current placement was due to processing deficits and hyperactivity. There has been much attention in special education to these so-called "neurological deficits" based on "soft signs" exhibited by the student (Carrier 1986, p. 33). The acceptance of such deficits as a cause of their learning problems effectively places the fault with the child since the deficits are considered to be genetic in origin or the result of undetected brain damage. This can lead to lowered expectations by the teachers combined with a sense of frustration, which is seen quite clearly in Ben's teachers. What is not so obvious is the long-term effect this can have on a child. Children have a sense of how people regard them and respond accordingly. Studies such as those by Rist (1970) and Cooper

(1979) have found that teachers' perceptions of a student's abilities lead to expectations for a student's achievement. Furthermore, children are aware of these expectations and tend to internalize these views, resulting in living up (or down) to the teacher's expectations. There is no way that Ben, who is constantly looking for attention, could be unaware of the at-best ambiguous and at-worst negative expectations all of his teachers seem to have had for him.

While attention deficit disorder (ADD) is somewhat controversial, it has become a catch phrase for any child who exhibits hyperactive symptoms. The fascinating aspect of ADD diagnosis is that the symptoms are all behaviors exhibited by normal children. The diagnosis is really based on a subjective judgment of what degree of aggression, movement, and distractibility is too much in a given environment. These soft signs are supposedly indicative of minimal brain dysfunction or MBD (Sigman 1987, pp. 52–54).

At this point I feel compelled to defend the teachers. The problem is not with the intentions or essential goodness of the teachers, for I do not believe they have had anything less than the best of intentions for Ben. The problem seems to lie with the theory they use to understand their students. Clay (1979) spoke of this problem when she stated that there is a need for reading teachers to be flexible in their use of theory when dealing with children with reading problems. She states that a teacher's adherence to one theoretical base or one instructional method results in a strict control over what a child is allowed to learn. In this case it appears that a deficit explanation and a bottom-up approach to reading instruction may be preventing Ben from experiencing the other types of instruction likely to improve his reading (i.e., more reading time in interesting texts, concept-building activities which also include meaning-vocabulary development, and instruction in the use of metacognitive strategies).

Another possible problem interfering with Ben's learning may be Ben's lack of sociolinguistic competence in a classroom situation. When speaking with his peers, Ben uses a strong black dialect which the teachers often do not understand. Ben does modify his dialect or change registers (DeStefano 1978) when speaking to adults, but not to the extent of his peers whom I either observed or interviewed. He does not have as much competency in these areas, and this can bring forth strong negative reactions from users of a different dialect, especially users of the dialect which is considered most appropriate in a given situation (Cazden 1988, pp. 17–18). For instance, in school the middle-class dialect of a particular region is normally favored. Ben may need to become much more aware of his speech and learn to switch registers when appropriate. Furthermore, Ben does not always seem adept at reading the non-verbal signals others give off in response to his behaviors, although I have found he is quite capable of doing so when given strong signals. He then adapts his behavior appropriately.

A powerful factor that has become necessary in his adolescent years if he is to make any educational progress is Ben's feeling of control over the events that affect his learning. It appears that in Ben's classroom, as in many classrooms, learning is a product which is handed out by the teachers and Ben is supposed to be a passive recipient of this product. In order to maintain a sense of control over his school experiences, Ben may be perpetuating his unacceptable behaviors. This brings him attention, albeit negative, and effectively puts any learning experiences under his control. Unfortunately the learning process is more likely to be subverted than enhanced (McDermott 1987; Willis 1977).

Ben's view of himself as an integral part of a peer culture is in direct opposition to the view of him given by the teachers, but it shows that he is unlikely to buy in to an adult-oriented school culture at this time unless he can find ways to feed his self-esteem in that environment. William Glasser (1986) addresses this problem of disaffectation of youth from what school is offering. In his discussion of control theory, Glasser states that schools do not satisfy the basic human needs for belonging and power. In fact, schools are set up to control interactions and keep them to a minimum. In this situation, adolescents must fulfill their need for belonging through peer cultures and gain power by resisting school rules within the peer group structure. The peer group determines how status is gained and maintained. Therefore, student energies are devoted toward counter-school interactions. Glasser suggests that schools must find ways to satisfy these students' needs for power by teaching them about the controls they are currently using to subvert schooling and giving them choices that include participation in structuring their own learning experiences. Cazden (1988) describes this as "relevance," that is ". . . ways to make connections between their words, and their meanings, and ours" (p. 73).

Of instructional interest was Ben's response to good children's literature which became a focal point of his reading tutoring. He was able to discover that books were fun and confirm his belief that they held wonderful things that he wanted to know about. Shumaker and Shumaker (1988) describe this liberating property well:

> Freed from drills whose purpose they may not see and from materials whose relevance they doubt, such students can find a new frame of reference for reading. Great stories by serious writers can disarm student resistance and begin the process of rebuilding self concepts. (p. 545)

Also of importance was the realization that Ben needed to know what words meant. William Smith (1980) stated that a knowledge of the meanings of words encountered in text is of vital importance to comprehension. Also the knowledge of word meanings supports the inference of more meanings from context. In Ben's case, his vocabulary deficiencies hinder him from independently engaging with more difficult texts from which he could learn new words. This has the effect of making him somewhat teacher dependent until there are a wide enough variety of books that he can read on his own. Then reading could become a "systematic tool for acquiring and developing language" (Smith p. 95).

Whether or not Ben reaches the point of independent reading is still an open question dependent on many factors. However, while these factors imply needed changes in our whole system of education, my sense is that a few concerned teachers who would open their hearts and leave behind preconceived ideas could achieve miracles with this young man. Erickson (1987) suggests that it is not so much what we openly do to students that keeps them from achieving, but what we do unknowingly based upon our ideas of how things are and how they have always been. He expresses belief in the ability of teachers to change these practices once they are made aware that such practices do frequently seep into their classrooms. I share his belief and hope that this study will help other teachers, as it did me, to critically analyze their own practices and to value their students' views on what will make schooling relevant and humane.

CHAPTER 4

Ways of Being At Risk:
The Case of Billy Charles Barnett

Thomas Barone, Arizona State University

The focus of this chapter is on Billy Charles Barnett, a child of rural poverty. Once again we see a young person who displays many of the characteristics we associate with students at risk. We also see, however, insight and wisdom, sense and sensitivity. These qualities challenge the author to dramatically rethink the whole notion of what puts students at risk.

We are the representatives of two subcultures, meeting at McDonald's along an interstate highway in northeastern Tennessee. Sitting across from me is Billy Charles Barnett, a tall lanky boy with dark hair, green eyes, a pug nose, and an infectious grin. He is a member of the rural "disadvantaged," a fifteen year old nominated by the vice-principal as the student least likely to remain in Dusty Hollow Middle School. I am a middle-aged urban academic who, secure in a tenured university position, will *never* leave school.

I am inclined to believe the warnings of others like me—teachers and administrators at Billy Charles's school—that this teenager from the hills will be "slow" and "hard to talk to." I am, therefore, surprised to discover almost immediately a keen intelligence and an eagerness to share his knowledge about his world. Even more jolting is a sudden realization of my vast ignorance about the ways of people who live within a two-hour drive of my home and about the fundamentals of a world no longer honored in the dominant culture.

Between slurps on a straw, Billy Charles speaks:

> You don't know what jugging is? When you go jugging, first you take a jug that bleach comes in. You rinse it out and tighten the lid and get some soft but strong nylon string. Then you need to get a two-inch turtlehook, real strong, and a three- or four-foot line. The best bait is a bluegill, cut in half. You know, you really should use the head part. It's better than the tail, because turtles always go for the head of the fish first. But you can [also] catch catfish, bass, like this. I caught me a seven-and-one-half-pound bass once, jugging. The jug just hangs in the water and nothing can get off the line unless they break it. I can catch a mess of turtles this way, and then I make turtle soup. Do you know how to make turtle soup?

I find myself squirming in my seat. But why should I? Why should I be the one feeling inadequate and defensive? No, I didn't know—until Billy Charles told me—that the market was bearish on coonskins this year, and that I could expect no more than forty dollars for a flawless one of average size. The topic had simply never arisen in any graduate course in curriculum theory. Moreover, E. D. Hirsch and his co-authors had included no such items in their *Dictionary of Cultural Literacy: What Every American Needs to Know.* So I take comfort: not only am I the better informed, but also apparently the better American of the two strangers chomping on their cheeseburgers on this unseasonably balmy January afternoon.

Although I know nothing about the price of coonskins, I am better informed about Billy Charles than he is about me. For example, I know that Billy Charles is spending a second year in the seventh grade. I know that he has expressed on numerous occasions his intention to drop out of school as soon as he can. And I know that, on occasion, he has entertained fantasies of dropping out of life, as well.

This last item is, of course, the most troublesome. "Specific suicidal ideations" is the phrase used by the school psychologist to characterize Billy Charles's morbid fantasies. Having ventured forth from my cozy, book-filled office to conduct a case study on what I thought would be a "typical" student at risk, I would soon be forced to rethink my tired notions about such fundamentals as, oh, the meaning of life, the purposes of schooling, and the various ways in which an adolescent can be at risk of not being educated. To explain what I mean, let me tell my own short version of Billy Charles's life story.

Billy Charles Barnett was born in the hills of northern Tennessee on 28 March 1974. When Billy Charles was two, his parents were divorced, and his mother received custody of him. His father moved to another part of the state, where he remarried and divorced several times, never receiving custody of any of the children from those marriages. When Billy Charles was eight, his father returned to live near Dusty Hollow. Billy Charles began to visit his father a few times a year. At age thirteen, in the seventh grade, he began to spend more and more time with a dad who passionately loved to hunt and fish and trap. Billy Charles decided to move into his father's house, located in (he still insists, even today) "paradise": a densely wooded area, thoroughly distanced from the world of convenience stores, gas stations, and book-filled schoolrooms.

What had begun to stir in Billy Charles is easily remembered by most former thirteen year olds. Billy Charles was beginning to think about who he was: the son, the grandson, the great-grandson, and maybe the great-great-grandson of frontiersmen in the upper South who remained in that region as the frontier moved on. Perhaps the sons of each succeeding generation felt what Billy Charles has hinted to me: violated and abandoned, as "civilization" barged in to distort the shape of their lives. But even today the allure of the woods remains intoxicating to many of the menfolk, who have traditionally been charged with providing their families with the necessities of life.

Some of these men (Billy Charles's stepfather among them) have managed to relegate outdoor activities to the margins of their lives, taking to their shotguns and fishing gear only on weekends. But not Billy Charles. At least not since he started to become a man. Billy Charles has always loved the outdoors, but what his mother calls his "obsession" with hunting, fishing, and trapping began a couple of years ago and accounts (she insists) for his initial desire to live with his father.

That was a glorious time, according to Billy Charles. He was ecstatic to finally have for his very own a father to connect him to the past that lived within him, a male parent versed in the ways of the wilderness to guide him into his own Appalachian manhood. Almost daily Billy Charles and his father went out in the wild, the two of them together, apprentice and teacher. Billy Charles was joyously receiving an education in the real basics, eagerly learning the time-honored skills of survival (as opposed to such pale school-honored imitations as how to write a check or how to fill out a job application). He was absorbing the fundamentals of the world around him. Almost daily for more than a year, rain or shine, this wilderness school was in session. Even after the master turned on his eager pupil. Even, at least for a while, after the beatings began.

The friction started early in the summer when Billy Charles's father introduced some female strangers into the household: a new wife and a nine-year-old stepdaughter. Billy Charles's version is that he was now burdened with cooking for four instead of for two. ("It's a lot more work, and all she [his stepmother] ever did was eat ice cream and watch TV.") The resentment probably runs even deeper, rooted in the slight Billy Charles must have felt as his father's attention was divided and shared with others. Whatever the cause, tensions rose, and the beatings increased in frequency and in severity, reaching a peak when his father attacked him with a horsewhip.

So a father turns viciously on a son, who, in a time of delicate adolescent need is reluctant to leave—until the final incident of abuse when the new family decides to vacation in Florida.

While in Florida Billy Charles wrote a letter to his mother, describing his increasingly unhappy life. His father somehow managed to read the letter, and Billy Charles awoke, he says, to the pain of being pulled from the couch by his hair and slammed across the room. Not even the memory of the exciting encounter with a hammerhead shark on a previous day's deep-sea expedition could prevent a second change of custody. Not even the picture of his father's face that, as Billy Charles poignantly admitted to me, now makes him depressed when it appears before him unbeckoned. So, on the verge of manhood, Billy Charles went back to Mama, back to a place strewn with so many obstacles to his escape.

Billy Charles has always resisted any encroachment of the school world on his freedom outside. Rarely, for example, has he deigned to do homework. But he is frequently reminded of his sins of omission, as his mother and three sisters collaborate on school assignments in the crowded kitchen. So he retreats further inward, into a bedroom shared with two young men in their early twenties—his cousin, Carl, and Teddy, a friend of Carl's. (Only temporary boarders, says Billy Charles's stepdad, only until Carl's parents "work things out.") What does he do there all night? Billy Charles corroborated what one of his teachers told me: "I asked him and he said, 'I crawl into bed. And I die.' That's what he said, 'I just die.'"

If Billy Charles feels cramped, is he ever tempted to create some artificial space for himself through the use of drugs? His mother once caught him using an amphetamine. He was promptly hauled off to the police station, and this experience, his mother believes, was sufficiently traumatic for him to swear off any further drug use. Maybe so. But an earlier, much more stunning incident seems to have produced a deeper fear, at least of harder drugs. Several years ago, as Billy Charles tells it, a good friend, while sitting right beside him, had injected himself with an overdose. Just a couple of nine year olds in northern Tennessee, one watching the other die— 1980s style. Recently the memory was revived when Teddy's girl-friend died in an identical manner. This, too, has depressed Billy Charles. I have wondered (but have lacked the courage to ask) about the possible relationship between these morbid memories and his own "specific suicidal ideations."

Billy Charles's imagination is his only source of escape during his self-described "imprisonment" by day. The school bus deposits him at Dusty Hollow Middle School at 8:15 every morning, and by second period—math, the period when the cage seems smallest—Billy Charles is gone. He leaves through his mind—but always on foot. "I am walking in the hills," he says, recalling the leaves and the ground and the foxes and the possums. "I love to walk." Before meeting Billy Charles, I had never known a fifteen year old without the slightest desire to drive a car. But driving is simply not of interest to him. Says Billy Charles, "I can walk to wherever I want to go."

Although Billy Charles is rarely present in spirit at school, he drifts less often out of social studies and reading classes. The social studies class is taught by Billy Charles's favorite teacher, a bright, inventive young man who attempts to inject some liveliness into classroom activities with various simulation games, films, and student-centered projects.

Billy Charles's interest in reading class may be surprising, for Billy Charles has never been an avid reader. There is an encyclopedia in his house, and there are dictionaries. But there are few books and no daily newspaper. Billy Charles has not been raised in a home in which reading is seen as a delicious way to spend idle time. Perhaps his relative success in reading class is due to the special attention that is afforded him there. Billy Charles scores fairly well on most standardized tests, but he was placed in a "special education" reading class because he had been "disruptive" in other classes and was considered more "manageable" in smaller groups. He is reportedly less abusive and obnoxious to the reading teacher.

For the most part, though, school and the world of Billy Charles do not overlap. On weekdays, he is locked in his school's embrace, but he is often dreaming of another time, another place, imagining that he is free, his own man in a future when every day is Saturday. His is a vision awash in nostalgia, adamantly culling out for celebration only the pleasant features of the past—the thrill of the catch, the pan-fried trout, and the time spent under his father's benign tutelage—while screening out the unbearable: his father's scowl, his friend's limp body, or anything (like, say, a car or a classroom) invented since the Industrial Revolution. But the selectivity of Billy Charles's memory is understandable, and it represents, I believe, a hopeful sign. For it is only when his defenses break down and the grim ghosts of episodes past invade his psyche that Billy Charles seems most seriously at risk of abandoning more than just a formal education.

Does his vision of the future include earning a living? Billy Charles is utterly convinced that his own talents at tapping the bounty of nature will be sufficient to provide the necessities of life. As if to seal his argument, he points to his father, who works only at odd jobs (currently selling bait out of a small store) to supplement his "natural" income. Others in the area are skeptical about the possibility of living only off the land these days, pointing to stringent enforcement of the legal limitations regarding season and size of catches.

And is Billy Charles foreseeing the possibility of a future family whose hungry mouths demand more than he can provide? Odds are that Billy Charles will once again find his hours divided into time lived and time served, as the time clock replaces the clock on the classroom wall. Still, his expectations are so robustly romantic, so close to those that even members of my branch of our frontier culture were so recently forced to abandon, that I have found myself hoping along with him: maybe there is a way. What if, for example, he changed his mind about the ethics of teaching for a living? Billy Charles recently forked over one hundred dollars for a weekend of instruction in a "trapping school." He found it rather useless (as would any advanced student in a remedial class). "But," I asked, "have you ever thought of opening a school of your own or of becoming a guide to earn your own money?"

With his infectious grin, Billy Charles answered, "Oh no, I don't believe it's right to sell just words, to sell what you know for a living."

When I pointed out to him that words are precisely what his teachers sell, his reply was another grin. But Billy Charles is young, so we may hope for future compromises of his rigorous ethical standards. Getting paid for opening up his treasure chest of backwoods wisdom to weekend sportsmen still seems to me both pragmatic and honorable.

Of course, Billy Charles wouldn't need any more formal schooling for such an occupation. On the contrary, if this were his goal, school might then be precisely what he already believes it to be: an unwarranted roadblock on the path to the "good life." This is an unsettling notion to those of us who work devotedly toward fulfilling the goals of universal mandatory schooling. But what are those goals? By the time such academically disinclined students as Billy Charles reach the middle grades, we think we see their future just up ahead. To paraphrase the vice-principal at his school, Billy Charles will, at best, become a common laborer like his stepfather, perhaps working nights operating a forklift. And seldom, if ever, will he read a newspaper or a novel or a book of poetry.

So we abandon any lingering hopes for Billy Charles's conversion to a world of erudition and instead focus on *our* version of the basics. Teenagers unlikely ever to attend college must, we assume, be equipped with the mental skills appropriate to a working-class life: minimal competence in the basics; maybe an additional dash of content from the dominant culture (what *every* American needs to know); the basic skills of a trade which we hope will be acquired in a high school vocational track; and, certainly, the employee's attitude, a demeanor tacitly encouraged by the organizational structure of the school and composed of a nexus of behavioral norms (such as perseverance, promptness, diligence, and intellectual docility) needed for the industrial work place. If the non–college bound acquire these learnings, we the taxpayers are placed at lower risk of having to fork over welfare money, and prospective employers are placed at lower risk of having to provide remedial education for candidates for employment.

But, I ask myself again, what of students such as Billy Charles who have equipped themselves to eke out a living (maybe even legally) within the cracks of the modern global economy? Billy Charles is not illiterate (and perhaps no more aliterate than the average citizen), and he possesses much more than the minimal knowledge and skills needed for his own way of life. Could it be that Billy Charles's economic well-being is jeopardized only by our persistent attempts to inculcate values and behaviors that are, in fact, counterproductive to the successful conduct of his line of work? What use after all, are passivity and punctuality to denizens of the forest?

Stated flatly, is Billy Charles at risk only if he stays in school? On those moments when I forget about the purposes of schooling that transcend the narrow focus on careers, my answer is yes. Then I am visited by Maria Montessori's vivid metaphor of students in rigid rows of desks as butterflies pinned to a display case. At those moments I confess to entertaining the impossible fantasy of pulling the pin and setting Billy Charles free.

How many other Billy Charles Barnetts are there—potential dropouts with the wits and wherewithal to survive financially in a world that worships the high school diploma? The conventional wisdom—the wisdom of my subculture, the legitimated wisdom—says "not many." There are other exceptions to the rule, of course, including the future stars of stage, screen, or playing field, the youthful heirs to family fortunes, or even the honest entrepreneurs-to-be. But I am incapable of imagining many stories like that of Billy Charles.

Nevertheless, I am reluctant to abandon the promises of schooling, even for such an exceptional case as Billy Charles. Indeed, his very exceptionality invites us to look beyond the narrowly pragmatic, utilitarian objectives of schooling to recollect a more substantial notion of the purposes of education. His case revives our fading dreams of a broader sort of empowerment that schools once hoped to provide for all American children, regardless of their economic or social backgrounds. This included the power to use the disciplines for penetrating more deeply into one's own past and present world, the power to imagine a wide range of alternative worlds in other times and places, and the power to express these understandings by employing many forms of literacy—verbal, visual, musical, kinesthetic, and so on.

This is where the exceptionality of Billy Charles ends and his commonality begins. For these are powers of thought and expression so often denied not only to the Billy Charles's among us, but also to many academically respectable students for whom schooling is merely endured for the payoff of financial security and social standing. Them I have known much longer, those classroom drones who remain (like Billy Charles) seriously at risk of never becoming truly educated. They may pass their courses, but they are just as inevitably failed by their schools.

The institution of the school has also failed to facilitate mutual acquaintance among the people who inhabit it. I will not document the obstacles that have kept teachers and administrators from seeing Billy Charles as I have been privileged to see him. I leave it to other essays to explore the kind of restructuring that is needed before school people can pay closer attention to the life histories of other students like Billy Charles. His relatively benign experiences in a less-crowded reading class and in a livelier social studies class only hint at the directions of that restructuring.

But even educators like Billy Charles's reading and social studies teachers will usually need help in acquiring the kind of knowledge that I lacked when I first met that scruffy stranger under McDonald's golden arches. Cocooned in the world of the middle-class educator, we are insulated from unfamiliar norms and ways of life. We have lost—indeed, have been systematically encouraged to lose—the ability to reach out to honor the places (whether the barrio, the ghetto, the reservation, the Appalachian "holler," or simply the peaks and pits of adolescence) where our students live.

Of course, a restructuring that gives teachers the time, the resources, and the motivation to learn about the individual worlds of their students will be only a beginning. Empathy alone is not enough. It is merely a necessary condition for a second element crucial to good teaching: the development of educational activities that can broaden students' horizons. Teachers in a school with a

Billy Charles Barnett will not only need to understand the importance of making turtle soup, they will also need to entice students to study other cuisines and other cultures. Math teachers will need the curricular finesse to lead students outward from field-and-stream economics to numeracy in other contexts. However, as John Dewey wisely noted long ago, one cannot effectively lead students outward without starting from the place where they currently reside.

Empowering teachers (and students) in this way may require more resources than our society is willing to provide. We will need to reeducate teachers, to reduce their workload, and to purchase material resources to link the local community with the larger one. Thus far, we have lacked the vision and the will to commit the resources necessary to this effort. Instead, we have sometimes resorted to gimmicks to lure our children back to school. In some Florida schools, pizza is offered as an incentive to attend classes. In one Kentucky district, a snazzy car is raffled off as a door prize for students with good attendance records. But should such bribery succeed in filling classrooms with warm bodies, will this no longer be a nation at risk of losing the hearts and wasting the minds of its young people? I think not.

I venture to suggest the heresy that we would not necessarily be better off were the dropout rate to decrease dramatically tomorrow. We conveniently forget the role of the traditional American school in perpetuating a seriously impoverished notion of what constitutes an education. Before we could say that a lower dropout rate is good news, we would need to know whether the lessons for not leaving school are valid ones. Are students remaining because we have become serious about introducing meaning into the life of the classroom? Are they staying because we have equipped our teachers with the means for knowing and respecting their students' pasts even as they attempt to open up their futures? And why would we need to know whether these things are occurring? Because Billy Charles has reminded us that doing anything less is still a very risky business.

CHAPTER 5

Ellen, A Deferring Learner

Karin L. Dahl, The Ohio State University

This chapter focuses on what the author calls a "deferring learner," a learner who early in her school experience lost interest in literacy activities and lost faith in her ability to master literacy skills. This chapter is not just a verbal portrait of a deferring learner, however. The author also creates images of the student's classroom and describes how the classroom environment helped create the student portrayed here.

What makes a child become discouraged with the business of learning to read and write in school? Are there critical events in the classroom that shape the learner's early school experience and affect the learner's perception of self as reader and writer? Is it possible to find the beginning of "learner shutdown" in school and trace its impact on early reading and writing development?

In this chapter I examine the literacy learning events in the first two years of schooling for an inner-city learner who appeared to lose interest in reading and writing and also lose faith in herself as a reader/writer during the first-grade year. She began as one of the higher-achieving learners in a cohort of inner-city children entering kindergarten in an inner-city school and ended first grade trailing many of her classmates. This worrisome and unexpected pattern prompted additional analysis in order to examine what happened. The chapter, therefore, is an attempt to see the instruction in reading and writing from Ellen's perspective, determine the patterns indicative of loss of confidence, and draw from it insights about at-risk learners and their interpretations of early school-based literacy experiences.

OVERVIEW OF ETHNOGRAPHIC INVESTIGATION

The data about this learner were drawn from a two-year federally funded ethnography which analyzed knowledge construction in reading and writing of inner-city learners in three urban mid-western schools with traditional skills-based literacy instruction (Dahl, Purcell-Gates, and McIntyre 1989). Focusing on children from economically poor families, the point of the study was to account for success and failure of these children in learning to read and write. The study included extensive assessment of written language knowledge at the beginning of kindergarten and the end of first grade. Further, the researchers engaged in close-proximity observation of focal learners in twice-weekly classroom visits across the two-year span of the study and gathered both audiotaped accounts of learner utterances during daily literacy instruction and artifacts produced by focal learners. Results of the study as a whole indicated that entering knowledge was an important factor in school success and the learner's stance in the classroom influenced what was learned.

For many low socioeconomic status (SES) learners in this study there was a mismatch between skills-based instruction, entering knowledge about written language, and children's evolving hypotheses about reading and writing. Further, learner transactive stance was shown to strongly influence reading and writing outcomes. Transactive stance referred to "the ways and the degree to which the children actively pursued the task of learning to read and write in these instructional contexts" (Purcell-Gates and Dahl 1991, p. 12). Results of the study indicated that the exploring and independent learners experienced the most success in skills-based beginning reading and writing instruction. Passive learners, particularly those entering kindergarten without a sense of written language as meaning centered, often failed to construct relationships between the skills presented during instruction, and they experienced the least success in beginning reading and writing (Purcell-Gates and Dahl 1991). Finally, the deferring learner emerged as a pattern in which a shift in transactive stance accompanied a decline in learner confidence.

KNOWLEDGE AT THE BEGINNING OF KINDERGARTEN

It was Ellen whose behaviors across the two years of the study led eventually to the identification of the deferring-learner pattern. Ellen was initially one of the more gregarious of the focal learners in this study. A stocky bright-eyed African American five year old, she usually was found in kindergarten talking and laughing merrily in the midst of a group of girls. When her friends were saying "look at this" to each other and making jokes and funny gestures, she would strike her Oprah Winfrey pose and make them laugh. She was an easy insider, one included in the leader group that formed during the opening days of school. Ellen and the other four girls who were in this group signaled their exclusiveness by sitting together at one table and making the thumbs-up gesture after they were seated.

The assessment of written language schemata conducted in the opening weeks of school showed that Ellen entered kindergarten knowing that a sentence written on a page was, as she put it, "for people to read" (Dahl, Purcell-Gates, and McIntyre 1989, p. 104). She recognized the original print and logo of some environmental print (*stop* recognized on a stop sign, *McDonald's* written on a cup, and *milk* printed on a milk carton). She knew a bit about the macrostructure of stories and generated an original story with some story elements when we played together with hand puppets. Her story began, "Once upon a time it was six aliens and they went up to the hill and they saw a old cricket and they say, 'Give me fifty cent' . . . ." She scored at the fourth stanine on Concepts of Print (Clay 1985) and appeared to be at ease drawing pictures and writing her name for the writing sample. Her spelling attempts documented a beginning interest in letter-sound relations as she wrote. For example, she produced the following letters for dictated words: *BP—pink, S—ask, B—trap.* Further, her scores on the written-register task assessing knowledge of book language indicated little experience with the language of storybooks. This general picture of entering knowledge was well above the average for urban children in this study. The mean total written language score across the study was 17.95 and Ellen's total score was 18.7, near the top of the cluster of scores. Thus, Ellen appeared to be a learner well prepared for the literacy instruction in her classroom at the beginning of kindergarten.

The curriculum she encountered in kindergarten was a traditional reading readiness program with the addition of a free-play period at the beginning of each day where literacy materials were among the available choices. In the free-choice period children chose among blocks, assorted books, magnetic boards, big books, chalkboard activity, writing materials, art materials, and beads. The instructional program remained separate from this period and utilized workbooks and dittos focusing on specific skills. There were ability groups for workbook sessions and children also worked with the teacher on pages that presented sight words and other specific skills—category formation, sequence recognition, and rhyming. Ditto sheets provided practice with letter formation, letter discrimination, and letter-sound relations, and there was a daily sentence (Today is [day of week, date]) which children copied from the board.

In the first half of kindergarten Ellen was particularly active during the free-choice portion of the kindergarten session. She experimented with writing and produced in one instance a nametag with her name and phone number written from memory and then wore that nametag for the rest of the morning. She picked up books and carried them around, holding them closed in front of her while she chatted with friends. In January she began to copy from the big books that were available and talked about each page in the book as she looked at its picture. She constructed her own books in which to write and later made greeting cards with messages written in letter strings. Her writing activity ranged in winter and spring from scribbling freely on the chalkboard to writing letter groups in her constructed books and talking about them. "That's a word," she said one February morning, pointing to *HRh* written on a page.

One day during February Ellen brought to school a set of homemade flash cards. Ellen shared the cards with the class, getting her friend Angel to whisper the words that she had forgotten. Ellen knew the cards for *boy* and *on* when she held them up and needed prompting for *carrot, can,* and *find* among others. A subsequent home visit confirmed that playing school was a regular activity between Ellen and her sister Crystal, a first grader. The concepts that Crystal knew appeared to be the substance of their play.

Ellen attended carefully to the directed-instruction portion of kindergarten. She could name specific letters when the teacher asked for volunteers and expected accuracy of herself as she copied from the board. When she made an error in copying the daily sentence, she destroyed her paper and began again.

By March, the instruction turned to sight words appearing in simple sentences and Ellen, still in the "top group," worked hard to identify the words when her turn came. She bent over the workbook and looked intently at every word, clearly finding the work difficult and important.

By the end of kindergarten Ellen had command of all the letters and knew some sounds. She could identify several sight words and use letter-sound relations to guess at the beginning sounds of an unknown word. She scored in the ninth stanine on the Metropolitan Achievement Test in reading and continued at year's end to write messages in invented spelling. She wrote a message (*I luov You*) in late April on a scrap of paper and shoved it into her pocket to take home.

ELLEN'S FIRST-GRADE EXPERIENCES

The first-grade curriculum was built around a newly adopted basal reader and its accompanying workbooks and dittos. The program required whole-class reading sessions with enlarged preprimers and used extensive boardwork where sight words or word patterns were copied. The program was designed to have skills instruction with the teacher using groupings based on mastery of specific skills. The groups were intended to be temporary and heterogeneous. While one group was meeting with the teacher, the remainder of the class was to complete dittos, workbook pages, and boardwork that reinforced specific skills. Included among such lessons were letter-sound relations, alphabetizing, forming contractions, and recognizing sequence.

The classroom teacher conducted the new program as directed by the school system, but expressed concern that the new skills sequence in this adoption was not the one she favored. She established ability-grouped round robin reading on a daily basis, "so she would know how each child was doing," and she added additional boardwork about vowel sounds.

At the beginning of first grade Ellen was successful in depending upon her knowledge of sight words to read the simple preprimer stories. Initially, she sat in round robin sessions waiting for her turn and read her sentence or page nearly without error. When she came to a word she didn't know, she used its beginning sound and guessed words with the same sound. In late September, for example, she was stuck on *fin;* she guessed *fair?* and was corrected. As Ellen gained confidence in the round robin reading routine, she began participating during other children's turns. Under her breath she read with the reciting child, mouthing the words she knew, guessing at unknown words, and being silent when that strategy didn't work.

Ellen's independent seatwork proceeded busily, though she was confused by the sight-word sentences that the basal series presented. The sight word was printed above the sentence and then the sentence showed the word in context. Ellen looked at the sentences:

   will   *not*   *can*

I will go.   I will not.   I can run.

She read them as meaningful wholes and repeated them to herself, "Will I will go," trying different intonational patterns to make each sentence sound plausible. She struggled with the phonics worksheets and appeared to stay with her "beginning sound and guess the word" strategy rather than sound blending as demonstrated by her teacher.

Ellen continued to keep up in the basal program until the preprimer stories expanded beyond her bank of memorized sight words and her guessing strategy became inadequate. She settled then into a less-active pattern during round robin reading. She took her own turn reading aloud and repeated the corrections when her word guesses were wrong. For example:

ELLEN: When the girls [long pause] come
TEACHER: came
ELLEN: came out of school, Pam [long pause]
TEACHER: asked
ELLEN: asked Jim is this my bike?

Ellen also sampled the text vicariously during the turns of others by reading a word here or saying a word there as the child read. Her view appeared to be that each word must be identified correctly and that reading demanded accurate performance. She also knew when she didn't know a word and remained silent when that was the case.

During seatwork she also began a more-passive pattern of activity and no longer read the boardwork to herself. Instead, she copied the text from the board letter by letter and simply turned it in. There were some individual interactions with the teacher when Ellen dictated a sentence, the teacher wrote it, and Ellen read and later recopied, but for the most part Ellen rarely read on her own. The other children in the top group, in contrast, were actively reading everything in sight—the words posted in the room, the print on their pencils, the print on their neighbor's paper. While Ellen was reading less and less in the course of doing her work, the others were creating opportunities to read.

In January and February the curriculum emphasized several skills, but especially focused on letter-sound relations. Ellen tried to follow the teacher's instructions. "When you come across a word that you don't know," the teacher explained over and over, "I want you to take the time to figure out what it is. Sound out the word." The teacher provided demonstrations of sounding out, "ssss nnnn aaaa kkkk," she would say running her hand under the letters of *snake* written in large letters on the board. Ellen would repeat each sounded-out word, but when she sounded out words independently she did not get beyond the beginning sound. "The mmm . . mow? . . . [*man*] will follow in a van," she read aloud at her desk.

The teacher presented rules for determining vowel sounds and Ellen listened intently. "How do you know that *write* is a long *i* word?" the teacher asked one day. Ellen offered, "Because it gots *i* in the middle." The teacher smiled and called on more children, looking for one that would state the rule. Finally, one offered a more elaborate explanation, "Cause it got a *i*, it got a *e*, and the *e*, it's not anything, just put the *e* right there, and the *i* IS the word." Ellen looked doubtful and scooted down in her chair.

Struggles with vowel-pattern rules continued during this period. For example during one particular observation, Ellen's teacher reviewed two patterns: two vowels together making the long sound of the first vowel and the silent *e* rule. There were lists of words conforming to these rules on the chalkboard and the class confidently chorused them together as the teacher pointed to each one. Seatwork for the day was to find the same patterns in the day's basal reader story and write them. Unfortunately, Ellen found the inevitable exceptions (*said, come,* and *wear*) along with some that did fit the pattern (*near*). She read them each aloud looking back and forth from her paper to the chalkboard, checking and rechecking. She erased the words that didn't make the long vowel sound, then wrote them again when she saw that they fit the letter pattern. She looked across words on her paper verifying that she knew the pattern, then wrote some words that had the long sound (*away, follow*) but did not fit the pattern and erased them. Finally, looking discouraged, she adopted a strategy that let her complete the lesson; she stopped reading the words to herself and simply copied any word that fit the letter pattern. When I asked if I could xerox her paper at the end of the morning she refused to let me have it and held the paper tightly.

The workbook pages during midyear emphasized word recognition and Ellen often guessed among word choices without understanding the sentence. For example, one workbook sentence was *He will come some (day, dear).* Ellen did not know the word *some* and did not perceive a word-pattern relationship between *come,* which she knew, and *some.* She looked at both word choices and then just circled *dear* as a guess.

While Ellen did not articulate how discouraged she was during reading, her demeanor indicated that she was doubtful that she could do well or that she could be accurate. She grew very quiet, her work was limited to what she could get right, and she worked slowly and deliberately. Sitting beside her, I could hear her sigh as she looked at the words she didn't know; she appeared to recognize that her answers were probably going to be wrong.

As other children became more successful than she, that is, more fluent readers and better at getting unknown words, Ellen developed a new pattern in round robin reading which allowed her to be successful—she specialized in being accurate. During her turn, she read the words she knew and then hesitated for just a second before attempting the words she didn't know. Because part of the point of round robin reading was to maintain the flow of the story, others quickly chimed in when she paused and Ellen could repeat *their* word, thus having a perfect round robin turn. Both the teacher and the other children supplied words and Ellen shifted her attention to answering the comprehension questions which the teacher asked at the end of the lesson, a feat which the children busy at sounding out were not able to do. Ellen remained a player in the top group using this strategy, no longer attempting new words and no longer reading along with others.

The children in this classroom who began the first-grade year with knowledge of written language similar to Ellen's developed personal strategies during these winter months that served them well. They read and reread everything in front of them—their basal stories, their worksheets, and even former basal stories—and they were flexible about the issue of accuracy. Ellen moved in the opposite direction, toward rigid rule following and silence when accuracy was unreachable. There was little reading that was self-sponsored. Close observation of Ellen found her doing exactly what she was told, sounding out words (e.g., /we:rr/ for *write*) and taking fewer and fewer risks. Her pattern of doing the paperwork intended for practice without actually processing the print became an everyday pattern. One day she copied four sentences perfectly from the board letter by letter, a process that consumed nearly all of her independent work time. She copied:

I was about to read that sentence.
I'm not afraid of a little frog.
After lunch we'll play.
Let's go shopping this afternoon.

When the sentences were completely copied, I asked Ellen what they said. She looked at me incredulously as if to say "we're not supposed to READ them," and walked up to the teacher's desk to have her paper graded. She returned with a one hundred percent and a smiley face sticker on the top of her paper.

Spring found a dearth of data indicating that Ellen was actively involved in her learning. She risked less and less in class recitations and began looking discouraged during seatwork. Her standardized achievement scores on the reading portion of the California Achievement Test showed her scoring in the thirty-fourth percentile. There were similar data on the written language knowledge tasks that I administered about the same time. Her Concepts of Print results reported a relative lack of close observation of word order in sentences, letter order in words, and punctuation. She showed little change in story understanding or written language schemata.

Interestingly, the alphabetic principle data on the post test reflected some increase in knowledge of letter-sound relations. For example, she spelled *pink* correctly, wrote *amke* for *ask,* and *hoip* for *trap.* The writing sample contained a list of twenty words (each numbered by Ellen), three of which were contractions, and two with invented spelling. She wrote:

1. cat, 2. dog, 3. mom, etc., ending the list with 16. ratt, 17. aane, 18. I, 19. love, and 20. you.

Her scores were not unlike the mean scores for the study on the post test, but they were markedly lower than the children who entered kindergarten demonstrating above-average written-language knowledge.

The table that follows presents pre- and post-test scores across the two-year period for Ellen. As can be seen, Ellen's scores were similar from the beginning of kindergarten to the end of first grade in many areas of written language knowledge. Other learners who entered with similar written language knowledge surged ahead in the first two years of schooling and were eager explorers of written language by the end of first grade.

TABLE 5.1.
PRE- AND POST-TEST SCORES
ON WRITTEN LANGUAGE TASKS

Task	Pretest Score (Kindergarten)	Post-Test Score (End First Grade)
Intentionality (1–5)	5.0	5.0
Concepts/Print (Stainine)	4.0	4.0
Alphabetic Principle (1–3)	1.7	3.0
Written Register (Stanines)	4.0	4.0
Concepts/Writing (1–6)	1.0	6.0
Total Written Language	18.7	26.0

Note. The numbers within the parentheses ( ) report the range of scores possible for each measure.

AN EXPLANATION FOR ELLEN'S PATTERN
OF DIFFICULTY

What accounts for the relative lack of growth for this learner, given her standing in the class at the beginning of kindergarten? We can only document the outward behaviors that Ellen provided, but there was evidence in her rumpled look, her close-to-the-desk posture as she worked, and her long silences that the inner thoughts during reading were failure messages. It may be that those inner thoughts were like these, I can't get this; I don't know what this says; or I don't think this answer is right.

While the other top-group children were noisily doing their work and ignoring the skills they didn't get, Ellen was noting her stream of failures. She knew what she didn't know and she appeared to be weighed down and limited by it. There were documented shifts in the scope of what Ellen attempted, given her assessment of self as one who gets it wrong. She attempted less, took fewer and fewer risks, avoided reading, and held to her "watch-the-teacher-and-memorize" strategy rather than moving toward phonemic awareness or toward other strategies that would have provided successful reading experiences or new insights. This pattern of self limiting led to less time spent reading and fewer experiences with written language. Ellen stayed with the worksheet that she was struggling with while others dashed off their careless answers and read independently in their basals.

Working concurrently with this pattern was Ellen's skill at doing school. She knew that teachers wanted correct answers and did not volunteer to recite when she didn't know. She raised her hand to recite the known words and got a smile from the teacher. Ellen also knew that teachers wanted correct papers that were neat and completely finished. She worked on ditto sheets for longer than other children did. When the weary teacher sitting at her desk with a stack of messy papers said, "Children, check your work before you bring it up here to be graded," Ellen redoubled her efforts to "get it right."

Other children who did not understand the skills in the program solved the problem by blurting out, "Hey, I don't get this!" or by asking their neighbor how to do it. Others abandoned the strategies that the teacher demonstrated and used their own ways successfully. They seemed to know what to keep and what to throw away of the instruction that was offered. They behaved less obediently and got up out of their chairs to go copy from someone whom they knew could do the work. They talked. They interrupted the teacher who was busy with a small group. These learners stopped the round robin routine and announced rudely, "But I don't know how to do it!" In contrast, Ellen was seated quietly, bent over her work, and stuck with the lack of understanding about letters and sounds that she needed. She was quietly engaged in a struggle that she was loosing and in a cover-up of that failure.

All of these patterns seemed to take their toll. Ultimately, Ellen appeared to lose confidence in her own language knowledge. In effect she sabotaged the intent of the curriculum which relied upon the learner to integrate new information with old and thereby reorganize knowledge (Purcell-Gates and Dahl 1991). The curriculum expected learner flexibility and synthesizing. Ellen instead deferred to the curriculum, took it literally (applying each rule) and was unable to resolve the conflict between her own language knowledge and the skills she was meeting in school. Her personal need to be accurate and get one hundreds outstripped the intent of the curriculum for correctness. Because Ellen was an able student in a class of many struggling learners, her quiet crisis went almost unnoticed and the teacher simply attributed Ellen's difficulty to carelessness.

Other aspects of the curriculum that could have compensated for Ellen's difficulties and raised her confidence were not present to any great extent during this particular year. In other years there would have been favorite stories brought out by the teacher, extended writing opportunities, and an activity period with some learner choice. But this year of the new adoption meant mandated deadlines for teachers and every spare moment spent working with the skills that the curriculum required. The teacher was concerned with meeting end-of-year goals in terms of skill mastery, and the class, even with its abundance of struggling beginning readers, did reach the designated unit by the deadline. Most children made steady progress in learning to read, and Ellen's pattern of decline was in large part lost in the shuffle.

REFLECTION

The most interesting characteristic of the first-grade year observed in this study was that so many children *were* moderately successful. The troubling part, of course, was that Ellen appeared to have decided by year's end that she was just not a reader, that reading was for someone else. Ellen's loss of confidence was subtle and quiet. Clearly, her case demonstrated that entering knowledge is not enough to guarantee success in learning to read and that learners—even those who are teacher pleasers—may not make it. The curriculum, partly because it was a first year of a new skills program, emphasized to an inordinate extent the skills of beginning reading. There were few story-reading experiences where children could laugh or predict the next event. There were few reading experiences that connected with learner experiences at home or in the neighborhood. Thus, children's store of prior knowledge was not tapped on a regular basis. Learners read in this basal about going up in a hot air balloon and exchanged glances that said they thought it was not very interesting. There was no time left in this classroom for reading self-chosen library books, lingering with a favorite story, or writing on a learner-chosen topic. Skill instructing filled the morning.

Further, Ellen did not appear to be doing the inner work that was needed. She was not connecting the concepts she met in skills-based instruction and weaving a personal cloth of literacy. Instead she was foregrounding accuracy and sounding out and receiving from herself a continuous stream of failure messages because she could not perform well.

It may be that Ellen will have a different kind of year in second grade, or that "playing school" at home will lead to reading proficiency. It may be that she will move away from rigid rules and become more flexible. If not, there is a real possibility that the quiet decline will continue and that Ellen will be among the many learners that could have become readers but didn't.

CHAPTER 6

Andy and Libby: At Risk or Undervalued?

Karen L. Ford, University of North Texas

Here the focus is on Andy and Libby. Both students challenge conventional assumptions about at-risk students. Both exhibit problems which require much more subtle solutions than the ones found in the literature on at-risk students.

I was a teacher of "at-risk" students for sixteen years. It was not until recently, however, that my common-sense middle-class perceptions of inner-city, "underprivileged" children were challenged. The challenge came from being a participant observer in a class with students who, for the most part, exhibited a majority of the factors commonly associated with putting students at risk of school failure (NCES 1990). Of the class of twenty students, ten lived in a single-parent family, thirteen were from families with incomes of less than fifteen thousand dollars, thirteen were home alone more than three hours a day, eight had parents with no high school diploma, and ten had a sibling who had dropped out of school before graduating.

I met these students when they were seventh graders and continued to learn from them until the end of their eighth-grade year. My most vivid recollection is the amazement that I continually felt as I watched them interact or talked with them; these were *really* not the students described in the literature that I had been reading. They may have come from a less than perfect home environment, but they brought a well-reasoned repertoire of literacy and learning skills to every learning situation. Two of these students, Andy and Libby, are described in this chapter.

ANDY

I can close my eyes and see Andy, rocking back on two legs of his chair, knees propped on the table. Andy was small for the last years of middle school and to make up for that he tried to be "cool." His army jacket was two sizes too big for him, but it was "cool."

Andy lived at home with his divorced mother and two sisters, one younger and one older. His older sister had dropped out of school two years ago so that she could work. He told me that she was really smart, but she just wanted to start making money. His mother worked as a secretary and usually arrived home after dark; since the older sister worked a second shift, Andy was responsible for his younger sister from the time they both got home from school until his mother returned. I asked him about this responsibility and he commented,

> Well, she's kinda a pain. I mean I want to play guns or work on our computer and she gets in the way, but I just sorta tell her to play around the house and she usually does. I'd like to get paid like some of the other kids here do, but Mom says there's not enough; once in a while she does though.

Andy typically chose to work alone on content-area tasks. He viewed the tasks as work that needed to be completed and so he did it. Through a self-report questionnaire and subsequent conversations, he consistently expressed confidence in his ability to perform in his classes. He told me that he was aware of the various course goals and felt comfortable with the goals, although he wasn't comfortable with all of the teachers. While he considered himself an active learner and indicated that he tried to participate in his classes, he also said that he only studied on occasion and wasn't worried about taking or passing tests. For him passing a content-area test or quiz was dependent upon listening in class. He commented, "Well we go over stuff in class and we review, so I just listen and do the stuff in class. Then I don't have to study. I mean why should I? I listened in class and so I just have to remember. Besides it's only a day or two."

Andy did not always appear to be listening in class. Often, when the teachers gave the class time to review for a test, Andy would rock back in his chair and stare out the window or simply get his paper ready for the test. At first his test scores were a surprise to me; he nearly always earned an A. I came to realize that, regardless of how it appeared, *his* method of approaching tests was apparently effective for him.

Normally Andy completed any homework that he intended to do during class. He told me he did the homework only because "it had to be done." During several of our discussions he told me that he "wasn't sure if doing homework would ever help him learn in a class." Several times he mentioned that the only homework that might ever help him learn was in his math class. He summed up his attitude toward homework by saying,

> I don't do homework much, sometimes just in class. I sure don't do it at home because I'd rather be working on our computer or outside playing guns. I just listen in class and get A's on all of my tests. F's on my homework grades and that still makes a C in the class. That's all I need!

Observation data supported the interview data. I remember one instance when Andy began to work ahead on a homework assignment and was chastised by the teacher for "not paying attention." After that time his approach was to still work ahead, but to cover up his answer sheet so that the teacher couldn't determine exactly what he was doing.

Although Andy typically worked alone, he did not refuse to help a classmate who asked him for help. One day the teacher had given the class ten minutes to review for a test over some chapters in *The Outsiders*. I watched as four or five students gathered around Andy as he told them from memory what had happened in those chapters. Another time when the class was trying to tackle a particularly difficult science activity involving probability, I noticed that Andy and two other boys were busily searching through the book and constantly turning back and forth to tell each other something. When I asked Andy what was going on he said, "Well nobody knew what to do so Jacob and Harold and me figured it our own way and then tried to come up with the best way. We was gonna tell the others, but Mr. Jackson stopped us before we got to."

As I looked more closely at Andy's approaches to learning I began to focus on how he used the skills of reading and writing. It was obvious that he always used reading as an information-gathering tool. In beginning an assignment for one of his classes he typically flipped through his text and appeared to gather the information that was needed to complete the task at hand. Once when I saw him skipping around in the chapter I asked what he was doing and he told me that he was, ". . . trying to find the things to fill in the sheet; they're not all right there, so I have to skip around to find them." When I queried why he didn't just read straight through, he said, "Why should I? They're just right here and I know that so I don't need to read all that other stuff."

Andy's use of reading regularly followed the same pattern. Once during a history assignment designed to have students trace the routes that the different explorers had taken, I noticed that Andy was not looking at the map in the book, but instead was thumbing through the chapter pages. When I asked him what he was doing, he said,

> I'm just trying to find the place in the book where it tells how DeSoto and Cartier went. See it's not on the map and sometimes it tells you in the book so I just have to find out where they started and finished. And I guess if they stopped anywhere along the way.

Another time I saw him frantically looking through the index of the science book. Later when I asked why he didn't just look in the chapter for the answer, he commented, "Well, sometimes it's just too slow. That chapter's got too many words and so I just wanted to find the page where the patterns were. Then I could just turn to it and get it done faster."

Although Andy typically used reading to help him finish homework tasks, his use of reading for studying was more difficult to pinpoint and describe. On only one occasion did I see him read something to prepare for a test. After the test was over I asked him what he had read before the test and he replied, "Just some notes that Mindy had taken on the day I was absent. I had to remember some causes, so she showed me and I read over them."

Andy's use of writing in content-area classes was similar to his use of reading—practical. Writing was used simply to record information. This recording of information involved writing answers to the chapter review questions, filling in maps, completing work-sheets, and copying notes that the teacher had written on an over-head transparency or the chalkboard. Typically the recorded infor-mation was turned in to the teacher and never given a second thought. I asked Andy about all of this writing and he told me, "It's just like the board work in elementary school. They just make us do it because that's what they have to grade. I never get my notes back because I just . . . I don't need 'em; they're for the teacher aren't they?"

LIBBY

Libby reminded me of a small tornado—always whirling around the room, trying to find help or finish an assignment. Although she always had a smile on her face, I had the sense that she was contin-ually troubled, as if something was nagging at her, causing her to feel anxious.

I asked Libby about her home and she responded by emphasiz-ing that she had a "good home." Her mother worked evenings as a nurse, but "not a real nurse, one of those LPN ones. She only got her GED 'cause she had to quit high school." Living at home with Libby and her mother were three other relatives, two older broth-ers and a female cousin who was pregnant. None of the other relatives were in school; the brothers had dropped out and were trying to find jobs, while the pregnant cousin worked afternoons at a nearby grocery store. Consequently, Libby was left alone for most of the evening. Every day after school she did some laundry, cleaned the house, and cooked her own meals—then she worked on her homework.

Libby was well liked by most of her classmates and during school hours was seldom seen alone. They described her as, "really busy and really worried" . . . "Libby's fun, but she always has to get everything right. She drives us crazy sometimes trying to make sure that everything is all right. I think Libby ought to be a teacher. She seems to know all the stuff to do and she's always talking to the teacher" . . . "She works real hard, but she never does that good; I think she only got C's last time and she works harder than just C's."

Libby was always worried about "doing" school correctly. Typically, she sought assistance from either classmates or teachers to help her get through various content-area tasks. Her responses to a self-questionnaire indicated a concern for doing well in school. This concern was, in turn, translated into a desire to score high on quizzes and tests or to receive high marks on homework papers.

While Libby constantly talked about her concern for doing well in school, she inadvertently indicated that she lacked total confidence in her performance as a student. In talking with her, she repeatedly said that she felt she should study more and that her study habits were not as good as they should be. She also pointed out that because she usually didn't know what was really expected in most class assignments, she constantly had to consult with class-mates who did know. In spite of this attitude, she said that she always attempted a "good" review before tests and quizzes, a re-view that she designed and which frequently involved constructing outlines and self-talking about the material on the tests.

My observations of Libby corroborated the information that she volunteered during our conversations. She constantly turned to classmates or the teacher for clarification about the assignments. On one occasion, the English teacher had given the students five or ten minutes to review for the daily quiz on one chapter of a novel that the class had been reading for two weeks. As soon as the review time began, Libby ran over to two of her classmates and began to ask them questions about the chapter. On another occa-sion, the problem-solving lab time was being devoted to letting students prepare for a unit test in American history. Libby spent this time again sitting and talking with another group of students as they looked at outlines and notes that they had copied from the board.

Libby's concern about doing well in school extended to a con-cern about getting credit for doing homework as well as receiving a high mark for the work. "I just have to ask somebody to help me," she said. "It helps me do better. I just have to do better." Although she said she could "sometimes get started on her own," she also indicated that eventually she "just had to get some help." Her typical approach involved a process of beginning to work and when she could not find an answer quickly, she would ask the teacher or call out to one of the other students in the class. Even when she was able to work through part of an assignment, she consulted with the teacher or teacher's aide to determine if her answers were "all right."

As I focused on Libby's use of reading and writing I was surprised to find that she used them more frequently and for different purposes than Andy. Libby read everything. When an assignment was made to read a chapter she read from beginning to end. When the questions at the end of the chapter were assigned, she looked first at the question and then went back to the beginning of the chapter and started reading to find the answer. Once she had answered a question she looked at the next question and then turned to the part of the text that she had just finished reading; she then began reading the section immediately following that section.

Although she read extensively, I observed that she did not always obtain the information that she needed from the readings. Often after reading, she literally ran to the teacher to ask where to look or how to find the answer. In talking with her, I realized that she expected the answers to be "right there" in the reading; her reading was directed toward finding the complete answer written in the passage of the text. On one occasion I asked her why she thought she was having trouble finding the answer. Her response was, "It's supposed to be in the chapter, but I can't find it. I found the word, but it's not talking about what this question is. So I can't find out what to put. Could you help me some?"

Libby was consistent in her practice of reading everything, even in her studying. She told me that she read over every chapter before a test. If the class had taken notes then she would also read over these notes. She was disturbed that all of the teachers did not return the homework in time for her to read over it while she studied for the test. I asked her to describe how she studied for a test. Her response was,

> Well, I done this right here [she flipped through the chapter]. We just had to read here and there. I read like a paragraph and then I just said what I read and then I read the next paragraph and did the same thing. But sometimes it's just easier to read. You get more. I'd read my homework too but we don't know if the answers is right. So I read the book and the timelines.

Libby used writing quite a bit more than Andy. While she also used writing to record information, I noticed that she tried to use writing to facilitate her own learning. She indicated that she "always made an outline before she wrote a paper and that sometimes she made an outline of things she knew she had to know for a test." When I asked why she did this she responded, "I don't know. I guess we just learned how to organize the stuff this way and then I figured it might help to keep doing it." Another time she indicated that she wrote summaries in her notebook because the teacher "made us do it anyway for some of those stupid questions at the end of the chapter, and since we were never getting our homework back, I wanted to have something else to study from."

CONCLUSION

Andy and Libby challenge conventional assumptions about at-risk students. Neither is unmotivated; neither lacks strategies for playing the school game. To the extent that Andy and Libby live up to the at-risk label that has been applied to them, their problems—and the solutions to these problems—are much more subtle than the literature on at-risk students suggests.

Libby needs to be weaned of her dependency on teachers and fellow students. There is little in the curriculum in Libby's school or in most schools, for that matter, to accomplish this purpose, however. Indeed, the school culture's emphasis on getting right answers and following teachers' directions would seem to reinforce rather than challenge Libby's less than functional proclivities.

There is also little in the school's environment to challenge Andy's way of doing business. In fact, it is hard not to see Andy's way of operating as an extremely rational, highly functional response to an environment in which homework is assigned even when it is not needed.

Andy's story—and to some extent Libby's—should make us question where the problem lies. Is the problem really with the student, the home, the family, the economic status, and/or all the other variables traditionally thought to be the culprits? Or is the problem really with schools that ask both too little and too much and that, in the process, put all students, in one way or another, at risk?

CHAPTER 7

Karen: An Interaction of Gender Role and Reading Disability

Raylene Kos, The Ohio State University at Lima

In this chapter the author tells the story of Karen, a truly nice girl. The story of Karen is also the story of how gender stereotyping can put students at risk.

The role of gender in education has been explored extensively in terms of whether or not teachers' expectations of academic performance differ in terms of their students' genders. Some studies have found few if any effects associated with gender (e.g., Prawat and Jarvis 1980), but some interesting findings concerning teacher responses to stereotypical gender-role behaviors have come to light. Dusek and Joseph (1983) found that elementary teachers tend to be somewhat more accepting of students exhibiting female stereotypical gender-role behaviors regardless of the sex of the student. However, these students were not expected to perform as well academically. Instead, academic achievement was found to be associated with masculine or androgynous behaviors. Benz, Pfeiffer, and Newman (1981) found that achievement also influenced teachers' perceptions of children. That is, high-achieving students were predicted to have more stereotypical masculine characteristics than low achievers who were predicted to have stereotypically feminine characteristics. The authors suggest that the tendency for achievement to decline for girls—declines that limit girls' potential

111

for life options—may be influenced by such teacher expectations. If a girl is very "feminine" she may not be expected to achieve highly.

Entwisle et al. (1987) propose that gender plays a more significant role than achievement in shaping the academic self-concept of girls. Unlike first-grade boys who stress individuation and academic competence, first-grade girls' self-concepts appear to rely on stereotypical gender-role behaviors such as nurturance, cooperation, and kindness. It is not until the end of first grade that girls' academic achievement begins to play a role in their perceptions of self.

Studies on special-education referrals also have relevance in the study of gender biases. The far more numerous placements of boys in special-education programs indicate the possibility of gender bias. In many cases academic achievement is not the main reason for special-education referrals (Kos 1989). Instead, behavior problems, particularly those acting-out behaviors typically associated with boys, were teachers' main concerns. The presence of academic difficulties, in a sense, simply facilitates the labeling and placement of the child. It has been suggested that there actually are as many girls as boys who would qualify for special services, but perhaps because of differences in behavior patterns, many of which are culturally accepted gender behaviors, the girls do not get referred (Shaywitz et al. 1990). Instead of acting out, girls have historically tended to be more passive and "nicer," and therefore, cause teachers far less trouble.

This research raises the question of what might happen to a poorly achieving female who has been successful in the female role when she realizes she is failing academically. One possibility is that she will cling more tightly to the stereotypical feminine roles as a means of maintaining positive social feedback from others and positive thoughts about herself—in a sense making feminine role playing a subconscious passing strategy similar to those described by Reuda and Mehan (1986). However, by doing so she may inadvertently foster low expectations from teachers, expectations that may inhibit the provision of badly needed academic support.

In this chapter, the possible interaction of teacher expectations with one girl's stereotypical gender-role behavior will be presented. While the data are tentative and based on one case study of a reading disabled adolescent girl, the case needs to be presented that stereotypical gender-role behavior, when examined on an individual basis, may indeed act as a moderator of teacher expectations and as a means of ensuring social acceptance by females who are achieving poorly in school.

KAREN

The student, Karen, was part of a qualitative multicase case study that explored the factors in schools that acted to maintained students' reading disabilities. She is a fourteen-year-old African American middle school student. She lives with her mother and a foster sister in a small stucco home in a lower-middle-class neighborhood in a midwestern metropolitan area. Karen lives amidst a close family, seeing her father frequently as well as many aunts, uncles, and cousins. When with her father, she is "daddy's little girl," and he speaks lovingly of her. Karen and her mother do "girl" things together frequently, such as shopping, cooking, and trying new hairstyles.

Karen loves to try new makeup and clothes, beaming when someone compliments her on her new looks. She once came to a research session with a sophisticated upswept hairstyle and a caftan and explained that she was going to school dress-up day as Nefertiti. Karen smiles frequently and speaks in a soft, warm voice. She listens when others talk and sometimes touches their sleeves or shoulders softly when she responds. She laughs readily. She has a softly rounded frame and carries herself gracefully. She is, in the traditional sense, very feminine.

Karen worked with three tutors in a reading clinic while I was a supervisor prior to our research study. It was interesting that none of the tutors made much progress with Karen's reading, but the first two tutors were quite fond of Karen. They would comment on how sweet she was, how nice. They praised the fact that Karen would do any of the activities they had prepared and that she always seemed so appreciative of their help. The third tutor agreed that Karen was nice, however, she was less accepting of Karen's passivity during the sessions. It was interesting to note that this tutor was a more aggressive woman than the other two, and she wanted things to move quickly, to bring excitement to the sessions. Unfortunately, excitement did not seem to be Karen's milieu. It was a less than satisfying quarter for both tutor and student.

Educationally, Karen began experiencing difficulty in reading in the first grade. There is no record that the teacher's were overly concerned with Karen's lack of progress. Her mother was concerned and had Karen tested by a private psychologist at the end of her first-grade year. The results of the WISC-R (Wechsler 1974) indicated a full-scale IQ score of 83 and a standard score of 69 on the reading portion of the Woodcock-Johnson (Woodcock and Johnson 1978). The other Woodcock-Johnson subtest scores ranged from 82 to 83. The school readministered the WISC-R in the middle of Karen's second-grade year, and her full-scale IQ score was 72, which should have qualified her for placement in a developmentally handicapped program. However, Karen's mother said she was told that Karen did not qualify, and, while the reason for nonplacement is not specified in the psychological report, the factor that may have kept Karen out of a special program was her high performance on scales of adaptive behavior. Karen was just a nice child.

On further testing in the sixth grade, Karen received a full-scale IQ score of 78 on the WISC-R and a standard score of 60 on the reading portion of the Woodcock-Johnson. Her sixth-grade district achievement-test results indicated that Karen was reading below the second-grade level. During her elementary years, she had received one year of Chapter 1 reading, but that was discontinued because she had made small gains.

When I began to work with Karen, she was reading independently at the preprimer level. Whatever gains she had made in elementary school had disappeared by the time she reached the seventh grade. Karen received no special help in reading in middle school, and she was placed in all regular classes.

When I first began a six-month-long study of Karen's school experiences, she appeared to be one of the many students whom we describe as falling through the cracks. However, the fact that she could read almost nothing from her textbooks and that she certainly was reading poorly enough that no teacher could have been unaware of her problems led me to feel that there was more to her story than just falling through the cracks. As a participant observer during reading tutoring sessions and through open-ended interviews, I began to explore how Karen felt about the lack of attention her poor reading received from her teachers. What I found was an unspoken agreement of silence that seemed to be based on a mutual system of teacher/student avoidance of a problem that neither knew what to do about.

Everybody liked Karen. She was nice. She was kind. She was such a sweet girl. She never caused anyone any trouble, and she never drew attention to herself. She had girlfriends and fitted into her niche of the school's social structure. She was clean and neat, and dressed and cared for herself like a nice young lady. And Karen was polite and accepting. She never questioned the teacher's actions. In fact, she found ways to rationalize the teacher's lack of attention to her problem and make the problem her own. The following excerpts from transcripts of interviews with Karen and Karen's current language arts teacher provide examples of Karen's role in the classroom:

> R (RAYLENE): Do you have to read very much in school?
> K (KAREN): No, not a lot.
> R: Do you read as much as the other kids do in class?
> K: Sometimes she'll pick other people and out of a whole day I don't read.
> R: Why do you think she doesn't always pick you to read?
> K: Because she, she knows that I'm slow and, I guess she doesn't want the kids to make fun of me or anything.

Mrs. Michaels, Karen's language arts teacher, had this to say about Karen:

> . . . she is delightful. The reason she has passed and made it to the 7th grade is because she is so congenial. She's nice, willing to work, and cooperative. And she doesn't stick out in class because she is so pleasant.

Mrs. Michaels explained her lack of attention to Karen by citing the many discipline problems she had in her class. She said she made no special accommodations for Karen because, "There's not time. What you do in class is try to control them." When asked about Karen's reading, she said that during silent reading Karen sits and quietly looks at the book. "I don't think she is actually reading. She simply cannot read and write." During oral reading, Mrs. Michaels says she probably avoids calling on Karen to avoid putting her in the spotlight. "I probably don't call on her, but I know she can't do it. Why should I make her uncomfortable?"

When asked what she thought would happen to Karen, Mrs. Michaels said Karen would:

. . . probably graduate from high school because she is such a nice person. She will get married and have a family. She will never be able to hold any kid of job besides very minimal jobs, unless she learns to read and write. Public schools are not going to help her read and write. Well, they could if she had one-to-one help. But I don't think that is available.

Karen is painfully aware of her reading problem and so are her teachers. However, neither find it prudent to address the problem at this point. Karen has found a means, either through natural inclinations or through trial and error, of receiving positive attention by being affectionate, cheerful, childlike, gentle, sensitive, cooperative, soft spoken, warm—all traits listed on the Bem Sex Role Inventory (BSRI) (BEM 1974) as denoting perceptions of desirable feminine traits. The teachers, on the other hand, have responded positively to their perceptions of Karen's femininity, rewarding her passive behavior by removing difficult situations from her school experiences. So flagrant is this acceptance of Karen's stereotypical behavior that Mrs. Michaels has even been able to chart Karen's life into a supposedly comfortable existence in which Karen will marry and continue to allow someone to remove life's difficult situations.

This is really what makes Karen's situation intolerable. The passive acceptance by school personnel of a life based on dependency shows a complete disregard for Karen's growth into a fully functioning adult. Proposing that Karen be directed into a work-study program, as was done early in the year, so that she may learn simple work skills, is simply a way for Karen to pass time until she finds a man who will take care of her. The school has failed miserably in addressing the needs of a student, needs that must be fulfilled if she is to become an independent person.

Karen, despite her seeming collusion in remaining comfortable, does not yet see herself as hopeless or helpless. When asked about her hopes when it came to her reading Karen related a remark made by her mother.

> K: My mom says you have to read or . . . or you won't get nowhere.
> R: What do you think about that?
> K: Um, I think, I think it's sad. An um, like Mom says that you, you might be having a night job and picking up trash and sweeping.
> R: Mm hmm.

K: And you wouldn't have a regular job like my mom and make some money.

R: Mmm. But somebody has to pick up the trash.

K: Yeah, *somebody.* But *I* don't know who!

Karen is also aware of the day-to-day humiliations of not reading. She made a list of how reading poorly affects people:

They can't read a menu.
They are sad.
They feel dumb.
They worry about someone telling others they can't read.
They make up excuses.
They feel uncomfortable.
They get lost sometime.

Reading for Karen is not just about employment; it is about her own personal psychological well-being. Being "feminine" is for Karen a double-edged sword. People like her and are kind to her because she is so nice. But those who could help her with her reading are able, albeit subconsciously, to justify not helping her because they think (or hope) she will be taken care of in the future.

While school itself, due to the large number of female teachers and its child-care role, has been characterized as a feminine environment (Benz, Pfeiffer, and Newman 1981), the essence of the feminine role, that of caring for relationships rather than individuality (Gilligan 1982) may sway teachers into responding in a nurturing, nonassertive manner to children who themselves behave in that manner. For the most part, this may be a positive response. However, if this response diverts attention from serious problems and justifies the diversion under the guise of being kind, then we will have students like Karen whose needs are not being met even though everyone says she is very nice.

CHAPTER 8

"Something to Keep the Relationship Holding": Victoria, A Pregnant Adolescent

Kathryn Herr, Albuquerque Academy

Victoria is a pregnant teenager. The author of this chapter helps us catch a glimpse of the world as Victoria sees it and to begin to understand why, in Victoria's world, becoming pregnant may be seen as reducing risk rather than increasing it.

A number of studies and surveys have documented the proportions of the national problem regarding teen pregnancies in the United States (Harris 1986; Zelnik, Kantner, and Ford 1981; Alan Guttmacher Institute 1981). The current state of the research is able to produce information as to whom is more at risk of becoming an adolescent parent and the interacting variables that impact on the problem. For example, the poor, female adolescent is three times more likely to become a teen parent than an adolescent who is not poor (Real 1987, p. 15); black teens, because they are more likely to be poor, are five times as likely as white teens to become adolescent parents (Children's Defense Fund 1987, p. 4). Yet, despite all the information generated, ". . . it is obvious to the researcher and frustrating to the treatment provider that some combination of personal, social, and environmental variables are impeding adolescent contraceptive use" (Bolton 1980, p. 35). The Children's Defense Fund (1987), in looking at the major barriers to preventing teen pregnancy, cites:

Teen pregnancy is not a single issue that affects all groups for the same reasons in the same ways with the same consequences. Thorough homework is required to define the overall problem carefully, to determine the common needs of all affected groups and then to realize how it affects each community and subgroup. We must struggle to disaggregate, to the extent possible, the varying contributing factors and consequences among blacks, whites and Hispanics, poor and middle class teens, boys as well as girls. We must subsequently design differentiated outreach and remedies carefully tailored and sensitive to the cultural needs of each group. . . . (p. 6)

In her critique of the available research literature on teen pregnancy, Stewart (1981) reports an underlying, taken-for-granted view that adolescent pregnancy is a psychological or social problem in need of explanation, and that pregnant adolescents had problems ("as evidenced by the fact that they were pregnant"). She attributed this to the consistent removal of the subjects in the studies from the wider structural and social environment in which the issue emerged; researchers focused only on the problematic side of the issue and ignored any normality. Stewart suggests that in removing the pregnant adolescent from the cultural demands which operate on her, as both an adolescent and a female, and in focusing on her as part of a deviant category, some of the contributing factors are distorted or denied. "If the adolescent is placed within her social cultural environment, much of what is viewed by researchers as indicative of deviance may well be reframed as a normal response to social expectations" (p. 453).

This research was an attempt at recognizing the student voice in discussion of their pregnancies and of their sexual decision making and at documenting their social realities. The question that took me into the field was: How do adolescent girls themselves perceive and make meaning of their pregnancies? I spent the better part of a school year in a large, urban high school located in a low-income area of a city in the Midwest. The specific focus of my research was a program within the high school designed to help pregnant and parenting teens stay in school until they graduated. While taking the typical course loads for their particular grade levels, these girls also rotated daily through one period of a special program designed to meet their immediate needs. The program focused on parenting skills, peer support, and health and social service information. Perhaps most importantly, it was a time in the school day for these young mothers to talk openly of their experiences of working to juggle it all—meeting the demands of parenting while hoping their own needs could be met as well. Pieces of their stories were gathered in these group discussions; other pieces came in lengthy, often tearful, interviews with individual girls in the program.

The following case study is one of a number of stories gathered in the course of this research. It traces the reflections of one adolescent girl, Victoria, as she works to make sense of her situation—becoming pregnant and then a parent at seventeen.

THE SETTING

Walking through the front doors of Jones High School is to step into noise and vitality, a swirl of students laughing, strolling, talking, trading teases with staff who monitor the halls. The building seems to burst at the seams; pupils are everywhere and space is at a premium.

The classes for the girls in the special program meet in a small room known as "the apartment." It is part of the suite of rooms allocated to the home economics department. Located on the first floor of the school building, the room is en route to the lunch room and adjacent to the auditorium. Because the apartment is very warm—getting its undue share of an old heating system—the door is often open and working around the noise in the hall becomes part of the classroom routine. Passing students call in greetings to the girls in the class. Because it is an interior room, there are no windows to throw open to escape the stifling heat.

The room itself is small and brimming with furniture and materials. The classes, up to ten students at a time, meet around a table, part of a wooden dining room set. A couch and two comfortable chairs fill the other end of the room; soft carpeting covers the floor. Peering down from a high, doll-sized playpen is a black Cabbage Patch doll; she is permanently suspended on the side of the playpen, tied in place, her big black eyes staring wide eyed at the rest of the room. Two colorful, handmade baby quilts are lapped over the sides of the playpen.

A cabinet, the type that displays the china in a dining room, displays pamphlets on toilet training, proper nutrition, safe sex, and various other topics. Applications for the WIC program are piled at one end; cards announcing a new drop-in center sponsored by Planned Parenthood are arranged at the other end. A bulletin board displays birth announcements.

For all of its drawbacks—the heat, the noise, the poor lighting—the first impression one has upon walking into the apartment is one of welcome relief from the long hallways of anonymous classrooms. It is smaller and hence more intimate, softer than the regular rooms with the usual rows of wooden chairs and desks. It is, in a word, inviting—a good place for the girls to share their stories.

THE AMBIANCE OF THE SCHOOL

Staff and students alike widely reported that "it's not a big deal" anymore to be pregnant while in this high school. One of the girls who is pregnant put it this way:

> . . . like a girl gets pregnant—she's sixteen—it's not like "Why, she is pregnant!" It's not like that no more. It's like at school, it's nothing. "Hey, everybody, Nikki is pregnant." That is it. That's all it is. It's not like back in the old days when somebody would get pregnant it would be around the school and everybody be talking about you and treating you—it will make you want to leave. But I don't feel like that because I see all these other girls walking around here pregnant. If they talk about me, they talk about them too.

Since Jones is a neighborhood school there is considerable overlap between the students found in class and neighborhood friends and gangs. As one girl explained it:

> Our neighborhood is filled with pregnant girls. All of them go here to Jones. They was just waiting for me to end up pregnant so it wasn't a shock or anything. Almost all of us—Christie was the first one to get pregnant and then comes me and then Micki and then I think Carmen; Micki and Carmen are sisters—one got pregnant and then the other.

THE STORY OF VICTORIA

At seventeen, Victoria seems older than her years. When she speaks, it's in a husky voice, focused and articulate. Reflective,

Victoria's thoughts on her pregnancy and subsequent parenting evolved and changed as she processed them in the space of the year that we knew each other. She shared multiple accounts of how she got where she was—an adolescent mother at seventeen. Her multiple accounts represent various slices of her reality and, when put together, make up the many aspects of her answer to my question: How do you perceive and make meaning of your pregnancy?

Victoria was pleased to be asked for follow-up interviews and saw herself as a spokesperson to the university community, interpreting her world to those of us in academe. She suggested we videotape some of our interviews in case I ever wanted to use them in a class at the university. We did tape, spending an afternoon in my living room, working around the logistics of her baby and mine. Me, an adult of thirty-five, a white woman; Victoria, a wise seventeen-year-old black adolescent. Her themes, whether they were about her relationship with her boyfriend, her relationship with her mother, or her new-found goals once the baby arrived, were echoed among the twenty-four other girls who participated in the study.

"Something to Keep the Relationship Holding. . ."

Of all the girls participating in my study, Victoria was the only one to tell me that she was happy when she discovered that she was pregnant, that she wasn't surprised at all. After a history of consistent contraceptive use, she went off the pill and within two months was pregnant. Sometimes when she spoke, she described it as a time when she and her boyfriend, then a committed couple, decided to have a baby. On other occasions, it sounded more like Victoria herself had just decided to go off the pill:

> I had stopped taking them [the pill] for two months. At first, you know, it wasn't mentioned . . then we agreed that things wouldn't change between us. . I had stopped taking them for two months and I ended up pregnant. Yeah, it was something to keep it holding, the relationship holding. But it didn't hold anyway. It's hard but he's done a lot of bad things. I let him get away with them and he's done a lot of things to my family and to me.
>
> We was going together for four years. I was going with him when I was thirteen. He was seventeen. And we knew each other's families. Our grandmothers lived next door to each other and he didn't have any kids, and he thought he could handle the

responsibility and I thought there wouldn't be too many problems. I knew I would have to have some kind of means so that the baby could go to the doctor and have milk and all that stuff. We figured it wouldn't be that much of a problem because he was working at the time and my family had some money so it wouldn't be that much of a problem.

We agreed that he would have to accept that while I would be pregnant my attitude would change because I had learned that from other girls. While I was pregnant, we had different attitude changes and we dealt with them. We never thought, "you own me"; it was just equal and then, after I had the baby, it got off balance.

It changed. I wanted to be more to myself after I had the baby and I just wanted to do things my way. I just didn't want to be by him. I just let him go. There was a lot of problems. He had problems with my family, adjusting to my family, and I had problems adjusting to his family. We didn't have any kind of communication after. He was eager. He wanted to take the baby out like the first day he came home. It was cold and the baby was born premature. Everything was so much in a hurry and I was trying to explain to him; he just wanted to do everything real quick. So I said I think we should cool it off for a while. Give you time to think and give me some times to be by myself. It is working. He comes around once in a while. We're something like enemies and friends.

The whole idea of a pregnancy being a way to effect a positive change in a primary romantic relationship was pervasive among the girls in the study. As Victoria explained it, it was a way to attempt to keep the relationship going. There is a considerable folk wisdom around the theme of "having a baby to save the marriage." While the girls in this study were not married when they became pregnant, the rationale appeared the same: that having a child would help pull together a relationship that was starting to crumble. In reality, the relationships rarely withstood the added strain of a pregnancy and baby, and the girls ended up disillusioned and bitter.

Consistent with previous research (Children's Defense Fund 1986), the girls in this study saw a solid relationship and a romantic commitment as a way to provide for their futures; marriage rather than jobs was their best way to escape poverty. When I asked Victoria what she had imagined for herself when she was pregnant and thinking ahead to the future, compared to the present reality, she responded:

> V: The luxury's the main thing. I imagine we still together. I imagine we living in this big old house. Have a lot of money. Getting to see my friends once in awhile.
>
> K: Were the big house and the money going to come from the person you married?
>
> V: Uhhuh. Yeah [laugh].
>
> K: And now when you think of it, do you still. . .
>
> V: It's a dream [pause]. It's a dream. But I would still like to have it.

"I Needed a Change . . . Just Something for a Decade or Two."

In other interviews, when asked how it was that she became an adolescent parent, Victoria's thoughts weren't directed toward her relationship with her boyfriend at all. She was thinking more about her own life and the direction she saw for herself. Having a baby seemed to allow her to make changes for herself that she couldn't manage before. School became a more serious part of her life; the street faded as a attractive place to hang out.

For many women, the fact of being pregnant brings with it feelings of self-esteem and accomplishment; in a country where one's worth is judged primarily in three areas—school, work, and family—it should not be surprising that adolescents who face little opportunity in the first two might consciously or unconsciously seek reinforcement of their self-worth in the third (Children's Defense Fund 1986). Chilman (1985) reports that motherhood itself is seen by many adolescent girls as having beneficial effects in helping them mature and gain status as women.

> I knew all about birth control. Knew all about them. And then I quit taking them. I needed a change. I was expecting it to be wonderful. I needed something new around, just something for a decade or two. That this person will be around. You don't have to worry about this person walking out and leaving you. Knowing that somebody else is there.
>
> Before I wanted to finish school. I was always looking forward to finishing school but in the meantime I was just with the gang and running the streets. . . Last year I cut school all the time. I think I only came to school three months out of the whole school year; I cut it that much. And then when I got pregnant I said it's not only good for me to graduate but my baby is going to

need that diploma too so I can get a job; I don't want to be on AFDC [Aid to Families with Dependent Children] forever. I see myself as being challenged, wanting to do a lot of things, wanting to improve myself. Wanting to prove to people that I can make it. Just trying to make things better for my son.

A typical day for me is getting up at five in the morning, leaving the house at six. My mom watches that baby. I go to school. I come home at 2:30. Do my household chores. Then the rest of the time is spent with my baby and the day starts over and over.

When I asked Victoria where she thought she'd be today, how her life would be different without the baby, she replied without hesitation:

I'd be out on the street, being in Franklin Park a lot, flirting. Not caring about tomorrow. Not wondering if someone needed me at home. I would depend on everybody else instead of myself. And I probably would have quit school. School didn't mean anything to me until I ended up pregnant.

Like if you have a baby and you are a teenager—and you probably didn't want to finish school before you got pregnant— that's a reason now that you do have to go to school. Me having a baby is like giving me more reasoning to go ahead with goals. Even though I might not want to do it, it is still giving me goals.

The highest teenage childbearing rates are in working-class neighborhoods and depressed urban areas. In these communities, where women have always married young, the generations are compressed; pregnancy may not be interrupting career plans but may be a plan in itself, one route to independence and adult status. Pregnancy serves the purpose of establishing the legitimacy of the lower socioeconomic female as a woman (Bolton 1980). There are whole sections of American society in which teenage pregnancy has been the norm for generations (Furstenberg 1976).

For me, everybody was into sex and everything. I just wanted to wait for awhile so I waited until I was about fourteen. It was a sexual experience but I didn't get anything out of it. And then I just waited another year and I thought I would try again. It was better.

When I was fourteen, I thought I would rather that I get some joy out of my teenage years. I got to have fun on my sixteenth birthday. Have some fun during my teenage life and then I thought, if I decide to get pregnant, I could deal with it better than being young and growing up with my child too. I said I'm not going to have any kids now because we have a girl in our neighborhood who is sixteen and she has three kids. I said no, I couldn't be like her. So I just figured I would wait until I got a little older, so I did.

I thought if I got older I wouldn't have a chance to have a child. I don't know why; I just felt like that. And it was so accepted; there was nothing wrong with it. I was in the right state for a child, to physically have a child. I just figured that this was the time rather than later; I figured that if I decided to have a child later there would be nobody around to have the child with. . . . So I figured I didn't know what was going to happen in the future so I didn't want to take that chance. I wanted to have a child now.

For many girls in my study, the birth of a baby was seen as a rite of passage, access into adulthood with the rights and privileges that go with it in our society and in their reality. A further fringe benefit in the eyes of the girls was the change in their relationship with their own mothers—from mother-daughter to "sisters or best friends or something."

My mom was mad when she found out I was pregnant because she had me when she was seventeen. So it is just like a family trait. She had to quit school because nobody would babysit for her. While I was pregnant she made me leave the house and I could finally come back when I was four months pregnant. She decided that she had to accept that I was pregnant and had no plans on giving it up or nothing like that. So, she decided to babysit while I would go to school.

Now our relationships is better—me and my mom's. Because before I got pregnant it wasn't good. We're closer now. It's not like a mother and a daughter. It is like sisters or best friends or something. We're sharing things. She get happiness out of babysitting and seeing me coming to school and doing my chores. Stuff like that. That makes her happy. We talk a whole lot more than we did before. So that brought us closer together. You seem to know what your mom went through when she had you, especially if she was a teenage mom. You seem to know what she went through when she had you.

It has brought my mom and me closer. We want to help each other. We give opinions a lot. It is not arguments. We just try to work things out a lot. It's one parent 'cause I wasn't raised by both parents. And since I was only raised by one parent I could understand how to raise a child by myself. I look at things my mom did.

"Thinking of How I Was Going to Raise This Child. . ."

Furstenberg's (1976) longitudinal study of pregnant, unmarried black teens found that they were more likely to marry if their boyfriends were employed. The availability of public assistance, while not a "cause" of adolescent pregnancy out of wedlock, does allow a teen mother another option and some limited economic security.

> It's not that hard taking care of a baby because you have WIC. We get milk from WIC and he's on diapers so we don't even worry about Pampers. They can put the baby on the health card but not the check yet (for AFDC) but that will help too. So there is nothing that you really have to get out and do right then. You can just wait awhile.

AFDC also allowed the girls' mothers to watch their babies while they were in school; given the shortage and expense of good child care, this was an integral piece for many of the girls in being able to remain in school. Victoria and the majority of the girls depended on their mothers in this regard.

Some resentment was expressed among teachers that only students on welfare could afford to stay in school, while students from homes where parents were employed could not afford to remain home and provide child care—so those students, they felt, were more likely to drop out. Field notes with the teacher of the special program illustrate this theme.

> I said that I was getting the impression that the girls relied heavily on their mothers, particularly to help with child care. Mrs. N. said that was true, although it was predominantly in those family situations where the parents were on assistance and could stay home. She said that those kids with working parents got "penalized" because those were the ones who ended up dropping out of school because there was no one at home to stay with their babies. She felt things were unjust in this.

Mostly unspoken was the implication that girls like Victoria have it easy, because they are having their babies at taxpayers' expense, i.e., working parents like the teachers are footing the bills for unmarried teen parents.

Increasing evidence has accumulated showing teen marriages to be financially unsound and generally fragile, with a high proportion ending in divorce. Research indicates that marriage may actually worsen a young mother's situation; she is likely to have more children at closely spaced intervals, is less likely to return to school, and has less child-care help from her parents and siblings, thereby reducing her opportunity to carry a job (Chilman 1985).

Victoria expressed her opposition to teen marriages for different reasons.

> I was tired of people always saying you are a teenager and you are supposed to get married . . . a lot of girls, they get married and they don't even want to. They just get married because it is their family tradition or something. I was tired of people always saying you are supposed to get married and *then* have kids.

"On the Borderline of Being Accepted. . ."

Depending on how she was feeling, Victoria gave varying reflections on how she felt society viewed her, first as a pregnant teen and now as an adolescent parent. At times she was cavalier, saying she had become pregnant because she was "seeing everybody have kids. It was just doing stuff like society did—being a teenager now." Most of the time, she gave two levels of answers, one reflecting her own personal slice of reality—her neighborhood and friends—and the other, with a view to middle-class America.

Victoria explained that her own friends were "happy for her" when they found out she was pregnant. "All my other friends were pregnant." As a cohort group, they wondered together "how I was going to take care of the baby and wondering if they had to drop out of school or who would babysit for them." They also gave each other moral support, a sense of them against the world: "They don't worry about what other people said about them. They just try to make things better."

But Victoria was aware that her circle of support and acceptance put her a slim line away from a larger societal view. Victoria described how she felt, traveling around the city as a pregnant teen:

> At first I hated it. People would look at you and stare, stare for a long time. They would come to you and say, "Are you pregnant?" They would stare at you for a long time. It would make me mad but then after awhile I was used to it and I was

more proud of myself, thinking about what people were saying and I just started thinking of how I was going to raise this child, things like that. Thinking more about myself than what other people thought.

Victoria demonstrated that she was well aware that she was walking in two worlds. She deftly figured out how to survive in two cultures—her own neighborhood and the middle-class value system of the school—with their sometimes conflicting rules. For example, when Victoria reflected on becoming pregnant at seventeen, she was pleased that she had intentionally waited that long: "I would say I was on the borderline to be accepted by society, eighteen, by being seventeen. Most people, they do wait until they are about my age, seventeen."

Her advice to those girls coming after her was that they should ask themselves "if they are ready."

> I would tell them to plan it better. If they want to have babies when they are a teenager, don't just think that because you met the man, you know him; you may know of that person but you really don't know him. It takes a long time to know a person. Just let things come by themselves. Let just one thing lead to another. Don't rush things. Make sure if you do end up pregnant, that you are in the eleventh or twelfth grade, because you can get you a tutor from the school and you can bounce right back and come to school and graduate.

DISCUSSION

Victoria, like the other girls in this study, would not consider her pregnancy planned, but she, like the other girls, expected to derive benefits from her pregnant status, should it occur. Luker (1975) formulates a series of decisions on the part of a risk taker, where individuals perceive options and assign values to them. She hypothesizes that a contraceptive risk is based on the immediate "costs of contraception" and the anticipated benefits of a pregnancy, which may be weighed differently once the pregnancy is an actuality. A pregnancy, at least in the abstract, was seen as moving women closer to other goals they had for themselves; these other goals centered around renegotiating relationships that were important to them toward some desired end, such as greater autonomy with their parents or a commitment from their male partners. Her formulation does not suggest that "rational decision making" is always explicit or clearly defined.

The implications from Luker's work as well as this research suggest that preventing a pregnancy may be one goal a girl has that is in competition simultaneously with other goals the adolescent has for herself. A pregnancy, while not planned per se, may be seen as facilitating those goals—greater autonomy from her parents, a step toward adulthood, a sealing of a personal relationship with her partner. Any program desiring to prevent adolescent pregnancies would need to address these various goals held by the girls as well as use of contraception.

The distinct feature of current teen births is the high proportion that occur out of wedlock.

> Birth rates among young women have fallen in recent years, although less than the rates for older women. . . . Illegitimacy, which has continued to rise among young women, even as their birth rates declined somewhat, casts a long economic shadow. . . . Among the young in the United States, illegitimacy is of substantial proportion and rising. . . . (Zelnik, Kantner, and Ford 1981, p. 19)

During the 1950s, only 15 percent of births, although not necessarily conceptions, were to unmarried teens; by 1980, 60 percent of the births to teens were to those who were unmarried (O'Connell and Moore 1981). Multiple factors have been singled out to explain the shift from married to unmarried adolescent parenthood. Births to single women are concentrated among low-income women. School dropout and unemployment rates for poor teenagers and young adults are very high. In terms of financial security for herself and her child, a young woman may be in a better position by not marrying. Between 1973 and 1984, the real incomes of males, ages twenty to twenty-four, dropped by a third; among black men in this age group, average annual incomes fell by 45 percent in real terms (Real 1987, p. 17).

For women, especially young women with children, marriage has been one of the key ways to escape poverty and avoid welfare dependency; contrary to popular belief, marriage, not employment, is the most common route off welfare for young mothers (Children's Defense Fund 1986). With a shortage of available young men who can support a family, the adolescent mother may not feel marriage is a feasible option. The most common route out of poverty and welfare dependency—marriage to someone who can offer a degree of financial security—is no longer an option to many adolescents. With the United States spending almost seventeen billion dollars a year on income supports for pregnant and parenting teens, we see the emergence of a social problem.

As practitioners, one of the range of interventions we use when working with clients is the idea of making the implicit explicit, drawing the decision-making process to consciousness so that it can be critiqued and evaluated realistically. Involved in this process is the development of a variety of approaches to a goal and a discarding of approaches that are unlikely to bring about the desired result. One of the foci, then, in working with girls like those in this study would be the decision-making process where the girls could evaluate their possible solutions in the light of other alternatives. For example, if a girl becomes aware that she has been bargaining for the right to be seen as an adult in her parents' eyes through becoming pregnant, she can focus on ways to achieve that end which will be ultimately less costly to her.

One of the tenets of feminists has been the translation of "private concerns to public issues." Rapp (1982) makes the point that in working-class communities founding a family is what people do for personal gratification and as a means towards gaining greater autonomy and a sense of adulthood for their lives. Traditional socialization has emphasized the role of nurturer for women; as she cares for her family, a woman will be taken care of herself, have a home, and be financially supported.

The benefits the girls expected to derive from their pregnancies are in keeping with those recorded in other research on lower- and working-class women (Rapp 1982). Unfortunately, these expectations are taking place in a society where marriage to a man who is employed and able to support her is currently less likely than it has been. What has been a fairly legitimate route to personal autonomy and fulfillment in the past is no longer a feasible option for many women. The larger societal question is whether alternate routes to the same ends—personal gratification, autonomy, a sense of adulthood—are being offered. If not, efforts need to focus not only on individual goal setting and planning but on the larger society as well in terms of opening up options for women. Self-determination truly takes place only in an environment of legitimate and diverse options.

CONCLUSION

One of the original reasons I decided to pursue the well-worn topic of adolescent pregnancy was my awareness—and puzzlement— that, despite numerous prevention programs, we as a country were not particularly successful in intervening. We continue to outdistance other comparable countries in our rate of teen pregnancy (Alan Guttmacher Institute 1981). My suspicion was that we were layering solutions on an issue without having the problem itself in focus. It made sense to me as a practitioner interested in preventative programs to go back and explore what it is we "know" about teen pregnancy and what it is we assume to the true.

I wasn't prepared for the therapeutic impact of the interviews themselves. After a few weeks of observing in the class, I asked to conduct some individual interviews and girls readily volunteered. Consistently I asked each one to "tell me about your pregnancy." While the girls took their answers in any direction they chose, the common denominator was the intensity of the interview experience. The outpouring by the girls was like a dam breaking, teary and cathartic, continuing past the time commitment I had originally asked them to give to the interview.

It was disquieting to me that many of the girls volunteered that this was their first opportunity to tell their stories. I puzzled over this since they were all participating in a special program with one of its goals being to prevent a second pregnancy while still in school. Had their stories, or the stories of girls like them, been considered in the design of the program?

Also unnerving to me was my own level of resonating with their stories. In putting them in context, their experiences as young black adolescents did not feel that removed from my own as an adult. I'd ask myself how this could be while simultaneously feeling we were women together with shared experiences. I found myself reviewing Stewart's (1981) work, which encourages us to put pregnant adolescents in context and find the threads of "normality." Stewart argues that what could be seen as deviant could be reframed as a "normal response to social expectations" (p. 453). In looking to understand the adolescents' responses to their own part of the culture, I hadn't expected it to strike chords with my own experiences.

Yet the sense of resonance as women together was unmistakable. And the implication in that was that they were not deviants, but rather young women making decisions for a whole variety of reasons and trying to negotiate difficult waters that many of us have been through: hoping to improve a relationship, wanting to be seen as an adult, buying a societal story line that our hope for the good things in life lies in the Prince Charmings that we find.

As we pull to the surface our reasonings and look at them in the light of day, we have the opportunity to hear what lies in back of the decisions we make and then see if there are other routes to the same desired end. Prince Charming may not be out there but the good things in life could become available as we work to expand opportunities, as we expose myths, as we hear stories, and are able to design programs and policies that meet the needs raised. Perhaps the real interventions for teens at risk of becoming pregnant are in listening to their stories and then expanding the routes to adulthood, to the good things in life.

CHAPTER 9

Andrew: The Story of a Gifted At-Risk Student

June Yennie-Donmoyer, Worthingway Middle School, Worthington City Schools, Ohio

Andrew, the subject of this chapter, is an unlikely candidate for inclusion in a book about students who are at risk of not graduating from high school. He is a truly brilliant adolescent from a stable, upper-middle-class home. His mother, however, confirmed just how at risk he really was.

The students took their places for the final scene of the readers theater production they were performing for the Ohio Association for Gifted Children, and I watched nervously from the audience as Andrew climbed the ladder that was positioned in the center of the stage. When he reached the top, he straddled the board where the two sides met, as if he had conquered the peak of a mountain. His extraordinary height and dramatic intensity were striking, and I thought he looked more perfect than anyone else who had done this role. Still, I wondered if he was wishing he could climb back off his perch, because I knew how much he hated to perform. At least that's what he had told me when he had finally agreed to fill in for an absent player.

Once in place, though, his voice rang out with no apparent qualms: "There once was an inventor who was a secluded sort of

135

person." The other actors, fellow students, were grouped below, looking straight out, isolated from the presence above them. Andrew went on, and I wondered when his voice would start to falter. "He could build things beyond his dreams. He could travel through the stars and up to the heavens in a machine he built himself." His pace was even, and his voice was controlled. He even looked up at the audience after his first few lines, and I began to relax.

"People said it won't work," the other actors shouted from the ground, turning in toward Andrew, fists raised.

"But he proved them wrong," Andrew replied, simply, confidently. I began to wonder if he was even nervous at all, and then I realized Andrew was totally comfortable in this role. Although another student (Andy Drake) had written this piece the previous year for a different class, the inventory was clearly a character Andrew knew well. In many ways, it was Andrew himself.

The groundlings continued, "But they didn't take notice, and he became even more and more withdrawn."

The taunting from below went on, and Andrew watched from atop his mountain with us, the audience, as the actors formed two distinct groups, and a "war" began. I started to become uneasy again as I thought about the stories Andrew had told me about his previous school, and I suddenly realized that I had put Andrew in a doubly difficult position. Not only had I asked him to perform when he was clearly more comfortable running the lights, I had also asked him to dramatize a role that bore an uncomfortable and, I feared, embarrassing, resemblance to his own life. I tried to remember why I hadn't thought earlier, when I was rushing to put this presentation together, about the irony of him doing these lines.

The reading moved on quickly, though, and I became absorbed again in the drama as solo voices continued the verbal riot. The noise built as voices were added to each other and the battle moved toward its climax:

> So, he set out to prove them all wrong. And, he built a motor that could power a thousand ships—or a million cars—and generate power for a hundred homes. Yes, he built the motor and proved them wrong.

"This time they did take notice." All fifteen voices were blaring now.

"They dove into the depths of his consciousness and drove away the seclusion," came from stage right, and then stage left took over: "They began to fight for his machines—a war."

"A bitter war," echoed the other side again, building the final volley. "Over a motor that could power a thousand ships" (left), "a million cars" (right), "or a hundred homes" (both sides).

"And when they were done, there was no one left," one plaintive voice said. "No cars, ships, or homes," the others gradually joined in, sinking one by one to the floor.

Then, quietly, Andrew spoke from his place above the crowd, in an ethereal tone I had not heard him use before:

> Just the inventor sailing in a machine they said would never work. High into the heavens he sailed, through time and space to places where a normal man could never go, in a machine he had built himself, that proved them wrong.

Silence, then applause, filled the room, and Andrew climbed down the ladder to join the others in a final bow. I was stunned. Not only had Andrew forgotten his stage fright, but he had turned in a brilliant performance, and I sensed he, as well as the rest of the class, knew his portrayal of the inventor had been extraordinary. Watching him join the others in a discussion with the audience about the performance afterwards, I remember thinking, "Something's changed these past eight months. Andrew is finally one of the group."

When I think of Andrew, my former eighth-grade student, I think of him atop that ladder, confident, self-aware, and happy, and I am reminded of how remarkable it is that Andrew had that experience. A quintessentially gifted student, Andrew was also, without doubt, one of the most at-risk students I had ever met. He was extremely unhappy, unable to make friends, and, it seemed to me, self-destructive. Just how at risk he was, though, I might never have known without investigating his story further for this chapter. His mother told me only recently, when I asked her for permission to portray Andrew as an at-risk student, that she had actually feared that her son, now approaching tenth grade, had been suicidal during the time that I had come to know him.

Today, however, only a year later, Andrew is a well-adjusted, productive student in a highly respected alternative program of the district's main high school. He has several good friends, is active in extracurricular activities, and is well liked by his teachers. Anyone meeting him for the first time probably would not suspect he might have once been classified as at-risk.

The critical question, of course, is what has caused Andrew to change so dramatically? According to Andrew, his parents, and his teachers, the answer is perfectly obvious: After years of being a pariah in school, he has finally found a place where he fits in, a place where he no longer feels the need to either flaunt or hide his talents, where being somewhat out of the mainstream is not a liability, but an asset. What follows is an account of Andrew's school experience, constructed from interviews with Andrew, his mother Carol, his eighth-grade principal, his ninth-grade principal, and several teachers. It is the story of a gifted child's lonely journey through endless hallowed, hollow halls of learning to the top of a ladder where he could finally soar away "to places where a normal man could never go"—and still land safely.

There were many things I didn't know about Andrew when he was my student a year ago, so recent conversations with Carol have been very enlightening. Apparently, Andrew was more like the inventor he played in our class presentation than I ever realized. He began taking things apart at a very young age, according to Carol, and she was soon afraid to leave him at friends' houses. Whenever anything broke, Andrew was automatically blamed, even if he was not responsible. Of course, he didn't earn this reputation without good reason. Once, for example, without being caught, he removed screens from the second-floor windows of the house where his preschool playgroup was meeting. He disassembled telephones as a toddler, found a way to make magnets out of nails in cub scouts, and, while still in elementary school, repaired a dishwasher and hooked up a compressor.

Andrew's parents appreciated that his curiosity and ability to fix things were often very positive, but they were also worried that their son had no sense of limits, and that some of his activities could lead to disaster. They tried to make their son live with the consequences of his behavior, but nothing seemed to deter him from what seemed to him to be perfectly worthwhile activities. At the end of seventh grade, for example, right after the family moved to their current location, Andrew decided he could fix a malfunctioning outdoor fountain by redesigning some plumbing in the basement. In spite of her skepticism, Carol agreed to let Andrew implement his very logical-sounding plan. Andrew moved a few pipes, and when he turned a faucet on to test his work, water began spraying all over the basement. Nonplussed, he tried to repair his leaking joints, first with solder, then with liquid nails, and finally with duct tape. When nothing worked, his mother told him he was responsible for the damage he had caused, and he would have to hire a plumber to repair the situation. Carol's hopes for teaching her son a lesson about what can happen when one assumes he always has all the answers were somewhat dashed, however, when the plumber made necessary repairs in only five minutes—using Andrew's original plan. "All he needed was a different solder," his mother sighed. The plumber didn't even bill Andrew for his time, so, in order to salvage some part of the original point she had hoped to make, Carol had to insist that Andrew send a "donation" to the plumber the next day!

From birth, Andrew was an exhausting child to care for, and when he was eighteen months old, Carol asked the pediatrician if Andrew might be hyperactive. The doctor replied that Andrew was quite normal, except that he was extremely bright, and he would "probably smoke cigars when he is an adult." Amused, but far from relieved, Carol continued to try to keep life organized around her busy, extraordinary child. In fact, Carol identifies herself as the "organizing parent," whereas she views her husband as the all-accepting parent who sometimes made it difficult for her to have a productive relationship with Andrew. "Andrew and I would get into power struggles, even when he was little," she said. "And often, I thought he was in control."

Later, when Andrew was three, Carol enrolled him in nursery school, hoping to help him develop some social skills. "He has always had difficulty communicating with his peer group," she explained. Before long, though, the teacher began complaining that Andrew did not function properly in "large group situations." "When we go to the gym, he goes berserk," Carol remembers the teacher saying. A friend tried to comfort Carol by reminding her that sometimes adults expect too much of children. "Think of him as being only thirty-six months old, instead of three years old, and you'll realize how little time he's actually been on this earth," she said. Carol says that somehow she found great strength in this thought, and it helped her to keep some perspective on what seemed to be developing into a chronic problem. She also began to believe that since Andrew was about twice as tall as most children his age, people would probably always expect him to act like children his size, not his age. "He seemed to have everything stacked against him," she reflected.

Andrew began public school in an extremely affluent community near Boston. His primary years were fairly positive, although there continued to be indications that Andrew was not a typical child. His kindergarten teacher was "a visionary," according to Carol, "who knew how to provide freedom with limits." Students were permitted to choose the interest areas they wanted to be in, and Andrew usually chose the big-blocks post, where he worked contentedly for hours. Still, there were difficulties, apparently, and there were some "screaming matches" between Andrew and his teacher. Fortunately, however, the teacher seemed to appreciate and understand Andrew in spite of the conflicts. "I'm not going to let you beat yourself up," Carol remembers the teacher telling her when she tried to apologize for her son's behavior. "You're doing the best you can."

Carol and her husband, Tom, held on to the hope that they would continue to find teachers who could work with Andrew, until they found out Mrs. Wilson was to be his first-grade teacher. "This was a woman who had a well-known reputation for hating boys," Carol said.

> We were sick. We worked all summer to come up with coping skills for Andrew so he could get through the year, sitting in an assigned seat and behaving like a conventional student. Finally, Tom came up with the idea of giving Andrew three big cards with the letters L, C, and V on them. Then he taught Andrew that each letter stood for a word that he would learn to remember when he looked at the cards. L stood for *listen*, C for *control*, and V for *volume*. On the first day of school, Andrew took the cards and put them in his desk where he could get them out any time he felt like he might need to think about those words. We also told the teacher about our plan. We were amazed because she seemed very impressed. It turned out to be a very good year. In fact, an eerie thing happened last week when I was thinking about all this: Mrs. Wilson called us to ask about Andrew! After seven years she decided to find out where we had moved and to see how Andrew was doing. She said she always thought he was a very special boy.

Although Andrew and his parents succeeded in developing a good relationship with Mrs. Wilson, however, other problems were clearly beginning to emerge that year. Andrew's family was not part of the socially elite community that dominated the school, and, as a result, Andrew was a bit of an outcast. One incident, in particular, made them wonder if Andrew was in the wrong school. Carol had heard about an extracurricular program for gifted students, and she asked Mrs. Wilson whether she thought Andrew might qualify. (Carol and Tom were just beginning to think that their son's restlessness in the classroom could be related to his naturally high academic ability, but they were insecure about promoting this idea.) Mrs. Wilson was very supportive and said that the program sounded like a perfect plan for Andrew, but the principal refused to endorse her recommendation. "We want you to know that we are in no way labeling Andrew as gifted," he announced, without giving further explanation. From that point on, Carol and Tom felt very much on their own in terms of looking after Andrew's best interests.

In second grade, Andrew had a teacher who was obsessively concerned about his thumb sucking. The teacher believed, according to Carol, that children who sucked their thumbs "had really big problems," and Andrew sucked his thumb for everything, whether he was happy or sad, relaxed or tense. He even sucked his thumb openly in class. Finally, in part to placate the teacher, Carol and Tom decided to have Andrew psychologically evaluated. According to Carol, the psychologist was "wonderful" with Andrew, who worked willingly with her. The only suggestion they got from the psychologist's analysis of the tests that something was "wrong" with Andrew, however, came from her comment that whenever Andrew drew a picture, he made the sky very dark. This meant, they were told, that Andrew was extremely threatened by his father's success. Not knowing what to do with this information, and inclined not to accept it, Andrew's parents decided to look elsewhere for help in understanding their son's problems.

Third grade was apparently uneventful, except that Carol remembers the teacher commenting to her one day that Andrew often sat reading a book at his desk while a lesson was going on, yet he didn't seem to miss a thing she said during the class. That summer, Andrew's parents decided it was time to challenge him with something that did not come so easily as school work, and they enrolled him in a softball league. Andrew was oblivious, they reasoned, to how most people learn, and to how he might eventually have to learn himself. "He had always learned by discovery, and he wanted him to have the experience of having to listen to instruction," Carol explained. What seemed like a good plan failed, however, because Andrew hated playing team sports. "We tried to get him to understand rules, teamwork," his parents said, "but he just sat on the bench and daydreamed. Other parents used to laugh at the way he watched the planes going by overhead while their sons were watching the ball." Andrew's softball career ended abruptly when he plopped himself into a big bag of balls after a game, totally humiliating his parents and finally convincing them that playing softball was not going to lead him to conform.

In the fourth grade, Andrew was finally placed in the gifted program. He only got to participate in the program a few months, however, because the family moved midyear to another district. While he was in the program, Andrew didn't talk much about it, and his parents didn't hear from either the regular classroom teacher or the gifted-class instructor. Finally, right before they left the district, Carol requested a conference in order to gather information on Andrew's progress for the file that would be taken to his new school. Carol remembers thinking during the conference that the teachers seemed to be talking about two entirely different children when they discussed Andrew. The classroom teacher barely knew how to distinguish Andrew from anyone else in the class, whereas the gifted teacher exclaimed that Andrew was one of the brightest and most enjoyable students he had ever known.

With this less than clear picture of his fourth-grade status, Andrew's parents enrolled him in his next school, which was similar socioeconomically to the school he had just left. One day, in his new class, he wrote an inventive essay called "13 Reasons Why You Should Never Move." The item Carol remembers best from the list was, "You don't get a birthday party that year." When Andrew's new teacher called his parents to share what he had written and suggest it be placed in a family archive somewhere, Carol and Tom were relieved to think that they might have encountered another understanding teacher who could appreciate their son. What they didn't realize was that, in spite of the good rapport he was having with some of his teachers. Andrew was becoming more and more unhappy at school, primarily because he couldn't get along with his peers. Socially and intellectually, he was simply too "different" to fit in.

Fifth through seventh grade, Andrew continued to be placed with kind teachers whom both Carol and Tom respected, but none of them were able to protect him from the cruelty of other students. These are the years Andrew remembers most vividly, and the story he tells parallels his mother's account of the same events.

"Schools should have 'insiders' and 'outsiders', so they can balance each other off," Andrew told me, as he tried to explain what had gone wrong for him after fourth grade. "This new school only had insiders—and me, and maybe a couple of others. But we weren't big enough to join together, so the few friends I did have couldn't stand by me if there were problems. They had to go with the insiders."

In addition to his fairly sophisticated, and undoubtedly accurate, analysis of the social dynamics of his school environment, Andrew also had a fairly clear understanding of why he became the main victim of the situation. Andrew knew that he hadn't done well socially, even in his first school, which he hated more than his parents probably realized at the time. Instead of worrying, then, as many children might have, when he learned they would be moving to a new house, he had actually looked forward to having a chance to "start over." But, unfortunately, when he got to his new school, and discovered the same kind of social elitism he had just left behind, he felt doomed. In fact, one of his most vivid memories of the new school is having been told by a student during the first week, "That's not how you cross your legs."

"That was my first sign, looking back," Andrew said, "that things weren't going to get any better. So I decided to do exactly the opposite of whatever anybody said I should do to conform. That's where the insider-outsider thing comes in."

Andrew's conscious decision to try to fight the social system made school an increasingly intolerable place for him. "It was World War III for me," he said. Although his parents were most likely unaware of how Andrew perceived his circumstances, or how he had decided to handle his frustrations, they were painfully aware of the accumulating incidents that were resulting from his behavior. In their view, Andrew was a victim of an out-of-control school, which, of course, he was—but for more complex reasons, perhaps, than were readily apparent.

There were many fights that both Andrew and Carol remember. Andrew speculates that he was in the principal's office two or three times a week in the end, in fact. Andrew recalls certain friends who helped him with various pranks, but Carol remembers John best of all. In fact, she believes moving next door to John's family was their fatal mistake. "He was as brilliant as Andrew. I think he had a photographic memory. But I think he's going to end up in prison someday," she said.

> His behavior was truly bizarre. Once, when he was left alone in his house, he literally chewed the woodwork in the family room. Part of the problem was that his father was a perfectionist professionally. He also signaled John that he could do or say anything he wanted to behind people's backs. John was really getting mixed messages. He needed friends, and he knew that, because he didn't have any. But he didn't know how to be a friend. He would sabotage Andrew, and Andrew wouldn't realize it and bail him out. John played Andrew like a violin, and unfortunately, they ended up in the same fifth-grade class.

By the time Andrew entered junior high, in the sixth grade, he had gained a reputation for being a troublemaker and a loner. At five feet, nine inches, he continued to be much taller than anyone else, and most of the students called him "Beaker," a name they got from a Muppets character. Andrew began to prize his outcast identity and lived by the motto "I'll get you back." In the end, though, they got him first. At the end of sixth grade, Andrew picked up his yearbook and discovered that on a composite page a picture of him had been drawn in which he had three very long necks. "Somehow, the teacher-adviser, who was a very nice woman, missed it," Carol said. "When a friend called me to warn me what had happened, I nearly threw up." To make matters worse, some students managed to talk Andrew into letting them sign his yearbook, and they marked it up with ugly slogans to "Beaker," in magic marker. The principal made them replace Andrew's yearbook, but they got the last word by organizing seventy-five students to jump him on the playground. It took five teachers nearly twenty minutes to pull Andrew, who was badly beaten and humiliated, out from under the pile.

In separate interviews, both Andrew and his mother identified the principal's ineptitude as a primary reason for the school's social chaos. They both described Mr. James, whom Carol called a friend, as having a good rapport with students but being unable to serve harsh punishments when necessary. Andrew recalls him once saying to students who had been fist fighting only moments before, "Now, you know you're not supposed to do that—okay, you can go." Carol recalls the disbelief she felt when Mr. James remarked after the yearbook incident that Andrew would just have to learn to laugh about the way he was being treated by other students.

Carol and Andrew also both listed the fact that Carol was a substitute teacher in Andrew's building as being a significant factor in Andrew's experience. On this issue, however, they saw things quite differently. Carol was constantly concerned about how her son felt about having her in the same building. She even offered to work somewhere else if it bothered him. He told her repeatedly he didn't mind, though, so she eventually concluded he probably felt more safe having her there. He, on the other hand, said that in retrospect he felt her presence just helped him "get hated more."

I met Andrew almost two years ago, when his family moved to our district and he was enrolled in the middle-school gifted and talented program, for which I am the teacher. Like the other eighth graders in the program, he was scheduled to divide his time between the gifted English class the regular English program (which was taught by someone else), spending two quarters in each. In addition, he spent two quarters attending an interdisciplinary seminar designed especially for the gifted students. Andrew also joined a few select students who traveled to the high school early each morning to take a tenth-grade geometry course.

Andrew's exceptional talents became obvious almost immediately, especially in the area of math. I couldn't help noticing, however, that his social skills were far less well developed than those of his peers. He seemed to have difficulty making friends and adjusting to his new environment. For one thing, he had a tendency to talk too loudly and too much, and this seemed to annoy other students. He also seemed overly judgmental, especially for someone who was new to the school, and he liked to talk about his previous school as if it had been superior in every way to where he was now. Students began to complain to me about his attitude in class, and eventually they started to tease him publicly. I noticed that the more he came in conflict with other students, the harder he tried to be impressive and create an image of superiority, which only made matters worse; he seemed incapable of making friends.

I spent the first month of school asking other students to be patient with Andrew, and to give him a chance, but before long it became clear that the situation would only deteriorate if Andrew's behavior did not change. I also discovered relatively quickly that although Andrew was a star math student, he was only a mediocre writer, which put him at real disadvantage in a class that spent a great deal of time creating, sharing, and publishing work. I had seen numerous other students gain peer respect and acceptance through their writing, but I was fairly sure Andrew wouldn't be one of them.

In October, the class began rehearsing its fall readers theater production, and I mentioned that I wished we could perform the program in a real theater with decent lighting equipment. (Readers theater is a technically simple, stylized form of theater that is greatly enhanced by artistic lighting.) In previous years, because we had no auditorium, I had gone to the trouble and expense of hiring a technician and renting professional equipment for a makeshift theater we built in the cafeteria. That year, however, funds had been cut, and I needed a new plan. In the end, it was Andrew who came to the group's rescue, and in the process he began also to rescue himself.

Andrew told me that he had worked the stage lights in his previous school and he could operate whatever equipment we needed if I could arrange to borrow the district's theater annex building for our production. Luckily, the schedule I needed for our plan worked out well for the other classes that normally used that building, and Andrew and I began to design the lights for our show. The production was very successful, and Andrew became a hero: he was clearly regarded as the mastermind and technician that had made it all possible. He didn't automatically gain popularity along with his new-found respect, of course, but there didn't seem to be any question any longer that he was part of the group, warts and all.

I began to know Andrew better during the time we worked together on that project. We traveled between the two buildings several times during free periods to set up the theater, and while we drove, he told me stories about his family and his previous school.

He talked mostly about the latter, which sounded like a Disneyland version of what schools of the future could be if money wasn't an issue. He described the state-of-the-art lighting equipment he had used there and the opportunities he might have had in technical theater at the high school if he hadn't been forced to move. I suggested he become involved the following year in our high school theater department, which is truly outstanding, but he didn't respond with any real enthusiasm. I remember thinking that he seemed almost hopelessly homesick. None of the stories he told me then revealed the fact that his experience in elementary school and seventh grade had actually been very negative, or that he had been victimized by his peers. I thought he only wanted to go back.

The next few months, Andrew became involved in a number of other areas around the school. Because he started his school day early with his geometry class at the high school, he ended up with an extra study hall period later in the day, and he eventually began spending this free period in the library. Before long, he let the librarian (Lillian) know he had great interest and considerable expertise in the area of computers, and she, needing whatever assistance she could get in installing a new catalogue system, invited him to begin working with the system. It didn't take her long to discover that she had met an expert, and Andrew soon became an assistant in both the library and the computer lab. Unfortunately, she also soon discovered Andrew's impulsive, assertive tendencies. I was often called upon to interpret what limits could and could not be expected of him, especially when he did things like help himself to equipment and install software on the hard drive without getting permission.

Lillian and I continued to negotiate Andrew's role, as a matter of fact, until the day he graduated, because there seemed to be a constant, seemingly unresolvable tension surrounding his much needed but also intimidating presence. In the end, however, our librarian contributed more than almost anyone else to Andrew's social and emotional development, because, although she became very frustrated at times by his take-charge behavior, she respected his talent and she seemed to view his "improprieties" as a function of his adolescence. Mostly, she became involved with him when she really didn't have to, spending lots of hours listening to his stories and allowing him to develop an identity as the technology expert in his new school.

Meanwhile, Andrew was beginning to have difficulties else-where in the school. Somewhere in the middle of the year, I began receiving reports from Andrew's other teachers that he was getting involved in fights in the halls. It seemed that although he had gained partial acceptance from members of the gifted class, his abrasive behavior was less tolerated by other students in the school. About the same time, Lillian alerted me that competition seemed to be developing between Andrew and some of the computer-oriented seventh-grade students in the gifted program who also liked to help out in the library, and, she said, it was getting fairly vicious. I remember collecting all this information and beginning to wonder if there were more to Andrew's history than we knew, or whether his apparently increasing problems were still only products of the fact that he was having trouble adjusting to his new environment.

I finally decided to ask Andrew directly why he was getting into fights, and why he felt compelled to dominate the younger students. We met one afternoon, and I began to question him about some of the reports I had been getting. I never expected the reaction I got. He began to cry, and then he told me all about his former schools. "I'm afraid it's starting again here," he said, "and I just can't go through it again. I just can't. You don't understand how bad it was."

Of course, I hadn't anticipated this passionate response, but I wasn't completely surprised by it either. And Andrew was right: I was unable to fully envision the incidents he proceeded to describe—How could seventy-five children be allowed to pile upon another child before someone stopped them? I believe the only thing I *was* beginning to understand was that Andrew's suffering had made him unsure of, maybe even hateful toward, himself.

It occurred to me that afternoon that Andrew's problems were much bigger than any of us had imagined, and I wasn't sure how to proceed. Before I could think, I merely responded to his distress by promising him things were going to change. "You won't ever have to worry about being treated like that again," I told him. "Not in this school. We simply don't tolerate kids being mean to each other. We expect people to accept each other in spite of their differ-ences, and you'll learn to do that, too."

What I told Andrew was true, at least in theory. I knew our school wasn't perfect, but I also knew "caring" was a priority. Not only were kindness and consideration for others explicitly required by that year's school theme, caring was also part of the pervasive atmosphere in the school. I was confident that I could assure Andrew that every effort would be made to give him a chance for acceptance. Although he seemed surprised, I sensed he trusted what I was saying, or at least he comprehended my intent in reassuring him. The rest of that afternoon, we talked about how Andrew's behavior turned other people against him, and we developed strategies for him to work peacefully alongside the seventh-grade students in the library. (For instance, he agreed to give other people's ideas a chance before arguing against them.)

That was the only time Andrew and I discussed his social life that year, but I heard a few weeks later that things were going well in the library, and I noticed that Andrew began to be quieter and more relaxed in class the next few months. He even started going out with a steady girlfriend. In the spring, about the same time he began rehearsing his role as the inventor for our conference presentation, he built the class a portable lighting system so we would no longer be dependent upon renting equipment or borrowing other facilities. We used the system for our spring production for parents, and Andrew was heralded as the genius behind the success of that program.

Eventually, Andrew became a regular member of a group of students who liked to spend free periods and lunchtime socializing and working in our classroom. He continued to be regarded as somewhat pig-headed and annoying at times, but any teasing he got, at least from his friends, was usually doused with liberal amounts of real affection. Simultaneously, tensions lessened in his other classes as well, especially as he began trying less hard to be noticed. Somehow, he was learning how to stop being a victim.

Andrew's parents and I began discussing his high school future early in the spring of that year, and, of course, a main concern was what would happen to him socially and emotionally once he left the middle school. This was a particularly difficult time for the family, because the corporation that had transferred Andrew's father to this area had just phased out his position, leaving him unemployed for many months. Andrew's parents seriously considered moving again to where employment opportunities were better, but they made a difficult decision to stay where they were for the sake of keeping Andrew in what seemed to be a positive environment.

They were very eager, then, to make sure that the progress he was making in middle school would continue in the ninth grade.

I suggested they look into the alternative program at the high school. I knew other students with needs similar to Andrew's who were flourishing there, and I was fairly sure he would respond well to the school's informal atmosphere, as well as to the students' tendencies to be both independent and yet appreciative of each other. The school has a reputation for attracting extremely bright students, as well as the nontraditional students who are more commonly associated with alternative programs. One of the school's most attractive features is its senior year Walkabout program which allows students to work as interns for three to six months in professional settings. In the past, students on Walkabout have traveled throughout the world to work in such settings as major universities, network television stations, national parks, and inner-city social agencies. This program plus others, such as interdisciplinary seminars and opportunities for independent study, made the school seem perfect for Andrew.

Though intrigued by my suggestion, Carol and Tom were skeptical at first. Like many parents, they associated "alternative school" with marginalization, the very last thing they felt their son needed. They were also concerned that a school that respected students' independence might not be able to help Andrew understand the limits he still also needed to learn. They agreed to visit the school, however, and were charmed and impressed enough by the students they met to decide to give it a try. In the end, they discovered their decision had been a good one, because only a few weeks after school opened the following fall, Andrew was a happy, well-liked ninth grader who was clearly flourishing in his new environment. Before long, his parents were exclaiming that Andrew had finally found his ideal school.

Today Andrew's principal and teachers report that Andrew has had an outstanding ninth-grade year. "Here, kids learn over a period of time how to gain respect from other kids," the principal said. He continued:

> Andrew is also learning how to accept and respect others. He benefits from our policy of mixing freshmen and upper classmen in courses. He is in a place where he can be an expert—and he is definitely that—and still be part of the group. He is a bit ar-

rogant at times and an occasional know-it-all, but that's only because he's inexperienced. We all understand that. It's no big deal.

Andrew is so involved in his activities and interests that he seems mostly unimpressed by the changes that have taken place in him over the past two years. He can barely even remember, for instance, the conversation we had when he first told me about his former schools. As we began to talk again last month, however, the anger and frustration crept back into his memory and he said through clenched teeth, "They got into my life so deeply—I would have killed them. Without guilt." Then he went on to reflect on how different his life is now. The difference, he says, is that he knows nothing will ever again be as bad as it used to be. When he has problems with people now, he says, he is more patient, because he has already experienced the worst.

Everything is not perfect, though, Andrew cautioned me in his final interview. "I still don't get along with everybody." Then as a postscript, he added, half joking, half thoughtful, that he may now be at risk in a different way, if being at risk means not working up to one's potential. "I'm involved in a lot of social stuff, now— especially theater. I studied a lot more in my other schools when I hated everyone and didn't have any other way to get my mind off them. I think my schoolwork is going down a little here."

For gifted students like Andrew, gaining acceptance from others can be more difficult and more crucial than succeeding academically. In fact, as Andrew's story tells us, students who are ostracized and humiliated primarily because of their special talents suffer in extraordinary and lonely ways that make them unique among at-risk individuals. American public schools generally do not celebrate differentness, nor does society, as *The Inventor* plainly illustrates. Ironically, therefore, many of this country's most promising students will be lost before they ever reach the potential we all need them to develop.

Thinking of Andrew sitting atop his ladder gives me hope that some at-risk students will overcome their difficulties. Still, there were others on the stage floor below Andrew that day—students with equal talent and intelligence—who I am less sure of. Although their problems were different from Andrew's, they suffered from their own forms of isolation. Tom was there, and he was still floundering in school the following year, unable to pass a single course because he couldn't discipline himself to do required, mundane tasks. Sam was there, too, a severly withdrawn student, overwhelmed by his own artistic intensity and a commitment to his Asian heritage that no one else seemed to understand or value.

And Jill was there; the final week of school we had to take her to the hospital when she withdrew into a silent fetal position under my desk. In spite of the help and understanding we had tried to give her during the previous eight months, she had become more and more depressed; a victim of sexual abuse, Jill's situation was complicated by her incredible intelligence and sensitivity. Although she is now in the same school as Andrew, and doing quite well, Jill is less fortunate than he is because she cannot count on any rational support from her parents at this point. It is not at all certain whether she will be able to keep from using her creativity to hurt herself.

Tom, Sam, Jill, and Andrew are students whom many would categorize as privileged because of their extraordinary talents and abilities. They attend school in one of the country's most highly rated districts, have well-educated parents who love them, and are economically well-off. In spite of these advantages, however, these students and others like them often fail to thrive academically, socially, and emotionally, for reasons that are not always obvious. What seems, then, at times to be a mysterious paradox often only exacerbates these students' problems of isolation and shattered self-esteem. As a result, unless schools learn to recognize the special needs of students like Andrew, many future inventors will probably fall before they "sail through time and space to places where a normal man can never go."

CHAPTER 10

Alston and Everetta: Too Risky for School?

James T. Sears, University of South Carolina

In this chapter portraits of Alston and Everetta are presented. These portraits may make some readers uncomfortable. Yet Alston and Everetta are no less at risk and no less in need of our understanding and support than the other students portrayed in this book.

At the 1990 national conference held by the Association for Supervision and Curriculum Development (ASCD), an organization of more than 150,000 curriculum specialists, principals, district administrators, and university professors of education, the membership passed a resolution which stated, in part, "ASCD urges its members to develop policies, curriculum materials, and teaching strategies that do not discriminate on the basis of sexual orientation. ASCD encourages schools to provide staff development training and materials to enable educators to better work with this at-risk student population" (ASCD 1990). While the National Educational Association, the American Federation of Teachers, and the American School Health Association had passed resolutions on student's sexual orientation, this was the first time that a major educational organization applied the "at-risk" label to lesbian, gay, and bisexual students.

Traditionally, at-risk students have been identified as those with one or more of the following characteristics: excessive school absences, discipline problems, reading or mathematic skills at or below one grade level, and/or academic underachievement (Mizell 1986). Studies of at-risk students—primarily those at-risk students in contact with the juvenile justice system—have focused exclusively on heterosexual behavior and have found these adolescents to have experienced heterosexual intercourse earlier and with greater frequency (Melchert and Burnett 1990; Farrow and Schroeder 1984). Sexual minority students have not been categorized as an "at-risk" population. They have been largely ignored by educators (Sears 1992) and rendered an invisible minority within the student population. However, as I have documented elsewhere (Sears 1989; Sears 1991) students identified as gay, lesbian, and bisexual are more susceptible than other young people to drug and alcohol problems, discipline problems, eating disorders, and youthful suicide. These students often report a history reflecting more fundamental problems such as a school curriculum irrelevant to their sexual and personal needs, family problems, and a lack of self-esteem or fear for their personal security.

Maxine Greene (1988), discussing the importance of the self in the student's journey toward self-understanding within the school curriculum, declares "I want people to name themselves and tell their stories" (p. xii). Within the predetermined, objective-based, test-driven curriculum evidenced in many schools meeting the questionable challenges of *A Nation at Risk,* there is little encouragement to "name the love that dare not speak its name" (Douglas and Hyde, 1973, p. 200); there are few educators willing to risk listening to this chorale of diverse voices whose stories of isolation, harassment and intimidation, despair—and love—fall silently in classrooms of loneliness. What follows are the voices of two such students, Everetta and Alston.

EVERETTA

Everetta, the youngest of three sisters, was reared during the mid-1960s in a sparsely populated county at the end of a dead-end dirt road. Her parents, Thurmond and Mandy, brought to their new family several additional children from previous marriages.

Everetta has vivid memories, though, of her Cinderella-like family relationship with her two natural sisters:

> Penny failed the seventh, eighth, and ninth grades, and the first grade, too. But Daddy never abused her. He never hit her or kicked her or anything like that. He bought her a car even though she had failed all those grades! The other, Julia Mae, was the prettiest and the wittiest one. She had health problems, though. She had sclerosis. She had to have surgery and a pin put in her back. She was untouchable, too.

In contrast to her two older sisters, Everetta enjoyed a less than charmed childhood. Short and husky with a determined smile and weather-beaten skin, she recalls her responsibilities at twelve years of age:

> First thing in the morning, when it was still not daylight, I had to get up. We had a farm and I had to do as much work as I could before I went to school. I rode my bike to the peach shed. I worked on a conveyer belt grading, working my way up to loading the trucks. Then I went to school. I came home and worked until it was dark. When I failed there was constant beatings from Daddy.

When Everetta wasn't doing her chores, working in the peach shed, or going to school, she would wander in the woods, walking along the nearby river journeying into "my own little space." She remembers going to bed as soon as possible to escape from the often heated arguments between her parents.

In first grade, Everetta experienced her first crush: It was on Louise, a third grader she came to know in her reading group. Everetta began writing little notes to her. "I wanted to be around her as much as possible. But, she thought it was sort of strange. She didn't really want to be around me that much. It went on for a while. I didn't give up real easy."

During elementary school, Everetta's teachers found her smart but disruptive. Though she earned A's and B's and was reading two levels above her grade, she was often punished by her teachers for engaging in playful mischief, such as throwing airplanes, that was considered unladylike in school. She recalls: "The boys liked to pick on me for some reason. I wouldn't let them. I would fight back. Most of the other girls, you know, they were just too femme." During recess, Everetta generally would be found roughhousing with the boys while her female classmates jumped rope, played on the swings, or talked quietly on the school steps. Seldom would a school day go in which Everetta, wearing heavy-rimmed black glasses bandaged together with tape, did not return home without soiled or torn clothes. Her parents, though, didn't seem too concerned with Everetta's tomboyish behavior. "It was like, 'You'll outgrow it,' so I wasn't really given a hard time about being a tomboy at that age."

As Everetta advanced in elementary school, her attraction to girls became stronger. Though she had no close friends, she had repeated crushes on other girls a year or two older than herself. Her second childhood sweetheart was Lynette. Everetta constantly followed her about school and sent her notes. "I nicknamed her 'Tally' because she was so tall," Everetta remembers. "She'd wear skirts. I would roll down the hill so I could see up under her skirt. It felt natural. She didn't like me either. It wasn't until later that I kind of understood a little bit about why she didn't like that."

As Everetta entered middle school, she continued to get into fights, play sports with the boys, and write notes to girls. Tracy became the target for Everetta's attentions:

> I had a baseball glove. I had her name and mine written all over it. I tried to explain to her how I felt. I remember being in school and telling her the only way I knew how: "There are three kinds of fruits. There is one where you are crazy. There is one that you eat. And, there is one where you are a girl and like other girls." That's how I explained it to her. I told her that I was the third one and that I liked her. She kind of went along with it for a while though we never touched or anything. Then, she got tired of it and asked the teacher to make me get her name off my glove. I told the teacher, "This is my glove and Tracy can't make me take her name off it." Well, teachers don't like that kind of attitude so, of course, I got into trouble.

Everetta's sense of difference became more apparent during middle school. And it was then that this sense of difference was first given a name.

> There was this kid named Billy. He decided he also liked Tracy. I thought that it was just too bad. Now, for some reason or another, Tracy and I ended up having to ride the same school bus home. He wanted to sit by her but I was sitting next to her. He told me, "Get up, 'four eyes'"—that was my nickname back then—"you shouldn't be sitting by Tracy unless you're queer."

We fought over her on the school bus. I got in trouble and ended up getting licks from the principal.

Still, Everetta really "didn't understand exactly what 'queer' meant. I just knew I was different. I went through a stage that I thought that somehow God had made a mistake and that I really would have rather been a boy."

Particularly after the school bus and glove incidents, Everetta had a difficult time fitting in with any of the groups at school.

> The kids just didn't accept me as much. The boys were getting old enough that they didn't like a little girl hanging around with them. The girls were all into their own thing. You know, being real pushy acting and talking like, "Ain't that boy cute?" and other things that I had no comprehension of. I was kind of an in-between. I didn't fit with the boys and I really didn't fit with the girls. I stayed mostly by myself.

Her continued fighting with boys (and often winning) earned her the nickname "Rock." Though Everetta continued to be the object of scorn and ridicule, her classmates' motivations were still uncertain. "I wasn't sure why they didn't like me. I didn't really think it had anything to do with my liking girls. I thought they were harassing me because I was little, wore patches, and wasn't good looking."

A welcomed relief during seventh grade was her teacher, Mrs. Munn. Everetta found her very friendly and supportive. "I always had a feeling that she knew something inside of me was gay," Everetta confesses. "She was the first teacher I actually ever connected with. I acted up and was late to her class a lot. I guess I was looking for attention. She'd reprimand me but she also understood why I did those things." Mrs. Munn, though, was an exception. Her other teachers, like Ms. Peagler, were less understanding.

> I always wore this blue jean jacket with fuzz inside. That jacket was everything to me; it was my identity. No matter what the weather was like, I would wear that jacket to school. Ms. Peagler would say, "That's not right, Everetta. You don't need to be wearing that kind of jacket, walking like a boy, talking like a boy, and acting like one." One day I left my jacket behind in her classroom. I went back later and asked her, "Did I leave my jacket here?" She teased me. She wouldn't tell me whether I left it there or not. Then she sat me down and told me how a young

woman should and should not act and what a young lady should and should not wear.

Although Everetta didn't date in middle school, she did write notes to one or two boys, let them accompany her to a class, and occasionally allowed them to kiss her. "I kept trying to like boys," recalls Everetta. "But it was never comfortable. But, I thought I just needed to keep trying even if I didn't like it or it wasn't comfortable." Her feelings for girls, however, persisted.

As her feelings deepened, Everetta started "taking pills, smoking a little pot, drinking vodka here and there." In eighth grade Everetta found herself in the same class as her former fifth-grade sweetheart, Tracy. She tried to get close to Tracy by moving their seats together during science class. As in the baseball glove incident years earlier, Everetta was rebuffed. "Tracy didn't want me being around her," recalls Everetta. "I honestly loved her. I wanted to hold her and kiss her. But, I knew I couldn't." Doing poor in her schoolwork, Everetta was harassed by other students and abused at home. At thirteen, Everetta could see no exit:

> I took everything I could get my hands on: cold medicines, Nyquil, Tylenol, a whole bottle of aspirin. I couldn't sleep at all that night. I'd break out in a cold sweat and then I'd get real, real hot. My ears were ringing constantly. The next morning, I told my father I was too sick to go to school. He said, "You're going anyway." I couldn't make it through the school day. I couldn't hold my head up and my ears were still ringing.

Everetta confided to her cousin, Linda, who told their teacher. Everetta was placed in the nurse's office and met with the school district's psychologist for the first of many sessions. During the next three years, Everetta and Dr. Dorothea Chapman developed a strong relationship, supportive to the point where Everetta would go and stay with Dr. Chapman:

> We kind of got close talking about different things at home: my mother, my father and him being abusive. That was when the first ideas of homosexuality came up. During that time is when it kind of fell into place. You know, I liked girls therefore I was gay, or homosexual, or lesbian. The terms came together at that time. I denied it when it fell into place. I wouldn't admit to myself that I was gay but I knew that I still had feelings. I didn't want any labels. At that time, I was still trying to be what I was supposed

to be. And, if you say you're a homosexual then you are and you can't change it.

Everetta's love and admiration for Dr. Chapman hasn't diminished over the years. "If she hadn't been there I probably would have killed myself. She really was a good influence and real supportive even though she couldn't give me the things I needed as far as being gay."

Troubled by the rumors of her classmates and the suspicions of her stepmother, Everetta decided that she "wanted to try to be straight again and to do what all the other girls were doing." Everetta decided to go on her first date. Gareth escorted his date to the cinema. *The Rose* was the feature film. "Have you ever seen that movie?" Everetta asks. "The bathroom scene hit me real good. I identified with that scene a lot. When you identify with something, that makes you understand a little bit." Gareth, though, was not interested in the cinematic virtues of the film. Everetta continues:

> It was half way through the movie and Gareth says, "Let's take off and go do something else." We wound up at the peach shed and it ended up being the same old thing. Again, I couldn't say "no." I felt like I had been used.

Her first and only high school date a fiasco, Everetta struggled with her sexuality. Her drug use became more prevalent and her studies continued to slide. She remembers "it was a constant struggle inside of what I should do and what I wanted to do. Drugs quieted the struggle. It quieted everything." One morning, Moose gave her a half a quaalude but "it was pure angel dust. I didn't know that at the time." It didn't take long for the drug to have its effect:

> I was sitting in junior English class and I asked the teacher if I could go to the bathroom. He bitched a little bit and said, "Yes." Some time went by and he said, "Why didn't you go?" I'm sitting there saying, "I'm a good desk." I finally was able to get up and I ran out of the class. I'm running into lockers and things. The school nurse found me. She knew that I had been taking drugs and the psychologist did too but they were trying to keep it quiet at this point. They didn't want me to get into any more trouble. But, they couldn't. I was totally out of it. The principal was pumping me for information. "Where did you get the drugs?"

He kept asking and I kept lying. Finally, I ended up telling him, "Moose!" I went into the hospital and got expelled.

ALSTON

Alston has come further than the mere fifty-mile distance between his home town and the capitol. He sports short blond hair with a rat tail, wears a suit and tie, and speaks in a distinctive southern accent. He vividly remembers growing up in a town of twelve hundred people: "There was one main street. Everyone knew what everyone did. There were few churches but lots of church activity and only a few blacks lived on the outskirts of town." More than a few of the town's inhabitants were related, in one way or another, to Alston. As far his eyes could see, there were aunts, grandmothers, uncles, and grandfathers. "I lived right among my father's relatives. One of his brothers lived on one side, the other brother lived behind us. His sister lived over to the side and his mother lived practically in our backyard."

Members of Alston's extended family did not get along with one another, just as he seldom got along with his brothers and sisters. "We all loved each other. But, I guess it was a kind of had-to-love." Alston and his brother, Luther, were the only two children from their parents' marriage. "Luther was very Civil War. He liked armies and guns." Within the family there was also a brother and two sisters from the parents' prior marriages. "My grandmother adored my father's first wife but couldn't stand my mother. Other southern families are very close but not my family. We were pitted against each other. Luther picked on me a lot. He was a lot like my father."

Bart, Alston's father, was an independent trucker spending most of his time on the road. Alston has few kind things to say about him:

> He was bald on top and had a pot-bellied stomach. If you did something wrong, he was usually there. He would let out a yell and stomp toward you in his bare feet and a tank top T-shirt. It was like a buffalo running up on you. With me, his favorite thing to do was to kick. He kicked me a lot. He beat my older brother, too—beat him so hard once with a stick he got welts on him and bled. He beat my younger brother with a folding ruler. He hit my sister once but he never hit my mother. He tried once. She told him she'd kill him if he did it again.

Alston's favorite forms of escape were bicycling and watching television. When his dad was at home, Alston was often seen riding around the six blocks on either side of Main Street:

> I was a loner. I only had a few times when friends came home and spent the night. The rest of the time, I stayed by myself and was left to my own imagination. I'd go places and put myself in different situations. I was also a TV-holic. I especially liked disaster movies and scary stuff. I'd sit down and write plays and skits.

In school, Alston spent little time on homework and had a lackluster academic performance. "There was no big emphasis placed on grades at home. Mom would just say, 'If you don't pass, they'll put you back a year.' So, all I had ever worried about was just passing at the end of the year." What he disliked most about school, however, was being around other kids—especially in the close and unsupervised setting of the school bus:

> It was a little scary. There were just lots of kids. The way the bus traveled we were the next to last people to be picked up. When we got on, the bus would be practically full. I was effeminate and there were people on the bus who did not like my older brothers and sisters. We didn't wear the better clothes; we wore hand-me-downs with holes in them. People didn't think us anywhere near their equals. I was picked on a lot. People didn't want me to sit down. They'd make a face or say something.

During recess Alston would play by himself or jump rope with the girls. Alston reminisces, "All the other boys were out chumming around and playing football or tag. The girls treated me a little nicer than the boys did." Alston was routinely harassed by his classmates. "'Sissy' kind of stuck with me until about seventh grade," he recalls. "Then it turned to 'fag'. I was a loner, an outcast."

Alston's relations with his teachers also were poor:

> I really didn't listen a lot to the teacher. She would tell the class to stop talking and I would still be talking. She would tell the class to stop drawing and I would continue to draw. She singled me out and made me stand in the corner and ridiculed me before the class. They all picked up on it and started ridiculing me.

Imagination was more important to Alston than homework. By third grade he was earning D's and F's. He simply refused to apply himself. "The third grade teacher came up with a new torture that I had not been exposed to before." Alston pauses, "She'd draw a circle on the board and make you stand in front of the board for ten minutes with your nose in the circle without moving while the rest of the class laughed at you."

Despite Alston's lackluster performance in the classroom, he was always placed in the "B group" in the class—"The kids who weren't the super smart ones but those that applied themselves in different areas." Not coincidentally, this was the same group to which his brother and sister had been assigned. Alston continues:

> My first grade teacher, Mrs. White, had had my sister, Tammy, and my brother. She knew from the moment I walked in there: "You're Tammy's and Luther's brother, aren't you?" She had me pegged from the start. "Well, I know you're going to be just like them." Others kids would come in and she'd say, "Oh! You're Linda's sister. We're going to get along just fine."

Alston's sorry school performance and his classmates' persistent badgering continued through fourth grade. Fifth grade was an important year for Alston, for he was assigned to the "A group." His teacher, Miss Langston, made a lasting impression on him:

> I liked her because she shaved her eyebrows off and drew them on with a big crayon. She had a big bouffant hairdo. I sat up front in the class. One day the principal's son, Derek, who was just a little hellion, took my books and threw them in the garbage can. I just broke down in tears and cried my eyes out. Miss Langston ridiculed Derek in front of the entire class for having mistreated me and made him apologize to me. With tears in his eyes, he apologized. Before when I was mistreated, it was overlooked. She was the first teacher I remember calling someone down.

Alston began to bring his schoolwork home and even started reading a bit. "Miss Langston," he asserted, "she made me see something."

One winter day Alston returned from Miss Langston's class and found his uncles and aunts sitting around the kitchen table talking quietly. The church lady, Mrs. Mosely, was comforting his mother. His older sister, Tammy, was crying, and Luther had tears streaming down his face. Alston asked, "What's going on?" "Your father passed away," he was told. Alston reflects:

> I just stood there and thought, "Oh." Then I went outside and walked around a bit. I thought, "He's gone." I was almost re-

lieved. He was out of the way now. He wasn't going to bother me. I wasn't going to be beat anymore. Everyone cried except me.

After Bart's death things changed for Alston in school. A potted plant arrived from Miss Langston's class. "That was kind of a point where there was a little recognition made, a little acceptance. But, people still made jokes about me and called me names." His appreciation for Miss Langston, though, was genuine: "Miss L. did a lot of changing in me. She sat me down and said, 'I'm going to pass you even though your grades are horrible. I think you can do better and you should.' I respect her because she had taken up for me."

Alston began his last year in elementary school as a sixth grader with high expectations.

> When I got off the bus and got in I walked around and looked for my name on the sheet. People who had been in the "A group" the year before were there. They all greeted me, "Hey, how are you doing? Welcome back." I came in and sat down. About an hour later the principal came and said, "You're not supposed to be here. We've made a mistake. You're supposed to be back in the 'B group'." He took me and put me back with the people I had been with the people I had been with in the fourth grade—kind of like being knocked back down and put into an old situation and surroundings. People in the "A group," like Derek, just laughed at me. They became the jocks and the cheerleaders in high school.

Despite this setback, Alston's grades continued to improve with the support of Miss Langston. He visited her frequently. "When I would do good on tests and things, I would bring them down to her. I'd say, 'Look what I've done.' She always offered encouragement." Alston also felt differently about his classmates' harassment. "It was getting to the point," he recalls, "the 'sissy' didn't hurt as much. I just kind of accepted that as a pet name." There were limits, however, to Alston's tolerance, as his most-memorable childhood tale reveals:

> Wilbur moved in new at sixth grade. He happened to be in the "B group". He went along with the crowd. He'd call me names and stuff. "Sissy" was his favorite. My teacher got up and left the room one day. Wilbur started in on me, "Sissy! Sissy! Sissy!" I was sitting two seats over from him. I got up from my desk and walked around to him and squeaked, "What did you call me?"

He sat there for a second and got a sheepish grin on his face and said, "Sissy." "That's what I thought you called me." Whack! I slapped him as hard as I could—backhanded. The class just roared. I walked back and sat down. The teacher came in. They all got real quiet. Wilbur is sitting there kind of stunned. Then the class starts tattling on me. "Alston got up and slapped Wilbur." The teacher just looked at Wilbur and looked at me. "Well," she said, "he probably deserved it." From that point on we became good friends. He was like one of my best male friends in high school. I think it also got me some respect. That was the first time I ever stood up for myself.

Though he continued to experience harassment at school, his grades steadily improved. In the seventh grade, Alston started being more of a "teacher's pet," doing extra-credit work in his classes and talking with the teachers in the library during recess. Soon he became a solid B student. He also became less introverted.

There were instances in which Alston's attraction for men surfaced. One day he borrowed a book from another freshman. "Tight Pants Ricky would bring bondage books to school. He gave me one about some girls' school where they would torture the girls and have sex. The cover had two good looking guys on it." Alston fantasized steamy sex scenes with the two guys. During this time, however, he had yet to associated his same-sex experiences with homosexuality, identify these fantasies as homosexual, or label himself as homosexual. But, he continued to endure the verbal and physical harassment from his fellow students. His experiences of humiliation were petty but constant. He recalls one typical incident at the school:

I had to go from the bottom floor to the top floor. If you were going up the stairs, you were against the wall; going down, you were against the rail. When I was changing classes I had all the books in my hands looking down and walking up. I'd hear someone mutter "Faggot" and have my books knocked down. People are walking over me as I am trying to gather my books. I don't have time to turn around and see who said it.

In Alston's high school of three hundred students, no subterranean gay group existed. At times, even Hollis and Wilbur avoided associating with Alston at school.

It seemed like every class had their *one* homosexual, their *one* scapegoat, their *one* outcast. I was the one in our class. I was picked on and harassed for it. Hollis had a different reputation. He didn't give a shit. He didn't do good school work and he was proud of it. He was caught in the ballpark with this girl one time so his reputation was okay. At times, I was comfortable "being gay" in high school. I just wish that I wouldn't have been harassed. What made me feel uncomfortable was hearing the word "faggot" and being hassled in the halls. That's what hurt.

Rocky Horror Picture Show was the "turning point" of Alston's young life:

Tim Curry changed my life. I went, "Wow!" The costumes, the grandness, the singing, the dancing, the decadence. I was just overpowered. My senses were blown completely apart. I left the theater going, "What a movie." Willa was like, "Yeah." I dropped her off at her house and went home. I thought about it and thought about it. I went a few more times by myself. Then I got the nerve up and bought a corset and got a costume together. I started going to the theater in costume. It started becoming a ritual. One day I ran into some people who I knew from my home town. There were like freaked that I was there dressed. They didn't recognize me because I had a big wig on. That's when I started developing these friends away from school. The movie just caught us and changed us all. It made life so much easier. It didn't matter anymore. I had something. I had meaning in my life.

Soon his nighttime activities became the object of jokes and sarcasm among his classmates. "Some of them, I heard, were in the audience on nights when I would strut down the aisle and do my little show. It got back to school and there were remarks made about it. But, they didn't hurt anymore. It all kind of stopped hurting. I had a shield, something to protect me." His mother also was aware of his dressing up, wearing makeup, and going to the theater. "I'd tell her, 'I'm getting acting experience, mamma.' She just kind of ignored it. She didn't want to face up to it."

Attending born-again church services three nights a week and playing to the *Rocky Horror* show audience on Saturday nights, Alston led a "double life." After several months, it began to take its toll:

One day I looked in the mirror and I didn't see me. All I saw was Mrs. Mosely. All I saw was the pastor. All I saw was the Congregation looking back at me. I couldn't see myself! I said, "This has got to end."

Within a short time, Alston had eased himself out of the church and became a weekend regular at *Rocky Horror.* A short time later, one of his *Rocky Horror* friends, Buddy, telephoned Alston to ask, "Do you want to go to a bar tomorrow night where there are shows and gay people meet?" Although Alston was only seventeen, he agreed. The next evening, Alston entered the Twilight dressed to go on stage:

> We walked into this bar and there were men kissing men, men dancing together, everyone was smoking cigarettes and drinking. It was like everything your mother told you about hell. Here it is. There were so many people that made me feel so much better and stronger. We walked in and I stood over in the darkness for a few minutes. Then they said, "Now welcome to the stage . . . What's your name?" I came out and did a show. I got a dollar tip.

Following this experience, Alston assumed the name "Velvetta Spike."

As his senior year progressed, Alston was increasingly unwilling to "take shit" from anyone. The little boy who had once stood up for himself in sixth grade once again adopted an offensive posture:

> I knew that people were going to pick on me regardless, even when I got out of high school, so I decided to give them something to pick on—something that was my shield. I had no qualms about stomping right up to someone and cussing them out if they looked at me the wrong way. I became a vicious, nasty, little queen. I didn't take shit from anyone.

Though he received little support from his high school teachers, Alston continued to entertain Twilight audiences as Velvetta Spike, for several years. He became mistress of ceremonies and head female impersonator. ("Don't call us 'drag queens.' We'll scratch your eyes out.") Besides choreographing the shows, he appeared doing Liza Minelli favorites such as *New York, New York, Cabaret,* and *City Lights;* he has also performed as Little Orphan Annie, who, nearing the ending of her song, is beat up by a band of hoodlums, as well as Sister Mary Magnum who quickly strips to reveal leather underwear and a T-shirt reading "Guns for Nuns."

Alston enjoyed scouting for new talent and teaching the "new girls" the fine art of female impersonation. One of his favorites was Timmy, known professionally as Foxie Ritz. Alston first spotted

Timmy when he had entered the 1983 contest for Miss Collard Festival in a neighboring South Carolina town.

> It wasn't supposed to be a contest for men. But Timmy just went there, did her talent, and won. She rode in this little redneck town's parade and her picture appeared in the state's newspaper. Another guy won it the following year. That's when the town fathers stopped having it. They said it wasn't right to have men get up in dresses to be judged by other men and looking better than the women.

Alston recognizes a freedom peculiar to the South. "People who grow up gay in the North are jaded. Even though it's hard down here, we're in the country. You can roam with your imagination here. It's a little bit more relaxed." The conservative views on gender and sexuality take on an air of ambivalence in the southerner's imagination. Alston remembers even his father engaging in this type of playful charade:

> We were raised hard-core Baptists. They hate fags. But, they still have this nutty tradition in my church called 'the womanless wedding'. There is a bride, a groom, flower girls—everything except women. Dad's favorite part of the play was the soprano soloist. He had this giant blonde wig and a purple sequined gown. It wasn't till years later that I realized that my dad did drag.

Alston quit working at the Twilight about two years ago. No longer a female impersonator, he wears a pin-striped suit, a fashionable tie, and short hair. It is difficult to envision him as Velvetta Spike.

> What you see before you is a different Alston. If you had known me two years ago, you'd be flabbergasted. That's why my mother is finally proud of me again. I've been through a 180 degree change on the outside. I used to have purple hair that stood out to here and shaved all around the back with a rat tail that hung down. I *was* Velvetta Spike.

Now a computer specialist, Alston has changed his name back and assumed a new image. He no longer belongs to the *Rocky Horror–* Twilight group:

> I've lost their respect. They feel I've sold out. But, I had to do something. I didn't want to end up a bag lady on the streets at the age of sixty. I didn't want to be living off my friends for the rest of

my life. I had to have a future and something to look forward to even if it doesn't fit with *their* image of who I am.

Alston does not regret any of his experiences. He has profited from them. From his relationship with Mike, Alston has now formed a mental image of a homosexual person:

This is someone who loves a member of his own sex intimately. It goes beyond the sexual. If it's indiscriminate sex here and there, a blow job in the park when the lights are dim, or some big truck driver or jock wanting to get into his own little fantasy world, that's just sex. You're really homosexual when you can fall in love with someone of your own sex and freely admit to yourself that you are in love with that person. Forget what the rest of the world thinks. You're in love. You may not want to tell the rest of the world, you may still be in your closet. But, if you can admit it to yourself that you truly love this person, then you've become a homosexual.

Alston still harbors painful memories of his harassment in high school:

If there had not been such a taboo on being gay or being feminine; if people had not ridiculed me for it as much, it would have been a lot easier. In dealing with myself there was no problem. Those were my feelings. They didn't embarrass me. The thing that was so hard and painful to deal with was all the name calling, the snickers and the laughs, the elbows in the side, knocking my books down or snatching them and throwing them in a garbage can. That's what hurt.

Reflecting on the importance of being oneself, Alston momentarily assumes the demeanor of Velvetta Spike. He snaps his fingers and crosses his legs. His raspy voice carries a reflective message:

If you don't really have to worry about risking your life or being stabbed to death, then be whatever you want to be. If you're young, you have the chance to do what you want, to be what you want, and to feel good about it. I've seen some wild things and been to some wild places, honey. But, I've met a group of people who genuinely loved me for who I was. And, babe, that's what is important.

CONCLUSION

Most elementary students and teachers hear the words "homo," "queer," "dyke," and "fag" bandied about in the schoolyard or uttered within the classroom. These words are strung together in brutish phrases used in the endless verbal warfare among children. These strings of barbed words—often unconnected with sexuality—are part of the cultural baggage picked up from siblings, parents, or other adults. They are taunts meant to offend but not to define; they are arrows expected to wound but not to maim. Only a few children, like Alston, are constantly barraged with such verbal abuse. These are most often the children whose behavior or appearance does not fit the gender-specific norms of their culture and community. These are the "outcasts."

A few outcasts are found in every elementary school. As adolescents or adults, many of these children will identify themselves as lesbians or gay men. There are other students who do not become outcasts until adolescence. These students, like Everetta, are viewed by their elementary classmates as distinctively different. They do not, however, become the butt of jokes or the target for torments with sexual innuendo. These are the "tomboys."

Other elementary children, not portrayed in this chapter, fit the norms for childhood behavior. Never experiencing sexual harassment, they may occasionally engage in such harassment themselves. During adolescence, they will eventually come to terms with feeling different—with being "queer." Until then, they experience what most teachers, counselors, and parents perceive to by typical southern childhoods. Beneath these surface appearances, however, lurk sexual feelings and untold experiences that will profoundly affect the manner in which they will cope with sexuality during adolescence.

At a very early age, children in the United States learn gender-appropriate behaviors through the assignments of household tasks and childhood toys, adult expectations for their dress and demeanor, and so forth. Despite this early, prolonged, and extensive socialization process, some children fail to comply with gender-role norms (White and Brinkerhoff 1981). Greater tolerance for such deviation, however, is extended to girls (Saghir and Robbins 1973). Whether she was reading *Hot Rod* magazine, disrupting class, or standing up against boys, Everetta's childhood behavior was not of great concern to her father or teachers—in contrast with Alston's experience.

In the South, where sexual and racial divisions are so pronounced, it would be unusual to find an elementary school that did not have its share of outcasts; boys like Alston, who fail to conform to social sex roles, face a particularly difficult time growing up in the South where Rambo-like strength and macho appearance are held up as an ideal. Like the effeminate Biff Brannon in Carson McCullers's (1940) New York Cafe, Alston, a thin young man with a soft face and a shrill voice, is the antithesis of this southern icon of manhood.

Alston and Everetta found out that the rigidity of these gender behaviors and roles is an artifact of the mind, not a reflection of the world. Yet most parents, teachers, and classmates believed that "being a man" or "being a woman" was biologically prescribed, not culturally constructed. Three misconceptions were commonly held.

First, that effeminate boyhood behavior continues into adulthood. Although not all children who engage in these cross-gender behaviors become effeminate adults (Harry 1985), some psychologists, educators, and parents seek to facilitate "defeminization." Practitioners such as Richard Green (1987) claim that counseling enhances these effeminate boys' social and psychological adjustment and their comfort with being male. Such an approach, of course, is not without its ethical and political dilemmas. As one critical reviewer of Green's work noted, "It's a little like trying to teach highly ghettoized blacks how to behave more 'properly' (don't jive too much, straighten you hair, whatever) so they won't get traumatized by the racists—without going after the racists" (Mass 1986, p. 56). Thus, other practitioners (e.g., Coleman 1986) assert that parents, teachers, and professionals should create an environment of respect and acceptance, assist the child in coping in a healthy manner with adverse reactions from less-sensitive persons and in understanding the reasons for such harassment. And, Money and Russo (1979) found that "nonjudgmentalism" was a critical factor that contributed to effeminate boys' healthy adjustment in adolescence and adulthood despite their continued "nontraditional" social sex-role behavior.

Since tomboyishness is "more common, more tolerated, and more likely to represent a passing phase than sissiness" (Saghir and Robbins 1973, p. 201), not surprisingly, Everetta was told, "You'll grow out of it." Generally, tomboys experience reprobation from adults only when their actions fall well outside the accepted behavior or if it continues beyond childhood. In the case of Everetta, her father, who wanted a son to do the chores, did nothing to discourage such behavior. It was not until the seventh grade that she was taken aside by a teacher, Ms. Peagler. Lectured on the appropriate demeanor and dress for "young ladies," Everetta's classmates distanced themselves from her.

Second, that gender roles and traits are the same everywhere. "Appropriate" and "inappropriate" gender behaviors are culturally based. Anthropologists (e.g., Mead 1935; Williams 1986) report a wide variety of human gender arrangements. Their findings portray a rich tapestry of male behavior and suggest that this great elasticity in gender roles and traits is culturally ordered, not divinely ordained. In New Guinea, for example, the interests of men in the Tchambuli tribe include art, gossip, and shopping while women adopt what we might consider masculine roles. On the Trobriand Islands, both husband and wife nurture and care for their children. In northern Madagascar, Yegale men assume their wive's surnames, perform domestic duties, and obediently comply with female demands.

Third, that cross-gender childhood trait signal adult homosexuality. Undergirding parental concern and peer harassment over cross-gender behavior among boys is its association with homosexuality. On both logical as well as empirical grounds the linkage of homosexuality to social sex roles is questionable. Michael Ross, a senior faculty member at the South Australia Medical School, succinctly writes:

> The view that homosexuality is associated with deviant social sex role implies that all homosexuals will contain attributes of the opposite sex. It is clear from past research, however, that there is little agreement on this. . . [G]iven the lack of empirical evidence of a consistent relationship between social sex role and homosexuality, it is important to understand the more subtle aspects of the relationship that may stem from social or cultural assumptions. (1983, pp. 3–4)

One of these subtleties is the distinction among sex, gender, and sexuality (Shively and DeCecco 1977). Like most effeminate boys, Alston has a male identity. Although he has no desire to become female, his effeminate characteristics were noticeable before he entered elementary school. His attraction to other boys began late in elementary school and he first labeled himself as "homosexual" at the age of fifteen. Like most tomboys, Everetta has a female identity. Although she has no desire to become male, her masculine characteristics continued beyond elementary school into adolescence. Her attraction to other girls began in elementary school but she did not label herself "lesbian" until she was sixteen.

Being born male or female, exhibiting masculinity or femininity, and desiring men or women are three human components which can be arranged in several distinct combinations reflected in terms such as hermaphrodite, transvestite, bisexual, sissy, tomboy, transsexual, and homosexual. While biological sex is established at conception, gender identity (personal conviction about being male or female) is thought to develop between eighteen months and four years; the internalization of cultural expectations for gender roles is believed to be established between the ages of three and seven; and the claiming of a homosexual identity is found to occur in the early twenties.

From a distance, at least, most at-risk students can appear to be tragic but still sympathetic figures. Victims of poverty and racism can easily earn our sympathy; those who are hearing impaired or learning disabled can make our hearts bleed. By contrast, Alston and Everetta may make some readers uncomfortable and squeamish. Yet Alston and Everetta are no less at risk than the other students portrayed in this book. They too must confront a school environment which is often inhospitable and even hostile. Furthermore, they seldom have the support of home, neighborhood culture, or peer group to compensate for an absence of support in school.

Somehow, Alston and Everetta managed to survive their school experiences. Many others like them do not.

CHAPTER 11

Paul: Differentiating Disorder and Intervention

John J. Gleason, Rhode Island College

This chapter focuses on the importance of professionals understanding their impact on individuals for whom they have responsibility. The chapter presents a story about Paul, an individual with severe and profound, multiple disabilities who is one of thirty-one residents on a ward in a state school for persons with mental retardation. The story is also about the staff of that institution and how staff members unwittingly contribute to escalating Paul's disruptive behavior.

The story calls into question some of our assumptions about the behavior of individuals with severe behavior disorders as well as notions that guide our interaction and involvement not only with individuals like Paul but also with less extreme at-risk individuals. It suggests a general principle which is significant not only for professionals in special education who hope to promote appropriate independent functioning of persons with developmental disabilities, but also for teachers, administrators, researchers, and policy makers concerned with the education and development of all at-risk youth: Professionals must consider the implicit meaning of the explicit behavior of *all* participants in an interaction and explain events in terms of the multiple patterns of meaning which inevitably come into play.

Following a description of Paul's interaction with staff, I provide a detailed explanation to highlight the nature of staff participation from two perspectives: first, from Paul's perspective as an expression of his needs, wants, and desires; and second, from the perspective of the staff who intervene in response to Paul's behavior. By highlighting both perspectives, I intend to clarify the relationship between the staff and Paul. Events in the interaction evolve as a spiral of action and reaction that serve to frustrate and confuse Paul, prompting the behavior viewed as "symptomatic" of his profound level of retardation and behavior disorder. However, his disabilities do not produce the event.

METHODOLOGY

The example of Paul details interactions between him and the direct care and professional staff. It is selected from a five-year anthropological study of the life experience of sixty-four residents from three different total care wards of a state institution. The study documents examples of learned and shared patterns of interactions among the residents prior to the introduction of federally mandated individualized educational programs. In the full analysis, what the residents do on their own is contrasted with their performance after professional staff initiate educational and therapeutic programs to teach appropriate skills (Gleason, 1984; 1985).

I entered this setting as an anthropologist interested in understanding the social interactions of individuals with the most severe developmental disabilities residing on the back wards of the institution. I characterized the environment as institutional because of the formal organization or roles and relationships among staff, the isolation of the ward, and the restrictions that the segregated environment and the profound nature of the resident's disabilities imposed. I anticipated that my previous professional experiences with persons with developmental disabilities would be helpful in the analysis and interpretation of their ability.

I adopted the role of complete observer; I became a participant occasionally when the residents of the ward actively sought me out. The ethnographic data in this study are the field notes of the residents' interactions with one another and with staff.

In the formal analysis and explanation of the data, I compared observational data with the record of more formal assessments from individualized educational programs. I contrasted the interaction of residents on their own with participation in the structured interaction with professionals during therapy and in lessons designed to teach a skill.

By continuous elaboration of the patterns in the residents' behavior, I was able to develop behavioral descriptions that revealed "messages" in what the residents did. By freezing the account and analyzing the meaning underlying the residents' involvement, I discovered intent and purpose in their actions. Explanations entailed identifying meaning in behavior, the messages in their communication, and the implicit patterns that constituted the course of their interaction.

In this setting, the distinguishing characteristic of professional practice is the explanation of what the resident is doing in terms of his or her disabilities. In this instance, however, the clinical understanding of Paul's disabilities does little to explain the event in which he becomes embroiled. Misunderstanding his initial behavior is compounded when staff fail to recognize the purposes for his actions.

In the example, the interactions between Paul and eight different staff develop over almost two hours. Each staff member contributes to the confusion by failing to recognize what disturbs Paul. When interpreted in the context of the interaction with staff, Paul's behavior reveals a pattern of meaning which makes his behavior understandable when interpreted from his perspective. Paul's behavior escalates in the face of repeated interventions to control his behavior rather than to understand what he is doing. The conflict is based on misunderstanding of the context of the event. This misinterpretation of the initial behavior confirms for staff their expectations of what he is like.

By explicating how the individual communicates and interacts within the constraints of his behavior disorder and the limitations of multiple disabilities, I came to understand the effect of the handicap on the individual in a different way. The irony is that Paul's actions are consistent with the context of events which he has previously experienced. He is demonstrating his ability in this instance, but staff view his expression as confirmation of his behavior problem. Staff do not see their behavior in relationship to his.

SETTING

The world experience of the residents in each of three total care wards is confined to two large living spaces: The Activity Area and the Sleeping Area. The Activity Area functions simultaneously as a dining room and living area. The room is partitioned into sections where residents are positioned on water beds, stretchers, sandbag chairs and mats during free time or for general activities. The Sleeping Area is a maze of crib-like beds separated by metal cabinets with facilities for bathing and toileting. Intersecting the rooms is a glassed-in office from which staff observe the residents who live there. Across the hall from these living areas are classrooms, offices, and therapy rooms for programmed activities.

POPULATION

Descriptions in the archive records reveal no simple specific clinical category to describe this population. A complicated array of physical handicaps constrains most aspects of an individual's functioning. The profound levels of mental retardation (I.Q. below 20), accompanied by impairment to the sensory modalities, modifies the processing of information and affects cognition. Many individuals are subject to random and debilitating central nervous system disturbances. In this setting, the medical and psychological consensus in the clinical description is that the stable and uncompromising nature of multiple handicaps necessitates total care and supervision through the individual's lifetime on the ward. The residents have not developed the skills of self-maintenance; they are unable to feed, dress, bathe, and even in some cases, move themselves. Professionals and caretakers can be heard to refer to these residents as the "lowest functioning on the grounds"; "they can't do anything"; "they're really bad off."

Due to his profound mental retardation, Paul was admitted to the institution in 1961 at three and one-half years of age. At the time of the study, he was 22 years old. His multiple disabilities manifested themselves clinically in terms of organic brain damage, microcephaly, seizures, and motoric disorders. A summary of progress notes and impressions from direct care and professional staff indicate he is a medically involved person whose medications (three anti-convulsants, Dialantin, Tegretal, and Phenobarbital) are very important to monitor. His behavior can be described as aggressive and combative when he is unfamiliar with staff and/or his environment. When he is non-compliant, staff use a structured behavioral approach. To assist Paul in controlling his own behavior, staff use parallel talk to explain events to him and relaxation techniques to increase his control over his own behavior.

DESCRIPTION: PAUL IN CONTEXT

When I arrive shortly after 8:30 a.m. to begin my observations, the thirty-one residents who live in the apartment are all present. The attendants and the teachers are finishing up feeding breakfast to the residents. Some have a bowl of oatmeal and a spoon in hand. Standing over the residents, the staff alternate a spoonful of oatmeal with a drink of milk. After the residents who go to school on the bus are fed, showered, and dressed, breakfast is never hurried for those who remain. They are the second shift. They attend school across the hall from the apartment.

After the meal, staff wheel residents into the showers for a washing down. From the shower, I hear screams of laughter, or singing, as residents and attendants wake up to the day. Dana yells when the water hits him. The staff in the activity area acknowledge to each other that Dana is in the shower.

After the teachers take these residents to their classrooms, the custodian washes the entire floor. The fact that the teachers will not keep off his clean floor is a constant source of tension for the custodian. Today, a teacher walks behind him on the floor he has just washed. Behind him, she grimaces and gestures, pointing her finger close to her head, and drawing tight circles in the air.

Paul sits in a lounge chair outside the office door quietly humming to himself. The janitor starts to wash the area in front of Paul. Three foster grandmothers enter the apartment. (Foster grandmothers are senior citizens who volunteer their time to provide assistance to the staff.) Paul's foster grandmother starts to walk toward Paul across the wet floor.

The foster grandmother approaches Paul. He turns his head toward her when she comments to the janitor, "Everything is confused here today. Everyone's all upset."

Paul gets up and starts to walk across the wet floor. The janitor tries to persuade him to sit down by pushing his arms against Paul's chest and backing him towards his chair. Paul resists. The foster grandmother calls out to a passing teacher, "Come and get him." The teacher replies, "Go get one of the ward staff. He's not my problem. I've got enough problems." The janitor, with a quizzical look on his face, says to Paul, "O.K., sit down." The janitor succeeds in backing Paul in the direction of the chair.

The senior woman attendant crosses the wet floor from the shower area, walks directly to Paul, grabs his arm and says, "O.K., Paul, come on, come and sit down." Holding his arm, she escorts him to his lounge chair. As she maneuvers him into the seat, she spins around on one leg to leave. Paul grabs her wrist. Her smile vanishes. "Stop that, Paul, stop it! Don't do this!" She exclaims, "Leave me alone!" She puts her head down as she swings herself back around to face him. She charges into Paul. He reacts by pinching her. "Stop it! Stop it! Stop it!" she repeats emphatically. "Don't pinch me. You better not pinch me." When she shakes loose, she heads straight for the office. Paul mutters, "Go, go, go."

Now in the chair, Paul begins to rock and clap his hands repeatedly, faster and faster, saying, "Go, go, go." The foster grandmother moves closer to him, sits on the arm of the chair next to him, and says out loud, "He's confused, they are all confused. Relax. Stop, Paul."

Paul gets up out of the chair and turns toward her. The foster grandmother jumps up off the arm of the chair and runs the few steps into the office. She calls from the office, "Stay there." Paul turns and walks back to the center of the activity area. The senior woman attendant comes out of the office and says, "Stay there." Paul claps his hands and walks in a circle. The foster grandmother reappears from the office and offers to take him for a walk if he puts on his shoes.

Paul is in his stocking feet. His socks slide down below his heel and bunch loosely at his toes to the front of his foot. He is wearing his football helmet to protect him should he fall due to a seizure. The older woman attendant grabs him by the arm and pushes him back across the activity area down into the chair. He says, "No, no, no," and grabs her arm. She continues, "I won't come in tomorrow if you pinch me. I won't come in tomorrow." Paul gets up from the chair and follows her as she pulls away. Paul keeps yelling, "Ge . . ha . . Ge . . ha . . ." The foster grandmother says, "They are nervous with the changes." (Many of the residents were recently changed from one apartment to the other.) The woman attendant shakes herself loose and runs into the office. "I'm not coming in tomorrow. No pinching." She inspects her arm. Paul follows her into the office. "No, go outside! No! No! No! Sit down." She pushes him out of the office and pulls her arm away.

A young male attendant, new to the ward and these events, casually, in passing, says to Paul, "Sit down." He enters the office without a pause. With this Paul circles around into the laundry room to get access to the office. He claps even harder. When the attendant commands, "Sit!", Paul starts to clap. With each successive command, he claps harder and sporadically hits the side of his helmet. The foster grandmother remarks again, "He is excited." Paul turns toward the foster grandmother. The three foster grandmothers who have huddled together to one side of the activity area disperse and run into the sleeping area when he starts toward them. Paul's foster grandmother continues as she retreats, "He's confused. He's confused. They're all confused today." Paul turns in the direction of her voice and yells, "Oh, no!" He turns away and goes out the door down the hall. The grandmothers yell, "He can't go down the hall without his shoes on."

The senior woman attendant comes out of the office and looks around, "Where is Paul? Where's Paul?" The foster grandmothers point down the hall and she charges out after him. When she overtakes Paul, she grabs him and pulls him back to the apartment. He spits at her. "Don't spit. No, don't spit. No. No." Getting him into the apartment, she exclaims, "I'm not coming in tomorrow. Look what he did to my arm." She holds out her arm for the foster grandmothers to see the scratch marks.

One of the three foster grandmothers goes over to Paul from across the room and sits him down calmly and quietly. The new attendant repeats, "Sit down." Paul grabs at him and starts to clap his hands. The attendant grabs him a second time. Paul pulls the attendant to him. In the strength of his withdrawal, the attendant pulls Paul out of the chair. Paul maintains his grip. The attendant frees himself only by shaking his hands very fast. When Paul releases him, the attendant runs into the office. Again Paul heads toward the office, but when he reaches the door, the two attendants push him out and shut the door.

He turns toward the laundry to go into the office through the back door. The new attendant pushes Paul back into the chair and runs back into the office and slams the office door. As if stunned,

Paul stays in the chair for only a minute and then gets up. He starts to clap and walk in circles once again.

The foster grandmothers have all collected at the edge of the sleeping area. One foster grandmother says, "The teachers can work with him. Where is the teacher? He doesn't like change. You can tell. He's a good boy. Just confused. I know him." One foster grandmother goes to get the behavior management specialist. When the behavior management specialist arrives, she walks up to Paul and talks to him in a calm voice. "Paul, what are you all upset about? What's the matter? It's all right. It's going to be all right." She then holds his hands; she does not pull his arms down to his sides, but instead follows their motion through the air. Paul stops clapping and repeating, "Ge . . ha . . Ge . . ha . . ." But his hands wave about. As they watch, the foster grandmothers comment to her, "Glad you came in." "He made us nervous wrecks," and "Good, that's it. He really listens to you." The older woman attendant gets his shoes and gives them to the specialist. His foster grandmother speaks to Paul, "That's it, put your shoes on and we'll take you out for a walk." The behavior management specialist leads him to the chair and the table, "Oh, you want to give him lunch?" Sitting him down, she stands over him talking quietly. He murmurs, "Ge . . ha . . Ge . . ha . . Ge . . ha . . " Paul sits quietly. The foster grandmother repeats, "He's such a good boy." She turns to get his food from the food cart. Paul gets up suddenly and starts across the wet floor. He heads for the door out of the apartment.

The new attendant yells, "Stop him! He can't see." Paul slips and falls to the floor. Reaching to grab Paul, the attendant falls over him instead.

"Oh, he can see," the foster grandmother corrects the new attendant. Then, suddenly losing her own balance, she herself falls over Paul and the new attendant. The three staff unravel themselves and get up off the floor. The new attendant then lifts Paul into the chair. The foster grandmother shakes herself off, gets the bowl of food, and puts it in front of Paul. Paul stares at the food. She ties the bib around his neck and asks, "Can he feed himself?" With no answer, she shrugs her shoulders and starts to feed him his lunch.

Almost a year after this event, Paul transferred to another state school.

EXPLANATION: UNRAVELING CONTEXT

In the example, we learn that the attendants know Paul by his reputation. What they know is confirmed by his behavior. However, an interpretation of the event which considers what he is doing from his perspective reveals another way of understanding the evolution of his behavior. Staff interaction with Paul, who is a new resident in this apartment, unwittingly creates the context for his behavior. His reputation is confirmed.

On hearing the foster grandmother's voice, Paul responds by getting up to go to her. He knows and reacts to the foster grandmother's voice and moves toward her. She routinely takes him out for a walk. This morning the janitor blocks Paul's way in an effort to prevent him from walking across a wet floor. Not wanting to walk across the floor herself, the foster grandmother sits on the arm of the chair on the other side of the room rather than continues toward him. The obstruction of the janitor is unannounced. What is happening to Paul is unexplained. He does not know what is new or different from previous interactions with the foster grandmother. The context which he knows is going outside with his foster grandmother. Being on a new ward does not change his expectation of his routine. Her voice is an invitation; he responds the way he knows.

The janitor tightens his restraint as Paul tries to move around him. Paul's efforts are thwarted. It is the janitor, not an attendant, nor the foster grandmother, nor a teacher, who stops him from walking across the floor and puts him back in the chair. Paul reacts. The foster grandmothers sound the alarm to alert a teacher. Unwittingly having created the situation with her invitation by coming for him to go for a walk, the foster grandmother is reluctant to approach Paul. The custodian attempts to quiet Paul. Once the behavior is identified as a problem, the custodian and the foster grandmother look for professional assistance. The professionals are the ones who will know what to do.

But the teacher indicates that she has her own problems and passes on. Surprised at the reaction, the janitor assumes responsibility. Simply, he backs Paul into the chair. For Paul, the context of his interaction with his foster grandmother has changed, and he does not understand the change.

The foster grandmother repeats, "Everything is confused here today." Because of changes on the apartments, she empathizes with Paul and provides a reason for his behavior. Her understanding of the immediate situation is voiced. But no one helps Paul to understand what is happening. How do events create Paul's confusion?

Unaware of the preceding set of events, the senior woman attendant comes into the apartment and places Paul back in the chair. Without a clue as to the situation in which Paul finds himself, she acts. What she understands is the necessity to control the situation. The event escalates. For Paul, she is a new person who thwarts what he is doing. The attendant frees herself and seeks the protection of the office. She relinquishes control of the situation.

Later reentering the activity area and reviewing the situation anew, the senior woman attendant decides to take charge, saying, "O.K., Paul, come on, come and sit down." Forcefully moved back into the chair, Paul grabs her. At this point, the interaction becomes a confrontation between the attendant's insistence and Paul's reaction to what is done with him.

The sequence of events which precipitated this confrontation are lost. Paul is confused. He reacts. His grabbing and pinching provoke the attendant's worst fears that she might be hurt. Paul reaffirms his label of "combative" with his actions.

As the attendant escapes from his grasp and retreats into the office, Paul shows his appreciation of his temporary freedom by clapping. With the attendant gone, the foster grandmother attempts to comfort him, "Relax. Stop, Paul."

Paul gets up and moves toward his foster grandmother. But now he has frightened her and she reacts by running into the office. His turning toward her is frightening to her now. The foster grandmother misinterprets his behavior. Paul's behavior is not necessarily unique to him nor directly attributable to the profound and multiple nature of his disabilities. Rather, his behavior is a result of the context in which he finds himself.

Leaving the office, the senior woman attendant tries again to assert her control over the situation by commanding, "Stay there!" Paul continues walking in a circle. The foster grandmother offers to take him for a walk a third time. Paul responds to the foster grandmother's invitation by going to her. But the senior woman attendant pushes him into the chair despite his protests. Paul resists. He pinches her again. She pulls away from him and turns into the office. Paul pursues her. She pushes him outside the office. Treating his behavior rather than the situation only serves to provoke him further.

Interestingly enough, the foster grandmother provides some context for Paul's behavior: He is confused because of the move and the changes in his routing. He seems bewildered about the change in the normal interaction between him and his foster grandmother. In his customary manner, he responds to the foster grandmother's voice by getting up to go with her. The senior woman attendant provokes his behavior with her own. Throughout the event both the attendant and the foster grandmother disregard their own involvement in prompting his response. They misinterpret his behavior. His actions quickly become misbehavior and symptomatic of his behavior disorder.

A new attendant on the scene initiates the same attempt at control through restraint. His demand to sit does not work either. Demonstrating his frustration with each new demand on him, Paul claps and pounds his helmet. (Paul wears a helmet both to protect himself from hitting his head during a fall from a seizure and also from hurting himself through self-abusive behavior.)

When the foster grandmothers scatter into the sleeping area, Paul disappears down the hall. The woman attendant charges down the hall after him. She resumes her efforts to establish control of the situation. After pulling him back into the apartment, the woman attendant examines her pinched arms. Paul starts spitting when he is brought back. Finally, the foster grandmother intervenes, calmly talking to him and getting him to sit in the chair.

Just when Paul appears calm the new male attendant returns and reminds Paul to stay seated. Paul grabs the new attendant. Unable to stop Paul from grabbing him, the attendant retreats into the office.

The foster grandmother calls a teacher to manage Paul. Surveying the situation, the behavior management specialist intervenes immediately. She reacts differently. She talks to Paul, asks him what's the matter, and offers reassurance. She expresses determined coaxing rather than forceful restraint, management that seems based more on understanding him than on gaining control over his behavior. Placing her hands on his flailing arms, the specialist follows his motion as she guides his hands to his sides. Paul responds to her overtures by sitting down. As soon as he does, she leaves.

However, she has not clarified the situation for staff. Although the disruptive behavior has stopped for the moment, the confusion in the situation continues. Paul has accepted a seat at the table, but is soon up and back on the newly washed floor. This time he slips, as do the two staff who rush toward him. The three entangled on the floor reflect the confusion of Paul's morning.

The significance of this event is that it happened at all. Each staff person responds to Paul's behavior idiosyncratically. The custodian enforces the rule not to walk across the wet floors. Paul does not understand that the floor is wet, or that there is a rule. The custodian does not know what is essential for Paul; Paul needs to be calmly introduced to what is expected of him. Quick or sudden moves which define limits that he does not understand escalate counter measures by Paul.

For the custodian, the context is clear: Paul needs to stay off the wet floor. For Paul, the context is unclear. The event puts the participants at cross purposes. Paul wants to go with his foster grandmother as he is accustomed. He does not realize alternatives.

The foster grandmother identifies a possible context for Paul's behavior. She gives meaning to the event from his perspective. But her voice and message are not incorporated into what the other staff do. Her understanding of the changes in the apartment and on Paul do not seem to be relevant. Even though the staff understand the changes, the situation they face is more immediate: to stop the behavior. The initial changes in the apartment which set the stage for the behavior are less immediate than the evolving set of interactions which maintain Paul's behavior.

The senior woman attendant reacts to Paul's hitting, grabbing, and pinching. The focus of her efforts is to control, that is, to get him to sit. Unfamiliar with Paul's needs and with the preceding events, she attempts to do something, but only compounds the problem. She is unaware of how she contributes to Paul's acting-out behavior. Paul's purposes may still be the same. A different context has been created. The new mail attendant on the scene provokes similar responses from Paul.

Not until the appearance of the behavior management specialist do events change for Paul. The behavior management specialist deals effectively with the immediate behavior, but once she leaves, her success is short-lived. She does not inquire about the precipitating events nor does she stay to evaluate her own efforts. Effective for the moment, her interaction changes the context for Paul. The behavior management specialist talks directly to him about what he is doing. She provides reassurance while mirroring his hand movements rather than forcefully restricting him. He cooperates, quiets down, and sits.

In this event, Paul's behavior is misread and misunderstood. Even when someone points out what could be the problem, others focus on the immediate behaviors. Paul's behaviors become symptomatic of an underlying behavior disorder, not the context in which it occurs. Misinterpretation of his behavior persists because Paul is fulfilling the clinical definition of his behavior disorder. The focus of how staff contribute to the escalation of his behavior is not considered.

With no new fundamental examination and understanding of the events that produce the behavior, the experience will repeat itself for both Paul and staff. Paul's behavior will remain an example of his disability. Staff will react to Paul in ways that precipitate his behavior, confirming their definition of who he is and what he does. What is known about Paul is what staff understand from their experience with him. The quality of Paul's experience and the understanding of what his capabilities are will not change very much until staff recognize something different about Paul.

IMPLICATIONS

This description challenges our notions of objectivity in understanding the behavior of the person with multiple disabilities as well as our assumptions of staff ability to understand the intent and purpose in the behavior. When staff explanations of behavior are themselves stereotypical, a problem exists when we rely on set procedures of behavioral intervention or prescribed management procedures. These procedures may inhibit our ability to intervene effectively with a single individual. When intervention restricts our perspective on events, behavior becomes something to control rather than something to understand. The measure of success is the exercise of control over the situation and the resident's cooperative response.

I suggest as a different starting place four principles of an interpretive framework that are key to understanding behavior and to avoiding placing students at risk because of our approach. They are:

1. The context of the interactional event must be understood over time.
2. The meaning of the event must objectively be described from the perspective of the student and in their own terms.
3. Initiation of involvement in interactional events must be undertaken commensurate with the experience of the person.
4. The intention or will of the person, the purpose toward which behavior is directed, becomes the definition of functionally appropriate.

Issues of control and management of behavior are not unique to staff in a state school for the mentally retarded. However, the consequences for individuals with severe and profound, multiple disabilities are numerous. Persons without their own voice are at risk because they are reliant on others for an accurate interpretation of what they are doing. Without understanding, they run the risk of being the object of our interventions. Without a fundamentally different understanding of what they are doing, we may perpetuate the limits of our practices by relying on inappropriate assumptions about disability.

We must use professional resources if we are to understand Paul's perspective and clarify the nature of our interaction. In order to reform our efforts we must ask ourselves: How do our interventions, what we say and what we do, perpetuate the very behaviors that we wish to modify, change, or ignore? Paul is "behavior-disordered" when he is frustrated. Viewed in a different way, his behavior is a form of communication in which he expresses his frustration, in this case his inability to tolerate confusion. He bangs his head, he claps his hands, he bites, he pinches. What is he telling us?

Three times Paul gets out of the chair in anticipation of his walk outside with his foster grandmother. When the context changes for him because of staff reactions to what he is doing, his intention is thwarted. The events do not match his previous experience. Because no one is able to translate events from his perspective, Paul faces the confusion alone. He is left to figure out what is happening for himself.

What does he learn from our reaction to his behavior? I argue that we unwittingly provoke his behavior in this situation. We provoke him into acting out the behavior that we expect and then we try to stop his behavior based on our assumptions concerning a behavior disorder, not Paul's experience. Not understanding his form of communication, we misunderstand his content. Paul's behavior, if viewed in context, reflects an aggressive response commensurate with the force used to control him. His pinching and grabbing are an expression of his frustration at being stopped from doing what he expects. He reacts in kind to what is done to him. Not understanding that he is demonstrating what he knows when he initially gets up to go to his foster grandmother, we participate in a misguided set of interventions.

The description of behavior disorder does not account for his behavior or his actions in this series of events. We must respect his lack of tolerance for ambiguity and clarify our actions. We must identify his needs and the role we play in frustrating those needs.

We must put as much effort into interpreting the meaning in his behavior as we put into controlling it. We respect his involvement in the interaction by seeing ourselves as active participants. Paul is not the sum of his disabilities, but a person acting within the constraint of his abilities. If we understand his needs in this situation, we can manage his behavior in a way that does not have to be time-consuming, exhausting, provocative, and self-defeating. The alternative is to start with an evaluation of the circumstances and to realize how what we do and say influences Paul. We must challenge our assumptions and examine the cause-and-effect relationships in the context of our interactions. Paul is not just an individual with an isolated set of behaviors that are symptomatic of a behavior disorder. He acts based on his needs and what he knows and understands about the situation. His behavior is shaped and influenced by others. Allowing Paul to meet his foster grandmother and go for a walk can be a way to manage his behavior.

SUMMARY

In this instance, we precipitate the behavior which we label as Paul's disorder. He acts out the behavior in the situation that we create. We must acknowledge the impact of our own behavior on the patterns which constitute his disorder. There are a variety of influences, factors, and situations which can place a student at risk, not the least of which is our interpretation of what he or she is doing. For persons with severe and profound, multiple disabilities, the probability of remaining at risk is heightened by their dependence on others. Their quality of life is based on our ways of making sense. The four principles suggested above offer the basis for a new framework to interpret behavior for all students. All students run the risk of being seen for less than what they are if we do not focus on what they do outside the context of our own involvement.

PART II

Policies, Programs, and Practices

CHAPTER 12

Structuring for Idiosyncracy: Rethinking Policies, Programs, and Practices for At-Risk Students

Robert Donmoyer, The Ohio State University

This chapter introduces the remaining chapters in part 2. The focus is on the metaphors we use to conceptualize policy making and program development, as well as teaching and learning in the classroom. Several emerging metaphors are contrasted with the social engineering metaphor which has dominated our thinking about educational policy, programs, and practice throughout most of this century.

The first section of this book contained a series of case studies—verbal portraits we called them—of very different at-risk students who are placed at risk by very different circumstances. In most books, some attempt would be made at this point to pull the disparate elements found in the case studies together. Most editors would engage in at least an informal cross-case analysis designed to identify common themes or build some sort of grounded theory. The remainder of the book would then be built around the common elements which were uncovered.

We have chosen a different tack. It is not that commonality does not exist in the verbal portraits found in part 1. Common themes and generalizations almost jump out at the reader:

- The perspective of the at-risk student (i.e., the way he/she make meaning) is too often ignored by the school.
- Implicit biases of teachers often have a negative impact on the learning of at-risk students.
- Schools are structured in ways that make it difficult for teachers to understand and attend to the perspectives of at-risk learners.
- The problems encountered by at-risk learners within our schools are not unique to them. Their backgrounds and experiences simply leave them more vulnerable than other students.
- Many teachers seem unable or unwilling to restructure the curriculum to facilitate the social construction (as opposed to the transmission) of knowledge.
- The social needs of children are too often considered educationally unimportant.

These themes, and others that might be generated, are undoubtedly important, and an explication and discussion of them might be useful to many. It is also possible, however, to emphasize the discontinuity among the cases and to consider how the policies, programs, and practices we fashion can accommodate the discontinuity we see. In other words, just as we can see a glass as being either half empty or half full, we can see, in the verbal portraits presented in part 1, either commonality or idiosyncracy. We have chosen the idiosyncracy option both because it is the tack less taken in the literature to date and because we believe that structuring policies, programs, and classroom practices so that they can accommodate the idiosyncracy of at-risk students is the major challenge facing educators today. The remainder of the chapters in the book explore how we might organize educational policy, programs, and practices to accommodate idiosyncracy. This chapter provides a general introduction to the structuring for idiosyncracy notion by focusing on emerging metaphors which may be useful for readjusting our thinking about educational organizations.

METAPHORS, OLD AND NEW

The whole notion of structuring for idiosyncracy is a bit of a paradox. Implicit in the very notion of structure are notions of regularity, standardization, and routine. The challenge will be to design structures with elbow room.

The way we have thought about policy, program, and practice in the past has made it almost impossible to design flexible structures or even to recognize the need to do so. As was noted in chapter 1, the social engineering metaphor has constrained the way we have thought about educational policy and programs, and even educational practice. While we are under the spell of the social engineering metaphor, we will see educational organizations in terms of hierarchies, control mechanisms (e.g., sanctions and rewards), and routines, all geared to producing a desired output. Equally important, at least for this discussion, as long as we are under the spell of the social engineering metaphor we will fail to see the organizational implications of the idiosyncracy so evident in the verbal portraits presented in this book.

Fortunately, new metaphors have begun to intrude upon our thinking about policy making, program development, and especially teaching and learning. Piagetian psychologists, for instance, conceive of learning in constructivist rather than mechanistic terms. Piagetians, for example, do not assume that learning will occur because a teacher or curriculum developer has carefully structured an educational program. For Piagetians, learning is itself a process of structuring which must be engaged in by learners themselves (see, for example, Piaget 1971).

Sociolinguists work from a similar constructivist view. They emphasize that learning is a product of social interaction and that understanding occurs through a process of negotiating meaning (Halliday 1975; Wells 1981). This is a significant departure from the mechanistic mindset which has dominated our thinking in the past.

New metaphors for learning suggest new metaphors for teaching. Bruner (1975) and Cazden (1972), for instance, have likened teaching to a process of providing scaffolding to assist students who are constructing their own understandings. The scaffolding image suggests an approach to teaching which is more reactive than proactive; more geared to responding to students concerns and utterances than to directing and controlling them; and more oriented to raising questions than making statements.

Piagetian psychologists' and sociolinguists' vision of teaching, of course, has emerged primarily from studies of one-to-one adult/child interactions rather than from studies of teaching and learning in group settings. Sociolinguists' notion of scaffolding, for instance, developed out of a study of how young children learned language from their parents. Consequently, Piagetians and sociolinguists have had less to say about such organizational phenomena as program development and policy making.

Implicit in the metaphors of scaffolding, negotiation of meaning, and constructivism, however, is a relatively clear sense of what should not be done in these areas: Program development should not be seen as a process of structuring a precise, carefully sequenced pathway over which all students must travel, and policy making certainly should not be seen as a process of social engineering. In addition, new metaphors have begun to emerge which allow us to talk about policy and program development in a manner which is compatible with the views of teaching and learning outlined above.

Elsewhere, for instance, I have suggested that we might think of educational programs as functioning much as a melody functions in improvisational jazz. The melody grounds jazz musicians' improvisations; it provides cohesion and direction. Each musician, however, is allowed to deviate from the notes the melody provides. Deviation, in fact, is encouraged as long as musicians idiosyncratic renderings remain within the general structure the melody provides (Donmoyer 1983).

We might also think of educational policy making in terms of improvisational theater (Spolin 1963). Policy makers' role is to specify situations and provide potentially useful props, to "set the stage" so to speak, for rich educational encounters. Their job is not to write the script. This must be done by teachers and students as they interact with each other in the classroom.

In addition to arts-oriented imagery, one other metaphor has begun to appear in the literature on organizations in recent years: the metaphor of culture. Organizational theorists have used the culture metaphor in recent years to help explain why certain organizations are successful while others are not (Brandt 1990; Deal 1990; Deal and Kennedy 1983; Greene 1991; Rossman, Corbett, and Firestone 1988). This focus on organizational culture represents a major departure from traditional views of organizational life. Traditionally organizational theorists relied almost exclusively on mechanistic metaphors to conceptualize organizations. The focus was on organizational form and structure; on standard operating procedures and routines; on formal authority and hierarchial relationships; and on sanctions and rewards (see, for example, Daft 1986; Morgan 1986).

By contrast, a cultural perspective directs our attention to ideational structures articulated in myths and stories; it conceives of routines as rituals which have symbolic significance for organizational life; and it views authority as emanating less from position and more from organization members' perception of legitimacy. Similarly, control is seen as being less dependent on extrinsic rewards and sanctions and more a product of socialization into a belief system.

This shift in perspective is significant for at least two reasons. First from a cultural perspective, members of an organization are no longer objects to be controlled and manipulated; they are human beings who think and feel and make meaning of the world around them. Second, since the source of control within an organization is new ideas rather than rules and regulations, there is considerably more room for individuals to adapt and adjust organizational activity and, in the process, to accommodate the idiosyncracy of particular situations and individuals.

In short, like the jazz and improvisational theater metaphors discussed above, the cultural metaphor seems consistent with constructivist and negotiation of meaning views of teaching and learning. Furthermore, all of the new metaphors discussed here seem to allow for greater elbow room to accommodate the idiosyncracy of individual at-risk students than one normally finds in social engineering ways of thinking.

BEYOND METAPHOR

New metaphors are useful because they provide a vantage point from which to critique conventional ways of thinking. At a basic level, they expose what we take to be natural and inevitable for what it really is: a human creation. They also provide visions of how we might recreate our current reality.

Ultimately, however, new metaphors can take us only so far. The possibilities they help us envision are not very clearly defined, for metaphors influence us primarily at the intuitive and feeling levels. That is their strength; it is also a major limitation for anyone who wants to act in the world. In the remainder of this book we will move beyond metaphor and explore the notion of structuring for idiosyncracy at the level of action. Once again many contributors utilize case study research as a way of grounding discourse. In this section, however, the cases are not primarily verbal portraits of individuals; rather the focus is on policies, programs, and classroom practices.

CHAPTER 13

Placing Children at Risk: Schools Respond to Reading Problems

Richard L. Allington and Anne McGill-Franzen, SUNY at Albany

The focus of this chapter and the two subsequent ones is on current policies and programs and more specifically on problems associated with the current emphasis on standard operating procedures within education. The focus of this particular chapter is on programs for students who have experienced reading difficulties. Implicit in the authors' critique is not just an indictment of the specific standard operating procedures dictated by existing policies and programs; the authors also challenge the very idea of thinking about literacy intervention programs in standard operating procedure terms. The authors also provide a glimpse of literacy programs that appear to be successful. The programs cited differ markedly from each other, a fact which the authors see as an asset rather than a liability.

Nothing is more likely to put school-age children at risk than failing to acquire reading and writing abilities with their peers. Difficulty in learning to read during the first years of schooling is a reliable predictor of several unfortunate futures. First, over 90 percent of the children placed in a first-grade bottom-reader group are still poor readers in the upper grades (Juel 1988). Second, primary-grade poor readers are amongst those children most likely to be retained in grade (Shepard and Smith 1989). Third, these children are the most likely to be classified as handicapped, particularly as learning disabled (Ysseldyke, 1982; Thurlow, Mecklenburg, and Graden, 1984). Finally, low academic achievement, retention, and special-education placement are all associated with dropping out of school, teen parenthood, and unemployment or limited earning power in adulthood (Edelmann 1988).

Common school responses to difficulties in learning to read and write have been not only largely ineffective in altering the status of the at-risk child but also enormously expensive. Schools have created a "pay me now and pay me later" response to literacy problems. We argue here that we need to rethink school responses to children with reading and writing difficulties, and we begin this chapter by discussing what schools typically do when faced with children who fall academically behind their peers.

Retention in grade

A common response—in fact the most common response in many schools—is retention in grade. Children who acquire reading and writing abilities more slowly than their peers are simply held back. Schools in the United States far outstrip those in other industrial nations in the frequency of use of retention. We have no national sample here, but we do know that about 7 percent of all students are retained in the states that collect such data. The cumulative effects of this rate (7 percent × 7 years = 49 percent) are such that by grade seven almost half of all students will have been retained! Early-grade retention seems now the most popular, with Florida reporting that 26 percent of the kindergarten through second-grade population was retained and Arizona reporting a 36 percent retention rate for those grades. In our work we found schools where nearly half of the students had been held back before third grade (Allington and McGill-Franzen 1991). Contrast this with the 0 percent retention in the United Kingdom and Japan, or the 1.9 percent rate in West Germany. Our current retention rates most closely approximate those reported for Cuba and Kenya (Shepard and Smith 1989). Retention seems to be gaining in popularity even in the face of mounting evidence of the almost wholly negative effects of the practice.

Closely related to retention is the use of "pre-first" transitional-grade classrooms between kindergarten and grade one or between grades one and two. Such placements are often described as an alternative to retention but still result in extending the school career by another year and the long-term results on student achievement are similarly negative (Leinhardt 1980). Both retention and transition-room responses are among the most expensive interventions schools could select and are doubly so because of the documented ineffectiveness.

The cost of retention can be fairly easily estimated by calculating the average cost per pupil for a year of schooling. In the United States, state average per pupil cost estimates vary from three thousand to six thousand dollars. Even if one could document positive effects for retention or transition-room placement, and researchers have not, both responses are expensive. The "gift of time" advocated by some supporters of retention or transition programs appears to be no real gift at all, although it too costs good money. Each student retained represents a substantial investment of extra educational resources to pay for the extra year of schooling. Retention is at least as expensive as tutorial intervention and significantly more expensive than options such as summer school, after-school programs, or remediation.

Likewise, the use of pre-kindergarten screening to delay school entry for some children has no reliable positive effects on student achievement or affect (May and Welch 1984). While there are no obvious costs if a child does not attend school there is the cost of testing all those children to inappropriately label a few as unready. While children obviously differ in their "readiness for schooling," leaving those deemed least ready (the children of poverty, for instance) in the environment that created the "unreadiness" seems an odd educational intervention. Parents, especially middle-class parents, are now more frequently delaying school entry for a year, especially for their sons. This "academic redshirting" has increased dramatically in the past decade but the effects seem quite different than what the parents might have hoped (Mergendoller, Bellisimo, and Horan 1990). The children who are held out, mostly boys, experience much higher rates of retention and special-education placements than boys who begin school on schedule.

Special-Education Placement

Classifying students who find learning to read difficult as handicapped is an increasingly common school response (Singer and Butler 1987), especially for young children. The substantial expansion of the learning-disability category in the past ten years has occurred primarily in elementary-aged children. Currently no federal or state agency seems to collect achievement data on students enrolled in these programs (Gartner and Lipsky 1987), but the accumulated research evidence suggests that participation rarely increases either the quantity or quality of reading instruction these children receive (Haynes and Jenkins 1986; Allington and McGill-Franzen 1989b). Too often children classified as learning disabled receive less reading instruction than nonhandicapped peers, experience substantially more fragmented reading curricula and instruction, and spend more time working alone on low-level instructional tasks. Not surprisingly, few learning-disabled children achieve normal reading abilities and return to regular education on a full-time basis.

In our observations of classrooms with Chapter 1 and special-education students we found that mainstreamed mildly handicapped students participated in fewer minutes of reading and language arts instruction than either remedial or normally achieving nonhandicapped students. In fact, the differences were striking, with the mildly handicapped students receiving thirty-five minutes per day less reading instruction than remedial students (Allington and McGill-Franzen 1989b). Most of this loss resulted from loss of classroom instructional time; these children did not participate in mainstream reading instruction. This lack of participation simply reduced daily instructional exposure dramatically. We have found it difficult to explain how offering less instruction to handicapped children would represent a more appropriate, or improved, educational experience. It has been even more difficult to explain why these students experienced the largest proportion of low-level seatwork time and the smallest proportion of direct teaching. These results just do not fit with any plan for accelerating learning that we have seen proposed.

Special-education programs would be expensive even if it were demonstrated that they accelerated student achievement. The *New York Times,* for instance, recently reported that it costs over three thousand dollars in New York City just to complete the initial screenings for referral to special education. This is money that is spent for assessment just to see if the referral seems sound and whether a full psychological assessment needed for consideration of a child as handicapped is called for. No instructional services are rendered for these funds. No teacher assistance is provided. No curricular modification is provided. But funds that could have been earmarked for instruction—enough funds for a semester-long daily one-to-one tutorial—are spent instead on a labeling process.

Even when mildly handicapped students are placed in mainstream classrooms for most of the day with an hour or less of resource room support each day, special education is expensive. Current estimates are that special education costs from 1.5 to 2.3 times as much as regular education. Of course, once children are identified as handicapped they rarely are declassified and returned to the mainstream full-time. Thus, the excess costs exist very nearly until perpetuity (actually only until the child graduates or leaves school). Unlike retention which is a one-time expenditure, hopefully, or remediation which also is likely to be of limited duration, special education costs are forever. Given the expense and the rising numbers of children identified as handicapped, we would argue that we should have good evidence that the best interests of children are being served by such placements. Unfortunately, such data are just not available from federal, state, or local agencies.

Remediation

Assignment to remedial classes is also a common school response to children experiencing academic difficulty. Federally funded Chapter 1 remedial reading programs are found in virtually all school districts and have been extensively evaluated over a long period of time. Slavin (1987) notes that, on average, participation in Chapter 1 results in a three percentile rank annual gain in achievement. While any gain is positive, participation in Chapter 1 too rarely results in any substantial shift in the child's status as a reader. Although poor readers do participate and may even improve slightly, they tend to remain poor readers and maintain long-term eligibility for remedial services. Here again, the available evidence suggests good reasons for the disappointing results.

Remedial classes infrequently increase the quantity of reading instruction that the child receives (Birman 1988). Participating children spend more time with paraprofessionals—the least qualified members of an instructional staff. The focus of remediation seems inevitably to be on low-level tasks with little evidence of either higher-order thinking activities or involvement in reading of text (Allington and McGill-Franzen 1989a; Rowan and Guthrie

1989) and again participants experience greater fragmentation of curricula and instruction than normally achieving peers (McGill-Franzen and Allington 1990). Finally, remedial reading teachers routinely serve from thirty-five to sixty-five students daily, a number so large as to virtually preclude the provision of any sort of tailored, personalized teaching.

Patterns of School Response

None of these three school responses—retention, special education, or remediation—reliably result in accelerated reading acquisition; none seems to alter the destiny of significant numbers of the participants: poor readers remain poor readers. However, such outcomes seem predictable when one considers that none of these school responses reliably enhances the reading instruction available to these children at risk. Rather, these school responses seem often to reflect a design that best serves the needs of administrators and teachers, not children (Allington and McGill-Franzen 1989a; Fraatz 1987). Unfortunately, this seems to be the case in many of the schools that we have studied.

For instance, we studied three small school districts where the use of retention, special education, and remediation varied substantially. The data in the table below are for single kindergarten cohorts across time in each district. In each case we report the percentage of children in the original cohort experiencing retention or special-education placement for a three year period. As illustrated in table 13.1, the cumulative retention rates varied, with 7, 15, and 40 percent of the cohorts retained before third grade. Special-education placements also varied with 6, 10, and 20 percent of the cohorts identified as handicapped before third grade. When the cumulative retentions and special-education placements are added together for each cohort we find that 13, 25, and, incredibly, 60 percent of the original kindergarten cohorts were removed from the statewide accountability testing stream!

In other words, substantial numbers of children would not sit for the state testing when scheduled, if ever. Perhaps it is just coincidence, but the reported passing rates for the state testing covary with the incidence of retention and special-education placement. The greater the proportion of children removed from the original cohort, the higher the reported passing rate. School district administrators could report higher levels of achievement in

TABLE 13.1.
CUMULATIVE RETENTION AND SPECIAL-EDUCATION RATES
IN THREE ELEMENTARY SCHOOLS IN THREE SMALL
COMPARABLE SCHOOL DISTRICTS.

| | School 1 | | | School 2 | | | School 3 | | |
	R	SPED		R	SPED		R	SPED	
K	3%	0%		0%	0%		0%	7%	
1	4%	3%		15%	0%		36%	6%	
2	0%	3%		0%	10%		4%	7%	
Totals	7% +	6%	= 13%	15% +	10%	= 25%	40% +	20%	= 60%

R = Retentions   SPED = Special-education placements

districts with higher retention and special-education placement rates since the lowest achieving students were removed from the state assessment stream. However, actual achievement of the students in these schools improved not one iota. Thus, this situation is, again, one in which schools and administrators seem better served than students by the school responses to low achievement.

Remediation is less an issue here since none of the districts offered much, if any, remediation below second grade. What does seem important is realizing that none of these districts had evaluated the effectiveness of retention or transition-room practices, nor had they evaluated the effectiveness of special-education instruction. Thus, the use of these responses was not based on district evidence of successful intervention data. Our analyses of the achievement data for these retained and handicapped students simply fit the patterns reported by others (e.g. Shepard and Smith 1989); the majority scored below the fortieth percentile for reading achievement at the end of grade three. In addition, children who were retained or placed in transition rooms were frequently identified as handicapped in subsequent years when achievement remained low.

The use of retention and special education seemed to better serve the needs of administrators and teachers than the needs of children. Retention was viewed as a way to limit the heterogeneity of student achievement. By holding the lowest achieving students back, the next teacher had a narrower range of achievement differences to plan for. Retention also allowed the school an extra year of schooling to raise achievement to state-mandated third-grade minimal competency levels. Special education served the same two purposes by removing the child from the classroom for part of the academic day, usually during reading/language arts instruction and by limiting school accountability for low achievement since handicapped student scores were not included in the state accountability reports.

What we found most fascinating was the differences in beliefs about children as learners and the attributions for difficulty in literacy learning. In School 1, where use of retention and special education was infrequent, teachers talked about their attempts to accelerate reading growth, usually through intensified classroom instruction. We observed real declines in low-achieving children (bottom quartile), from about 35 percent of the children at the end of grade one to less than 5 percent at the end of grade five, with fewer than 15 percent of the children experiencing retention or special-education placement. In School 3, on the other hand, a number of the grade-five students who had experienced double retentions or double retention and special-education placement were creating some not insignificant problems for teachers and administrators and their achievement remained low along with their motivation for academic work. The use of special-education placement had increased to the point where there was a special-education teacher for each 120 students (or roughly 1 for every 100 nonhandicapped students).

These three schools represent some sense of the range of incidence we have observed, but we must admit that too often we were simply unable to construct such profiles for schools because the necessary information just was not retrievable, even from hand searches of student records, and some schools simply denied our requests for access to such information. Each of the three schools presented in the table were truly interested in the question of effects and worked with us to locate the data presented above. We suspect that some schools exceed the incidence data for School 3 and are even less successful with their responses to literacy learning difficulties. Finally, we need to note that virtually all schools retain some students and identify some as handicapped. In that sense these schools were not all that different from others. More telling is the almost complete lack of data on such placement patterns in school districts or state education agencies, and in our view, an irresponsible lack of any evidence of positive effects of such re-sponses on children. Yet district and state policies produce such patterns.

RECONCEPTUALIZING RESPONSES TO READING FAILURE

To begin, we must recognize that we can design instructional pro-grams that virtually eliminate reading failure. Several examples come immediately to mind and represent substantial variation in size and nature. Each is discussed briefly below, and the descrip-tions are followed by an analytic summary of the shared critical features.

The North Warren Project

Walmsley and Walp (1990) describe the evolution of the North Warren Project, an upper-grade-level curricular redesign in a small poor rural district that began as an attempt to restructure the remedial program and evolved, ultimately, into a comprehensive restructuring of the grades three through six language arts curricu-lum. Central to this redesign was the principle that genuine reading and composing were to be the primary language arts activities and that they should occupy the largest portion of the language arts curriculum.

They adopted a "skills through application" view of the lan-guage arts curriculum, as opposed to the traditional "skills first, application later" model that has dominated curriculum design for the past half-century. They created a daily ninety-minute integrated language arts core curriculum that balanced reading and writing activities and substantially trimmed the time traditionally allo-cated for reading and writing skills in isolation activities. Thus, instead of 70 percent of the classroom language arts block being spent on skill worksheets and drill (Shannon 1989), 70 percent was spent on reading books and stories and composing stories, biogra-phies, and summaries.

The role of specialist teachers was to support progress in the literature and writing activities of the classroom. The specialist teachers work in the classroom during the regular language arts period, for thirty minutes each day, providing in-class assistance to the low-achieving students. Later in the day, outside of the regular language arts period, the specialists again work with those children in another location. During this pull-out period the core curriculum tasks and activities are the focus of the instruction. Specialist teachers, having worked in the classroom, have a strong sense of what the child is finding difficult and plan support lessons accordingly.

This project evolved over a five-year period and involved participation of classroom teachers, specialist teachers, librarians, and consultants. In many senses the project could be viewed primarily as a curriculum redesign effort rather than an effort to solve the difficulties some children have in reading and writing. While the school drew from a student population in which over a third of the children qualified for free or reduced-price lunches, the project focused more on finding ways to include the reading of tradebooks and composing activities in an already full language arts block. However, the difficulties that remedial and mainstreamed mildly handicapped students had in both reading and writing was a central concern from the beginning. Related concerns were the role of the remedial and special-education programs in a curricular redesign and the issue of curriculum access for all students. All children benefited in the effort but the academically at-risk students have benefited the most. Today virtually no child falls below the state minimum-performance levels at grade six and all successfully participate in the school's theme-based book reading and composing curricula. Retention in grade or special-education placement is infrequent (below 2 percent) across the grade levels (three through six) involved in this integrated approach to literacy.

The Success for All Project

Slavin (1987) discusses Success for All, a program in the Baltimore City Schools. This effort is based on the principles of prevention and immediate and intensive intervention. The goals are that all children will be reading on grade level by the end of grade three and no child will be retained or referred to special education because of reading difficulties. This project originated in a school where three-quarters of the children qualify for free or reduced-price lunches based on family poverty. There are several program elements that are critical; no single effort seemed sufficient.

To begin, there are reading tutors who work in the regular classroom during the daily ninety-minute core reading and language arts period. These tutors are certified teachers, reading teachers, special-education teachers and experienced primary-grade teachers. The use of tutors in the regular classroom reduces the teacher-child ratio to about one to fifteen. The tutors also work with selected children in a one-to-one tutorial for twenty minutes each day, focusing on individual difficulties children have in the core curriculum tasks.

The program regroups students by achievement levels for reading and language arts instruction so that each teacher has children at one level for the daily ninety-minute block. This was done to eliminate the need for seatwork skill assignments, tasks often used as management devices to busy some children while the teacher works with others. The core curriculum emphasizes direct instruction on decoding, story structure, and comprehension skills, active reading and rereading to partners, integrated reading and writing, and cooperative learning activities. In addition, every eight weeks each child is assessed and an individual academic plan is rewritten.

Success for All has created family support teams of two social workers and a parent liaison. The parent liaison and one social worker is provided by the school district, the other social worker is provided by the social services department of the city. This team provides parenting education, monitors families experiencing difficulties, and intervenes when eyeglasses are needed, or attendance is irregular, and so on.

Finally, the school has a program facilitator who works with the building principal to ensure implementation and to see that teachers needs are met. The facilitator may offer demonstration lessons, tutor or assess children who puzzle others on the staff, and so forth. The primary tasks involve coordinating the efforts of everyone and ensuring that no child falls through the cracks.

This project has demonstrated success: The average grade-three student scored at the forty-seventh percentile (compared to an average seventeen percentile performance in the control school nearby); retentions have been reduced to zero; special-education referrals have been reduced from thirty to six; and special-education placements have been reduced from twelve to three. Even though retention and referral rates decreased dramatically, keeping the neediest children within the mainstream, the lowest scoring 25 percent of the school's third graders outperformed the average students in the control school.

The added personnel did effect an increase in cost, but it seems that is but a temporary situation. Already the school has eliminated the need for one special-education teacher and the reduction in expenses for children not now retained are substantial. What has happened, by and large, is the redistribution of resources from specialist programs to the classroom. While this project was focused on the low achievers from the beginning, the redesign involved substantial changes in the core curriculum and regular class instruction.

The Ohio Reading Recovery Project

Pinnell, Lyons, and Deford (1988) detail the implementation of this intervention in the Columbus City Schools and its dissemination as a statewide effort. This project originated in New Zealand (Clay 1985) and involves intensive tutorial intervention with the lowest-achieving first graders (students in the lowest 20 percent of their class). In the Ohio adaptation of the program, the students participate in their classroom reading lessons and then meet with a highly trained Reading Recovery teacher daily for thirty minutes. During this latter period the children read and reread predictable language books, write a response, and receive a mini-lesson on some decoding or text-processing strategy identified in that day's performance. The tutorial involves constant active reading and direct instructional intervention based upon a contextual assessment.

In the Columbus schools implementation, teacher teams were trained in the Reading Recovery procedures. The teams included a first-grade classroom teacher and a specialist teacher. These teachers shifted roles at midday with the specialist teacher taking over the classroom and the classroom teacher becoming the Reading Recovery teacher. In the statewide implementation effort it has been more common for a specialist teacher to be trained and then to work as a Recovery teacher in the morning and return to the traditional small-group pull-out role in the afternoon.

The initial Columbus three-school implementation project has provided dramatic longitudinal evidence of the success of this early intervention with 75 to 85 percent of the participating students "recovered" (reading on par with achieving peers) and released from the program in an average of fifteen weeks. At the end of third grade the recovered children were reading better than the average third grader, an edge they had maintained since they were released from the program in first grade. A full-time Recovery teacher would serve about twenty-five children per year and about twenty of those children would become good readers and stay good readers.

As in other successful programs, reductions in retention in grade, special-education placements, and later remedial interventions reduce school costs over the long term. In the Lancaster (Ohio) schools, for instance, grade one retentions dropped from thirty-two pupils to fifteen when Reading Recovery services were expanded from seven students served to sixty-three students served. The district, then, saved the expense of an extra year of schooling for seventeen first-grade students and some unknown costs for reductions in later-grade retentions, decreased the need for future remedial services, and lowered special-education identification rates. Even if Reading Recovery were half as expensive as a full-year retention in grade, and we suspect it is not, over half the cost of the intervention would be saved in the first year as a result of dramatically reduced incidence of first-grade retention.

The New Haven School-Community Project

Comer (1988) provides a candid discussion of the successful effort to revitalize urban schools in New Haven. In this project, poverty was again widespread, with 70 percent of the students from families that received Aid to Families with Dependent Children. School attendance and reading achievement were both very low. Comer first targeted family-school relations for the intervention effort, arguing that educational reform activities in urban schools particularly, and schools with predominantly minority enrollment especially, too often failed because of mutual distrust between parents and educators.

Thus, for each building implementing Comer's program a school governance and management team was created, comprised of about a dozen people including the principal, elected teachers and parents, a mental health specialist, and a member of the non-professional support staff. This team created policy on issues concerning the academic program, the social programs, and school procedures that were central to academic and behavioral problems.

All decisions were by consensus, not by majority vote, to ensure all listened, compromised, and collaborated. In addition, the focus of team meetings was on deriving solutions rather than identifying who was to blame.

Specialists, including support teachers, psychologists, social workers, and regular education teachers worked in mental health teams to solve problems rather than working independently as before. Parents whose children attended the school were hired for nonprofessional jobs. These parents encouraged others to participate in school activities and the special projects, such as the potluck dinners for staff and parents.

Comer (1988) discusses the difficulty that educators experienced initially and the mistrust that permeated the atmosphere, with parents and teachers each blaming the other for the difficulties children experienced in school. After five years, student achievement in one building—earlier the lowest of the city's thirty-three elementary schools—had moved up among the highest-achieving elementary schools in the city. Student attendance increased so much that this school led all other schools.

WHY DO THESE PROJECTS WORK?

Access to Large Amounts of High-Quality Instruction

In each of these effective projects, reading instruction is intensive for the targeted children. Unlike in other studies, these projects provided children experiencing difficulty in reading with access to larger amounts of high-quality reading instruction. In the Reading Recovery Project the children received 150 minutes of tutorial instruction each week and they read substantially more stories and books than did the good readers. In the North Warren Project, low-achieving children benefited from the upgrading of the core language arts curriculum and the enhanced amounts of reading and writing the upgrading included. In addition, they benefited from the instructionally coordinated remedial and special-education efforts that accelerated achievement in the core literature program. In the Success for All and the New Haven projects, participating children had access to a variety of instructional personnel and program options which ensured that opportunity to learn to read was expanded.

Currently, children who experience difficulty in learning to read on schedule are likely to be retained, remediated, or classified as handicapped, but none of these responses reliably enhances their opportunities to read and write nor their access to greater amounts of higher quality instruction. The successful projects, however, reconceptualized issues of access to opportunities and expectations for learning.

Collaboration and Shared Decisions

In each of the successful projects collaboration between instructional personnel, regular, remedial, and special educators occurred. In other words, it was not simply an add-on effort by a few specialized staff. This collaboration took many forms but involved curricular and instructional collaboration most critically. For instance, rather than viewing the difficulties that some children had learning to read as a problem for someone else to address (a problem for the Chapter 1 teacher, for instance), those difficulties were viewed as shared responsibilities.

Rather than presenting a fragmented instructional effort with several different curricula offered by the several different teachers who might be working with a child, the focus of all instruction was success in the core curriculum. In the North Warren Project, for instance, the remedial and special-education teachers simply support progress in the literature and the common writing activities of the classroom. Rather than defining an arbitrary list of "basic skills" to be remediated, the specialist teachers offer added instruction on those aspects of the classroom reading and writing assignments that the children experience difficulty with. Their skills through application approach represents the best translation of recent research on facilitating reading and writing acquisition (Walmsley and Walp 1990). Similarly, in the program classrooms of the Reading Recovery Project, the classroom and reading teachers exchanged roles at midday. That is, the classroom teacher became the Recovery teacher and the reading teacher became the classroom teacher. In these shared classrooms there existed much shared knowledge about the children, the curriculum, and the instructional interventions most appropriate for easing reading acquisition. In the Success for All schools the tutors also teach the classroom program and offer tutorial support on that program later in the day. In New Haven the specialist worked within teams and, perhaps more importantly, the building governance and management team worked collaboratively to identify problems and interventions.

In these project schools there were attempts to clarify the role of instructional support programs and an effort to enhance shared knowledge of the instructional activities of the professionals who worked with those children at risk. The support instruction was designed to support the efforts of the child in the core curriculum. Unlike less-successful schools, these schools designed responses that alleviated the fragmentation of the school day and the instructional effort. The shared knowledge reflected the shared professional responsibility of all members of the instructional staff.

Effort and Time

In each of the project schools an enormous effort was put forth to achieve the desired outcomes, and in each case, the projects faltered, floundered, and those involved regrouped to address the problems. It is important to recognize the intense effort involved, if for no other reason than to assert that such programs cannot simply be packaged and slipped into other schools. Too often, it seems, the level of effort necessary to achieve such results is tremendously underestimated by those in other schools. These projects involved multiyear plans for implementation, not one-shot in-service or a single three-day retreat. These projects were not simply imported into the school but involved the efforts of many, if not most, staff members. In other words, it was not just a "super principal" that came in and cracked the whip. The final shape of the effort was negotiated and refined across time. These projects involved rethinking and then reeducating professional staff, not simply fine tuning existing systems or redeployment of a few specialist teachers. It was not the case that these schools needed only to have a poorly designed remedial, or special-education, program redesigned. The schools were failing their constituency, the children, and it was the whole approach that needed to be recast, not just a few parts.

However, it must be noted that the changes were largely incremental in nature, changing across time and not all in one fell swoop. These projects tended to start small, in a few grades, or in a single school within a large district. The projects involved teachers working on the problems, not just administrative mandates to change in particular ways. These efforts took energy and time, both of which cost money. However, in all cases the costs were actually trivial given the outcomes, and actually ended up as cost saving. Because fewer children were being retained, because fewer were being placed in special education, and because fewer were qualifying for remedial services, less excess funding was needed to support those who failed. Unfortunately, federal and state funding is more often tied to failure than success. Thus, in some cases the success was more expensive for the local district though more cost effective overall. Hopefully, recent recommendations to eliminate the disincentives found in many federal and state funding activities will be heeded (Allington and Johnston 1989; McGill-Franzen 1987, 1993).

No Single Answer

These four projects were selected in an attempt to illustrate that there is no one best way, no single answer, to the problem of educating at-risk children. These projects differ on a variety of attributes; they are perhaps more different than similar. They represent efforts in different communities, with different school personnel, different histories of reform, different funding opportunities, and so on. None of these efforts is probably wholly exportable to another site. While American education has a yearning for the quick fix, the single, simple, and straightforward answer to all the ills that beset us, there are no simple answers.

These projects shared, first, a belief that improvement was possible and necessary. Each also involved the leadership of key administrative personnel in supporting the change. All of these projects involved university personnel working collaboratively with school personnel. While university involvement is obviously unnecessary in theory, in these districts a large part of the effort came from outside the public school.

Commitment and Beliefs

In each of these effective projects someone believed that virtually all children are capable learners. This belief is a critical characteristic of places that support the literacy development of all children. In many schools the dominant belief is that children differ in their aptitude for literacy learning and some must inevitably fail

(McGill-Franzen and Allington 1991). The number of children who fail varies by school, according to local norms that have evolved within the school communities. In some schools few children fail, whereas other communities tolerate the failure of more than half of their children before the end of grade three.

Even within the same school with children from the same community some first-grade teachers manage to teach the reading curriculum to all children, while others do not (Gastright 1985). Some first-grade teachers believe that they have fulfilled the job requirements satisfactorily if they get the top group through all of the books, the middle group through most of the books, and the bottom group at least halfway through the grade-level work. As long as teachers do not believe that it is their responsibility to teach the curriculum to all children, we should not be surprised that many do not. As long as school administrators do not believe that all children can learn the expected curriculum they will communicate this to teachers, and design and support school responses that validate these beliefs.

Likewise, some kindergarten teachers believe that school readiness is more a physiological function than an educational one. These teachers retain three to five times as many children as do teachers who believe that their educational interventions are the primary determinant of school readiness (Shepard and Smith 1989). When teachers have a low sense of self-efficacy and a belief that some children are not helped by instruction, we need not be surprised to find they offer slower-paced, lower-quality instruction in relatively small amounts (Ashton and Webb 1986). We should not then be surprised that some children in these rooms learn less and become candidates for retention, remediation, and special education.

In some districts we studied, as many as two of every three regular education teachers believed that the instruction of children who were enrolled in remedial reading programs was the primary responsibility of the remedial teachers, even though the remedial teachers worked with the remedial students less than two hours per week! In these schools the classroom teachers offered substantially less reading instruction to these children than in other schools. In some schools, over 80 percent of the classroom teachers believed that teaching reading to mainstreamed mildly handicapped students was the responsibility of the special-education staff. Classroom teachers in these schools rarely involved mainstreamed children in classroom reading activities, and these mainstreamed children received the least amount of instructional time (Allington and McGill-Franzen 1989b). These beliefs were typically institutionalized; that is, they were widely held by members of the staff.

Beliefs about the inevitability of reading failure undermine efforts to reconceptualize school response. Such beliefs may account for the distressing finding reported in the most recent evaluation of the Chapter 1 program (Birman 1988). Classroom teachers in schools with many poor children were found to schedule approximately 25 percent less reading instruction each week than the teachers in schools with few poor children enrolled. While the educators who work in schools with large numbers of poor children often attribute low achievement to parental, community, or child factors (Winfield 1986), the available data more directly address the limitations of the instructional effort. Simply put, when some children routinely receive substantially less instruction than others, one does not have to look outside the school for determinants of lower achievement. Likewise, when both administrators and teachers believe that failure is inevitable for many children, we cannot be surprised that substantial numbers of at-risk children are routinely retained in grade or classified as handicapped. When regular education personnel believe that it is someone else's responsibility to teach children at risk, we cannot be surprised that these remedial and mainstreamed mildly handicapped children receive less instruction than their more-able peers and thus rarely catch up or keep up with their normally achieving peers.

Beliefs about how best to teach children who find learning to read difficult drive the instructional plans of teachers and the design of instructional support programs. For at least fifty years, the most prevalent belief system has held that children who find learning to read difficult need a slower pace, not more instruction and increased opportunity to read. As we have slowed the pace and decreased the instructional time, we have ensured that these children fall further behind. As we attempted to break the reading activity into smaller steps we have ensured that fewer children will ever see the point of reading. As we increased the drill, we decreased actual text reading and ensured that these children would become more easily distracted from the low-level tasks that dominated their day. As these children failed to learn to read we retained them, identified then as handicapped, and blamed them and their parents for the failure of our efforts (Allington 1991).

By contrast, in schools where more effective responses to children in trouble have taken hold, teachers and administrators raised questions about the efficacy of their instruction rather than simply questioning the abilities, maturity, and readiness of the children. They questioned the long-term effects of remediation, retention, and special-education programs, but the key question became: What does this child need instructionally to achieve at a level comparable to his/her peers?

Beliefs about learners and learning drive our plans and actions. Until belief systems shift and educators believe that virtually all children can and will learn to read and read well, there is little likelihood that instructional programs will be redesigned to make that outcome possible. Until our beliefs about the most appropriate instructional activities reflect the last half-century of research, we will repeat the "slow it down and make it concrete" myths of the past. As we continue to actualize these myths in our instructional interventions, we make learning to read more difficult for those we are trying to help.

In each of the successful programs that we have described, teachers' and administrators' beliefs about children changed, and this may, in fact, be the critical first step. As long as those in schools believe they are accomplishing all that can be expected there is no reason to change (Ashton and Webb 1988). As long as schools believe that there has to be a bottom group, they will produce one. As long as the locus of problems in learning to read remains in the supposed deficiencies of children and their families, schools will continue to fail children and place them at risk.

SUMMARY

Schools respond to literacy learning difficulties in ways that are as likely to increase the risk associated with such difficulties as to ameliorate it. The most common school responses—retention, remediation, and special education—offer unenviable records of sustaining the at-risk status of participants. Remediation is the least expensive and most-often effective, but the most common remedial programs provide too little, too late. Changing school responses have proven to be difficult but not unattainable. Changing schools responses involves time, effort, and leadership. The sad truth is that there is no quick fix.

CHAPTER 14

"Teacher, Why Am I Failing? I Know The Answers": The Effects of Developmentally Inappropriate Assessment

Pamela O. Fleege, University of North Texas Rosalind Charlesworth, Louisiana State University

Standardized assessment is one of the most potent tools policy makers have for influencing classroom practice; policy makers in many states have not hesitated to use this form of control. The authors of this chapter examine the impact of standardized testing in one classroom and on one student in particular. The data they report suggest the costs associated with using this potent control mechanism. The data also call into question the validity of standardized procedures which do not allow students to demonstrate what they know in formats which are comfortable and appropriate for them.

A controversy exists concerning the validity and reliability of group-administered standardized testing when used at the kindergarten level. Considering the serious decisions that are frequently made on the basis of such tests, it is important to consider the effects of such tests on the children to whom they are given and on the teachers of those children. This chapter offers some insight into these effects by focusing on the experiences of one at-risk child, Luke, during a week of standardized testing and the environment in which that testing occurred.

BACKGROUND

Luke attended Laurel Meadow Elementary which is located in a small town outside a large metropolitan area. Laurel Meadow Elementary houses 699 students in grades K to 5. The socio-economic range for the school is lower- to lower-middle class. Fifty percent of the children are on the federally funded free and reduced-price lunch program. Also, 32 percent of the students participate in federally funded remedial or special education programs. Of the total number of students who attend Laurel Meadow, 51 percent are African American and 49 percent are white. Within this school there are five sections each of grades K to 3 and three sections of grades 4 to 6.

Twenty-four children were enrolled in Luke's kindergarten class, ten white and fourteen African American. The children came from low to middle socioeconomic backgrounds. Sixty-three percent of the class participated in the federally funded free and reduced-price lunch program, while 58 percent participated in the Chapter 1 and speech therapy programs.

At the time this research was conducted during the spring of 1989, Luke was a bright, mischievous, seven year old who wore hearing aids in both ears. He was small and blonde with a slender build and a quick smile. This was his second year in kindergarten. Luke's hearing impairment (discovered during his first year in kindergarten), low achievement, and behavior problems were cited as causes for his retention. His teacher reported that Luke's family had gone through a difficult divorce and a recent remarriage the previous year. At the beginning of the 1988–89 school year, the severity of Luke's behavior problems resulted in a psychologist being brought in to work with his family and the school. By the spring of that year his teacher reported that his behavior had improved. In her words, "He's just like the other kids; he has his good days and his bad days. His behavior is comparable to that of the other children in the class."

Luke's hearing problem did not seem to affect his progress in the classroom; while he was not a top student, his teacher considered him to be average. He participated in group discussions, read aloud for the teacher, and responded to jokes told by his peers. Luke spoke softly in front of the class, but he could be found yelling and screaming like his peers on the playground. He received speech therapy and Chapter 1 services. However, after observing Luke for four weeks, it was hard to remember that he had a hearing problem. His behavior, both inside and outside of class, was similar to that of his peers.

LUKE AT TESTING TIME

Four weeks of observations were conducted beginning on a Monday, early in the month of April, and ending the middle of May. The observations were conducted before, during, and after administration of the California Achievement Test. The test was administered each morning for one week for approximately two hours. The children were tested in two groups of ten with the other four children sent to the Chapter 1 teacher for testing. While one group was tested, the other group worked in self-selected centers. The teacher orally read each test item and then gave the children time to fill in a circle.

During the observations, I served as a monitor in the classroom. It was my duty to make sure the children were on the correct page and question as the teacher read the test questions. If pencils were dropped or broken, I supplied new ones.

It was as a monitor that I noticed a difference in Luke's behavior. The change in his behavior was noticeable on the first day of testing, and it continued to grow in magnitude until testing was completed. On the first day when Luke's group was called to begin the test, he took the booklet, headed for his seat and told me:

LUKE: You're going to have to help me with my test.
PAM: I will.
LUKE: My whole test.
PAM: I'll make sure you're putting your marks on the right row.
LUKE: No, you have to show me what to put. [voice rises as he clutches my hand]
PAM: I can't do that, Luke.
LUKE: But, I have to know!

I assured Luke that everything would be fine and that I was confident that he would be able to do the test. He let go of my hand but the look on his face told me he did not believe me. During the administration of the first day's questions, Luke asked for almost all the questions to be repeated. After a while, he did not ask; he would only point and wait for the teacher or me to repeat the question. He seemed to need the presence of an adult for reassurance; when we walked away to answer a question for another child, he looked around for us and motioned for one of us to return to his side.

On the second day of testing he played with his pencil and test booklet and watched the other children in centers for a while. When he finally began to attend to the test he copied many of his answers from the others sitting around him. Luke was not the only child engaging in this particular behavior. In fact, the majority of the children copied answers from their peers more than once. Luke's agitation seemed to be increasing as evidenced by the escalation in Luke's demands for confirmation of the responses that he marked and the number of times he copied answers from other children.

By the third day, when his group was called, he began crying. He told the teacher, "I don't want to do the test. I hate tests." Luke laid across his table, cried, and refused to complete his test. After being comforted by the teacher, he continued with the test.

Luke's change in behavior seemed to reach a peak on the fourth day. That morning Luke had to be led into the classroom by his mother. He was crying, and his mother told the teacher that he had refused to come to school. When his mother attempted to leave, he tried to go with her. Luke's teacher put her arm around him to offer him some comfort and she tried to position herself between Luke and the door so he could not run out of the room. After a while he calmed down but seemed subdued. He was no longer the smiling child of several weeks ago. When his turn came to be tested, he seemed to mark answers at random. He no longer looked at his peers' test booklets or asked for assistance.

On the last day of testing, as Luke's group was called, he began to cry. "I don't want to do this," he said while taking his booklet to his seat. His teacher told him that everything was okay and that there were only two pages left to complete. Luke stopped crying and was silent. After the teacher comforted Luke for a few minutes, the testing began. As the test questions were read Luke did not mark his answers. The teacher asked him to please mark his answers but Luke gave her no response. After a few minutes, the teacher repeated the question and asked him to point to the answer. He did point to the answers and the teacher marked what he selected. The test was finished with the teacher reading the questions aloud to the class and marking Luke's booklet as he pointed to the answers. When the testing was completed many of the children clapped and yelled. Luke was very quiet but wore a very large grin.

KINDERGARTNER'S RESPONSES TO STANDARDIZED TESTING

This vignette clearly demonstrates the negative responses Luke had to the testing situation which appeared to indicate feelings of anxiety and stress. Luke's behavior was unusual, dramatic, and over the course of the week seemed to escalate. His behavior during testing in no way resembled what had been observed before or after testing, times when he appeared to be a capable student. He did not require an inordinate amount of teacher time, and he was able to complete the classroom activities with little or no help from the teacher. No other incidents of crying were witnessed. He gave evidence of being a happy, energetic, albeit soft-spoken, boy.

Luke's behavior, while more extreme, was not the only incident of stress-related behaviors observed during the administration of the test. Many of the children chewed on pencils, twisted their hair, played with their clothes or test booklets, and squirmed almost constantly in their chairs. Several of the children wanted constant reassurance that their answers were correct. All were reluctant to work on the test each day.

The stress levels for all the children tested appeared to increase during testing. Some of the comments the children made included the following: "I hate tests" and "Do I hav't [*sic*] to take it?" When I finish this I'm never gonna take another test.

DISSONANCE BETWEEN TESTING AND CLASSROOM BEHAVIORS

Luke and the other children engaged in behaviors which would question the validity of the test, copying and calling out answers during the administration of the test. It should be noted that while these behaviors were inappropriate for the testing situation, they were considered appropriate for the regular classroom setting. In this class the children did much of their work orally, and peer tutoring was encouraged. An example of a typical activity included the teacher holding up an object and asking the class to name it. The teacher would then call on one of the students to tell what sound was heard at the beginning of the word. If the student had trouble a peer was asked to lend assistance. Sometimes, peers would respond spontaneously. Students were encouraged daily to collaborate and help each other. Therefore, in this particular setting the assessment methods, which required totally individual effort and silence, did not match the instructional methods currently being used in the classroom. This type of dissonance appeared to produce confusion and anxiety in Luke and his peers who had not become accustomed to testing situations.

INACCURACIES IN THE MEASUREMENT OF CHILDREN'S UNDERSTANDINGS

During interviews conducted after the testing period, the children were told that we would discuss some of the questions they found difficult. The children were given the opportunity to orally respond to many of the questions they had marked incorrectly and were often able to verbalize correct answers. For example, when Luke was asked to tell what word rhymes with *pear*, he replied, "Oh, that's easy, *bear*." These behaviors were exhibited not only by the low-ability children as one might expect, but also by high-ability children. Some of their frequent comments during this interview period were:

> "Oh! Oh! I know that one." (hands waving frantically)
> "That's easy."
> "That's not hard. Give me a hard one."

After several minutes of questions and answers, one child said, "Miss Pam, these aren't hard." As I looked at the expressions of the children seated in the circle, they seemed to say, "Teacher, why am I failing? I know the answers." The children were clearly puzzled as to why they missed these questions on the test but now knew the correct answers.

THE EFFECTS OF TESTING ON TEACHERS

Not only was the situation stressful for the children, but for the teachers as well. Daily, the teachers reported growing incidents of behavior problems. The scene in the teachers' lounge resembled the aftermath of a battlefield. The teachers were all worn out and statements like the following could be heard:

"I don't know if I can last."
"This week seems like it will never be over."
"I can't believe what they're doing! We've been over that, but they're getting it all wrong."
"I may just scream."

Many of the teachers at this school reported that they, as well as colleagues at other schools, felt pressured to raise test scores. As one stated, "It's hard not to feel pressured when they're publishing them in the paper." This pressure appears to lead to inappropriate instructional and assessment practices. It's not surprising that there are reports of teachers teaching the test or teaching approximations of the test. Luke's teacher said some teachers were so concerned about the test scores that they practically gave the children the answers.

Perhaps the teachers' levels of stress and that of the children could be due, in part, to the importance that the principal of this school placed on test scores. The principal believed, as do many, that her school would be judged on the basis of how high their test scores were. This principal encouraged her teachers to teach the format of the test throughout the year. Meetings held after school for the teachers included in-service on strategies to be used with the children to increase the scores. The principal repeatedly told the teachers that they must raise the children's test scores. As Luke's teacher put it, "The only thing she hasn't said is teach the test." In addition to pushing the teachers to increase test scores, the principal also gave students reminders at the beginning and ending of each school day during the testing period that it was important to do their best on the test. It was not surprising that at the end of the testing week tempers were short and behavior problems had increased.

OBSERVATION ON TESTING IN THE EARLY GRADES

The emphasis that the principal at Laurel Meadow and others put on testing was not always the case. Prior to 1965 standardized tests and achievement tests in particular were rarely used in the primary grades. According to Vito Perrone (1990), there was a unanimity within the field of early childhood professionals that the primary grades were unique and the children should be given time to develop naturally. Testing did not usually begin before third grade. By the mid 1970s testing was on the increase and showing up in the primary grades. However, a major expansion in testing came with the publication of *A Nation at Risk* (National Commission on Excellence in Education 1983).

Developmental Inappropriateness

As the amount of testing has increased, so has the criticism. Pencil and paper achievement tests are considered to be developmentally inappropriate because they require children to make as yet unmastered types of responses. In most primary classrooms, instruction and assessment rely heavily on oral discussion and demonstrations by the child to determine mastery of a concept. A test that requires a child to respond mainly in a motoric fashion (such as pointing), to verbalize, or to react to auditory stimuli would be considered one that asked for developmentally appropriate responses at the kindergarten level.

The validity of these tests with young children has been questioned due to the behaviors they exhibit during testing. Wodtke, Harper, Schommer, and Brunelli (1989) reported that the kindergarten children they observed copied and called out answers while taking the Metropolitan Readiness Test, Holt Basic Reading Series Management Program Readiness Tests, and Clymer-Barrett Prereading Battery. Fleege, Charlesworth, Burts, and Hart (1991) also reported observing these kinds of behaviors during testing, as well as an increase in behaviors said to be stress related. Furthermore, the children who were tested marked answers incorrectly, but when interviewed, they could supply the correct response.

Many achievement tests are considered inappropriate because they require the child to respond to questions by marking an X on a picture or coloring in a small circle that can be graded mechanically. Using this method to respond to questions creates a hardship for children who do not possess the fine motor capabilities that allow them to respond. The test does not assess whether the child knows the correct responses but whether he/she can color within predetermined circles or make an X. Some research suggests that paper and pencil responses should only be used at that age to check perceptual-motor functioning (Charlesworth 1985), and to obtain responses, the examiner should use concrete materials and pictures (Bredekamp 1987).

Effects of Standardized Testing on the Curriculum

Not only do the testing practices often not match the instructional practices, but it has been reported that teachers spend an inordinate amount of time helping young children become test wise. Some of the strategies taught are (a) teaching how to transfer answers to separate answer sheets, (b) teaching how to finish within time limits, (c) teaching the content of the test, and (d) practicing on parallel forms of the tests (Smith 1991a). Many of these practices were in existence at Laurel Meadow.

It has been reported that achievement tests often do not match the curricula used in schools or current teaching methods (Wortham 1990; Fleege et al. 1991; Fleege 1991). Arizona found that the instrument they used only covered one-quarter of the state's curriculum. They also discovered that the teachers had a tendency to teach primarily what was on the test thus narrowing the curriculum (National Center for Fair and Open Testing 1990).

Effects of Standardized Testing on Teachers

Testing affects teachers as well as children. The teachers observed in this study felt pressured to improve their children's scores for accountability reasons. The teachers observed by Smith (1991b) reported the same pressures, in addition to feelings of shame and embarrassment if their students did not score well and anxiety and guilt for using this type of assessment with young children.

CONCLUSION

Observations of Luke and his classmates suggest criticisms concerning validity and reliability leveled against standardized tests are indeed valid; standardized testing did not provide a clear picture of these kindergartner's achievement. Furthermore, the use of standardized testing with young children becomes particularly problematic when standardized test results are used to make decisions concerning which children are held back and which children are placed in transitional classes—classes which have not been shown to be effective. During the fall of 1990, the Texas Education Agency held hearings on the transition-class issue. At these hearings, parents indicated their children exhibited a loss of self-esteem and had feelings of failure when placed in these classes. Parents reported teasing by peers and tears because friends were passing to the next grade. The children also made references years later such as "If I had been given a chance, I would be in third grade now" (Johnson 1990). The children discussed during these hearings were aware that they were not continuing with their peers and exhibited behaviors usually associated with stress. Their comments and Luke's responses to the testing situation suggest that inappropriate assessment can socially construct at-risk students, not only organizationally, but psychically as well.

CHAPTER 15

"A Different Kind of Responsibility" Social and Academic Engagement of General-Track High School Students

Sandra B. Damico and Jeffrey Roth, University of Florida

The focus in this chapter is on well-intentioned, seemingly sensible policies and programs designed to keep students in school. The authors demonstrate that what may seem sensible to adults will not necessarily seem sensible to students. Consequently policies designed to help at-risk students may have a decidedly opposite effect. The need to ascertain students' perspectives and the need for flexibility so that policies and programs can be modified accordingly is stressed.

> I enjoy playing in the band. It gets my feelings out. It gives me something I can be proud of. I like doing it for my school. It gives me a different kind of responsibility than I get from class. You're responsible for homework because they tell you to. In band, I practice not because I have to but because I decide to. No one tells me I have to.
>
> —White Female

> I'm small and would have liked to play on a team but you have to be really good to be on a team here. The stuff you have to do to get on a team isn't fair; there is too much. There should be two teams. Now they have JV football but they don't have this for

other sports. There are a lot of kids who would like to play sports but can't. You almost have to be a professional to play.

—White Male

Five years ago, in response to high dropout rates, Florida re-structured its efforts to meet the needs of at-risk students. How-ever, the comprehensive programs supported by the 1986 Dropout Prevention Act meet the needs of only a small percentage of Flori-da's student population, those most at risk of dropping out. Conse-quently, Florida's graduation rate has remained unacceptably low because students other than those defined as "at risk" also drop out. Thus if Florida schools are to increase their graduation rates, they need to move beyond reliance on special programs for those at the bottom and determine why average-achieving students drop out of school. Responding to this need, the Office of Policy Re-search and Improvement in the Florida Department of Education commissioned a study to determine whether any school policies or practices might be unwittingly pushing students out of school (Damico et al. 1990, 1991). This chapter focuses on a portion of that study—general-track students' reactions to policies and prac-tices governing extracurricular activities and attendance. The first set of policies seeks to provide students with opportunities to bond with school through participation in the extracurricular activities of the informal curriculum, while the second is concerned with ensuring that students are in classrooms to receive the formal cur-riculum. Paradoxically, these policies frequently have the obverse effect and result in student disengagement with the life of school. How and why does this occur?

School improvement efforts directed toward increasing the graduation rate of general-track students have been hampered by lack of research on those dimensions of education which are most likely to push these students out of school. Studies of differing curricular tracks have tended to emphasize the basis on which students are assigned to them (e.g., Jones, 1987; Oakes, 1985; Rosenbaum, 1976) or contrast academic experiences of those in college-preparatory courses to those in vocational or remedial courses (e.g., Adelman 1983; Davis and Haller 1981; Natriello, Alexander, and Pallas 1989; Vanfossen, Jones, and Spade 1987). The educational experiences of those in the middle have been left largely unexplored. And yet, in the decade between the late 1960s and the late 1970s, the percentage of students in the general curriculum increased from 12 percent to 42.5 percent (Adelman 1983). And there is no indication that these percentages are declining.

While scant, there is evidence in the research literature supporting the proposition that educators need to examine more closely the experiences of those in the general curriculum in order to increase high school graduation rates. As the size of the student population assigned to the general track has grown, it has begun to set the "tone" of a school's social-learning climate (Adelman 1983), and students enrolled in it are more alienated from school and have less focused aspirations than those in either the academic or vocational tracks (Echternacht 1976). A national study using follow-up data from the High School and Beyond study (Vanfossen, Jones, and Spade 1987) found general- and vocational-track students, as compared to those in the academic curriculum, were less committed to academic goals, had poorer classroom discipline, and received more negative treatment by teachers. These authors concluded, ". . . students in nonacademic tracks **are not** [emphasis in original] given an environment that encourages them to increase their performance and their educational and occupational aspirations" (p. 116). But what type of environment *are* they given?

In an effort to understand the ways in which a school's policies and practices may contribute to students' physical or psychological withdrawal from school, the concept of engagement was employed in this study. Engagement may be thought of as a continuum with integration into the life of the school on one end and alienation or disengagement on the other (e.g., Farrell 1990; Farrell et al. 1988; Fine 1986; Miller, Leinhardt, and Zigmond 1988; Newmann 1989; Wehlage 1989). Academic engagement describes the ways in which students respond to their schools' formal curriculum, including its content, academic demands, and learning tasks (Miller et al. 1988; Wehlage et al. 1989). Social engagement, on the other hand, encompasses interpersonal relationships and participation in the life of the school, including its cocurricular and extracurricular programs (Miller et al. 1988).

Students who are academically and/or socially engaged with their schools' programs are likely to persist to graduation, while those who are estranged from them are most likely to drop out. This leaves a large body of students in the middle—those for whom we have difficulty predicting the likelihood of their graduation. They have some degree of engagement with the academic and/or social components of their schools, but their engagement is tenuous and academic difficulties or confrontations with the school's authority structure may convince them to leave before graduation. Those who study disengagement make the point that, "While at-risk students make their lack of engagement obvious, observers generally agree that it is a problem among a majority of high school students" (Wehlage et al. 1989, p. 177).

The research on which this chapter is based looked at the majority group in high school, general-track students, in an effort to corroborate the degree to which disengagement was to be found in high schools with varying graduation rates. If we are to increase graduation rates of general-track students, we need first to understand the signals which trigger the process of disengagement. The researchers sought to provide these students with a voice through which they could reflect on various aspects of their school experiences that affected academic and social engagement. This chapter focuses on two aspects of the school environment—policies surrounding extracurricular activities and classroom attendance. Policies in these two areas have been promulgated to increase student engagement with the social and academic life of school.

METHODS

Most studies of high school graduation rates have been quantitative, relying on either questionnaires or secondary analysis of large data sets. These approaches assume that researchers know the appropriate questions to ask and the range of possible answers. Additionally, many of these researchers have not bothered to administer the instruments directly to students, but have assumed that educators could accurately report student experiences for them. When qualitative approaches have been used, they have tended to be confined to small populations of students who are either most likely to drop out or who are enrolled in alternative education programs (e.g., Fine 1985; Miller et al. 1988; Wehlage et al. 1989). In response to the limitations of previous research, data for this study were collected during in-depth interviews with 236 individuals. Consequently, this study presents an insider's view of school policies and practices; it tapped the perceptions of students, teachers, and administrators as they reflected on their experiences in schools.

Data were collected from six high schools in three of Florida's countywide school districts. The schools were selected to reflect variations within each county. One district was selected from those with graduation rates above the state mean, one from those at the state mean, and one from those below it. In addition to graduation rate, sociodemographic information, such as geographic region, variations in racial/ethic composition of the student population, and urban-rural setting, was considered in final sample selection. In each of these six high schools a sampling of administrators, counselors, teachers, and tenth- and twelfth-grade students were interviewed.

In-depth interviews were completed with 178 adolescents in the six high schools. Interviews ranged from ninety minutes to slightly over two hours. Individual interviews were conducted with 101 general-track students, while 77 honors and advanced-placement students were interviewed in groups of 4 to 6. The group interviews were designed to examine the extent to which perceptions of school varied across achievement levels. One of the researchers was bilingual and thus able to interview students in Spanish or English, depending on their preference. All interviews were conducted during school hours in quiet, private rooms. Interviews were typed directly into laptop computers rather than being tape recorded.

Interview protocols were developed based upon a review of the at-risk and dropout literature. The purpose of the student interviews was to tap perceptions of school in terms of both academic and social engagement. The interview protocols were open ended enough to elicit individual experiences and beliefs of those being interviewed while containing enough structure to permit comparisons across respondents. A full description of the methodology is available in other sources (Damico et al. 1990; Damico and Roth, 1991). This chapter focuses on general-track students' responses to policies and practices in the areas of the informal curriculum and the enforcement of the schools' attendance policies.

THE INFORMAL CURRICULUM

The informal curriculum refers to those occasions at school outside of regular classes which provided opportunities for students to learn skills necessary to function effectively as responsible adult members of society.

> You learn things not just in class but in the halls: How mean some people are, how ignorant some people are; how some people take advantage, how some people are easily taken advantage of.

Skills such as leadership, cooperation, and planning were not necessary for success in academics. The nonacademic dimension of schooling supplied the occasions for exercising valuable inter- and intra-personal skills.

Two areas within the nonacademic dimension were examined to assess the extent to which these skills were acquired and mastered by general-track students: (1) cocurricular activities, and (2) extracurricular activities. Each of these areas required that students make a contribution to a group enterprise. Learning how to engage in socially valuable interpersonal transactions was conspicuously absent from the decontextualized intellectual demands students routinely faced. Success in school was determined for the most part on students' individual and isolated effort. Rare was the classroom teacher or school district that had devised a grading system which included performance on cooperative learning or group problem-solving tasks. Therefore, those occasions where students learned to work toward a common goal deserved close scrutiny.

Cocurricular Activities

The cocurricular activity that most closely approximated the behavior of adult citizens was student government, specifically, the process of choosing class leaders and student council representatives. Could it be that the phenomenon of voter apathy which has reached alarming proportions in local and national elections has its roots in the campaigns for high school class officers? How skeptical were average students about the people who ran for office? The answer was very interesting. They reported that the same few people, usually the "preps" (college-bound students whose parents know the value of a service-laden resume), appeared on the ballots every year.

> Student government is for the really smart kids, the more popular ones. If you're smart, you're popular here. The same people run the student government from the 9th grade on. They always win.

> Lower social class can't find anyone they can trust, so they don't vote. My friends never get a chance.

Once elected, these officers did not stand up on behalf of the student body to protest unpopular decisions made by school or district administrators; instead they busied themselves with innocuous matters such as choosing the color scheme for the prom or the amusement park for senior-class night.

> Student Council doesn't have any voice. I think they should be able to vote on what kind of clothes we wear and whether we can go off campus. All they do is decide when we are going to have prom or dances. They hardly bring up any issues about what they want to change.

> I really don't know why they have it. They do the ring ceremony and the president makes a speech. They have no power at all. They say they can change things but they have done nothing.

> . . . really don't know when they have their meetings. They have to elect officers and get candidates. I haven't heard much about it. They are supposed to listen to complaints but what good comes of it, I don't know. They have an answer for everything. They do dances for juniors and seniors. Important things they don't do.

Because they perceived student government to be an organization without any power or consequence, most general-curriculum students regarded running for office as a school-sanctioned popularity contest for overachievers.

> The popular group go for attention. Same people get in every year. It makes me sick. They aren't even nice.

Another intriguing similarity between school and bipartisan politics was the fact that students running for a school office incurred considerable expense. Only a few of the students interviewed knew someone who had run for office (none of the general-curriculum students interviewed was a class officer); several commented on the cost of mounting a campaign. They realized that students whose parents could defray the cost of papering every available inch of wall space with hundreds of posters and distributing pins and balloons to supporters had a better chance of winning an election than someone who did not have a large war chest with which to capture the crowd's eye.

This inequality in resources was recognized by one school in the high graduation-rate district. Its response was to simplify the procedure for getting on the ballot (just tell the homeroom teacher, no need for signed petitions) and, for candidates in the final election, to subsidize the costs of campaigning. This intervention on the part of the school produced greater involvement in the electoral process by a wider spectrum of the student body, but it did not end the monopoly on government offices by college-bound students.

The school newspaper and yearbook were likewise staffed almost exclusively by college-bound seniors. Because these publications were routinely entered into state and national competitions by their faculty advisors, there was a press to recruit and retain only top-notch writers and artists. The degree of professionalization now required for these media productions meant that ordinary students, who might not be familiar with the latest computer graphics or desktop publishing packages, were not likely to be invited to fill these high-visibility positions.

The low levels of involvement of general-curriculum students in cocurricular activities indicated that, with the exception of one school in the high graduation-rate district, administrators and teachers were overlooking the power of service to strengthen large numbers of students' sense of affiliation to school.

Extracurricular Activities

Student participation in extracurricular activities depended on a number of factors: the methods the school used to publicize the availability of clubs and teams; the recruiting zeal of the faculty advisor or coach; the tradition of peer group involvement in certain interest areas. Methods for publicizing available options ranged from a list students said they knew existed somewhere in the guidance office to special rush programs featuring booths set up during an extended lunch hour. Schools that did not stage an official club-shopping expo relied instead on the informal system of faculty sponsor recruitment or peer invitation. For students unaffiliated with veteran club participants, or who by chance were not in the class of a faculty sponsor, the chances of being invited to join a club were slim.

There is ample evidence that students bond to their high school through their participation in extracurricular activities (Ekstrom et al. 1986). Service clubs and athletic teams, in particular, have long been known to serve as vehicles for students eager to excel in nonacademic activities which are valued by the community at large. With this association in mind, one might assume that schools would try everything possible to facilitate participation of low-achieving students. However, this emphatically was not the case. In the low-graduation district, students reported that overcrowding had forced school officials to eliminate club meetings from the lunch schedule. Postponing club meetings to after school meant that those students who had no transportation home save the school bus could not exercise the option to stay late and try out for teams or attend club meetings. "My cousin wanted to try out for the tennis team but his mother doesn't have a car so he couldn't." The high-graduation district recognized the importance of scheduling extracurricular activities during school hours. Twice a month the last period of the day was set aside for club meetings.

Other obstacles faced students who might have otherwise found in school-sponsored peer collaboration the motivation to persist to graduation. One was the minimum GPA requirement. For varsity athletics, a 1.5 GPA was required for team eligibility; service clubs set their admission criterion at 2.0. Thus, historically underachieving students were effectively excluded from the very kinds of activities which engender a sense of affiliation. Instead these students were given the message that their academic troubles prohibited them from participating in the civic life of the school and the larger community.

Another obstacle preventing many ordinary students from entering the social life of school was the cost of participating. Membership in highly visible, highly competitive, all-school group activities such as athletics, band, and cheerleading required expenditures (which could run to several hundred dollars a year) for uniforms and training camps. Such costs effectively discouraged students whose parent(s) lacked discretionary income. Once again, that same school in the high-graduation district which had acted to level the playing field for student elections made a commitment to its economically disadvantaged students and subsidized the purchase of their instruments and uniforms. Funds for these subsidies came from companies and organizations in the community who understood (as a result of the principal's lobbying) that these showcase teams were the basis for generating school and community pride. Because these teams were able to recruit from the whole spectrum of the student body, they enjoyed the enthusiastic support of every segment of the populace. There was a powerful incentive to stay in a school whose teams' triumphs and setbacks were followed avidly by nearly everyone in the community.

ATTENDANCE POLICIES

Of all the policies within a school's student handbook, probably none occupy as much time or attention as those surrounding various aspects of attendance—behaviors ranging from being tardy, cutting a class, leaving school grounds, and being truant. Given this attention, it was surprising to discover how little research had been completed on attendance policies. Studies on this topic have focused almost exclusively on the correlation between frequency of truant behavior and dropping out of school (e.g., Ekstrom et al. 1986; Hess et al. 1987; Rumberger 1987; Wehlage and Rutter 1986). No studies of the attendance behavior of general-track or college-bound students could be located. Yet since these policies impact directly on every student in a school, they have the potential to directly affect all students' engagement with learning.

Though the research out of which this chapter emerged (Damico et al. 1990) obtained descriptions of student discipline codes and their enforcement from principals, counselors, and teachers, attention here is focused on these issues from the student perspective. Three attendance-related issues emerged from the analysis of the student interview data. First, students had *never been asked why* they might be tardy or cut class; yet students felt they frequently had legitimate reasons. Secondly, the determination of whether an absence was excused or unexcused was seen by many students as discriminatory. And finally, students in the low- and medium-graduation district provided evidence that their schools' policies were differentially enforced, with high-achieving students receiving lighter punishments than those in the general track. Consequently, reliance on descriptions of a school's attendance policies and the punishments for their infractions fails to convey the ways in these policies inadvertently "push" some students out of school. Each of these three attendance issues will be considered in turn.

Tardies and Cutting Class

Student explanations of tardiness to classes centered on the physical difficulty of getting from one class to another in the allotted time, a felt need to socialize with friends, and perceptions of teacher indifference.

> For me to get from the portables, upstairs to my locker and then to class can make me late. Inside the school you can do it, but then you don't have time to talk to friends. Five minutes just doesn't seem like enough time.

> I have one class out at the end of the portables and then the next at the front of the school and I can just barely make it, but if I have to go to my locker or there is a fight in the hall, I can't make it on time.

It was not surprising that students felt they were being unfairly penalized when distance between classes resulted in referrals for being tardy. Even when schools managed to accommodate all their students in a single building, the crush of a large number of students trying to move through hallways frequently made passage during the time between bells impossible.

Students expressed a real need to socialize with peers during the school day, and yet most found little time in their schedules to do so. Without meaning to be late for a class, students reported they would begin talking to a friend in the hallway and then suddenly find they were going to be tardy. This press for social engagement was not surprising given the strong evidence that adolescents view school as a site for emotional as well as intellectual stimulation (Fine 1986). Social engagement also was one of the reasons adolescents gave for cutting classes. As schools have become overcrowded and lunch periods split, students often may not see friends any time during the school day. Thus, classes scheduled during lunch shifts were among those students frequently cut. Students at one school claimed there were those who stayed in the cafeteria for all three lunch shifts rather than going to any fifth-period classes.

Students also cut, or were late to, classes in which they felt their attendance didn't make a difference—either the teacher didn't care or so little instruction was going on that they weren't missing anything by being late. Other research (Pokay, Jernigan, and Michael 1990) also has found that students are selective in the classes to which they are late or cut. These choices have to do with their relationships with teachers, evaluations of the quality of instruction, and the importance of being in class to learn new material.

> On the first day of school a good teacher will pass out rules and what you need to be prepared for this class. Others say "well, I didn't really want to come back today and I'm sure you guys didn't either."

Excused and Unexcused Absences

Unexcused absences are those for which there is no officially sanctioned justification. Students may accrue unexcused absences through a history of repeated class tardies or by being counted absent from a class without pre-arranged permission. Efforts to increase class attendance and reduce the number of unexcused student absences had taken two approaches in the schools studied. The high-graduation district had instituted a series of positive incentives to encourage students to be in class on time. For instance, they had inaugurated a policy excusing from midsemester exams those students with a C or higher grade average and fewer than a specified number of absences—the number of absences varying by the student's course grade. Since academically less-secure students are especially frightened of tests covering large amounts of material, this policy had the double effect of convincing them to come to class and to keep their grades up.

The other two districts used a punitive approach to decreasing tardies and unexcused absences. Under these arrangements, students' grades were reduced either an entire letter grade or a specified percentage for unexcused absences; a certain number of tardies translated into an unexcused absence. Unfortunately, these policies were not working to get students to class on time, but rather were forcing some of them to drop out. A senior discussed this process:

> Taking 2.2% off somebody's grade doesn't help a child want to come to school. If you work hard and you have lots of points

off, then you don't want to come to class because you are failing or getting really low grades even though you are working hard.

In a similar vein, an honors student in another school commented on this process in the following way.

> The attendance policy encourages kids to drop out. They want to lower the truancy rate but then tell you if you miss a day your grade will go down. Sometimes teachers don't report attendance accurately and you can have your grade lowered even if you were in class.

At this school the policy of reducing students' grades by a letter for every unexcused absence had a major impact on high-achieving students as well as those in the general track. This problem arose because teachers at this school were not always sure what constituted an unexcused absence, students weren't marked in attendance when they were, or the office hadn't notified teachers that students were excused. To protect students there was an appeal process; one school had four hundred appeals of first-semester grades. Many general-track students, however, didn't feel they would be able to make a case that would be accepted.

School policies defining the difference between excused and unexcused absences clearly discriminated against some groups of students. The most blatant of these was the district where an absence, even of one day, had to be supported by a written note from a doctor in order to be considered "excused." This policy sent the message to all parents that their word was suspect. The general-track students were particularly hard hit by this policy because many of their parents could not afford to take them to a doctor even when they had missed several days with the flu. What should have been an excused absence was translated by the district as unexcused.

Even when schools accepted written excuses from parents, some students still encountered problems. Most schools had a deadline within which written notice had to be received from the parent or guardian for an absence to be excused. Unfortunately, many students came from homes where parents could not be relied upon either to write a note or to write it in a timely manner. Where these policies were adhered to strictly—a note received after the deadline was not accepted—students who could least afford the penalties associated with an unexcused absence regularly accrued them. One tenth grader reported that he was going to leave the state and live with his father for the remainder of the academic year since his school's calculations of unexcused absences would result in his failing many of his courses.

Equity and the Enforcement of School Rules

Wehlage and Rutter (1986), using the High School and Beyond data, found that high school graduates did not differ from dropouts in their perceptions of teachers as uncaring or in their evaluation of the disciplinary system as unfair and ineffectual. This study found also that honors, advanced-placement, and general-track students all held very similar views on the ways in which their schools arbitrarily enforced their student conduct code. In fact, a consistent theme running throughout all our data was that "what happens to you in school depends on who you are." Life in our sample high schools was very different for general-track and advanced-placement students, especially in the medium- and low-graduation districts. In these schools students didn't complain about the rules per se, but rather about the unfairness with which they believed they were enforced. An honors student in a low-graduation district high school commented:

> If you play in sports or some teachers like you, you won't get into any trouble at this school. Hugo and I were messing around in the atrium, and if we had been anyone else, they would have thought we were fighting. Even if we said we weren't. And they would have been written up. But no one said anything to us.

A general-track student added additional confirmation to this perception.

> I know someone who got into a fight and nothing happened to him, and another person was horsing around, not exactly fighting, and he got suspended.

Students also reported that the monitoring of movement through the hallways during classes was unevenly enforced. For instance, student leaders and high achievers admitted they were less likely than others to be asked to present hall passes. These students indicated that they frequently cut classes they found boring—and that this was easy for them to do. No one questioned where they were going because of their reputations as high achievers and school leaders. The student government president, in one school, stated, "I'm in good with the administration. And I roam the halls and they [administrators] don't say anything to me." High-achieving students frequently commented on how other students must feel when they were constantly challenged while moving through the hallways during classes.

One of the sharpest distinctions between the high-graduation district and the other two was the extent to which students attending high-graduation district schools knew their schools' rules, knew the consequences for infractions of these rules, and reported that the same consequences befell everyone who broke the rules. Moreover, they did not feel as though they were engaged in a battle with an administration convinced that they were always in the wrong. In contrast, students in the medium- and low-graduation districts reported that their schools were suspicious of their motives and presumed them to be in the wrong.

> If you get a referral they don't listen to your side of the story. Teachers have lied and I've seen this when I've been in a class and then in the office. They say "I don't want to hear it" when a student tries to tell their side of the incident. Every person has their own version and they have a right to say what happened.

> "The teacher is always right." Sometimes they make mistakes—but not according to the school.

The differential responses of the three school districts to student misconduct reflected, in a broader sense, their general orientation to their student population. The high-graduation district took a more proactive or counseling approach and the others a punitive one. An honors student in the low-graduation district stated, "There is no way here you can ever wipe the slate clean. No matter what you do, they always hold it over your head." In contrast, a student at a high-graduation district school talked about the assistant principal in the following terms:

> People are more likely not to get into trouble. They know she's strict, but she's nice . . . She asks if we're making good grades and keeping them up. She doesn't favor people. Not like the assistant principal we had before.

Students interviewed supported the need for rules governing school conduct. In fact, they reserved their harshest criticism for teachers and administrators who did not maintain control. However, this desire for orderliness was counterbalanced by a recognition that some rules were overtly punitive and others were applied differentially to varying groups of students. In schools where this was the case, even the high-achieving students played games with the rules to see how much they could get away with. The implementation of attendance policies can affect directly students' engagement with learning.

DISCUSSION

This study pursued a line of questioning that ideally would be included in any assessment of the impact of new or revised educational policies. The researchers had been asked to investigate the intended and unintended effects on a target population—general-track students—of new regulations designed to ensure that greater numbers of them would persist to graduation. After more than five hundred hours of interviews, it became clear that schools did not have in place any mechanisms for assessing the full impact of these new regulations on students and teachers. Regularly listening to what students and faculty had to say about unforeseen problems or inequities created by new school rules was not an established procedure in any of the six high schools visited.

Yet if we are sincerely interested in school improvement in general, and policies and practices that lead to higher graduation rates in particular, then we need to listen to the voices of those most directly impacted by those policies and practices. Over ten years ago Fred Newmann pointed out that "student involvement-engagement is necessary for learning" (1981, p. 548). Among the measures Newmann proposed to reduce student alienation was participation in the school's policy decisions and management. Our respondents agreed. What may sound like a reasonable requirement on paper (e.g. a minimum GPA in order to participate in extracurricular activities) in practice may act as a disincentive in the very population we are seeking to encourage to bond more strongly with school. Without institutionalizing some procedures for securing student and faculty feedback, we are not likely to notice, for example, when a policy is counterproductive or inequitable, as in the case of absence forgiveness resting upon the ability to produce a doctor's note.

Another means of strengthening the commitment to student graduation is to expand the range of those able to participate in the social life of the school. This is not only an issue of equity (in that general-track students are underrepresented in leadership positions), but also a means to increase the likelihood of engaging the interests and affiliation of students who seek compensation for disappointments or lack of distinction in academic affairs. There was no question in this study that the overwhelming majority of students did not identify with school. As Finn said, the ability to "manipulate participation in school activities may provide a handle through which increased levels of identification may become accessible" (1989, p. 127).

The quality of the experiences at school of general-track students was generally ignored by school officials because such students presented few problems or demands. They did persist in coming to school even though they found their classes boring and their participation in school activities obstructed. These conditions demoralized them, but those who had been selected to be interviewed had made the decision, at least the day they talked to the researchers, to persevere. For those students who had not been selected because they were known to be disgruntled or who could not be found because they had already left the building, there remained the strong possibility that they soon would be gone for good, without anyone at school having become informed about why they chose to leave.

CHAPTER 16

Direction with Discretion: Reading Recovery as an Example of Balancing Top-Down and Bottom-Up Decision Making

Patricia L. Scharer, The Ohio State University at Lima
Nancy C. Zajano, Legislative Office of Education Oversight, Ohio General Assembly

The focus of the previous three chapters was primarily on problems with existing programs. This chapter presents a success story. It is the story of Reading Recovery, a program which was briefly mentioned in chapter 13. Reading Recovery is a tutorial program for first graders at risk of not learning to read. The program was first developed in New Zealand and is now utilized in thirty-seven states in the United States and in several other countries. In this chapter, the authors cite Reading Recovery as a concrete example of the sort of balance between local discretion and top-down direction which is required if teachers are to have a sense of how to proceed while accommodating student idiosyncracy.

The authors gratefully acknowledge the assistance of Sharon Gilbert and Vicki Bell in the development of this chapter.

Educational policy analysts have been begging for a new type of reform strategy which will combine the merits of "top-down" mandates with "bottom-up" teacher discretion (Boyd 1987; McLaughlin 1987; Odden 1987; Soltis 1988). Researchers have argued that external reforms which control the everyday decisions of teachers can do more harm than good (Boyd 1987; Conley 1988; Darling-Hammond 1988; Elmore 1987; McNeil 1988; Wise 1979). Yet leaving all decisions to teachers will not necessarily bring about reform or equity (Murphy 1988; Odden 1987).

The question becomes who shall control what goes on in classrooms? Will teachers control the content and form of instruction that takes place with their students? Will legislators in state houses direct what and how students are taught through state-mandated curriculum, textbooks, and tests? Will administrators feel the need to centralize and control what is taught in each classroom in order to respond to increased demands for accountability?

Some maintain that if control rests outside of the classroom, there are grave consequences for teaching and learning. Attempts to externally legislate learning undermine the essential and legitimate authority relations between teachers and students in the classroom (Elmore 1987; Wise 1979). Elmore argues that an essential quality of the teacher-student relationship is that students give teachers authority to influence their (student) lives because students recognize and accept the teacher's knowledge and the teacher's commitment to student learning. When teachers are seen by students as mere functionaries, carrying out decisions made by someone else, this authority is eroded (Elmore 1987).

Without the essential relationship between students and teachers, instructional content becomes fragmented and reduced to narrow "lists" of facts which teachers lecture from for ease of presentation, students memorize for ease of learning, and schools and states use in multiple-choice tests for ease of assessment and accountability. Teachers do not bring their personal passion for the subject matter to their students; controversial topics are kept out of classroom discussions; the emotional environment of the classroom is flat; teachers and students make a bargain not to disrupt the work lives of the other; and neither is engaged in the educational process (Elmore 1987; Goodlad 1984; McNeil 1988; Powell, Farrar, and Cohen 1985).

If, on the other hand, all curricular and instructional decisions are left to individual teachers, how will all students be guaranteed access to classroom conditions which promote learning? Who ensures that female and male students are treated equitably; that students in the "low" groups receive lessons as carefully planned and implemented as those in the advanced groups; that outmoded methods of teaching are replaced by strategies based on new understandings of student cognition and literacy development (Allington 1991; Murphy, Hallinger, and Lotto 1986; Sadker and Sadker 1984; Stanovich 1986)?

Given that the most important aspect of education is the interaction between teachers and students, and that true and lasting reform has to take place in the classroom (Cohen and Ball 1990; Darling-Hammond 1990; Elmore and McLaughlin 1988; Glickman 1989; McLaughlin 1990; Richardson 1990), what is needed now are policies and programs which support a balance of external pressure and internal autonomy in schooling. Recognizing that equity and excellence concerns will not be realized by a complete reliance on laissez faire classroom and local control, and that excessive centralization and regulation will not bring about the type of student-teacher interactions that further intellectual and emotional growth, a combination of top-down and bottom-up policies is needed.

Such policies would encourage, not undermine, the professional expertise of teachers to wisely make the day-to-day discretionary choices most important to the instruction of students and the improvement of schools. Since legislators and administrators cannot mandate what matters between teachers and students, they need to find the policy and administrative tools which support those who do matter in their exercise of professional judgment (Boyd 1987; Darling-Hammond 1988; Elmore 1983; McLaughlin 1987; Soltis 1988).

The search is on for policies and programs which combine an overall direction for schooling with educator discretion to deal with idiosyncratic student needs and the unique personalities, histories, and conditions which shape the distinctive context of each classroom and school. Odden captures the need for this delicate balance between external direction and teacher discretion: "[T]he administrative trick . . . is to determine the appropriate mix of necessary regulations made at the top with the professional decisions made at the bottom" (1987, p. 234).

READING RECOVERY: TOP-DOWN AND BOTTOM-UP

The Reading Recovery program is offered as an example of an educational program which appropriately balances top-down direction and bottom-up discretion by: (a) providing an overall structure and set of goals; (b) requiring teacher decisions in daily interactions with pupils; and (c) developing teacher capacity to make those decisions through intensive professional development sessions focused on improving teachers' practical reasoning.

Reading Recovery is an intervention program for at-risk first graders supporting accelerated reading progress within a one-on-one tutorial setting. The prescribed procedures provide overall direction for teachers, yet also require teacher decision making before, during, and after each lesson. Although there is a suggested framework for lessons, within each lesson the teacher can, and indeed must, respond to the idiosyncratic nature of learning for each individual child. The fundamental strategy relies upon the teacher's careful observation of the child's reading and writing behaviors. The teacher's next move is based on her analysis of the child's actions during each lesson. In other words, the teacher's decisions are not tightly prescribed but are, instead, based on a constantly increasing knowledge base concerning the individual child's strengths as a reader and writer as the lessons progress.

Reading Recovery procedures were first developed by Dr. Marie Clay, a New Zealand child psychologist interested in early literacy development. Clay's research focused particularly upon children who, in their second year of formal schooling, appeared to be at risk of failing to learn to read. She developed an intervention program of one-on-one, daily thirty-minute tutoring sessions to provide intensive instruction, based upon the individual needs of at-risk children, that would enable them to progress as readers in an accelerated manner. The overall goal of the program is for children to become independent readers with a "self-extending system" (Clay 1991, p. 345) which ensures both the accelerated development of reading behaviors during tutoring and the continued reading progress after the tutoring sessions are ended. Most Reading Recovery children are discontinued from the program after twelve to fifteen weeks of lessons. Typically, Reading Recovery teachers serve four children per half-day. As each child is discontinued, another child enters the program.

Teaching Materials

Unlike the commercially prepared basal textbooks and workbooks used in over 90 percent of today's elementary classrooms and in many remedial programs (Allington 1991; Shannon 1989), the Reading Recovery program is not a set of materials for the teacher to assign sequentially. Basal reading programs typically feature consumable workbooks, anthologies of stories bound together into single texts, and teachers' manuals describing not only the sequence of assignments but the very words the teacher might say.

In contrast, the teaching materials used for Reading Recovery lessons are quite simple: paper, pencils or markers, and books. Rather than workbooks requiring fill-in-the-blank responses from students, Reading Recovery students use a "writing book" made of blank, unlined sheets of paper. Magnetic letters are used occasionally to help students focus on the visual properties of letters and words.

Characteristics of the books read during Reading Recovery lessons also contrast sharply with those found in many basal reading programs. In an effort to make reading easy, most basal materials for young readers depend heavily upon strict vocabulary controls with the easiest stories defined as those with the fewest words. Gradually, words are introduced, incorporated into stories, and repeatedly practiced. Textbook writers find it difficult to write appealing stories with strict vocabulary controls. Consequently, such texts have been criticized for their stilted, unnatural language and uninteresting stories (Goodman et al. 1988; Larrick 1987).

The books used in Reading Recovery lessons, however, do not have strict vocabulary controls. The easiest stories support young readers, not by controlling the number of words, but by providing predictable texts written in natural language patterns with illustrations that assist the reader in making sense of the written words (Peterson 1991). *Toot, Toot* (Wildsmith 1984), for example, includes words not commonly found in preprimer basal texts, but features a repetitive pattern ("'Moo,' said the cow. 'Baa, baa,' said the sheep. 'Woof, woof, woof,' said the dogs."). This is combined with colorful illustrations that clearly identify the animals featured on each page in ways that support the early reader's attempts at reading the book.

Many of the books used in Reading Recovery lessons are small, single-story paperbacks which are interesting for children to read. The books are organized into levels of approximate difficulty to assist the teacher in selecting appropriate texts. Within each level there are numerous titles from which the teacher selects the child's next book. The number of books children read from any level will depend upon the observations the teacher makes of the child's current reading behaviors. Teacher discretion is essential to the choice of the reading material to be used next (in contrast to simply moving on to the next story in the basal reader). Furthermore, the teacher's choice of the next book is dependent upon observing the child's moment-to-moment performance as a reader.

The Reading Recovery Lesson

The format of a typical Reading Recovery lesson includes five sequential parts:

1. *Rereading of Familiar Text.* At the beginning of each lesson, the child rereads several familiar stories from previous lessons to develop confidence and fluency as a reader.

2. *Taking a "Running Record."* The child reads the story which was introduced during the previous lesson while the teacher records the child's reading behaviors using a coding system called running records. Daily running records provide documentation of reading behaviors that may be examined within the context of a single lesson and over time to determine the instructional needs of each child.

3. *Writing a Story.* During the writing portion of the lesson, the child verbally composes then writes a message with the help of the teacher. As the message is written, there are many opportunities for the child to closely examine the visual properties of words and the relationships between letters and sounds. The rapid, fluent writing of high-frequency words may be emphasized during this portion of the lesson. The message is read many times as it is written.

4. *Cut-up Story.* The child's message is also written by the teacher on a strip of paper that is cut apart and reassembled by the child. During this activity the child carefully examines the details of print and rereads the message with fluency.

5. *Introduction of the New Book.* Based upon careful observation of the child's reading behaviors during the lesson, the teacher

selects a book for the child to read that is slightly more difficult than previous texts. The teacher introduces the book in ways that will assist the child in reading the text by discussing the plot and illustrations or talking about unfamiliar concepts.

Within this lesson structure the teacher must constantly make decisions regarding how to respond to each child's reading and writing behaviors.

Student-Teacher Interactions During Lessons

We can witness the workings of this combination of program direction and teacher decision making by focusing on three parts of a Reading Recovery lesson. In the first vignette, early in the lesson, Mike is rereading a familiar story, one he has read several times. In the second, we observe Mike's reading of yesterday's new book as his teacher takes a running record. Finally, the teacher selects and introduces Mike's new book.

VIGNETTE ONE

Each page of Mike's familiar small book features a photograph of an animal and patterned text.

MIKE (READING): I like the dog. I like the bird. I like the chicken. I like the rooster.
TEACHER: Which is it, chicken or rooster?
MIKE: Rooster.
TEACHER: How do you know it's rooster?
MIKE: Because I can tell by the red stuff [in the picture].
TEACHER: All right, you can tell by the red on the head. It looks like a rooster. What letter would you expect to see at the beginning of rooster?
Mike: R.
TEACHER: And is there an R there?
MIKE: (Nods his head yes.)
TEACHER: So, not only do you check those pictures, but you check that first letter. Good for you.

As he reads this text, the teacher encourages Mike to monitor his reading by considering the pictures in the book (the red stuff) as well as the visual elements of the print (r at the beginning of "rooster"). Each of the teacher's responses is based upon her observation of the student and requires rapid decision-making skills. Her overall goal is for Mike to become an independent reader with strategies enabling him to know whether he is right or wrong and to problem solve when he encounters unfamiliar words. Within this brief exchange, the teacher is following step one of the Reading Recovery lesson (rereading of familiar text) while making instructional decisions in response to Mike's reading behaviors.

VIGNETTE TWO

During previous lessons, the teacher noted that Mike would occasionally ignore the visual aspects of words during his attempts to reread familiar stories. He might, for example, predict a word by focusing solely on the meaning of the story without checking to see if his prediction was consistent with the letters in the word.

While taking a running record during this lesson, the teacher noticed that Mike consistently skipped the word "my." He read "I love father" and "I love mother" rather than "I love my father" and "I love my mother." Mike's version of the story made sense and was supported by the pictures but demonstrated a lack of attention to print that would have rendered a more accurate reading. Based upon Mike's previous difficulties and his most recent visual omissions, the teacher decided at this moment to use a variety of instructional techniques to encourage Mike to focus on the details of printed words in conjunction with the meaning of the text. Her goal during this part of the lesson is not for Mike to memorize the letters of the word "my," but to help him use the physical properties of the printed words in conjunction with the meaning of the story.

> TEACHER: Mike, find "my" on this page. Read the sentence.
> MIKE (READING): I love . . . [locates the word] right here!
> TEACHER: All right. There is "my." [Turns to the next page.] Where is "my"? Read it again.
> MIKE (READING): I love my sister.
> TEACHER: Where's "my"? "My" begins like Mike, doesn't it. What letter is that?
> MIKE: M.
> TEACHER: I'm going to mix up these [magnetic] letters. Make "my" with these letters. What word did you make?

MIKE: My. Just like in *My Puppy.*
TEACHER: Yes, just like in *My Puppy.* You're right. Good job! What word did you make?
MIKE: My.
TEACHER: My. You said it was like in *My Puppy.* Read *My Puppy.*
MIKE (READING): *My Puppy.* No, my puppy. No, my puppy. No, my puppy. No, my puppy.
TEACHER: Yes, Mike. You really make it sound like that mother is saying, "No, my puppy." Everybody wants that puppy. Read your story from yesterday.
MIKE (READING): My whole family is at home.
TEACHER: Find "my" in your story.

In this portion of the lesson, the teacher responds to Mike's difficulty by giving Mike different ways to examine "my" in isolation as well as within familiar texts: she asks him to identify "my" in a different, yet familiar book; she connects "my" with the first letter of his name; she uses magnetic letters to form "my"; she has him reread a story (*My Puppy,* Cowley 1986) which Mike connects with "my"; and she finds "my" in the story he wrote in his writing book the previous day. Each activity is done quickly and is intended to provide Mike with many opportunities to focus on the details of print.

The teacher uses her observations to help Mike make important connections between what he already knows (his name; other familiar books; what he wrote yesterday) and what he needs to know regarding the word "my." Her decisions, then, are not based upon a generalized scope and sequence chart or predeveloped word list, but on the specific needs of *this* student at *this* moment in *this* context.

VIGNETTE THREE

During the final step of the lesson (introduction of the new book), the teacher must choose a new book for the student to read. Clay provides specific criteria for Reading Recovery teachers to use when selecting an appropriate new story.

> Choose the reading book very carefully. First off take meaning and language into account. Then from the possible texts select one that is well within the child's control, uses words and letters he knows or can get to using his present strategies. There should

be a minimum of new things to learn if the teaching goal is the integration of all these aspects of the task. (1979a, p. 68)

Since Reading Recovery books are leveled according to characteristics of the text rather than tightly sequenced, the selection of the new text is not mandated by a teacher's manual, but is controlled by the teacher. The selection of the new book is usually made before the lesson, but it can be changed based on what the teacher observes during the lesson. To make the selection, the teacher combines her knowledge of the reading process, the available texts, and the child's responses during the lessons. The new book reflects the teacher's attempt to both support and challenge the reader. Texts that are either too difficult or too easy are not suitable selections for the new book.

In this part of the lesson, Mike's teacher uses her knowledge about Mike as a reader and the available stories to select the new story. *I Can Read* (Malcolm 1983) deals with family members with whom Mike is familiar, has predictable qualities similar to the stories Mike has successfully read during previous lessons, and provides Mike with an opportunity to use what he has learned during the lesson. To introduce the new book, the teacher discusses the pictures and the characters' names in order to support Mike's attempt at reading this unfamiliar text.

TEACHER: Your new book is called *I Can Read*. And this little girl is going to tell you about how I can read to all these people in the family. Let's see who she is going to read to. Who do you think this is? [Points to a picture.]

MIKE: Her mom.

TEACHER: Yes. That's one person she can read to. Who else?

MIKE: Dad.

TEACHER: To Dad.

MIKE: Grandma.

TEACHER: It looks like grandma. In this book they call grandma, Nana. Have you ever heard anybody call their grandma, Nana? Sometimes little children who can't say grandma will call her Nana. What letter would you expect to see at the beginning of Nana?

MIKE: N.

TEACHER: Find N. Find Nana. Who do you think she is reading to here?

MIKE: Her sister.

TEACHER: That's another person she says I can read to. Who else?

MIKE: Her teacher?

TEACHER: Yes. Look, you can see all the things in the background [of the picture]. It looks like a classroom, doesn't it?

MIKE: And to myself.

TEACHER: Yes. Myself. Read *I Can Read*.

MIKE (READING): I can read to my mom. I can read to my dad. I can read to Nana. I can read to my sister. I can read to my sister [appeals to the teacher for help].

TEACHER: It could be another sister by the picture. We can't really tell. What letter would you expect to see at the beginning of sister?

MIKE: S.

TEACHER: S. You have checked the picture and you think it might be sister, but there is no s there. What's going to make sense?

MIKE (READING): I can read to my friend.

TEACHER: Could that be her friend? Does that sound right? Yes. Good for you!

MIKE (READING): I can read to myself.

The teacher's focus during this lesson is completely on Mike. The teacher is learning his strengths, weaknesses, and habits as a reader, and his interests, personality, and concerns as a person in order to make decisions about how best to help him learn to read. The idiosyncratic way Mike approaches a story is all important to the pedagogical decisions his teacher makes during each lesson.

The strength of Reading Recovery is its coupling of this concentration on the individual student with the overall direction provided by the lesson framework and the teacher's authority to expertly decide the next instructional move. Program direction and teacher discretion merge to focus on the needs of individual learners. An essential feature of Reading Recovery is its preparation of teachers to make these expert instructional decisions.

PROFESSIONAL DEVELOPMENT

In the previous vignettes, the role of the Reading Recovery teacher is that of an active decision maker, capable of making rapid choices based upon a professional understanding of the reading process, the components of the Reading Recovery lesson, the individual characteristics and capabilities of each young reader, and the materials available for instructional purposes. This role is in stark contrast to that of teachers who are guided exclusively by basal manuals. These teachers are characterized as abdicating such decision making to the writers and publishers of the basal materials (Durkin 1979; Duffy and McIntyre 1982). Such teachers are described as holding a manual "clutched in [their] arms" (Hoffman and O'Neal 1984, p. 143), which is used as a script until it is internalized and routinized over time. With the explicit guide of the basal manual "there is no active decision making going on at this level because there is no uncertainty" (Hoffman and O'Neal 1984, p. 143).

Historically, the use of the basal teachers' manual was particularly important in the first half of this century when teachers were often poorly educated. The extensive use of the teachers' manual was promoted by Gray (cited by Shannon 1989):

> . . . prepared materials are, as a rule, more skillfully organized and are technically superior to those developed daily in classrooms. Because they follow a sequential plan, the chance for so called gaps in learning is greatly reduced. (Gray 1937, pp. 90–91)

Although the level of teacher preparation has risen significantly in recent years, teachers continue to be encouraged to use basal materials by those who argue that teachers do not have "the time, energy, or expertise to develop the types of materials and activities required to meet the goals set by parents and legislators" (McCallum 1988, pp. 205–6).

If teachers are to move beyond the role of a technician monitoring student progress through sequential basal activities to that of a professional decision maker basing decisions upon the needs of individual children, it is necessary to consider ways in which teachers might gain the expertise McCallum contends teachers lack. Peterson proposes that teachers need "time, support, access to new knowledge, and encouragements to learn and develop [their] own knowledge" (1990, p. 295). For Reading Recovery teachers, these needs are met through a year-long professional development program.

The Need for Time

Teachers learn about Reading Recovery through a graduate-level professional development program that lasts an entire school year. In weekly classes held after regular school hours, teachers meet to learn about their role as Reading Recovery teachers. Instructors for the classes (called teacher leaders in the United States) complete an intensive, year-long program in order to teach other teachers about Reading Recovery.

Beginning sessions are typically scheduled in August and focus on learning to use the observational tools Clay recommends for learning what children know about print. When school begins, the new Reading Recovery teachers select four first-grade students who appear to be at risk in the process of learning to read. Through the use of the observational tools they practiced during the August in-service, the teachers begin to learn about each student as a reader. For the rest of the year, the teachers continue to work with individual students during daily thirty-minute lessons and also participate in weekly classes to assist them in making instructional decisions concerning their individual children. Clay encourages teachers to use their observations of children in conjunction with their growing repertoire of strategies discussed in training sessions to

> . . . design a superbly sequenced programme determined by the child's performance, and to make highly skilled decisions moment by moment during the lesson. (Clay 1979a, p. 53)

Time is required in a variety of contexts to learn how to make such "highly skilled decisions." School districts adjust instructional schedules to provide Reading Recovery teachers with time for daily thirty-minute lessons with individual children. In some states, legislatures help fund the tuition needed for graduate classes that are both intensive and extensive. Teachers themselves spend many after-school hours attending classes and preparing course assignments. Preparation for Reading Recovery teachers, then, is not as simple as opening a manual or attending a single in-service session, but requires significant time and financial commitments by administrators, legislators, and teachers.

The Need for Access to New Knowledge

In order to become an effective decision maker, the Reading Recovery teacher must be knowledgeable not only about Reading Recovery procedures, but also about ways to observe and document the specific needs and strengths of the student, and ways to most effectively respond to those observations. New Reading Recovery teachers read Clay's (1979a, 1979b) theoretical works on how children learn language, the relationship of language to reading, and the implications of recent research concerning young readers.

The overall intent of the graduate classes is to provide teachers with a great deal of knowledge about early reading behaviors that will assist them in making decisions within the context of individual Reading Recovery lessons. As their knowledge base increases, Reading Recovery teachers develop their sense of practical reasoning. That is, they provide evidence and theoretical groundings for their moment-to-moment decisions about which instructional move to make next (Rentel and Pinnell 1987). In addition, Reading Recovery teachers report a growing sense of empowerment that they are able to use their knowledge to help children become better readers and also experience a greater degree of respect from colleagues and administrators for their professional abilities (Rinehart and Short 1990).

The professional development sessions for new Reading Recovery teachers are unique in organization as well as duration. Although commonly used teaching techniques such as lecture, recitation, and discussion are sometimes used by teacher leaders, most of the sessions focus on observing a teacher and student during actual Reading Recovery lessons through a one-way glass. The window functions as a mirror in the room where the lesson is being taught but as a window in the adjoining room where the rest of the teachers and the teacher leader are observing during the lesson. A microphone placed close to the mirror enables the voices of the teacher and the child to be heard. During the lesson the teachers and the teacher leader discuss their observations without disrupting the teacher or the child on the other side of the glass.

The use of the one-way mirror facilitates the development of knowledge about children as readers and the role of teachers during Reading Recovery lessons by placing teacher development sessions squarely within the context of an authentic lesson. As the lesson progresses, the teachers observing the lesson are challenged by the teacher leader to closely observe both the teacher and the child and to freely discuss their thoughts and ideas about how the lesson is progressing. Decisions made by the teacher during the lesson are sometimes questioned by the teachers on the other side of the mirror. Such opportunities to critically evaluate instructional decision making during a lesson provide teachers with occasions to clarify emerging notions about how lessons are organized and to examine their own beliefs about the quality of the decisions made by the teacher as the lesson progresses. The role of the teacher leader during this process is to assist teachers in analyzing their observations rather than to provide simple answers to questions or concerns.

For example, in the following vignette, the teachers observing the lesson have noticed that the student appears to be consistently looking at her teacher for confirmation that she is reading correctly. One of the teachers (Sally) has a similar problem with one of her own students and asks the teacher leader about ways to handle these situations.

> SALLY: Would that be a good point to say, "What do you know?" Or try to get the kid to go back and use the picture?
> TEACHER LEADER: And what is your purpose when you say that?
> SALLY: I want the child to figure it out.
> TEACHER LEADER: Is accuracy your concern?
> SALLY: For me, right now, it's not so much accuracy as dependency. I mean, I have one that "plays tennis" [looking back and forth] with me right now. I want him to know the first thing you don't do is look at me. Try something else. I'm trying to break that pattern right now. It makes me wonder if I'm giving too much help.

For Sally, observing another teacher's lesson and talking about her thoughts and concerns provides an opportunity to think reflectively on her own practice and to critically examine not only the decisions being made by the teacher behind the glass, but her own decisions as well.

After the "behind the glass" observation of one or two lessons, a follow-up session is usually held with the teachers who presented the lessons behind the mirror. Questions from teachers on both sides of the glass are thoroughly discussed. It is a time for teachers to integrate theoretical literature, information from lectures and recitations, and their own practice during daily lessons.

In an 1980 analysis of two hundred research studies examining the effectiveness of staff development programs, Joyce and Showers identified five components typically found in effective programs: (1) presentation of theory or description, (2) modeling or demonstration, (3) simulated or actual practice, (4) feedback, and (5) coaching. They concluded, however, that the use of individual components was much less effective than a combination of two or more. All five components are found in the program to support the professional development of Reading Recovery teachers. The first four are most commonly found within the graduate classes. The fifth, however, coaching, takes place during site visits as the teacher leader travels to individual schools to observe lessons by each teacher.

The Need for Support

The organization of the Reading Recovery professional development program supports teachers by providing ample time and opportunity to develop the knowledge required for successful decision making. The program also provides a great deal of support for new Reading Recovery teachers in a variety of ways. Classes are typically small (four to fifteen teachers), enabling teachers to rapidly get to know the teacher leaders and fellow classmates. During the year, a sense of camaraderie develops among the teachers, particularly as each takes a turn teaching behind the glass. Such close observation of a single teacher's practice is not common within education today and demands a level of professionalism that ensures teachers that the risks they are taking will contribute significantly to the knowledge of the group as a whole.

As they study and learn, the teachers also develop a shared vocabulary that is easily understood by other Reading Recovery teachers, but not always understood by casual observers. An administrator, for example, once observed a lesson behind the one-way mirror and remarked that trying to understand the discussion was like listening in on a discussion in a foreign country. Developing a common vocabulary (e.g., "monitoring," "in-the-know," "discontinuing") enables Reading Recovery teachers to talk about their enhanced understanding of their practice in precise and mutually supportive ways.

Additional support is offered during the training year as teacher leaders visit each teacher at least four times. Within the context of the actual school setting, teacher leaders observe each teacher during one or two lessons and provide individual opportunities to reflectively discuss the instructional decisions made during those lessons. Teacher leaders are also available for individual conferences concerning students who are progressing more slowly than expected and to assist the teacher by observing and sometimes teaching the student in question.

Although the support offered to Reading Recovery teachers is most intense during the first year of implementation, the program also maintains continuing contact to assist teachers in their professional growth during subsequent years. Small and large group meetings are organized by the teacher leaders and held several times each year, and site visits continue to be scheduled yearly. Attendance at the yearly three-day Reading Recovery conference is an additional opportunity for teachers to continue to refine their decision-making skills.

Professional development within Reading Recovery offers teachers the chance to gain expertise. With the addition of time, access to new knowledge, and support, teachers can change from being technicians dependent on the basal reader to professionals making expert decisions.

CONCLUSION AND IMPLICATIONS

Reading Recovery is offered as an example of the effective combination of four different ingredients in the current educational reform movement. Top-down direction, in the form of a carefully designed lesson framework based on a particular theoretical understanding of the reading process and the strategies needed by successful readers, is combined with bottom-up discretion, relying on teacher's moment-to-moment observations of the learner and split-second decisions about what instructional move to make next. These attributes combine to focus on the individual student, recognizing that each at-risk learner may be confused about different reading strategies and a lesson aimed at all of them may help none of them. Finally, the program invests deeply in teacher professional development, acknowledging that teachers must develop their capacity for improved practice if they are to improve schools.

The success of Reading Recovery has two important implications for other programs and policies aimed at educational reform. First, there must be a serious investment in the development of teacher capacity to make expert professional judgments in the rapid-fire context of the classroom. The typical "everybody-come-to-the-cafeteria-Wednesday-after-school" in-service must be replaced with intensive instruction in new ways of thinking about and observing student learning, coupled with well-coached practice and ongoing collegial support. This type of professional development is costly and time consuming, but necessary if teachers are to become professional educators rather than just the delivery team for textbooks.

The second implication concerns the development of district- and state-level policies which support the type of teacher-student interaction represented in Reading Recovery. Notice the time to focus solely on one learner; notice the availability of different books to meet the instructional needs of different students; notice the time and opportunity for collegial reflection on what the student is thinking and how best to intervene; notice the expectation that teachers will constantly improve their expertise as facilitators of emerging readers.

These characteristics are rarely found in schools in the United States. Current district and state policies often act on the assumption that if teachers are not with groups of students, they are not working. They may assume that planning time is "free time," without value for instruction. Schools are not structured to enable teachers to develop personal relationships and come to know how individual students attempt to learn. Nor are they organized so that several teachers could simultaneously observe the learning behaviors of a student and confer on how best to help him or her. Currently, time and money for ongoing teacher development make up a minuscule part of the yearly school schedule and budget.

To support teachers interacting with students in new and effective ways, there needs to be a serious reconsideration of how we organize teacher-student time and contact. If what really matters in the reform movement is the nature of the teacher-student interaction, we need to reconsider such current policies as: teachers working alone in classrooms with large numbers of students; dividing the school day into subject-matter periods; and one-shot, short-term in-service sessions. Instead, we must organize schools to enable teachers to focus on the individual characteristics of their students and to support teachers' professional growth through intensive staff development efforts.

In the Shadow of the Excellence Reports: School Restructuring for At-Risk Students

Andrew Gitlin, Frank Margonis, and Heather Brunjes, University of Utah

This chapter reminds us that the direction/discretion balance discussed in chapter 16 in the context of Reading Recovery is a delicate one, particularly when we move from one-on-one tutorial programs like Reading Recovery to building-level programs involving site-based management. The authors of this chapter describe an attempt to restructure a school along site-based management lines. As was noted in chapter 1, site-based management is often lauded as a way to make schools more responsible to the needs of particular at-risk students since it puts decision making in the hands of those who apparently know students best. This chapter reminds us (1) that the decisions over which locals have discretion must be educationally significant and (2) that considerable time is required when decisions must be made by a collective.

The excellence reforms of the 1980s have been followed by school restructuring and at-risk movements. Both trends might be viewed as compensations for the excesses of excellence. While the excellence reform process was notoriously top-down, school restructuring purports to be bottom-up. While the excellence movement focused upon raising standards so students already succeeding in school might do better, recent at-risk reforms concentrate upon preventing the expected failure of students.

The current wisdom in policy-making circles links the goals of school restructuring or site-based decision making with the need to serve at-risk students. The excellence reforms led to the successful passage of laws in state capitols, but such reforms were likely to hurt, not help, students already being failed (National Coalition of Advocates for Children 1985; Shor 1986). Alterations in teaching practices, which might benefit these students, have not resulted from the excellence reforms. Top-down reforms simply are not suited to altering the school practices that most concern the students targeted in at-risk reforms (Odden and Marsh 1988).

Since we believe that local control of school curriculum, instructional approaches, and teachers' responsibilities would improve the success rate of public schools with students presently being failed, we were optimistic about school restructuring programs for so-called at-risk students. Influenced by the literature focusing upon the character of teachers' work, we believed that reforms which improve teachers' working conditions and give teachers greater authority to make fundamental educational decisions would simultaneously serve teachers' and students' interests (Apple 1979; Gitlin 1983; McNeil 1988). Teachers—in consultation with parents, principals, and students of specific communities—would be able to design educational programs tailored to local circumstances and to students' cultural backgrounds.

To examine our assumptions about local control, we decided to study one school's attempt to implement site-based decision making. In particular, we wanted to see if community control would indeed make schools more sensitive to diverse student populations. Unfortunately, in the school we studied, changes in teachers' decision-making authority and teaching practices changed only minimally. As the faculty at the school attempted to implement at-risk reforms, state and district mandates, the intensification of teachers' work, and the partial exclusion of parents operated to restrict the democratic potential of the reforms as well as limit possibilities for altering the relation between schooling and students viewed as being at risk. Understanding why this particular reform effort had such a limited result requires not only a close look at the school studied and its historical relations with the district, but also the literature that links site-based decision making and at-risk students.

SITE-BASED DECISION MAKING AND AT-RISK STUDENTS IN THE POLICY LITERATURE

We begin our story with a review of this literature. While the school restructuring and at-risk movements appear to compensate for the shortcomings of the excellence movement, these current reform movements are, in fact, heavily influenced by both the laws passed and the ideology of excellence established during the excellence reforms. In many districts, laws mandating the use of standardized testing and a core curriculum restrict site-level decision making. And the portrait of so-called at-risk students guiding many reform movements—far from providing a greater sensitivity to diverse student backgrounds—lumps a heterogeneous group of students into one category according to their shared inability to be excellent.

The limitations placed upon local control of schools is apparent in the school restructuring literature. Indeed, there is some evidence that the current popularity of site-based decision making reflects an attempt to find more efficient ways to achieve centrally determined educational goals. For example, the influential governors' report, *Time for Results,* advises that state and local authorities "be explicit about expected levels of academic performance" and then "allow teachers, administrators, and parents to devise ways to meet these levels" (National Governors' Association 1986, p. 39). The governors' recommendation that central authorities determine the goals of educational programs while practitioners develop the means of reaching those goals is commonly echoed in the at-risk literature (see, for example, Committee for Economic Development 1987, pp. 14, 48).

Modest decentralization is prescribed to fully utilize the knowledge and energy of teachers, principals, and parents and to induce their ownership of educational programs without a qualitative shift in control to the community and school. Numerous observers have traced the trend towards site-based decision making to contemporary management principles, which attempt to enlist the aggressive engagement of employees by giving them some autonomy (Conley, Schmidle, and Shedd 1988, pp. 206–61; Swanson 1989, p. 272; Timar 1989, p. 266). Neither democratic nor pluralistic sentiments appear to be guiding the trend towards school restructuring, and the preservation of centralized mandates threatens to make schools less responsive to local needs.

Our concern that site-level decision making might be a managerial technique intended to preserve the authority of top-down decrees heightened as we studied the guiding concept of many reforms, the idea of "at-risk" students. Far from enlarging the realm of acceptable educational objectives and thus compensating for the narrowness of the excellence movement, the assumptions established during the excellence reforms shape the very meaning of at risk.

Two central assumptions of the excellence movement play a pivotal role in defining the meaning of at-risk students. The excellence reports combined economism with a reassertion of a common curriculum. The economism of the excellence movement was blatant: reformers threatened the fall of the United States empire if means of reviving the economy were not found. Individual students were promised upward mobility if they would only improve their performance in math and science (National Commission on Excellence in Education 1983).

The excellence reforms also invoked the need for a standard curriculum, thus reasserting knowledge sanctioned in the Western tradition. Conservatives were highly critical of child-centered pedagogies—what one commentator called "the romantic self-indulgent follies which crippled American education in the 1960s and 1970s" (Uzzell 1984, p. 177). Reported declines in student achievement were blamed on the alleged ascendance of "soft" pedagogies. And reformers sharply criticized Afrocentric curricula and bilingual programs that celebrated students' heritage, culture, and language. (See, for example, Finn and Ravitch 1984; pp. 245–46; Hirsch 1987, pp. xiv–xvi; Twentieth Century Fund Task Force on Federal Elementary and Secondary Education Policy 1983).

The power of the excellence assumptions and institutionalized policies is apparent in the official meaning of the notion at risk. The influence of excellence economism can be found in both the national and individual objectives in the at-risk literature. National concerns shaping the meaning of at risk focus upon increasing the productivity of the workforce while minimizing social expenditures. Students likely to fail "either in school or in life" (Frymier and Gansneder 1989, p. 142) are targeted because such failure is likely to slow the country's growth. "We cannot," according to the nation's governors, "maintain our standard of living or perhaps even our security if we have more incapacitated or underutilized people than our competitors have" (National Governors' Association 1987, p. ix). Reformers reason that, given their present life courses, at-risk students are unlikely to be productive laborers, likely to become welfare recipients, and given worst-case scenarios, could become a large group of disgruntled citizens who would turn to violence (Levin 1990, p. 286; National Governors' Association 1987, p. 38).

Hence, many of the arguments given in favor of at-risk policies focus upon the economic advantages of integrating more citizens into the workforce. Predictions of a contracting workforce have led political leaders to seek ways of tapping pools of workers, specifically African Americans and Latinos, who have been kept out of the economic mainstream (National Governors Association 1986, p. 6; Hudson Institute 1987, p. 114). Numerous authors attempt to demonstrate the economic need for at-risk programs by tabulating the wages and tax revenues lost due to unemployment, noting in a fashion quite true to Horace Mann that "this does not include the billions more for crime control and for welfare, health care, and other social services that this group will cost the nation" (Committee for Economic Development 1987, pp. 3–4; see also: Levin 1990, pp. 286–87; National Governors' Association 1987, pp. 37–38; U.S. Department of Education 1987, p. 5).

For the individual student, the economistic legacy of the excellence movement means that occupational mobility, a decidedly middle-class value, is often assumed to be the supreme educational goal (Ehrenreich 1989; Bellah et al. 1985, pp. 142–51). Reformers commonly pay tribute to the "American dream," that is, the ability to "pursue a satisfying life, reap the benefits of economic prosperity, and partake of the privileges and responsibilities of citizenship" (Committee for Economic Development 1987, p. 1).

The excellence reformers' emphasis upon a standardized curriculum has also shaped the at-risk movement. At-risk reformers need not ask whether the knowledge presented in classrooms includes certain students while excluding others, because the standard curriculum embodies the ideal of excellence—not the traditions of particular groups. Indeed, so called at-risk students are said to be most in need of rigorous academic standards. The reestablished "consensus that schools should teach standards of right and wrong" is also directed toward at-risk students (U.S. Department of Education 1987, p. 3; Hirsch 1987, p. xiv).

With the authority of traditional curricular standards reinstated, students are stereotyped according to their success in school. Extra-school factors are considered only as a means of explaining why students are not accomplishing what excellence reformers set out for them. Little thought needs to be given to adjusting curricula to divergent student backgrounds or developing multiple conceptions of "excellence" as Maxine Greene (1984) had advised, because the out-of-school lives of "at-risk" youth are portrayed in the most dismal terms. For example, the National Commission on Children states that,

> More and more families, overburdened and debilitated by the conditions of their lives, struggle to survive in settings where poverty, unmarried childbearing, absent fathers, unemployment, alienation, and violence are common. Under these circumstances, it is difficult for parents to teach children the value of marriage, steady work, and a healthful lifestyle. Children have few opportunities to acquire the skills, attitudes, and habits that lead to success in school, productive employment, and strong, stable families. They have few models to show them that character, self-discipline, determination, and constructive service are the real substance of life. (National Commission on Children, 1991, p. 4)

Combining the influence of excellence economism and rigid curricular standards into one statement, William Bennett sums up the mainstream approach to at-risk students: "Our faith is that a good education can help children overcome even the most severe effects of poverty, and can provide our children with the traits of character and the shared knowledge and beliefs necessary for personal and economic success" (U.S. Department of Education 1987, Introduction). The underlying vision directing the movement posits a successful student who assimilates Eurocentric ways of thought and feeling via the subject-matter curriculum and whose achievement translates into upward mobility and economic productivity. It's this ideal individual that haunts the at-risk literature, that appears everywhere as an absence. Diverse students are

compared to this ideal and found wanting, and they are characterized by those traits which do not conform to this ideal type.[1]

While the reform literature does not explicitly describe the
ideal student/worker, we can easily recognize the positive characteristics assumed in a sampling of reformers' descriptions of at-risk
students: "Children who are born into poverty or overly stressful
family circumstances often suffer from a wide variety of physical
and emotional problems that can delay normal social and intellectual development or impair their ability to function effectively in
the typical public school setting" (Committee for Economic Development 1987, p. 21). "Home conditions that contribute to being
educationally at-risk include poverty, low educational attainments
of parents, single-parent families, and non-English speaking families" (Levin 1990, p. 284). "Young people who are experiencing
school problems such as chronic truancy, disruptive behavior and
suspensions are among those at-risk. . . . Youth who become teenage parents without the education or skills to support a family also
are at-risk" (National Governors' Association 1987, p. 39).

If these quotes are read for their absences—for the ideal informing the description of at-risk—a portrait emerges of a student
who is middle class or better and English speaking. She or he is
well nourished and from a nuclear family with two well-educated
parents. She or he follows school rules and either abstains from
intercourse or practices safe sex. Starting with this implicit vision
of an individual thought to satisfy current "national needs," policy
makers have *deduced* a characterization of "at-risk" children. The
"problem" is defined by determining which component of the
ideal type a particular group of students is missing. Since the process of thought begins with an assumed ideal and considers individual people only insofar as they do not meet the ideal, we should
not be surprised that the resulting conclusion is a deficit conception.

Thus, the definitions of at-risk students that one finds in the
national policy-making literature groups a diverse population of
students according to their shared failure. "At risk" has become an
adjective characterizing a broad variety of people. Some are
deemed at risk because they have low incomes or live with one
parent; others because they sell drugs. Some are said to be at risk
because they are a minority or their primary language is Spanish;
others because they spend their afternoons without parental super-

vision (see, for example, Frymier and Gansneder 1989, p. 142; Levin 1990, pp. 284–85; National Commission on Children 1991, p. xxv; National Governors' Association 1987, pp. 38–39). The National Governors' Association defines at-risk students according to the one characteristic this varied group is said to share in common, a deficiency in basic skills: "A lack of adequate basic skills— the ability to read, write, compute, and communicate—is the one characteristic that the school dropout, the teenage parent, the criminally involved, and the socially dependent youth typically have in common" (National Governors' Association 1987, p. 39).

The governors' deficit conception of at-risk students is of doubtful educational value. Students of significantly different characteristics are grouped together in accordance with their failure to achieve educational excellence. The specific reasons for specific students' failures are ignored. If, as many people have argued, there is a mismatch between the culture of students' homes and the culture of the school, the concept at-risk will only obscure the problem (see, for example, Heath, 1983). Or if, as many other researchers have suggested, particular students are doing poorly because they consider the schools a threat to their cultural identity, the concept at risk will only indicate that students are failing (see, for example, Ogbu 1978; Dehyle 1991). Policy makers' tendency to define at-risk students according to their shared failure suggests that mainstream at-risk reforms are unlikely to be built around the specific cultures of the students in question.

SITE-BASED DECISION MAKING AND AT-RISK STUDENTS: A CASE STUDY

While we were suspicious of the national trends in policy making, such movements do not predetermine the character reforms taking place in particular schools. Some districts have significantly altered teachers' authority and the students' educational experiences through the school restructuring movement (Timar 1989). However, the trends in the national policy-making literature which we found most problematic had an unmistakable influence on the site-based reforms that we studied. The centralized state and district policies played a fundamental role in shaping the reform process. The curriculum content was not altered by the reforms. A strong district role led teachers to propose modest reforms in keeping with the mandated curriculum, while other teachers withdrew from the reform process altogether.

The use of the category at-risk served to blur important distinctions between diverse groups of students, leading to the assumption, for example, that cooperative learning is good for at-risk students. The reforms we observed allowed for no distinctions between Anglo low-income students and Tongan students, or girls and boys, while our data indicated that these groups had significantly different relations to the school. Although site-based decision making includes parental input, the parents at the school we studied did not have sufficient influence in the reforms to make the school program more responsive to their children.

Methods

We embarked upon a two-year study of the site-based reforms targeting so-called at-risk students at an elementary school, which we will call Yellowtail, to determine whether school restructuring promised to make the curriculum more supportive of these students. Yellowtail is a Chapter 1 school, located in a moderately sized western United States city, with a population of approximately six hundred students, a high proportion of whom are living below the poverty level. Many of the students are considered to be at risk based on determinations made with Chapter 1 assessment criteria. Parents often have several jobs, little time to attend school functions, and move in and out of the community based on economic need.

To trace the process of reform we interviewed all the people who were influential in conceiving, administering, and planning the Yellowtail reforms. We conducted semistructured interviews with the superintendent and assistant superintendent instrumental in supporting the reforms in, what shall be called, "Valley" District. We also interviewed the principal who implemented the program in her school. These extensive interviews focused upon three types of questions: the individual's understanding of the Yellowtail reforms, their interpretation of the program's essential features, and their role in the process of reform.

Because the site-based reforms at Yellowtail depended upon coordinated efforts by parents, teachers, and administrators, we sent out questionnaires to a sample of seventy-five parents, to all the teachers, and to the principal. These questionnaires primarily addressed three types of questions: the person's understanding of the reform, the role they played in the decision to adopt the program, and their attitude toward the school and others involved in the reform.

All students from the fourth, fifth, and sixth grades were asked to fill out multiple-choice questionnaires designed to gauge their feelings about the teacher and students in their class. These questionnaires were analyzed using Factor Analysis and Discriminant Analysis.

To trace the steps whereby the Yellowtail faculty translated their understanding of the reform into specific practices, we followed all the events related to the implementation of the reform. Specifically, we attended and took extensive field notes at all the faculty meetings and subcommittee meetings where the reform was discussed, and we collected all the documents from those meetings. Further, we observed classroom practice two half-days per week for fifteen weeks. For each observation, extensive field notes were taken and informal interviews were conducted to get teachers' and students' views on the lessons observed.

As we collected data, the three of us read and discussed interview transcripts, questionnaire responses, and field notes. We attempted to integrate understanding gained from administrators with the perspectives voiced by teachers, students, and parents. When we disagreed, we either discussed the matter until agreement was reached, or we threw out analyses upon which agreement could not be reached.

District-School Relations

The division of labor between centralized authorities and the school recommended in *Time for Results* accorded well with the vision articulated by Valley District's superintendent. The superintendent favored site-based decision making because it gave schools "maximum flexibility, with respect to the means of inducing learning and achieving learning objectives, while also providing great accountability for results" (Superintendent, interview 1989). Site-based decision making, therefore, enhances school accountability while leaving the district's role in place.

> There are some givens. There is the state core [curriculum], there are district objectives. How they [schools] get to those objectives, that would be up to them . . . the board felt secure moving to

site-based as long as there was some assessment and some accountability. (Assistant Superintendent, interview 1989)

In the area of curriculum, for example, the "district-wide curriculum committees identify state and district core learning objectives and develop assessment instruments to monitor student progress" (School-Based Management Document 1988). Site-based decision making then takes place within these boundaries. The schools have the option to develop materials themselves that are better than any available from publishers, but they must do so with the understanding that they are responsible for teaching the core objectives and will be responsible for any district-wide assessment of student progress (School-Based Management Document 1988).

Local decision making within these boundaries was encouraged. However, this increase in administrative responsibilities and accountability was not accompanied by a reduction in teachers' and administrators' already burdensome workloads. Instead, teachers were urged to find creative ways to operate within their current work structure.

[One way is to use] the ten contract days that are non-teaching. Then another way is using career ladder money to pay for some committee work. They can also use some money, in unusual circumstances, to hire substitutes. (Assistant Superintendent, interview 1989)

In contrast to district administrators, the principal at Yellowtail had an expansive conception of the possibilities of site-based decision making. In her view, a site-based program "can be whatever we want it to be, and, for me, that is very exciting" (Principal, interview 1989). The principal did worry, however, that the authority of the Yellowtail faculty would be compromised by the never-ending stream of requirements handed down from the district office. She complained of recent district actions, saying, "The words are site-based—but I don't know that the actions of the District are site-based—and that's a real dilemma for us at the school" (interview 1989). In contrast to the district's position, the principal wanted local schools to make nearly all educational decisions. She mused, "I suppose, in the ideal, there wouldn't be anything the school couldn't decide upon if you had enough help and enough time and expertise" (interview 1989).

The Reform Process

The Yellowtail teachers shared the principal's frustration with the authority of the district, and showed their dissatisfaction in a number of different ways: some stated their distrust, others took a cynical attitude towards reform, and some became disengaged from the process of reform altogether. Such reactions, however, did not prevent a committed core of teachers from launching ahead with plans of reform. Once district office approval for pursuing the at-risk reforms at Yellowtail had been received, the faculty voted to pursue the reform and immediately began working on a mission statement outlining the goals of the school.

The question posed by the principal at the first full faculty meeting was, "Are there central issues [of concern] that we can do something about?" As the discussion proceeded, it became obvious that teachers' perceptions of the school-district relationship composed a formidable obstacle to identifying these issues. The teachers did not expect the district to let them determine their own agenda; they suspected that their goals would have to be modified to fit within district guidelines. Were they to proceed with their designated goals, the teachers thought their decisions might be reversed at any time and replaced by district programs (faculty meeting, observation 1989). With this sort of distrust expressed frequently, it was not surprising that the goals the teachers developed were modest and self-protective. For example, they initially identified the following issues of concern:

1. Everyone has a job that creates work for others (this is a not-so-subtle assault on those with "career ladder positions," [the name for Valley District's merit pay program])
2. Too many meetings
3. Machines don't work (copying, etc.) and the work room doesn't function

After a second meeting which focused on areas of stress, a smaller group of teachers, personally selected by the principal, started work anew on the mission statement. This hand-picked group had far fewer critical comments about the district and other teachers (e.g. those holding career ladder positions) and instead focused on the development of goal statements. A statement broader in scope and more clearly directed at students and school policy was constructed:

1. Children's work should be relevant to real life
2. Fifteen-minute silent, sustained reading should be part of school day
3. More emphasis on social skills
4. Unified school discipline policy
5. Cross-aged tutoring
6. Make goals clear to parents

The site-based committee continued to work on the mission statement over the next few weeks. Specifically, this committee focused on defining goals in the area of life skills and academic skills. Eventually, they determined three broad goals:

1. Each year academic growth will be increased so that students are on grade level by third and sixth grades.
2. Students will learn to use life skills, such as constructive decision making and effective communication, which promote dealing with problems appropriately, positive self-image, responsibility, independence, and growth.
3. Parents and community will be involved in supporting and developing academic growth and life skills for each student.

To achieve these goals, the school decided to start with the following types of intervention:

1. Develop a tracking system in math so that teachers can know what skills students have mastered and where they are at in terms of grade-level standards. Purchase manipulatives in math.
2. Introduce, where possible, cooperative learning approaches into curricular areas.
3. Involve parents in school—specifically helping their children with homework.
4. Where possible, begin a "whole language" program.

The site-based committee shared these goals and strategies with the entire faculty, and the principal asked the faculty to accept the goals with a consensus vote. Although there was a great deal of discussion on the exact wording of the goals, most teachers favored the proposal. Several, especially those in the lower elementary grades, felt the mission statement did not speak to the needs of young children. At first, one teacher refused to go along with the mission statement, but after some tense moments the faculty as a whole decided to adopt the mission statement (planning meeting, observation 1989).

At this point each faculty member chose what area they wanted to work on and began to pursue that goal in the classroom. A math group explored incorporatng manipulatives into the instructional program, meetings were set up with parents, and one of the senior teachers discussed ways to develop a skill-tracking system. The university also played a role at this time. Specifically, two professors were asked to give two- to three-hour workshops, one on math and the other on cooperative learning.

Reform at the Chalkface

At the level of practice, the major impact of the reform effort during the first two years was the introduction of cooperative learning strategies into the classroom. Yellowtail employed Robert Slavin's (1990) model of cooperative learning, which involves heterogeneous grouping so that more-able students help those who need assistance. To facilitate implementation of cooperative learning, as mentioned, the teachers received a three-hour workshop on it from a university faculty member who was knowledgeable about the process. After this workshop, some teachers began to experiment with the process in their classrooms.

The paucity of staff development support—namely, having only one in-service—in the process of implementing cooperative learning helps explain the erratic use of the method in classes. Indeed, given the inadequate support, it's impressive that several teachers were able to implement a cooperative learning program that was beginning to make a difference for some students. Many teachers, however, were not using cooperative learning at all, and those who did generally utilized this approach only a few times a week in nonacademic areas.

Teachers we observed and informally interviewed for the most part followed Slavin's standard cooperative learning procedures using tangible reinforcers and competition between groups to motivate learning. In certain cases the competition seemed healthy and motivated students to work hard and lend a helping hand to those who were struggling to do the assignment. In one math class, for example, where average-achieving students were grouped with bilingual students and students who were low achieving, the higher-achieving students took time to explain the math process to the struggling members of their team in a caring and patient way. In contrast to the regular teacher-led classroom, these students received more attention with less wait time. The students doing the "teaching" were learning the process more thoroughly by articulating it to others. Further, the cooperation between students appeared to encourage an appreciation of differences between cultural groups.

However, the implementation of cooperative learning rarely altered the basic authority structure of the classroom; most classrooms, even classes where students worked fairly well together, were still teacher directed and controlled. And in some cases, the emphasis on competition transformed the cooperative part of the activity into a facade and created anxiety and anger among the students:

> The students are working with math manipulatives in their cooperative groups. Groups are set against each other in a race to see who can finish first. The winning group receives a "funny money" bonus of $5, all the other groups receive $1 for getting the answer right. Individuals in each group press each other to perform quickly and correctly. As the activity progresses, a dominant child emerges and takes over the problem solving. The other team members are excluded but seem to concede leadership to the more aggressive member. Groups seem to be falling into hard angry feelings. (observation 1990)

When used in "pull-out" classes, where students thought to have special needs are pulled out of the regular classroom, cooperative learning for the most part didn't make a difference. In one classroom, for example, the struggle to get the students to agree on teams and work together appeared to be such a burden for the teacher that often the cooperative process got no further than allowing students to sit together but work independently (observation 1990). When these students returned to their regular class-room they often were not actively engaged in the cooperative learning occurring there.

> While the majority of students are diagramming sentences as part of a cooperative language lesson, the two Latino students who have just returned from the E.S.L. classroom are silently working from their math books. The teacher does not seem to expect them to participate nor are they ever acknowledged. (observation 1989)

In a few pull-out classes, however, the cooperative learning process was rich and enabled groups of students to actively engage in their learning.

> The teacher has designated student experts within each team to teach the other students a concept which they are cooperatively working to learn. Each student has a chance to be an "expert." They are interacting with each other in a warm and helping way and the children seem to feel knowledgeable and important helping one another learn. (observation 1990)

In summary, cooperative learning at this beginning stage appeared at best to have had an uneven effect on the school. In a few classrooms, remarkable changes had begun to take place that have the potential to alter the success of students by challenging the competitive, individualistic curriculum that many have argued is unsuited to building on the strengths of some minority and working-class students (see, for example, Connell et al. 1982; Weis 1985). In most situations, however, the cooperative learning process being implemented became a brief interlude that did not challenge the authoritarian learning structure typical of teacher-directed classrooms. Instruction also remained competitive and, in a few classrooms, the cooperative learning process seemed to cause further labeling and differentiation of minority and poor students, which led to anger and frustration rather than accelerated learning.

Reflections on Site-Based Decision Making and "At-Risk" Students

While local control of school curricula and instructional practices would, in our opinion, make it so teachers could better adapt school activities to the specific needs of particular student populations, the reforms at Yellowtail did not involve substantive local control and, as a consequence, did not allow the development of an educational program tailored to the specific needs of diverse student groups. As some of the teachers' work literature (for example, McNeil 1988) would lead us to predict, state and district restrictions on Yellowtail teachers' authority to develop and implement educational programs translated into definite instructional results. In keeping with the excellence emphasis upon a standard curriculum, the content of the curriculum at Yellowtail remained unchanged, thus neglecting one of the means schools have of connecting with students who are not presently engaged by classroom activities. Classroom teaching methods were changed to a degree, but even here, the limitations on teachers' authority and time militated against a significant change in teaching practices.

With Yellowtail's flexibility limited by state and district policies, the targeting of so-called at-risk students justified a single instructional approach with a broad diversity of students. The set curriculum and cooperative learning were deemed appropriate for all "at-risk" students, as if any instructional approach would be equally helpful for the quite different groups of students to be found at Yellowtail. And the potential for site-based decision making to allow for meaningful relations between teachers and parents, informing the school's instructional practices, was not realized.

Limits on Site-Level Decision Making

In the Yellowtail reforms, most teachers felt little "ownership" of or commitment to the reform effort; and parents played a very limited role in decision making. Instead, a dedicated but small core of teachers along with an ambitious and open principal seemed to forge ahead independently of the general school community. This restricted participation is partly explained by Yellowtail's relations to the district office.

Because the district controls resources and determines in large measure the policies schools must follow, it sets the parameters for the relation between the schools and the district. Within these parameters, power struggles occur, which in certain instances, lead the superintendent to redistribute resources and authority. For example, the superintendent notes that:

> When I came to [Valley] the tradition of shared governance had been in effect for about eleven years . . . the focus was at the school level with a relatively weak central office . . . . Accountability was defined as everybody setting a couple of goals and then at the end of the year each person deciding whether he or she had met them. So in my first two or three years there was a lot of district-wide effort. But there was a backlash because for years schools had not been used to much direction and leadership from the district office. At the same time we were closing [a school] . . . . It was a time of very high conflict and difficulty and . . . so that was one reason that we got launched on a site-based decision-making study. (Superintendent, interview 1989)

While authority relations between the district office and schools are made and remade through human agency, the shifting balance of power rarely alters the basic hierarchy. The conflict surrounding the closing of a school referred to by the superintendent, for example, resulted in the decision to implement site-based decision making; it did not challenge district authority to make this type of decision, to set the guidelines for the process, or to distribute the resources. Instead, simple forms of control, where mandates from the central office allowed no choice at the school level, were replaced with bureaucratic rules that determined the parameters in which decisions could be made (Edwards 1979). School faculties now had increased choices, but policy requirements, such as the core curriculum and centrally mandated assessment devices, maintained the institutional hierarchy. Site-based decision making thus involved more hidden and possibly more powerful forms of control. Site-level meetings gave teachers, parents, and the principal the illusion of greater autonomy while, in actuality, decision making was tightly coupled to performance-based outcomes. Rules and regulations bound teachers in the way mandates did previously.

With the rules of site-based decision making set in place, district administrators and the Yellowtail faculty struggled for control within this structure. From the superintendent's point of view, Yellowtail's decision making needed to be kept within the established limits of site-based decision making to

> . . . avoid a return to days in which there was a loose federation with each school doing their own thing; some doing good things, and, at least from my point of view, some doing not so good

things and no particular consequences either way. (Superintendent, interview 1989)

Yellowtail's reforms, however, required a more dramatic shift in resources than was possible under the established site-based policies. Teachers needed the resources and authority to allocate significant amounts of time to learning difficult new teaching methods (whole language and cooperative learning) and developing new curricula. Yellowtail was expected to implement these significant changes with few additional resources and within the existing curriculum and testing policies. The hierarchical structure between district and school limited the implementation of Yellowtail's reforms and reinforced teachers' negative beliefs about the district.

At the first meeting called to discuss the reforms at Yellowtail, teachers' distrust of the district surfaced quickly. Teachers worried that the initiative would be accepted merely as one more recommendation that would be underfunded or lose support abruptly (planning meeting, observation 1989). Such distrust was reinforced as the district continued to make centralized decisions over matters that might have easily been turned over to schools. Because of this distrust, many teachers did not fully participate in the reform process, while others withdrew from the effort altogether. Those who participated approached the reform effort, at least initially, in a self-protective manner. The first draft of Yellowtail's mission statement identified activities and goals that would make teachers' work easier.

Believing they had already made significant shifts toward site-level decision making, district administrators did not appropriate further resources or grant greater decision-making authority to the Yellowtail faculty. On the other hand, many Yellowtail teachers, long distrustful of district policies and well aware of the structural limits to their authority, viewed the reform effort as another disguised attempt to further intensify their work without adequate support. They tended to withdraw from the reform, to limit its scope, or to simply go through the motions. Teachers' resistance to district authority served, paradoxically, to limit their own participation and to reinforce district administrators' belief that educational reform depends upon leadership from the central office (Superintendent, interview 1989). In the process, the possibility for significant school change was limited.

For example, in designing their math goals, the Yellowtail faculty adopted an approach that was structured by the state core curriculum. Teachers limited their efforts to devising a tracking system which would monitor student progress on the predetermined state objectives. These objectives, at least in this case, acted to limit school change to a consideration of educational means.

Likewise, mandated standardized tests limited the degree to which teachers could alter the curriculum. A survey of teachers' views, for example, indicates that such tests operate as constraints, by focusing class time on tested rather than untested material, decreasing the amount of writing assigned, and emphasizing the coverage of material (Darling-Hammond 1985, p. 209). The implicit goals embedded in the tests are thus likely to shape identified aims and the choice of interventions used in the classroom, thereby constraining the range of decision making and potential changes taking place at the school site.

A combination of too few resources, too little time, and too little commitment to the reform process help explain the approach taken towards cooperative learning in many classrooms. The intense nature of teachers' work made critical reflection on current beliefs and examination of the consistency between school goals and practices nearly impossible. The shortage of time for teachers to reflect on their beliefs played a particularly important role in shaping the reform. For most teachers, the brief in-service on cooperative learning was insufficient to problematize their existing understanding of teaching. Teachers viewed cooperative learning as one more method, without considering how this method might fit within a general set of established goals and aims. As a consequence, teachers tended to integrate cooperative learning into an established framework formed by many years of experience and the rigors of large classes with mandated homogeneous grouping. Most cooperative learning lessons, as a result, maintained the traditional teacher-to-student interaction. While this is not a problem in itself, there is some evidence that this trend toward supporting the status quo had more to do with the teachers' underdeveloped view of the nature of cooperative learning, rather than a firm commitment to traditional teacher-student relations. In one meeting for example, a teacher described cooperative learning as a "peer tutoring" system—something she said they had been doing for a long time (site-based meeting, observation 1989). No member of the faculty appeared to have problems with collapsing a novel proposal into an already existing practice. Cooperative learning, in general, was remade in accordance with teachers' already existing strategies. Such an outcome was predictable given the overburdened schedules of teachers and the limited staff support received at Yellowtail.

"At-Risk" Students and a Standard Curriculum

The category at-risk was central to defining the nature of reform at Yellowtail. In practice, this category served a function demarcated in the national policy literature, highlighting students who are unlikely to assimilate the subject-matter curriculum and to become productive workers. At-risk did not identify the distinctive character of students' cultural backgrounds, thus challenging the relevance of a standard curriculum. Yellowtail students and their parents referred to themselves as "Mexican," "Tongan," or "Navajo," while the category "at risk" groups students and their parents according to their shared failure in the system, not according to their cultural background. As a result, the recommended instructional processes, cooperative learning and whole language, were thought to be appropriate a priori for *all* students regardless of their diverse backgrounds.

One of the limits of treating students from different ethnic backgrounds in the same manner became clear in the student questionnaires. Our analysis of these questionnaires indicates that students of different ethnic backgrounds had significantly different relations to the Yellowtail faculty. Students of color thought they worked significantly harder than white students but also thought they were expected to do much less by their teachers.[2] Lumping ethnically diverse groups of students into an apparently homogeneous group of at-risk students neglects the way race influences the relation between students and the school, creating specific needs and problems for particular groups (Fine 1989; Ogbu 1987).

The category "at-risk" likewise obscures important differences between males and females. Cooperative learning, for example, may encourage gender stereotypes where boys lead the group process and girls act as recorders or secretaries. While we do not have any systematic data on this issue, our observation notes indicate that boys took the lead in cooperative learning activities far more often than girls. At-risk in this case acts as a gender-neutral category that washes out important differences between girls and boys, leaving the whole issue of patriarchy outside the scope of the reform.

Ironically, even the needs of low-achieving students at Yellowtail may have been neglected by the assumption that a standard curriculum and cooperative learning would aid all "at-risk" students. While processes such as cooperative learning and whole language have the potential to significantly change educational content, acceptance of the standard curriculum reduces these processes to nothing more than efficient methods of instruction. At Yellowtail, cooperative learning and whole language were viewed as instructional techniques more than as encompassing philosophies that alter both process and content. Not surprisingly, the reforms at Yellowtail did little to make schooling more relevant to students. Because our student questionnaire revealed that low-achieving students were much more likely than high-achieving students to consider school lessons irrelevant to their lives,[3] this constrained interpretation of cooperative learning and whole language neglected one of the basic needs of low-achieving students at Yellowtail: to make the curriculum relevant to their lives outside school.

Parental Participation

While the guiding category of the reform and acceptance of traditional course content were not responsive to the diverse character of students, the provision of parental and teacher involvement promised to build cultural sensitivity into the decision-making process. But, parental input at Yellowtail did not have an important role in the school-based reforms. As previously noted, parents played a very small part in the reform process; only a few parents were invited to attend the planning meetings, and those who were invited attended only sporadically. The Yellowtail faculty's apparent unwillingness to encourage widespread parent involvement was partly explained by teachers' views of parents. Our questionnaires and observations contained several comments suggesting that parents were thought to care about their kids, but that parents had "little time for their kids" and often "don't have the skills to help them do well in school." Teachers also were quite explicit about the limited role parents should play in the schools. In early planning meetings, for example, they suggested that parents were to help with their children's homework assignments (planning meeting, observation 1989). Similarly, the mission statement notes that parents are to be "involved in *supporting* and *developing* academic growth and life skills for each student" (mission statement 1989). Not surprisingly, parental commitment to and understanding of the reforms appeared difficult to generate. Of the small group of most-active parents, only one-half knew about the reform effort, and no parents played a role in setting the reform goals.

Parents' beliefs and practices, however, are partly explained by structural conditions. As Connell (1982) points out, the inability to move to another school area and the inflexibility of school schedules all play a part in keeping working-class parents out of the school. On the other hand, teachers often view parents critically because their work is so intensified that they have little time to communicate with this group, address special-needs students, or make significant changes in the bureaucratic structure of the schools (Apple 1982). The extra burdens likely to develop if parents were given a role in school governance are simply too great. Structural conditions have encouraged a tense and at times conflictual relation between teachers and parents: teachers view the parents as uncaring and the parents feel disenfranchised from the school.

CONCLUSION

Our review of the relevant literature along with the empirical evidence provided by our case study of Yellowtail school suggest some significant tensions in current attempts to use site-based decision making to alter the nature of schooling and better serve so-called at-risk students. One such tension is that although site-based decision making promises a significant shift of decision making to the local community, it is still structured by assumptions and related practices coming out of the excellence reforms. The result of this tension is a mixed message to the local constituents. On the one hand, local participants expect a significantly greater say, while on the other hand they are expected to follow procedures that standardize teaching practices and are determined in large measure by those at the upper end of the educational hierarchy. It should not come as a surprise, therefore, that teachers, such as those at Yellowtail, may be less than totally enthusiastic about site-based decision making. They may correctly see this reform effort as an attempt to make teachers and others more accountable without providing the resources or the decision-making responsibility necessary to alter the nature of education at their school.

An example of this type of mixed message is evident in a current document on reforms put out by the state in which Valley District resides. This document clearly combines outcome-based education—which among other things is intended to increase student achievement, improve behavior, and help implement the core curriculum—with school restructuring, a form of site-based management.

> [W]hen fully implemented, outcome-based education (OBE) provides instructional philosophy based on learning outcomes, driven by instructional management procedures and delivery systems which enable all students to learn and demonstrate those skills necessary for continued progress. The Shift in Focus adopted by the State Board of Education outlines a hope for school restructuring requiring unprecedented cooperation and teamwork. (Painter 1991, p. 28)

Cooperation and teaming at the school level goes hand in hand with facilitating an outcome-based approach that will likely use a standardized curriculum and give greater weight to the sequence of objectives outlined in the core curriculum.

A second tension is that in an attempt to help those who have been neglected in the excellence reforms, current efforts often combine into one category students who have very different needs and cultural backgrounds. Further, this constructed notion of at risk becomes a deficit model that associates excellence with white middle-class values. By seeing all students who do not thrive in school as at risk, across-the-board teaching practices are recommended without consideration of how they relate to a particular cultural background or specific set of experience.

The popularity of whole language programs for at-risk students provides a good example of the potential limits of implementing across-the-board practices without concern for cultural background. Whole language in many ways is a needed corrective to the overreliance on phonics in the learning of reading and writing. However, as was true of the students at Yellowtail, the educational issue or problem, if you will, for many minority groups is not only learning to read and write, but to see value in their native languages and the way these languages construct meaning

(McLaughlin 1991). Whole language is unlikely to meet these needs unless it is adapted to the particular cultural backgrounds of the students receiving it. In the Yellowtail reforms, the concept "at-risk" justified the limitation of whole language to a set curricular content, limiting the potential effectiveness of a valuable instructional approach.

The deficit view embodied in the notion of at risk also skews the solution to educational problems toward the individual. While we don't want to suggest that so-called at-risk students couldn't benefit from extra support of one sort or another, correcting the almost obscene dropout rate among minorities (see, for example, Deyhle in press; Fine 1991) would require a reliance upon Connell's (1982) position, suggesting that we seek to understand school failure as the result of a relation between schools and their community. The central problematic within this framework focuses upon an alteration of a dysfunctional relationship. School practices are scrutinized in relation to students' cultural backgrounds—neither stands apart. The question associated with "at-risk" students is not only how to get them up to speed on some determined criteria, but also how to examine these criteria and the way they inform a set of practices which may contribute to student failure.

In summary, current efforts to increase local decision making to meet the needs of "at-risk" students are hampered by the legacy of the excellence reforms. Significant change will only occur, in our opinion, if we break completely with the influence of the excellence reform movement. In particular, the need for standardized procedures and practices constrains the possibility for a local decision-making reform effort which significantly refigures the relation between community and school. Finally, while the term "at-risk" may seem different than the outdated term "disadvantaged," unless we move away from a deficit model we will not see how common school practices contribute to the making of student failure.

NOTES

1. From different theoretical perspectives, Foucault (1982) and Poulantzas (1978) argue that the state works to develop a type of subjec-

tivity or individuality that will serve state needs. The concept "at risk" provides a strong example of this tendency.

2.   At Yellowtail, according to our analysis of student questionnaire data, students of color thought they worked harder than white students but were expected to do less by their teachers (approximately $F (1, 217) = 7.146, p < .01$).

3.   Our student questionnaire revealed that low-achieving students were much more likely than high-achieving students to consider school lessons irrelevant to their lives (approximately $F (2, 133) = 7.824, p < .01$).

CHAPTER 18

Emergent Spanish Literacy in a Whole Language Bilingual Classroom

Irene Alicia Serna and Sarah Hudelson, Arizona State University

With this chapter the focus shifts to the classroom level. The emphasis, however, is still on the importance of balancing direction and discretion. Here direction is largely intellectual and ideological; direction comes from a particular philosophical orientation toward bilingual education and from a whole language philosophy of literacy learning. Because philosophies normally are somewhat abstract and, hence, less restricting than rules, regulations, and standard operating procedures, the teachers discussed in this chapter, although constrained somewhat by their philosophical commitments, still have considerable discretion to respond to the particular needs of particular students. Discretion also is enhanced by the whole language movement's philosophical commitment to student-centered teaching. The chapter, in fact, documents how two quite different students—both of whom would be at risk by virtually any criteria currently in use—grew and developed over the course of two years at radically different rates and in somewhat different ways. It is unlikely these differences could have been accommodated in classrooms governed by rules, regulations, and routines.

In many Spanish-English bilingual education programs, a central feature of instruction is initial literacy teaching in Spanish. Bilingual educators who advocate native-language literacy development do so because they believe that children who come to view themselves as readers and writers in their native language naturally come to apply these understandings to their second language, English (Hudelson 1987). Traditionally, Spanish reading and writing have been taught from a part to whole skills orientation, where learners first learn vowels, add on consonants to create syllables, and then move from syllables to words to sentences to paragraphs to stories. In this approach early writing consists basically of copying, manipulating syllables to create words and filling in the blanks in incomplete sentences. Original writing has not had a place until learners have "mastered" standard orthography (Freeman 1988). In many classrooms, this approach to Spanish literacy is still being used (Goldenberg 1990).

However, a significant number of bilingual educators have rejected this part to whole orientation and instead advocate and work from a whole language approach to Spanish literacy (for example, Barrera 1983; Edelsky 1986; Flores et al. 1985; Freeman 1988). One place where such an approach is being utilized is William T. Machan Elementary School, a public school in the Creighton School District in Phoenix, Arizona. Machan's population is about 90 percent Hispanic; about half of the non-native English speakers have been designated limited-English proficient; and over two-thirds of the children have been designated as at risk for school failure. A few years ago many of the Machan teachers, under the leadership of Principal Lynn Davey, decided to move to a whole language philosophy of education, including their bilingual program which utilizes and values Spanish.

Machan's commitment to a whole language philosophy and the utilization and valuing of Spanish influenced us to involve ourselves in the examination and documentation of Spanish-language literacy development at the school. We chose to do this by developing some longitudinal case studies of Spanish-speaking children learning to read and write in Spanish. Since the 1989–90 academic year, therefore, we have spent at least one day a week in selected bilingual classrooms at Machan, both documenting the classroom contexts for literacy and focusing on how specific children are becoming literate in Spanish.

We began by spending some time in two kindergarten rooms, getting to know the children and selecting certain at-risk children for observation and case studies. The Spanish-speaking children selected represent the full range of literacy development (in Spanish) that could be expected in kindergarten classrooms: from those who created stories through pictures to children already writing short sentences in invented spelling; and from those who could neither retell a story from a picture book nor construct an original story to those who were retelling stories from familiar books and had the beginnings of stories in their journals.

On a weekly basis we have worked with the children in whatever classroom activities they were participating in, or we were asked to assist with by the teachers. We have made copies of the writing produced throughout the kindergarten year for each child. We have made audio recordings of each child reading familiar and unfamiliar books, and we have taken notes on what occurred in the classes each time we were there. We have followed the same children, except one who moved away, into bilingual first-grade classrooms. To demonstrate the range of Spanish-language literacy development evidenced by the case study children, two children with widely varying reading and writing abilities have been selected for discussion in this chapter. We begin by summarizing the classroom settings and the instructional strategies in use, and we then move to detailing each child's growth as a reader and writer within the classroom context.

TEACHERS' BACKGROUNDS, LITERACY GOALS, AND TEACHING PRACTICES

The bilingual kindergarten teachers, Ms. E. and Ms. M., were trained in early childhood education. Their classroom environments, curriculum, and instruction reflect an understanding of child development, child-centered programming, and developmentally appropriate practices. Both teachers are bilingual and have an understanding of how young children acquire a second language and develop bilingualism and biliteracy. Philosophically both teachers believe that first language and literacy development will facilitate children's acquisition of English and literacy development in the second language.

The first-grade teachers, Ms. G. and Ms. L., are both certified in elementary education with endorsement in bilingual education and are bilingual. One of the teachers has had extensive experience in early childhood education, having taught in a Montessori school in Spain for several years. The other first-grade teacher is in her second year of teaching and had student taught in a bilingual, primary-grade classroom. Both teachers are pursuing master's degrees in bilingual education and have taken graduate-level courses in second-language literacy development and language arts instruction. Through in-service workshops and collaborative problem solving with the other primary-grade teachers at Machan, these teachers are developing a language arts curriculum based on whole language philosophies. They concur with the kindergarten teachers, whose children they received as first graders, that children should develop as fluent readers and writers of Spanish first, and that literacy abilities in Spanish will be applied to developing literacy in English.

The literacy goals the kindergarten teachers wanted to accomplish included having each child become familiar with books (concept of story and how to read books); enjoy reading familiar books; learn to write meaningful text for multiple purposes, on different topics, and to various audiences; and publish an original story or report in book form. Both first-grade teachers wanted the children to become independent readers and writers, to read for enjoyment and information, to read often, to write for multiple purposes on different topics to different audiences, and to publish original stories and reports. Many different methods were utilized to accomplish these goals.

In both the kindergarten and first-grade classrooms, from the beginning of the year, a variety of children's books (both fiction and nonfiction) in Spanish and English were read to the children daily. From having books read to them, the children gained an understanding of story elements. They learned that print tells the story and that the story can be interpreted from the illustrations. They also became familiar with the story language in familiar and predictable children's literature books, and began to retell the story and/or read books. The children were encouraged to discuss the books read to them, to express their interpretation and appreciation of a book. Frequently, they asked for favorite books to be reread, and took familiar books home to share. During free time they read books alone or with another child. As children became familiar with books and felt confident doing so, they read to the class as the teacher did, usually retelling the story from the illustrations and incorporating much of the story language in their retelling. As the children gained receptive knowledge of English, they understood and responded to books read in English, though the discussions occurred in Spanish about the English text.

Furthermore, in Spanish-language literature studies (Peterson and Eeds 1990), the children discussed elements of stories such as setting, theme, characters' feelings and motivations, and plot. They also shared their individual responses to and interpretations of each piece of literature. Nonfiction texts were used extensively as resources for thematic units in science and social studies, and teachers read aloud from these books. Children dictated stories and observations from their science and social studies projects which were incorporated into classroom charts; the language experience charts were also part of the classroom reading materials available to the children.

Additionally, the first-grade teachers made use of highly predictable big books for reading instruction. Using the same book for at least a week, the teachers would read it many times both to establish familiarity with it and to demonstrate multiple strategies for making sense of text. These strategies included predicting what would happen next in the story, interpreting the story from the illustrations, completing an incomplete sentence based on syntactic and semantic cues, reading ahead to predict an unfamiliar word, and using grapho-phonic information to phonetically analyze a word.

To help the children understand that one of writing's purposes is to communicate a message, the teachers implemented various writing process activities (Calkins 1986; Graves 1983; Harste and Short 1989) which encouraged children to communicate through written language. Through dialogue with a teacher or peer, children organized their thoughts. Then they drew pictures and wrote letters, words, or sentences to describe the depicted idea. Peers helped each other write by identifying letters and letter-sound associations for words. Children gave each other feedback as they developed their stories or reports. Revision, editing, and publishing resulted in final books and charts. Texts produced included classroom messages, notes to each other, letters to other persons, journals, stories, and learning logs for science and social studies projects. Most of the writing that occurred throughout the year in the kindergarten and first-grade classrooms was narrative (in the form of the children's stories) and expository (learning logs and reports providing information and explanations of findings from the topics studied in science and social studies).

CECILIA: BECOMING A FLUENT READER AND WRITER OF SPANISH

Cecilia was born in Mexico. Her family had moved to Phoenix about a year before she started school. The language of her home is Spanish, and Cecilia would often talk about Spanish-language television programs. Her mother had studied to be a teacher in Mexico and expressed interest in Cecilia's academic development. Cecilia was read to at home in Spanish and received encouragement and support from home in terms of her schoolwork.

Cecilia's Kindergarten Experience

Cecilia arrived at Machan at the beginning of the school year. When she first joined the kindergarten class, she was not particularly happy to be there. For the first few days she cried when her parents left her and frequently asked when school would be over. Initially, as Cecilia became accustomed to the school environment, she was more comfortable with adults than with children, and she developed a close attachment to the instructional aide. She developed friendships with children slowly; she was slow to play with other children until January. By the end of the year, however, she had become much more outgoing and could frequently be found in the middle of whatever activity was going on. While Cecilia was reserved with people she did not know, she became quite sociable once she felt at ease with someone. At home she participated in such activities as preparing grocery lists and helping her mother do the shopping. Cecilia has been described by all of those who worked with her as an achiever, as a child who set high standards for herself, as a child who stuck to whatever task she was doing until she completed it to her satisfaction. Cecilia began kindergarten as one of the most academically advanced children.

Development As a Writer in Kindergarten   During the kindergarten year, Cecilia made remarkable progress as a writer, both in terms of the conventionality of her work and in the quality, quantity, and variety of products. Early in the school year (late September and October), when Cecilia wrote in her journal, she created multicolored drawings. If asked a question about her drawings, she generally responded with another drawing or with a string of letters. While she made use of both capital and lowercase letters, the letters did not represent a particular meaning for her. Her meaning was expressed in her drawings.

During November and December, she went through a brief period of sometimes creating lines and circles rather than letters. Additionally, her pictures became more detailed, and gradually more letters appeared to accompany her drawings. Cecilia also briefly utilized a strategy of copying titles of books from the class library or environmental print around the classroom into her journal.

By mid-December, Cecilia started to provide labels for some of the objects in her pictures. To do this, she used invented spelling, making guesses about how words were spelled based on her knowledge of letters and sounds in Spanish. For example, she drew a picture of a fish and labeled the fish *psacad,* her invented version of the Spanish *pescado* (fish). From her earliest inventions, Cecilia used both consonant and vowel sounds in her spellings. Her journal work continued through February, and she moved from writing isolated words to creating sentences that described the central action in whatever picture she had created, as seen in figure 18.1. In her earliest writing many of the sounds Cecilia wrote in Spanish were vowels, which were standardized. The dominance of the vowels in this child's early writings is due in part to the morphophonological structure of the Spanish language, with vowels occurring in each syllable and receiving equal or more stress than consonants; whereas, descriptions of early spellings in English have found consonant and long-vowel sounds written more frequently than short-vowel sounds (Bissex 1980; Chomsky 1979; Dyson 1983, 1986). Within a month and with minor assistance from an adult in slowly saying the words she intended to write, Cecilia was able to hear and represent most sounds in her invented spellings.

In late February, Cecilia moved from working in her journal to creating stories. She brainstormed story topics and decided to write a story about her dog (*Mi perro*). Story writing occupied her for the rest of the year. For her dog story (written through the first of April and summarized here in standard Spanish orthography), she produced a series of facts about her dog and family activities:

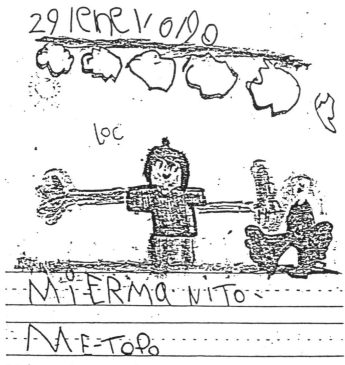

Mi hermanito me topó

(My little brother hit me.)

FIGURE 18.1.

Mi perro estaba corriendo y se me escapó. (My dog was running and he ran away from me.)

Mi perrito andaba conmigo. (My dog was with me.)

Mamá me estaba cuidando mi perro mientras que yo venía de la escuela. (My mother was taking care of my dog until I came home from school.)

Mi perro estaba jugando con mi papá afuera en la noche. (My dog was playing outside in the dark with my father.)

Un carro machucó a mi perro y lo llevé al hospital. (A car struck my dog and I took him to the hospital.)

Mi hermanito y yo estábamos felices porque mi perro salió del hospital. (My brother and I were happy because my dog came home from the hospital.)

Mi hermanito estaba cuidando a mi perro y mi perro estaba jugando con la pelota. (My little brother was watching my dog and my dog was playing with a ball.)

Cuando se me escapó mi perro, lo extrañamos mucho, mi hermanito, mi mamá, mi papá y yo. (When my dog ran away we really missed him, my brother, my mother, my father, and me.)

As her writing progressed, it came closer to standard Spanish in terms of spelling. Cecilia also demonstrated that she understood that there was a difference between the way that she spelled certain words and the standard spelling. When she would ask an adult for assistance, she often commented on differences between her spelling and adult spelling and would change hers to reflect the adult standard. In April, Cecilia figured out how to insert spaces between words, which she did by putting in lines or points. In May, her writing included periods. Just before school ended, she began to use accent marks appropriately.

Cecilia also used writing in several different ways both in and out of school. In addition to her early journal writing and the personal narrative about her dog, Cecilia also wrote an informational piece about the habitats of turtles as part of a science unit; a Mother's Day card; entries in an interactive dialogue journal where she both responded to questions from and asked questions of her teacher; entries she shared about her daily life in a personal journal; and entries in a science log where she observed and recorded the development of a plant. Since Cecilia was the most fluent writer in the class, the children often let her write any group report. For instance, when the group studying *tortugas* (turtles) reported on the species' habitats, Cecilia wrote as her peers dictated that turtles live in the desert, in prairie grasses, and in water (see figure 18.2).

The content of Cecilia's texts is readable because she approximated standard spellings in Spanish phonetically and wrote most words completely. However, she did not rewrite her message, no revisions of content were made, and only a few instances of editing form (grammar or spelling) were evident. In summary, Cecilia wrote as she thought, verbalizing her message as she wrote, producing fairly comprehensible text which could be deciphered by a

Algunas tortugas viven
en la tierra y otros viven
en la agua

(Some turtles live on land and others
live in the water.)

FIGURE 18.2.

fluent Spanish speaker; her purpose was to encode her message and she was not concerned with form.

When Cecilia began to write, she was not always able to read back what she had written, or she would read by approximating what she had written (reading for the meaning) rather than by reading word for word. By April, Cecilia could read her own writing word for word. She was able to sound out each word syllable by syllable and then blend the syllables back into words and the words back into sentences. She was able to read both her own handwriting and the final typed version of her story.

Development As a Reader in Kindergarten   From the beginning of the kindergarten year, Cecilia was very interested in books. She could often be found reading to herself a book that the teacher had read aloud to the class. During read-aloud sessions, Cecilia was attentive, focusing in on the book and often responding verbally to the text with her personal reactions. She attended to books read in both English and Spanish and often verbalized her understanding of English books by responding and commenting in Spanish.

By February, when she read familiar predictable stories such as *Alguien se está comiendo al sol* and *Eres tu mi mamá?*, Cecilia demonstrated not only that she had a clear sense of the story line or plot but also that she was attending closely to the literary language or book talk of the story. She read the story by remembering the plot from the pictures and then utilizing vocabulary specific to the story, for example words such as *picoteando* (pecking), and the sentence structures of the stories. If she substituted one word for another, for example the verb *ver* for *mirar* or the verb *hablar* for *decir,* she was able to use the substituted word in the appropriate places with the correct tense. She also reflected the dialogue in the story by changing her voice to indicate different characters talking. She read with fluency and enjoyment. However, she did not read by looking at the words.

While in April she read a typed version of her own text using the grapho-phonic cues, in May she applied this strategy to both familiar and unfamiliar book. This was the first time that she really focused on the print in books. Her reading became much less fluent than it had previously been, because she was now slowing down and focusing on the grapho-phonemic system, pronouncing each syllable and then blending the syllables together to form words. After she had sounded out everything in the graphic display, she went back and reread the sentences smoothly. Since she had figured out how the code worked, she seemed to need to practice it, even if it took her a very long time to read something. She also knew some words and phrases by sight and these she read fluently.

Summary of Cecilia's Literacy Development at the End of Kindergarten

By the end of kindergarten, Cecilia was well on her way to becoming a proficient reader and writer in Spanish. She understood that writing can serve various purposes and that writers can write to different audiences. She attended to such mechanical aspects of the language as spelling and punctuation, but she did not let concern for these aspects of transcription interfere with expressing her message. She was concerned first about writing her message and then about the standard forms. She knew how to read a book and how the print was arranged on a page, how books are supposed to sound, and how the individual letters and words relate to the telling of stories. She was able to both read and write independently, but she was also interested in working with adults to refine her work. She worked cooperatively with others who viewed her as a good reader and writer and as someone who could help them write and read.

Cecilia's First-Grade Experience

For the first month of school in first grade, Cecilia again cried and said she did not want to go to school, often complaining of head- and stomachaches. A new teacher and a new classroom environment had shaken the confidence of an otherwise socially and academically competent young child. However, she adjusted to her new teacher and classmates and became quite a leader within the group, easily associating with her peers and the adults who worked with her. Cecilia was perceived as a competent learner by her classmates, who often sought her assistance with many projects involving reading and writing. She was often in the company of four girls, three of whom had been her classmates in kindergarten. Her first-grade teacher perceived Cecilia as one of the better readers, an independent writer and learner, who was achieving well academically.

Development As a Writer in First Grade   From the beginning of the year, Cecilia wrote her texts independently and fluently, vocalizing each syllable in a word as she wrote phonetically. She continued to write for various purposes to varied audiences. In writer's workshop she created personal narratives about herself and her family. Throughout the year, these stories became more elaborate in content, more complex syntactically, and more conventional in orthography and in segmentation. Cecilia also utilized a dialogue journal to carry on written conversations with her teacher. By November, she had become a participant in the construction of the weekly classroom newsletter, actually taking dictation from others in the room who utilized her as a scribe because they viewed her as a good writer. Through the remainder of the year, Cecilia produced more fluent and still coherent personal narratives and expository texts. By March, she rewrote her text to expand invented spellings as needed, to revise the content by adding more information, and to edit grammatical and syntactical structures.

Development As a Reader in First Grade   Early in first grade, Cecilia was able to read her own written texts and the language experience charts the teacher produced. Because these were familiar to her, Cecilia read them fluently rather than disfluently as she had at the end of kindergarten when she had used the slow graphophonic decoding strategy when first attending to print. At the end of one semester in first grade, having participated in predictable book activities in her class, Cecilia read familiar texts with fluency and meaning. Her decoding strategies included recalling the story language, reading on, and using linguistic knowledge (syntax and semantics). Her phrase, "*No suena bien,*" (It doesn't sound right) indicated her awareness of using a linguistic strategy to decode. While her early reading in kindergarten was based almost exclusively on a grapho-phonic strategy, Cecilia now used some of the other strategies her teacher had instructed. Cecilia was only reading books which were familiar to her at the end of the fall semester in first grade. These titles included a number of Spanish translations of well-known picture books, such as *Donde viven los monstruos* (*Where the Wild Things Are*) by Maurice Sendak and *La oruga hambriente* (*The Very Hungry Caterpillar*) by Eric Carle, in addition to the predictable big books. During the second semester of first grade, she continued to read a wide variety of more complex Spanish-language children's literature, but she had yet to start to read in English. Cecilia was reading Spanish texts fluently and as she continues to develop in her reading abilities, she will probably begin to read familiar and predictable children's literature books in English.

DIANA: EMERGENT LITERACY IN SPANISH

Diana was born in Guatemala where some of her relatives still live. She comes from a Spanish-speaking home and spoke only Spanish at the time she entered school. Neither of her parents was well educated in Guatemala, and the family is struggling economically in this country. Prior to kindergarten Diana did not have a pre-school experience in Head Start or in a private preschool. The younger sibling of others already at Machan, Diana comes from a family of children who have struggled academically. An older sister and some cousins attend bilingual special-education classes.

Diana's Kindergarten Experience

When Diana entered kindergarten, she was an extremely quiet child, so quiet that the teacher noted that it would be easy to forget that she was there. She appeared confused about school, as though she wasn't sure why she was there and what she was supposed to do. Throughout the year, her style was to hang back and observe what was going on in the classroom rather than participate in an activity. She required a lot of individual attention in terms of repeated explanations about and assistance with whatever the work happened to be. Without this individual assistance she often did not attempt or complete tasks on her own. She also seemed to work better when she was not surrounded by others. Since the presence of a lot of other children distracted her, Diana worked more effectively with one or two other children and/or with the assistance of an adult. Diana began kindergarten as one of the children who had the least familiarity with school-related tasks.

Development As a Writer in Kindergarten   Diana's class began writing in journals at the end of September. Her first entries were multicolored pictures. When asked a question in writing, Diana sometimes responded with letter forms. The early forms looked like *P, T,* and *O.* Later, she began to use forms that looked like *I, E, S,* and *F.* However, these forms did not represent sounds or words. By late October, her journal pages contained multiple lines of letter forms that filled each page. Then in November, the majority of her journal entries contained drawings but no writing. Although the adults were still asking her questions in writing, she did not respond with letter forms. Her drawings continued. Letter strings reappeared in January, but Diana attached meaning to her drawings rather than the letter strings.

In February, Diana's teacher decided to provide her with larger sheets of paper on which to draw and to encourage her to tell stories orally since she was unwilling to write on her own. Because she had more space, her drawings became more complex, and she was willing to dictate stories about what she had drawn. However, from one day to the next, if asked to retell or continue her story, she changed the story. After working with single large sheets of paper, she began to use several sheets of paper per story. This enabled her to separate out the parts of each story and to dictate specifics about each part of the story. She continued to respond to requests to read or retell what she had dictated by adding on or changing the story. However, if an adult began to read her dictation, she could complete the sentences as originally dictated. Thus, she demonstrated that she remembered what she had dictated.

Late in April, Diana told her teacher that she wanted to create her own book, which was something that many of the other children had been doing. She chose to write about an imaginary friend, Erica, and the life that Erica would like to have. Diana worked on this book for more than a month. Some of the events in the story as they were written (but rendered here in standard Spanish orthography) were:

> 5/3/90 La nina grañde se enamoró de su papá. (The big girl loved her father.)

> 5/4/90 La niña vivía con su mamá y el papá quería llevarla a la casa de él. (The girl lived with her mother and the father wanted to take her to his house.) Es el cumpleaños de Erica, tiene cinco años. Ella quería una muñeca. Dijo, "Yo quiero el regalo." Su papá y su tío le dieron el regalo y chocolates. Cuando abrió su regalo encontró una muñeca. La niña tenía sorpressa. Se comio su pastel. (It is Erica's birthday, she is five years old. She wanted a doll. She said, "I want the present." Her father and uncle gave her the present and chocolates. When she opened the present she found a doll. The girl was surprised. She ate her birthday cake.)

> 5/10/90 La niña le regaló una pelota a su papá porque era su cumpleaños. Le dijo a su papá, "Yo te quiero mucho," ye le regalo' una pelota. (The girl gave her father a ball because it was his birthday. She told her father, "I love you very much," and she gave him the ball.)

5/11/90 Y ella ya era grande y le llamó por teléfono a su papá y le dijo que se quería ir a vivir con su papá. (And when she was big she called her father and she told him she wanted to live with him.)

5/17/90 La niña anda llorando porque su mamá fue de compras y no quería llevar niños. Su papa le dijo que se durmiera. (The girl was crying because her mother went to the store and she did not want to take the children. Her father told her to go to sleep.)

5/18/90 Cuando la mamá le dio un chocolate Erica ya no estaba enojada. (When her mother gave her a chocolate Erica wasn't mad anymore.)

5/23/90 La Erica es buena. (Erica is a good person.)

This was the first time Diana generated text which encoded a message by writing some of it herself. In creating the book sometimes she wrote independently and sometimes with assistance from an adult. She began each session by drawing a picture and then articulating a sentence or the sentences she wanted to write. She would then consider the words individually, trying to sound them out and making some guesses about what their beginning sounds were. Since she did not know most of the letters of the alphabet, if no one told her what the correct letter was, she would pick a letter at random from her personal Spanish alphabet chart and write it down. This strategy resulted in sentences that could be read only by someone who had been there during the writing or by Diana herself, who remembered what she had written. But what was significant was that Diana had seen the other children sounding out and finding letters, and she had figured that that was part of what had to be done during writing. She demonstrated awareness that words have sounds represented by letters. She could begin to identify beginning and ending sounds auditorally, but she still needed to learn the visual representations. When rereading this type of text she would tell the story for the picture rather than attend to the print. By May, Diana wrote three words on the next to the last page of her story, "Erica," "mama," and "papa," from memory (see figure 18.3), demonstrating that not all her writing was composed of random letter strings.

Frequently Diana had adults assist her in her writing. When

Cuando la mamá le dio un
chocolate
Erica ya no estaba
enojada.

(When her mother gave her a
chocolate
Erica was not mad anymore.)

FIGURE 18.3.

working with an adult who helped her sound out words, she would ask which letters represented which sounds. When these were pointed out on the alphabet chart, she was able to copy them on her paper. For instance, in figure 18.3, Diana was able to hear and say each sound in *chocolate,* but needed help in identifying each letter on a small Spanish alphabet chart. She also needed assistance in sequencing the syllables in *chocolate* as she wrote each letter sound association. Thus, with the assistance that she began to seek, Diana produced texts with some letter-sound correspondence rather than just random letter strings. Diana also received assistance from adults in the form of shared writing, where an adult (as seen in figure 18.3) would write some of what Diana wanted to represent, sharing the responsibility for transcription with the child.

When she reread her story, Diana retold it by relying on the pictures. She could remember from day to day what she had written, and when she read the final version of her story aloud to the class, she remembered all but one sentence of the story. The story itself was quite sophisticated in that part of it went beyond the usual string of isolated facts to describing the beginning, middle, and ending of an event, and the main character's feelings.

In addition to her personal narrative, Diana was able when working with another child to produce an informational piece of writing about the life cycle of the butterfly. This piece took the form of a book, based on *La oruga hambriente* (*The Very Hungry Caterpillar*) by Eric Carle. Diana produced pictures for the piece but no written text. The other child dictated the text. However, when the children read their book to the rest of the class, Diana was able to alternate with the other child in reading aloud the pages of the book.

By the end of the year Diana also produced pictures and some writing in the learning log that each child kept in connection with a science unit on plants. Diana observed her plant and noted growth and changes. When she wrote without assistance she used letters of the alphabet to express her meaning, but there was no clear sound-symbol relationship between the letters she chose and the text she produced. However, she could read her text to an adult, indicating that she associated a particular meaning with the letters she had produced. Diana also dictated some of her observations, and her pictures recorded the information accurately.

Development as a Reader in Kindergarten At the beginning of the year, Diana did not respond verbally to books read aloud either in Spanish or in English. She was quiet and nonresponsive in the reading circle. As the year progressed, Diana remained quiet in the reading circle, but she began to pick up books on her own and look at them. She became increasingly interested in books. Toward the end of the year, she would frequently find a book that the teacher had read to the class and sit with it, reading it to herself from her memory of what the teacher had read and pointing to the lines of print, moving her finger from left to right.

In May, she read two familiar books, *La oruga hambriente* (*The Very Hungry Caterpillar*) and *Manzano, manzano* (*Apple Tree, Apple Tree*). The first, as mentioned, is a predictable book that describes the life cycle of the butterfly, and the second is a predictable rhyming book about an apple tree bearing fruit. Diana read both of these books by examining the pictures and recalling the text page by page. Her reading was quite accurate, both in terms of the plot and of the language and patterning of the story. In the first book, she remembered that there was a repetition of the pattern *se comió* (he ate), and she used this pattern in her reading, producing a rendition of the text that was close to the text itself: "*se comió una manzana, se comió dos peras, se comió tres uvas, se comió cuatro fresas*" (he ate one apple, he ate two pears, he ate three grapes, he ate four strawberries). The second book used a rhyme scheme which Diana remembered and utilized. In these ways, Diana demonstrated an awareness of the connection between the pictures and particular words, that is, the book talk or literary language of the text.

Also in May, Diana read an unfamiliar book, *José el gran ayudante* (*Herman the Helper*). She was able to construct a story for this unfamiliar book using only the pictures. She demonstrated that she knew that books tell stories and that she could use the pictures to help construct the plot. However, she did not use the written text to assist her in telling the story, nor did she ask what the written text said.

Summary of Diana's Literacy Development at the End of Kindergarten

Diana came into the kindergarten with very little knowledge of reading and writing. She made considerable progress during this year. She was willing to create her own stories, producing both illustrations and written text. While she still needed to learn most of the letter-sound correspondences in Spanish, she understood the function that letters serve, and she was willing to take risks to get a message down on paper as best she could. She was beginning to understand that writers can write for different purposes, and she was becoming more willing to write for different purposes. She had a clear sense of what books were for and of how illustrations and words can work together to produce a story. She demonstrated a sensitivity to the language of stories and was able to remember much of the story language for a familiar, predictable picture book. She knew that the letters (the squiggles on the page) represent the words of the story, indicated by her underlining of the sentences with her finger as she told the story for a familiar, predictable picture book. Diana sought the assistance of teachers in writing but was beginning to be able to work on her own in the generation of pictures, letter strings, and family names. At the end of the year, she still needed continued immersion in Spanish-language literacy and content-area studies so that she could continue to figure out how the written language works and what reading and writing are for, and to write her understandings of content examined in science and social studies projects.

Diana's First-Grade Experience

In first grade Diana was still a reticent child, but she did not look as lost; she knew how to approach the learning tasks. She made friends with two girls who had been in her kindergarten class and chose to work and play with them. With them she was more verbal and outgoing. Diana related well to her teachers and worked with them effectively when they noticed her, but she did not seek out their assistance. Diana appeared comfortable in her new class, but she was still a quiet individual and was sometimes overlooked since she did not seek her teachers' help.

Development As a Writer in First Grade   Diana began the year writing texts which were similar to the texts she had produced in kindergarten, that is, by producing first pictures and then lines of letter strings that had no letter-sound correspondence but to which she attributed meaning. She continued doing this into October.

By the end of October, it became clear that there were significant differences between what Diana could do when she worked with an adult and what she produced when working alone. On October 24, 1990, working by herself, she first produced two lines of letters strings with no letter-sound correspondence (see figure 18.4). When her teacher asked her what she had written, Diana told her a story about going trick or treating for Halloween. With her teacher's assistance in sounding out the words and identifying the letters which represented the sounds, Diana was able to write the sentence, "*Yo ui a W*" (I went to Halloween). The next day Diana completed the story by creating two more pictures and six lines of random letters, which she read as she and her siblings trick or treating, receiving chocolates, and then going to bed. Thus, Diana did attach meaning to each line of text. When asked to practice writing key words from her story, she could not reproduce "Halloween," but could write "trick-or-treat." However, when two other children needed these words for their stories, Diana retrieved her journal, found the page where she had practiced writing them, and read the two words correctly for her peers to copy.

By November, Diana's writing began to reflect some knowledge of sound-letter relationships. For example, on November 15, Diana produced three lines of text which contained invented spellings that were partially interpretable (see figure 18.5). When Diana interpreted the text, it was clear that she had written "*Yo y mi hermano estabamos jugando en el campo*" (My brother and I were playing in the country). Thus, Diana produced several words using invented spellings; however, she was not able to use letter-sound relationships to write the entire sentence. Perhaps if Diana had verbalized as she had written the sentence, as did most of the other case study children, she would have been able to write more than a few words using letter-sound associations.

Since Diana had demonstrated that with assistance she could produce text using some letter-sound correspondences, the adults in the classroom decided that they would no longer accept her production of random letter strings. Therefore, when later that same morning Diana wrote in her science journal the letter string "AebNA" which she read as "*El pescado se cayó del agua y se murió*" (The fish fell out of the water and it died), an adult asked Diana to look for the word *pez* or *pescado* in print within the classroom. She found *peces* labeling the fish food container (with a picture of a fish on it) which she copied onto her page. She used the

Yo *fui a* Halloween.

(I went out on Halloween.)

FIGURE 18.4.

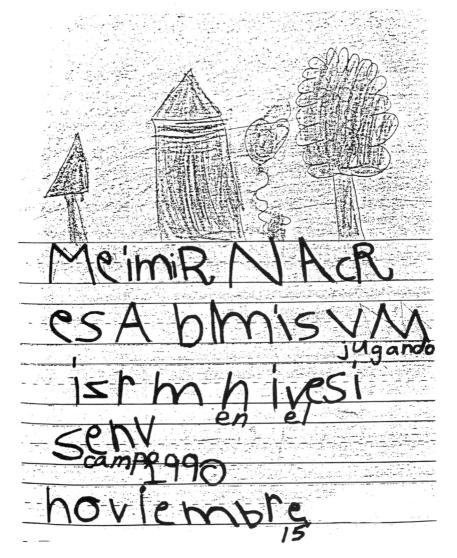

Yo y mi hermano
estabamos jugando
en el campo

(My brother and I
were playing
in the country.)

FIGURE 18.5.

letter name *c* for *se,* copied *cayo,* and the other children helped her spell *agua* as "AUA." In this instance, Diana knew the content of her text and was ready to begin working with other children to sound out words and identify sound-letter associations. Diana appeared to be making progress since with help from an adult and other children she could encode her message using invented spelling.

The adults working with Diana also realized that she had a lot more to tell than she could encode herself. Therefore, a process of shared writing was initiated in which an adult would write most of Diana's story and Diana would write key words. While more complex stories resulted from this strategy, the only written text that Diana was able to read was what she had written herself. Shared writing continued through February. Beginning in March, Diana chose to write personal narratives about events in her family's life. First, Diana wrote a story about her mother's accident in which, with assistance in hearing the sounds within words and identifying the corresponding letters, she encoded a sentence describing the action of each picture. This story was published as a book, and Diana could read both her handwritten (invented spellings) and the typed (standard spelling) versions of the story. In April, she created a story about her grandparents, once again with assistance in analyzing words phonetically (see figure 18.6). Throughout the remainder of the year, adults no longer produced text for Diana but continued to assist her to write alphabetically. In summary, only with assistance could Diana produce invented spellings which were readable, but she could read all her text.

Development As a Reader in First Grade   During the first semester of the school year, when asked to read a familiar book, Diana chose three familiar books, *Sapo y sepo* by Arnold Lobel, *Pájaros en la cabeza* by Laura Fernandez, and *Federico* by Leo Lionni, all books the teacher had read several times. For each book Diana accurately told the story from the illustrations. While she underlined the text with her finger, moving left to right and top to bottom, as she retold the story, she did not maintain voice-print match. While reading *Sapo y sepo,* which had more print on each page than the other two books, Diana read the right page before the left page many times, and even skipped reading some pages.

The only text she actually attended to were the printed words for the sound the bird makes in the illustrations, "*pío, pío, pío*" in *Pájaros en la cabeza*. Thus, just as she had in kindergarten, Diana continued to interpret the story from the illustrations and did not attempt to read the printed text. Again, Diana focused on the whole story, the meaning of the text, rather than attending to the words, the smaller parts of the printed text.

During the second semester of first grade, the adults working with her decided to focus Diana's attention on the print in a familiar book that she frequently chose to tell the story for. Using the highly predictable book *Un cuento curioso de colores* by Joanne and David Wylie, Diana would read along with the teacher while pointing to the individual words in the story. Immediately after the reading, words in each patterned sentence were written on sentence strips and Diana was asked to sequence the words to form the sentences of the story. Diana also created her own set of handwritten word cards which she used to practice reading the words of the story. Color names are a prominent feature of the story, and Diana contextualized these names for herself by writing each name with the corresponding colored marker.

Diana was able to return to the text and read it accurately. She also was successful in reading word for word several highly predictable patterned Spanish readers, where only one word in a sentence is changed and where the illustrations assist the reader in figuring out the change. For example, in the book, *El pastel de cumpleaños* (*The Birthday Cake*), the phrase on the first page reads "*Un pastel rojo*" (a red cake) and the phrase on the second page reads "*Un pastel amarillo*" (a yellow cake). The illustration makes clear the color of each new cake layer as the text progresses. Reading the familiar predictable book and the patterned readers gave Diana some success in reading, although she was still most successful at reading her personally created stories. While phonetic analysis to produce invented spellings made sense in her writing of personal narratives, she did not yet use this strategy for decoding texts other than her own. She relied on syntactic and semantic cues and the illustrations to construct the meaning of the text. At the end of the first grade, Diana was still an emerging reader in Spanish, reading whole texts for meaning, and paying little attention to the grapho-phonic display.

An unknown man came
My brother Panchito
My little sister Cindy and I
were at home
by ourselves. An unknown man came.
We went into the bedroom.
We looked out the window.
It was a friend of my father's.
We opened the door.
The man came in.
He asked for my father.
We told him that my father was
working with my mother.
We asked him his name.
It was my uncle Chepe.
He had put on a mask.
And his children also had on masks.
It was Halloween.

FIGURE 18.6.

MShSe b P m a qu3 Nov Vi em b re 19

Vino un señor desconocido

MI ERMANiTO PANCh HI
TO,

Mi hermanito Cindy y yo

estabamos en la CASA

sditos Vino un señor desconocido

Nosotros furmos al cuarto

Vimos por la ventana

Era un amigo de mi PAPA

Abrimos la puerta

Entró el señor

Pregunto por mi papa

Le dejimos que estaba trabajando

con mi MAMA.

Le preguntamos que era su

nombre

Era mi tía Chepe Se

había puesto una mascara

Y sus hijas también se habían

puesto mascaras

Y era el día de HALOWIN.

DISCUSSION

What do Cecilia and Diana demonstrate about how literacy develops for Spanish-speaking children identified as at risk within the context of a whole language philosophy in a bilingual program? First, their experiences suggest that a whole language perspective, while varying in instructional implementation across classrooms, provided Cecilia and Diana with opportunities to figure out how written language works and what it is for. In these whole language bilingual classrooms children have been able to read and respond to good children's literature; to write various types of texts, for multiple purposes, and to different audiences; and to use their first language and literacy abilities to mediate their learning of meaningful content. The instructional strategies and materials provided in Spanish were not simplified nor did they emphasize isolated skills. The contexts, purposes, and authenticity of the texts read and written allowed the children both to construct their own meaningful texts and to construct meaning from texts written by others. These Spanish-speaking, "at-risk" children came to understand reading and writing by engaging in reading and writing.

Second, Cecilia and Diana demonstrate that there are significant individual differences among children when they enter school. These differences have an effect upon individual rates of development, including how children come to be independent readers and writers. Different children need different amounts of time and support to accomplish literacy. Cecilia and Diana began their kindergarten experiences with different understandings about reading and writing and with different strategies for coping with school. When Cecilia began school, she had been read to frequently at home, and she had experimented with writing at home. She related well to adults and interacted with them easily. In contrast, Diana had not been read to at home; she had few, if any, previous experiences with writing. She was frightened at school, a reality illustrated poignantly by Diana when early in first grade, while walking with Irene Serna one day from the cafeteria, she confided to her, "*Ya no tengo miedo de la escuela*" (I'm not afraid of school anymore). Diana coped with this fear and confusion by withdrawing. She did not seek out others, either children or adults, for companionship or assistance.

Over the course of two years, both children made progress

although they progressed at different rates. By the end of kindergarten, Cecilia had become a reader and writer in the sense that she could make accurate use of grapheme-phoneme relationships both to create her own messages and to construct the meanings of texts that she herself had not created. During first grade, she became a more fluent reader, relying less exclusively on the graphophonic cuing system. She continued to write different kinds of texts for various purposes to varied audiences. She also continued to develop her appreciation for literature in both Spanish and English.

Diana's development was slower than Cecilia's and at times perhaps less consistent, but she did make remarkable progress. During kindergarten she developed a love for books and a sensitivity to the language of stories. As a kindergarten writer, she gradually became willing to create her own texts, employing pictures and strings of letters. She also became willing to seek out the assistance of others who knew more than she did. And it was with this assistance that she became able to produce a very few key words utilizing sound-letter correspondences. In first grade, Diana's literacy continued to emerge slowly. Diana continued to enjoy books and to pay close attention to her teacher's reading of stories. As she wrote a variety of kinds of texts, she gradually learned for herself the sound-letter correspondences she needed to use to represent her text phonetically so that it could be read by other people. She learned the letter names and sound-letter associations through her own writing. She also began to be able to read a few highly predictable texts word for word utilizing the syntactic, semantic, and illustration cues employed by efficient readers. By the end of first grade, reading and writing were no longer a mystery to Diana. While one might wish that she were at the same place as Cecilia at the end of first grade, this is simply not realistic. And to evaluate Diana's achievements by comparing her to Cecilia is also unfair. Each child needs to be considered in light of her own progress.

Third, Cecilia's and Diana's stories make clear that the adoption of a whole language philosophy is not a panacea in terms of equal achievement for all learners. Even when teachers instruct from a paradigm that focuses on meaning and that moves from authentic wholes to parts, not all children will progress at the same rate, nor will all have equal success (just as they would not were the teaching being done from a skills paradigm). But teaching from this paradigm does mean that teachers are taking their cues from the learners and basing their instruction on what the learners demonstrate they know and need to learn, rather than from a set of grade-level objectives or materials created without specific learners in mind. Particularly in the case of someone like Diana, the focus on her individual strengths and needs and the classroom environment that affords her both individualized instructional support and the time she needs to figure out how written language works have been critical to her progress so far and will continue to be so.

Fourth, teaching from a whole language philosophy does not mean that all children receive exactly the same amount or kind of instruction. For example, in kindergarten Cecilia was able to utilize some adult assistance in sounding out the words in the stories she was writing and to ask adults to assist her with spelling and rereading her work. By the end of her kindergarten year, she had figured out how to represent the written language alphabetically, and she was becoming an independent writer and reader who could benefit from an adult conferring with her about the content of her texts. In contrast, for much of kindergarten Diana needed first to work with an adult on the creation of dictated stories so that she came to understand that an oral story could take a written form. After she understood this, she needed extended and continued assistance in first grade both in sounding out the words in her stories and in identifying the letters that represented the sounds she could hear to produce invented or conventional spellings. Thus, Diana received more direct, individualized instruction in transcribing her message than Cecilia did, although this instruction always came from Diana's own work in progress.

Finally, Diana and Cecilia (and their classmates) point out the importance of promoting native-language literacy. These two learners have been given the opportunity to construct knowledge of reading and writing processes in Spanish, their first and dominant language. Almost certainly Cecilia and Diana would not have developed their literacy to the extent that they have had they received instruction only in English, their nondominant language. In Spanish, both children have constructed grapheme-phoneme relationships initially needed for producing written texts. They would have had more difficulty analyzing words phonetically in the language they did not even speak fluently. They have been able to use their fluent oral-language abilities to read and to discuss books, to investigate content, and to plan and discuss their own written texts. If they had had to accomplish all of this exclusively in English, they would not have understood as much of what they read and/or had read to them; they would not have been able to discuss the content studied in as much depth; their own written texts would have been simplified, reduced to the few words and sentence patterns that they were taught and could produce. In the second language, Cecilia likely would be a less fluent and independent reader and writer, and Diana would more than likely have failed to read. While Cecilia probably would have been promoted to second grade, Diana's failure would have been remediated either through retention (a practice of many schools), promotion to second grade with Chapter 1 programming, or referral for screening for special-education services. To promote native-language literacy is to recognize and take advantage of the strengths children bring to learning in school rather than to suggest that they are not ready for school because "they" don't speak, read, or write in English.

CHAPTER 19

"It's Not a Perfect World": Defining Success and Failure at Central Park East Secondary School

Mark A. Faust, University of Georgia

This chapter plays counterpoint to chapter 17. It contains the reflections of a former teacher at New York's famous Central Park East High School, a school which was freed from the bureaucratic rules and regulations which constrain most New York City schools and is "governed" instead by philosophy of education, a philosophy which bears at least a family resemblance to the whole language orientation discussed in the previous chapter. The teacher's account describes a vibrant educational environment overseen by a dedicated hard-working administration and staff, a school which more than deserves the attention and praise heaped upon it. The chapter, however, also demonstrates how a philosophy—even a child-centered one—can blind teachers and administrators to the special needs of particular students. The story, in short, functions as cautionary tale: It challenges, at least somewhat, a major theme in the second half of this book by indicating that building programs around philosophical tenets rather than bureaucratic procedures is certainly no guarantee that the idiosyncratic needs of at-risk students will always get addressed.

Central Park East Secondary School (C.P.E.S.S.) is located in an area of Manhattan that continues to be known as Spanish Harlem even as the gentrification of the Upper East Side swells past ninety-sixth street, once a reliable boundary. As always, the city is on the move, neighborhoods are shifting, and perhaps as never before, images of success abound in stark contrast with the grim, everpresent spectre of failure. Here, in this volatile and troubled neighborhood, I imagined, was an opportunity to take the next good step away from a teaching position that had become just a bit too predictable. Here was a school that appeared to be a place where I might share with others a sense of purpose and a spirit of innovation. You see, C.P.E.S.S., which opened in 1985, is not a typical inner-city high school but a daring educational experiment, "a small, non-specialized, non-elitist high school . . . incorporating the ideas of progressive education with an emphasis on academic learning and inquiry" (Perlez 1987). Deborah Meier, the school's founder and principal, fervently believes that this kind of education, which is ordinarily an option only for the affluent, ought to be made available to families living in our nation's most troubled neighborhoods. Furthermore, she believes that the presence of schools like C.P.E.S.S. can make a difference for many in a population that by all reasonable measures is simply not being served by our educational system as it presently exists. Students will not drop out, Debbie claims, from a school where they are respected and challenged by the best that we can offer.

When I arrived on the scene in the autumn of 1987, virtually every aspect of the school's operation was open to question and revision. In this climate, we found ourselves constantly confronted by overwhelming questions, such as: What is the best that we can offer? And who are our students, most of them black and Hispanic, that they should want to collaborate with us, and what ultimately are we collaborating for? How will success and failure be defined in "our" school, and how will this be connected with the larger issues of success and failure in our lives? As we struggled to create a curriculum and a community, the staff at C.P.E.S.S. often took comfort in Debbie's famous line, "remember, it's not a perfect world." A few of us, however, felt it only highlighted our burden of responsibility. After all, it was only because we were trying so hard to envision a perfect world (or at least a perfect school) that we constantly had to confront the certainty that where we were was far from perfect. Nonetheless, as educators and journalists traveled from as far away as California to catch a glimpse of what we were doing, and as Debbie returned from numerous speaking engagements with glowing reports indicating that our school was gaining national prominence, we redoubled our efforts to actually be as good as the claims that were being made on our behalf. I do not for a moment mean to suggest any conscious dishonesty in articles bearing headlines such as "An East Harlem Learning Citadel Where Openness Rules" (Teltsch 1987), "A Harlem School Stresses the Basics" (Perlez 1987), or "Year of Honor in East Harlem Schools" (Perlez 1987a), but, sometimes, a determination to see the half-full rather than the half-empty glass evolves into a strategy for ignoring the fact that the glass is indeed not full.

In the pages that follow, I will speak about this program based on the two years (1987 to 1989) I devoted to teaching students "humanities" at C.P.E.S.S. I want to say at the outset that I applaud the efforts of Debbie Meier and those others who have dedicated their lives to creating a school that responds to the needs of inner-city students, their families, and the people who become their teachers. In some respects, C.P.E.S.S. constitutes the best teaching/learning environment I have ever known. Unquestionably, those who are responsible for bringing this school to life are justified in feeling a sense of accomplishment. Nonetheless, nagging questions linger in my mind, questions about how success and failure are defined, about how needs are defined and addressed, and about the limits of so-called progressive education in a society at odds with many of its foundational values and assumptions.

Generally speaking, the staff at C.P.E.S.S. is made up of people who have cast themselves as social activists working to change the face of American society. It would be wrong, however, to visualize the school as a haven for radicals. On the contrary, C.P.E.S.S., in theory and in practice, is rooted in traditional democratic ideals. Among the most significant of these is the belief that education can be a force for change in a society whose leaders must respond to the organized efforts of educated people. When the school's first graduating class departs this June (1991) for college or careers, you can be sure their teachers will be hoping that, in addition to being well prepared for "success," they will be persons who will "ask not what their country can do for them but what they can do for their country." Like most other American high schools, C.P.E.S.S. claims to be a place where adolescents are prepared to be good citizens and productive workers. What sets this school apart from most others is the high degree of seriousness with which these ideals are pursued, the nontraditional means employed, and the fact that most of the students come from backgrounds that at best would indicate a limited chance of academic success.

Teaching at C.P.E.S.S., I felt immersed in an uncertain mix of liberal idealism and a hard-nosed acknowledgment of social, political, and economic realities. Yes, we told ourselves, we were working within the boundaries set by our society in order to make it more humane and just, yet we resolutely refused to judge ourselves according to the values and standards dictated by that same society. Most of the time, I felt as though I was floating between claiming that accepting the norms of society leads to empowerment and arguing that empowerment entitles us to challenge the norms of society. Of course, if one takes the long view, this contradiction can be made to disappear. One of the great virtues of a democracy is the indisputable freedom its citizens possess to initiate change. Ample evidence both at home and abroad supports this claim, and what could be more uplifting than dedicating oneself to helping those who have traditionally been disenfranchised to claim their rightful place in a society that is gradually but definitively improving itself? My aim is not to criticize this idealism per se. The broad question I wish to raise here is whether or not the highly politicized agenda which exists at C.P.E.S.S. can be commensurate with fashioning a curriculum that is truly appropriate for many of those students who constitute the population that C.P.E.S.S. claims to serve.

SOLVING THE "MYSTERY"/JOINING THE "CLUB"

A dominant metaphor in the vocabulary of those who teach at C.P.E.S.S. links academic success with membership in "the club." Let me be honest and say that I do not care much for clubs and as a rule try to avoid them, but this one seemed relatively benign if only because it was so ill defined. To this day, I continue to be mystified as to who club members actually are and what privileges they enjoy. It is one thing to claim that "the club" welcomes all of "us" who are "functionally literate" (whatever that means), quite another to claim that access is closed to all but an inner circle of scholars. At C.P.E.S.S., we attempted to draw the line somewhere between these extremes, but it was never clear to me and certainly not clear to our students precisely what the metaphor is intended to communicate. According to Debbie Meier, membership has something to do with developing "intellectual habits," which "are not quite 'facts,' 'skills,' or 'concepts'; intellectual habits are a 'way' of approaching almost any serious inquiry; such habits of mind presume the need for knowledge, skill, and appropriate concepts" (1987, p. 2). We at C.P.E.S.S. relied upon this notion of inculcating "habits of mind" as opposed to transmitting a predetermined content to justify our leap of faith in generating a curriculum that challenged traditional assumptions about time, ownership, and assessment.

Debbie Meier encouraged us to think of the curriculum at C.P.E.S.S. as "a good detective story" (1987, p. 3). We were expected to "set out an arena for our mystery," including the "big question." Then, we were to identify the "appropriate modes of inquiry" needed to disclose "the sequence of events that unravels the mystery." Although our curriculum was traditional in that we preselected topics and set tasks, our decidedly nontraditional aim was to model what "scholars" and "citizens" in the "real world" do when confronted with gaps in their understanding. Time was of the essence to us, but not in the usual sense. Our students were not to be pressured into lock-step procedures. Each was to be granted time to "unravel the mystery" at his or her own pace. Taking to heart the slogan, "less is more," we set out to show each student how to respond to very specific questions related to an overarching thematic concern ("the big question"). Our claim (our hope? our dream?) was that the students were "learning how to learn" and that this kind of knowledge is infinitely more valuable than the content-area knowledge to which they would be exposed in more typical schools.

Before offering a more detailed glimpse of what our curriculum involved, I would be remiss if I failed to acknowledge the small number of students (usually between thirty-five and forty divided into morning and afternoon groups) each of us had to work with, as well as the extraordinary autonomy we enjoyed not only to design a curriculum, but to make decisions about allocating time and resources. For instance, its original staff members decided to make C.P.E.S.S. a 7 to 12 high school with two-year course sequences taking the place of the usual grades. As part of this decision, they determined to divide the academic portion of the curriculum not into the usual five or six content areas but only two, math/science and humanities, each to be designed and implemented by a team of teachers. Debbie Meier deserves most of the credit for engineering this minor miracle within a school system noted for its rigidity, and hers is an interesting story. Nevertheless, I will only add (and only because it is so often perceived to be an issue) that Debbie always insisted that the per-pupil cost of running C.P.E.S.S. never exceeded by more than 10 percent that averaged by other New York City high schools.

To clarify what we meant by "curriculum as detective story," I will quote from a memo Debbie wrote in 1988 concerning the major components in a 7/8 grade course then being revised. Following this, I will share a few specifics about classroom procedure at C.P.E.S.S., including procedures for assessing student performance and progress. In this context, I will present some portraits of success and failure, and raise some questions about whose needs are really being served by the kind of innovative and demanding program being developed at C.P.E.S.S.

The theme or "mystery" unifying one-half of the two-year 7/8 grade course of study in humanities concerned "the peopling of America." Various strands or lines of inquiry were defined by "essential questions," such as: Whose country is this anyhow? What makes someone an American? Are blacks just another example of an immigrant group? In what ways has their story been the same as well as different? Are all differences okay? Are there limits to acceptable differences? The team of teachers working with this group were responsible for helping kids explore ways of answering these and other similar questions. A major part of this responsibility involved specifying what "knowledge/information/facts" the students needed to acquire in order to carry out their investigations. For instance, students would be expected to learn about the old world and the new world, that there were people in the old world before there were any in the new, that the first people to arrive in the new world were ancestors of the people we now call Indians or Native Americans, that these native Americans built civilizations, cultures, governments, languages, etc. long before any Africans or Europeans appeared on the scene, and so on. In addition to handouts, visual media, and library research, students were provided with fictional and nonfictional texts that were connected in some way with the overall mystery to be solved.

My role, as a teacher in this type of curriculum, was to be an expert in the sense that an athletic coach is an expert (another dominant metaphor) capable of helping students to achieve "ownership" in the same way young athletes develop the ability to perform. Using a combination of independent study, one-on-one guidance, small- and large-group activities, modeling, and peer assistance, I tried to help each of my students achieve some degree of mastery of the core curriculum ("habits of mind" plus specific knowledge) as well as to become more competent in the four language arts: reading, writing, speaking, and listening. Like a good coach, I did not expect all my students to perform with equal proficiency, nor did I expect them all to learn at the same rate. Still, I was expected to have a clear understanding of what constitutes excellence and to be able to challenge my students while exhibiting patience with those of lesser ability. I was expected to monitor each student's individual progress and in collaboration with the other members of my "team" to plan and coordinate classroom instruction.

Three times each year, students presented what we called an "exhibition," in which they brought to completion various projects we had designed for them to work on. This format allowed us to negotiate individualized study plans spanning many weeks and at the same time promote seriousness by imposing schoolwide deadlines. Exhibitions consisted of written work, oral conferences, class presentations, and artwork all devoted to demonstrating each student's degree of mastery of the year's curriculum. Although "distinguished" work was acknowledged as such, we tried not to rely on grades as a primary stimulus. To supplement our ongoing encouragement and guidance, following exhibition week, each student received a comprehensive written evaluation of his or her progress that along with the written portion of their exhibition was reviewed in conferences with their parents. Achievement was noted and goals for the immediate future established.

What we claimed to be offering was a kind of all-purpose curriculum, a one-size-fits-all approach to education in the context of which no one could be categorized as "at risk." We believed that given enough time and the right kind of encouragement and support, every child is capable of success in school. We constantly told ourselves that any failures ultimately would be our responsibility, our failure to provide what a particular child needed. In this environment, I found myself torn between the responsibility to set high expectations and the responsibility to label virtually any performance as a degree of success. Most of the time, I felt overwhelmed by the difficult task of tailoring a predetermined program to fit the varied needs of even the relatively small number of students I had to work with. The difficulty of this situation was compounded for me (and I was not alone in feeling this way) by the truth that I really could not claim to have a clear, unqualified grasp of what constitutes excellence in humanities (in fact even the subject, "humanities," was and is vague to me; at C.P.E.S.S., "humanities" seemed to mean "social studies" with extras). Neither could I claim to know precisely what steps were involved in helping students, many of whom could barely read and write, to achieve "mastery" of a "mystery" as complex as "the peopling of America" or any of the other broad themes that defined and unified the curriculum at C.P.E.S.S. As a result, assessment was always an extremely muddled business that left those students who cared in a perpetual state of confusion and those who seemed not to care in a comfortable zone where blatant irresponsibility would be tolerated. Debbie always claimed that our students had a more realistic awareness of their ability than we gave them credit for, but in my experience, we neither set clear standards nor communicated very realistic goals for most of them.

Looking back on the experience, I now recognize deep contradictions in the teacher as coach metaphor. While I remain as opposed as anyone to the idea of teachers transmitting knowledge to masses of students via endless lectures and phony discussion, I am troubled by the notion of teachers operating out of an assumption that kids (no matter who they are) can be as easily motivated to learn about science, history, and literature as they are to succeed in athletics. Motivating kids on the playing field simply is not commensurate with motivating students in a classroom. Moreover, my experience of being cut from more than one team in high school has taught me that coaches rarely lose sleep over the failure of aspiring athletes. In addition, I am troubled by the notion that a core curriculum, any core curriculum, can be designed in such a way that everyone's needs are being addressed as vigorously as possible. Yet, this is precisely what we claimed to be offering at C.P.E.S.S. And this, rather than our unique curriculum with its implied social agenda, was the utterly mainstream carrot that brought the kids in. The truth is that many parents and students possessed a very limited concept of what the school was supposed to be all about. Clearly, the school owes its extraordinarily high rates of attendance more to the promise that success in life follows from success in school allied with the claim that, at C.P.E.S.S., everyone who wants to succeed can succeed, than to its innovative approach to education. Parents want to enroll their children in C.P.E.S.S. because the word is out that "their approach works." My only claim is that this assessment is premature. Like most schools, C.P.E.S.S. generates some dramatic success stories and, considering where the school is located, this is no small achievement. Nevertheless, it has and will generate notable failures as well, despite all the claims to the contrary.

I could tell you a story about Thomas, who was expelled for punching Debbie Meier, or about Jamall, who was arrested for pushing drugs, or another one about Jimi, who I heard was finally expelled after disrupting classes (including mine) for years and wasting countless hours of my own and other peoples' time in school and family conferences. Then there was Alex, whose entire final exhibition one year consisted of a brief description of cutting school and spending the day in a video arcade. I remember three girls—Cary and Pam, who were very bright and Cynthia who was not so bright—all of whom elected to transfer to other schools because they and their parents believed they just were not learning anything of value. I could go on, but I prefer not to dwell on such obvious instances of "failure." Instead, I will offer you three brief portraits depicting the experiences of boys I knew at C.P.E.S.S., who clearly benefited from the program offered there. I have no doubt that all three would have dropped out of any of the other city high schools they might have attended. Of course, it is better for them to be in school, any school, than on the street, but in spite of this evidence of success, I question whether C.P.E.S.S. offers the best program for students like them.

James transferred to C.P.E.S.S., or to put it more accurately, he was "placed" there with a warning that the next step would be some kind of reform school. As a result of excessive truancy, he had been expelled from the high school in his neighborhood. James responded positively to the friendly atmosphere he found at C.P.E.S.S. and from the beginning attended regularly. His parents were thrilled and we got credit for turning him around. At first, he did very little schoolwork, but gradually began to show signs of involvement. Although he never took much of an interest in the "mystery" (the questions were "boring") and his work was never better than perfunctory (the assignments were "stupid"), he did attend school and he did "complete" his exhibitions. James' dream in life, as he constantly reiterated, was to attend the N.Y.U. Film School and become a director of horror movies. The improbability of him ever realizing this dream notwithstanding, his performance at C.P.E.S.S. was a far cry from Debbie Meier's image of "youngsters digging into real issues and recognizing the excitement of being educated."

At age twenty, Carlos was quite a bit older than most of his 9/10 grade peers. Despite his enormous size and strength and his habit of "looking tough," you could not ask to meet a gentler, more-caring person than Carlos. After living for a number of years with his mother literally in a homeless state, he had been taken in finally by relatives. Once back in school, Carlos was determined to work hard and make up for lost time. His previous teachers at C.P.E.S.S. had encouraged him to believe that college and a career in architecture were within his grasp if only he applied himself. After working with him myself, I questioned this advice and, with sadness, I observed Carlos's growing sense of discouragement as the distance he had to travel became more apparent to him. No one had helped him develop a realistic sense of his limited ability to read and write. All he ever heard was how wonderful his progress had been.

English was a second language for Amir, who was born in Morocco and came to the United States at the age of eight. An enthusiastic and diligent student, he clearly made some progress toward becoming fluent in English during the year I worked with him. I wish I could take some credit for this, but the truth is, I actually spent very little time with him. It would be easy to say that I gave him room to grow, but if anyone deserves credit, it ought to be his mother because she made him read every night and Amir was not the type of boy to rebel against this pressure. I think he enjoyed complaining about it almost as much as he enjoyed the reading. C.P.E.S.S. was certainly not a bad place for Amir, but I have to wonder what he might have accomplished in the hands of a person with experience in ESL, who was not harried by students with more visible if not more urgent needs.

The mere presence of students like James, Carlos, and Amir (and their stories are by no means atypical) in a school boasting the high-powered, academically serious program such as that being offerred at C.P.E.S.S. seems wonderful from a distance and even from a brief close-up view. In suggesting that things are not quite as wonderful as they seem, I do not wish to give the impression that these students had any alternative. I have no doubt that C.P.E.S.S. represents the last, best hope for many of its students, even those who remain bewildered by the "mystery" and uncertain about whether they have or ever will be able to "join the club." Perhaps it is enough to hope that, as one of my colleagues at C.P.E.S.S. put it, the mere fact that some of these kids stay in school and have positive feelings about the experience is a measure of success. Perhaps it is, but unless we are willing to say this to the kids directly and let them choose to come to school on those terms, then we are being dishonest.

Clearly, what students like James, Carlos, and Amir needed was more latitude on our part as we selected books and designed activities for them. For the life of me, I fail to grasp the logic in asking a nineteen-year-old Hispanic student, who is neither a fluent reader nor a fluent writer, to read and respond to *The Daughter of Han* (a nearly three hundred-page transcription of the verbal autobiography of a chinese peasant woman) simply because the core curriculum happens at that moment to be focused on China. Yet this is precisely what I did with (to?) Carlos. With an already vast and still-growing amount of scholarship suggesting that *how* we read, write, and talk is more important than *what* we read, write, and talk about, I see no impediment to reaching for anything and everything available in the interest of promoting literacy—no impediment, that is, but an outdated overestimation of the importance of preserving a core curriculum. Although we discussed and sought to establish "proximal goals" for our students (see Bandura and Schunk 1981), these were driven entirely by our predetermined content rather than the emerging interests and concerns of the students. For students like Carlos, James, Amir, and, I suspect, even those others, who "failed" to survive at C.P.E.S.S., the core curriculum served only to bolster the very socioeconomic distinctions it supposedly was designed to break down.

There is more I want to say about how we struggled to define success and failure for our students and ourselves, but first, I need to talk about the unique support system built into the program at C.P.E.S.S. and the role that is claimed for it in making the road to academic achievement open to all.

SCHOOL AS COMMUNITY/COMMUNITY AS SCHOOL

At any given moment, kids and teachers are doing the best they can to do what is right for them and others they care about. We at C.P.E.S.S. did our best to act on this belief and the corollary belief that problems concerning motivation and/or behavior present opportunities for growth as long as these are confronted honestly and with genuine care rather than the strong arm of impersonal, institutionalized constraints. We believed that our students wanted to succeed and that when appearances suggested otherwise, it was our responsibility to help them get back on track, even if this required a huge expenditure of time and energy, and, as it usually did, superhuman degrees of patience. Our claim was that by helping kids cope with social and/or emotional problems in the context of school, we were enabling them to be more productive when they finally did concentrate on their schoolwork. Several "systems" were in place at C.P.E.S.S. to help individual teachers fulfill this mission.

First of all, there was what we called the "advisory" period. For one hour at the end of each day, I met with my ten to fifteen advisees. In addition to developing a camaraderie, I was expected to offer one-to-one guidance, discussion groups, and various activities aimed at exploring issues in the students' personal lives and their connectedness to the life of the school community. I was also expected to initiate and sustain a dialogue with each student's family. My responsibilities also called upon me to serve as an individual student's advocate in conflicts involving other teachers or students that threatened the community as a whole.

Secondly, if and when conflicts became unmanageable, a family conference would be scheduled. Ideally, everyone directly involved in the conflict would be asked to attend and an effort would be made to resolve the conflict without blame placing or punishment. In extreme circumstances, a trained family therapist could be called in to assist in these conferences, which most often would take place between seven and eight in the morning to accommodate parents and teachers. It was not uncommon, however, for these to interrupt the school day, in which case other staff members would cover for those involved in the conference.

Thirdly, the entire school staff would meet weekly from three to six in the afternoon to discuss current issues and future plans. Twice each year, the full staff would convene over a full weekend for discussion and presentations. Content-area teams also met weekly for four hours to plan curriculum. Also, as you might imagine, these teams met almost daily in ad hoc sessions to share ideas and offer support. At least once each week, advisors working with a particular age group would have lunch together and discuss advisory issues. Advisory periods, family conferences, and staff interaction were intended to, and for the most part did, promote the sense of a cohesive and caring community.

As we sought to identify ourselves as a school community, we also sought to establish links with our neighborhood and New York City at large. One facet of this has already been mentioned, namely, the effort we focused on reaching out to the families of our students. Another we called "community service," which consisted of sending our students out into the community once a week to perform various functions in local establishments such as hospitals, libraries, day-care centers, outreach centers, other schools, and businesses. Students received two placements per year that provided them with valuable experience in "real-world" settings and contributed to our visibility in the community. This program also created preparation time for science and humanities teams.

Finally, I need to mention our policy of routinely taking kids on field trips to museums, theatre performances, and points of interest around the city. Visits to the Metropolitan Museum of Art, the Museum of Natural History, the Museum of the City of New York as well as several other local museums, performances of *Macbeth,* and *Sarrafina,* outings to the United Nations building, the Queens Museum, and the movies (*Stand and Deliver,* and *Mississippi Burning*) were incorporated into our curriculum during the two years I taught at C.P.E.S.S. There also were outings to local libraries, bookstores, and parks. What all this added up to, on the bright side, was an impressive array of potentially stimulating and educational experiences, especially given the consideration that many students at C.P.E.S.S. would not otherwise have known even that these places existed. From another, more-sobering perspective, however, we can see a crazy quilt of activity that instead of providing support and enrichment served only to make an imposing curriculum even more inaccessible than it already was for those many students whose ability to read and write could be described as rudimentary at best.

To assist you in imagining what is involved in actually functioning within such an all-inclusive set of expectations, I will tell you about Dorene and what I think her story discloses about C.P.E.S.S. When I arrived on the scene, Dorene had already achieved legendary status among her peers and the school staff. Awe-inspiring energy and verbal dexterity made Dorene a formidable presence in any situation. Those who challenged her domination found themselves involved in conflicts that quickly turned brutal and in some cases physical. There simply was no way to resist her; one had to find a way to work with her, or risk a confrontation that was sure to escalate beyond all reasonable bounds. Getting along with Dorene would have been difficult even had she been a dolt, but she was, in fact, quite perceptive. As a member of my humanities class and my advisee that year, she made herself the center of attention, period. Do not think for a minute that we did not undertake numerous family conferences involving Dorene, her mother (her father had disappeared), myself, the school's assistant director, and often times, a trained therapist. Every appearance indicated that these sessions were going nowhere, although we gained a clearer understanding of how Dorene was using all of us to sustain an illusory sense of control over her life. I could not begin to calculate the cost of our intense involvement with Dorene and a handful of similar cases. Students like James, Carlos, and Amir faded into the background and the few academically capable students we had were rendered invisible by people like Dorene.

When, the following year, it became apparent that we were in for another round of incidents, the staff elected to expel Dorene. We had given her our best shot, and we did not know what else we could do for her. Clearly, she was not benefiting from the school and her antics were inhibiting the progress of others (truly an understatement!). Her mother was informed of our decision and the reasons behind it, and she received assurances that Dorene would be assisted in her effort to find another school. No sooner had we breathed our first sigh of relief, when we were notified that Dorene's mother was threatening to sue the school on the grounds of racial discrimination. Not wishing to expose the school to potentially harmful publicity, Debbie insisted that we quietly readmit Dorene. Things went on much as before, although Dorene did show signs of exercising more self-control than she had in the past. When I visited the school a year ago, I heard that she had continued to improve so much that there was talk that hers eventually might be counted among the school's "success stories."

Whether or not Dorene ultimately gained personally from what can only be described as an excessively tolerant and nonjudgmental approach to her antisocial behavior is a moot point as far as I am concerned. At the time, I found myself rebelling inside against having to devote so much of my time and energy to her at the expense of other students. On the other hand, I said to myself, if not her, then someone else. There always seemed to be something preventing me from sustaining in my classroom an atmosphere of focused inquiry in which kids might legitimately be said to be taking responsibility for their own learning. The expectation that I be prepared to adjust my teaching style and procedures to meet the varied needs of a multicultural, multi-everything student body, combined with all the networking and interaction associated with building a "school community" and implementing a "high-powered curriculum," created from my perspective a perpetually frenzied environment that eventually left me exhausted and demoralized. I had to wonder who, if anyone, was really benefiting from my labor. How could a program so thoughtfully conceived to be academically respectable and at the same time egalitarian in spirit result in the kind of disorientation and dishonesty observable at C.P.E.S.S.?

TWO CHEERS FOR CENTRAL PARK EAST

Paradoxically, writing about the program at C.P.E.S.S. makes me feel again some of the excitement that attracted me to the school in the first place. For all of its problems and limitations, there is a vibrancy and sense of mission there that is decidedly absent from the atmosphere of other schools with which I am familiar. For those with a strong will, lots of energy, an inexhaustible tolerance for constant questioning and revision, all combined with a genuine love of teenagers, C.P.E.S.S. is a wonderful place to teach. I wish I could say it is an equally wonderful place to be a student. For some, it undoubtedly is, but many of the boys and girls I knew at C.P.E.S.S. would have been better served by other kinds of programs, and, not surprisingly, most of these would have been labeled as "at risk" by any of the other schools available to them. While C.P.E.S.S. may have motivated them to stay in school, these students needed something other than a loosely structured and in reality undemanding course of study that placed a premium on political awareness and "personal growth" at the expense of more immediate and practical concerns.

There are three (at least) powerful rejoinders to the points I have been making. The first would accuse me of deliberately highlighting the "half-empty" glass, while downplaying the fact that, during the years 1987 to 1989, the school was still in a "start-up" phase and had yet to produce a single graduate. Since then, a Senior Institute has been created for students entering the final two years of the program, and teachers will have had an opportunity to fine tune courses of study that were being taught for the first time only a few years ago. There is also the consideration that what appears to be an excessively tolerant approach might pay off in the long run as students mature. My answer to this consists of two parts. In the first place, I think it is crucial that we acknowledge that the students not being served because the glass is half-empty are the very students elsewhere being labeled "at-risk." There is no doubt that C.P.E.S.S. is generating opportunities for some students who might otherwise have few or none, but there is a danger in overgeneralizing, which leads me to the second part of my response. I do not believe that any amount of "fine tuning" can make an academically rigorous curriculum, grounded as is the program at C.P.E.S.S. in the liberal arts, appropriate for *all* students, especially for those whose intellectual and emotional problems can make them appear to be uneducable.

A second rejoinder might argue that "disorientation and dishonesty" describe what goes on at many schools and that Debbie Meier and her staff deserve praise for confronting issues ignored or suppressed in other institutions. To this, I could only say, "here, here!" My intention has never been to discredit the ambitiousness of the educational experiment being carried out at C.P.E.S.S. My only aim has been to forestall premature conclusions about the program, in particular concerning the needs of at-risk students.

A third rejoinder might be directed at me personally and question whether or not my doubts about the program at C.P.E.S.S. say more about my own than its limitations. Without question, my brief experience teaching at C.P.E.S.S. made me aware, as no other position has, of my limitations, both personally and professionally speaking. Equally beyond question, as I hope is clear based on my account of the program, is the fact that Debbie Meier expects a great deal from her staff and I think we all felt overwhelmed most of the time. At least that was my impression. My decision to leave the school, however, was prompted more by a sense of failing my students than of failing Debbie Meier. Too often I felt that what I was asking them to do was disconnected from what they needed to be doing. Too many of them simply did not understand why we were doing the things we did and seemed to trust that, as long as they got that nod of approval from me (which given the belief system imposed on us was inevitable), they were destined for success. Their confusion is understandable, in part as the result of our confusion about how to maintain an emphasis on "learning how to learn" within the context of a predetermined and detailed core curriculum. Beyond my earlier call for a more flexible and open-ended definition of "content," I remain, in all honesty, unsure about precisely what kind of program would be right for these students, but I am quite certain that our wonderful "essential questions" were never in any way "essential" to them.

If "at risk" means on the verge of failing and/or dropping out of school, then the label can apply as well to teachers as it does to students. Teachers, too, can become oppressed by the weight of incoherent expectations and the absence of meaningful measures of what constitutes "success." Teachers too can become confused about the connection between success in school and success in life. I have been challenged by these issues throughout my career as an educator, but answers that worked for the middle-class, predominantly white, college-bound students I taught before joining the staff at C.P.E.S.S. simply were inadequate for the likes of Thomas, Jamall, Jimi, James, Carlos, and Amir. It is not enough to say to these boys, "We're not elitist. We have the same high expectations for you as we would for any other bunch of American teenagers, so let's get to work, and don't worry, you can't fail." Given the intensity and diversity of their needs, and the inadequacy of my response, I felt myself to be at risk almost from the day I started teaching at C.P.E.S.S.

I firmly believe that by eliminating all possibility of failure, we at C.P.E.S.S. undermined the credibility of any claims we might make regarding the success of many of our students. As a matter of policy, we chose to ignore the fact that the terms are mutually defining and thus interdependent. Ironically, this policy was at odds with one of the major points of Theodore Sizer's (1984) book *Horace's Compromise,* which in other respects was enormously influential in the development of the program at C.P.E.S.S. On more than one occasion in his book, Sizer makes the startlingly sane claim that education beyond basic literacy, numeracy, and civic understanding ought to be *voluntary* (pp. 84–88, 136, 233). According to Sizer, clear standards ought to be established as preconditions for high school level study. Furthermore, he argues, a variety of programs ought to exist to assist students in meeting these standards and to offer alternatives for students who do meet them but do not desire a traditional liberal arts education. Imposing a rigorous program of academic learning and inquiry on students who are either unable or unwilling to meet that challenge is unfair. Telling them they are succeeding when really they are not is dishonest. At C.P.E.S.S., I felt as though I was guilty on both counts.

A popular television ad exhorting kids not to become dropouts features a well-dressed black man saying, "The more you learn, the more you earn. Stay in school." Ignoring the fact that the validity of this claim is open to question, is it the message we want kids to hear? Do we want to measure success in monetary terms? And why not? Are politicians suddenly concerned about the dropout rate because people are not being educated, or is it that uneducated people can no longer be absorbed into the economy as easily as they once were? Why should kids stay in school? What is school for? For all those in our country who are not doomed to success no matter what their educational background consists of, these are real questions. We owe ourselves and our children real answers.

For all the talk about "empowerment" that circulated at C.P.E.S.S., we did not, in my opinion, do a very good job of sorting out the various interpretations of that word. For instance, the power to read difficult books is not synonymous with the power to earn money, and while the two are by no means mutually exclusive, it is dishonest to suggest that one necessarily leads to or is connected with the other. My father used to say to me, "A good education is valuable in and of itself. Even if you choose to be a ditch digger, you're better off with an education." Beside the fact that this advice appears to assume that a person could actually choose to be a ditch digger, it is suspect because it appears to deny the very real connection between education and the world of work. Romantic notions about education for self-actualization are acceptable for those who already have choices about how to live their lives. Those who do not require additional options and clarity.

I am not one of those who would turn inner-city schools into training centers that would track minority students into low-paying, low-prestige jobs. On the other hand, I also think it is wrong to simply open the doors of our universities in the name of equal opportunity. In the context of this issue, I think C.P.E.S.S. deserves two cheers, one for seeking to offer inner-city kids an academic program of high quality and high expectations, and another for creating an innovative support system to help able students realize their potential. I have to withhold the final cheer, however, because too many students who are either not ready or not interested in such a program are being allowed to consume too much of their teacher's time and energy. I am not suggesting that these students ought to be abandoned. I am suggesting that we cannot expect one school and its individual teachers to be all things for all people.

CHAPTER 20

Creating a Culture of Writers with At-Risk Students

June Yennie-Donmoyer, Worthingway Middle School, Worthington City Schools, Ohio
Robert Donmoyer, The Ohio State University

Previous chapters focused on how philosophical beliefs functioned to create a school culture which provided direction for teachers but permitted more discretion over classroom decision making than more bureaucratic modes of control. This chapter, which was co-authored by a classroom teacher, describes how one teacher quite consciously used the notion of culture to organize and structure life in her classroom. Data are presented which indicate (1) how this orientation played out in practice, (2) how it helped accommodate student idiosyncracy while providing the sort of direction and order all classrooms need, and (3) what effect it had on students.

Process writing is an approach to the teaching of writing which assumes that students learn to write primarily by writing. Rather than emphasizing the teaching of grammatical rules and rhetorical techniques, process writing emphasizes the need for students to become actively engaged in the processes of composing, critiquing, editing, and rewriting.

The notion that students learn to write by writing makes intuitive sense to many middle and secondary school teachers, and we have seen large numbers of teachers adopt the process-writing approach in their classrooms. We have also seen many of these teachers quickly become frustrated. Their frustration seems to have resulted from one of two erroneous assumptions which they made in the course of implementing the process-writing approach. Either they assumed that middle school and secondary students would take to writing much as ducks take to water, or they assumed that the process-writing approach could be fit into traditional teacher-directed modes of instruction.

The first assumption underestimates both the native ability and the intrinsic motivation of many middle and secondary school students. For most of us, writing is a difficult, laborious process, and many students—particularly those who have had little success in playing "the school game"—require assistance and motivation to become successfully engaged in the writing process.

Traditional modes of instruction, however, are not necessarily compatible with the process-writing approach. We have seen teachers try to package the process-writing approach into a three- to six-week writing unit. We have seen them provide no other incentive than the promise of a good grade (or, as is more often the case, the threat of a bad one). We have seen teachers assign topics and titles, require a certain number of paragraphs, specify rules for composing opening paragraphs, and even, in one instance, dictate the opening and closing sentences of a story. While those under the influence of the "ducks to water" metaphor provide too little structure and direction, those who attempt to fit the process-writing approach into traditional modes of instruction generally provide too much. They fail to realize that writing is an extremely personal, idiosyncratic and serendipitous process which cannot be easily fit into six-week units and cannot readily accommodate teacher directives and demands.

This chapter describes one teacher's attempt to find a middle ground between too much structure and too little. The description results from an action research project involving collaboration between a classroom teacher, June Yennie-Donmoyer and a university professor, Robert Donmoyer, who also happen to be married to each other.

THE EXISTING LITERATURE

Teacher effectiveness studies endorse direct instruction as the best way for teachers to teach. These studies, however, did not focus on the teaching of writing. Writing appears to be far too serendipitous and too personal a process to be translated into precisely crafted, carefully sequenced behavioral objectives which can be transmitted directly from teacher to student and which will add up to writing ability.

The literature on process writing (see, for example, Graves 1984, 1983; Calkins 1986; Atwell 1987) suggests a more promising instructional model; its emphasis on learning to write by writing, critiquing, editing, and revising is certainly consistent with the way writers actually work. The process-writing literature, however, often seems vague, incomplete, and overly optimistic. The assumption of this literature seems to be that all teachers need do is set the writing/critiquing/revising process in motion and students will respond enthusiastically and improve in their ability to write. It is probably significant that much of the work in process writing has focused on the elementary school years, when students are more likely to want to do what adults ask them to do, and when great refinements in writing skills are not expected. At the secondary level, it seems reasonable to expect teachers to take a more activist role both in motivating students and in helping them perfect their skills. The question, of course, is, How can teachers influence students yet avoid the pitfalls associated with using a direct instruction approach?

An answer to the problem of teaching a highly complex skill like writing is suggested by the literature on organizational culture. Organizational theory suggests that organizational members can be influenced in one of two ways: (1) Leaders can clearly articulate what behaviors are expected of members, monitor carefully to see whether expected behaviors are displayed by group members, and reward and punish members on the basis of this monitoring, or (2) leaders can articulate a set of cultural norms which provide the basis for member socialization and which predispose socialized members to behave in certain ways. The former approach may be effective in organizations such as factories, which lend themselves to regimentation and precisely defined standard operating procedures. However, in other sorts of organizations, the latter approach, which focuses on the development of organizational culture through the use of culturally significant myths, rituals, symbols, and models has begun to be recognized as being effective. Robert's research on effective schools and effective school principals, for example, revealed the importance of the cultural dimension at the school building level. His speculation that cultural variables could also play a significant role at the classroom level ultimately led to the project described here.

RESEARCH PROCEDURES

Neither of the authors of this chapter initially conceptualized their work as a research project. Initially, they were merely responding to a real-life situation: June had decided to return to secondary school English teaching after working for years as a writer and editor, and she wanted to know how to teach writing to ninth- and tenth-grade students, many of whom had had little academic success in the past and little motivation to play the school game at present. (An average of four or five students in each class had failed the course the previous year and were repeating; honors students, as well as students enrolled in gifted and talented programs were placed in separate classes taught by teachers with more seniority.)

The English department provided a prescribed curriculum, but there was sufficient flexibility in what was required of students to allow for a process-writing program to be implemented effectively. Before the school year began, it was decided that students would keep portfolios of writing that they produced independently throughout the year. Minimum requirements would be set at the beginning of each quarter (usually two to three polished pieces which had been revised several times), but it was hoped the students would voluntarily exceed these minimums. In addition, special portfolio days would be scheduled throughout the quarter. On these days, students would be expected to either write quietly by themselves, critique each other's work, or confer with the teacher.

Both Robert and June realized that for these rudimentary procedures to be successful, students would have to be socialized into a classroom culture where writing was valued, but neither of them had precise ideas about how to do this. Ideas emerged through trial and error and during almost nightly consultation sessions.

By midyear, there was evidence that the program was at least somewhat successful. It was at this point that the team began to reconceptualize their work. Slowly they began to think of the project as action research and to increasingly reorient their almost daily debriefing sessions away from pedagogical problem solving and toward data collection and analysis. Robert served as a participant observer in June's classroom, collecting interview and questionnaire data. The project was interrupted for a year, which was spent on sabbatical in New Zealand, and it was begun again with a new group of ninth and tenth graders in 1987. Longitudinal data were then collected on the first group of students who were now juniors and seniors.

The research focused on two questions: (1) Did the evidence support the assumption that the program was successful, and (2) if so, what classroom characteristics appeared to contribute to success?

FINDINGS

Evidence of Success

In attempting to assess the success of the writing program, the team focused on six questions: (1) Did students, in fact, begin writing more as a result of being in the immersion-type setting that was provided by this classroom? (Given the assumption that students learn to write by writing, this question seemed by far the most critical.) (2) Did students begin to write for themselves, rather than to simply meet course requirements; did they, for instance, write for intrinsic rewards such as feelings of increased self-esteem, or for other personal goals such as applying for jobs? (3) Did students begin to regard themselves as professionals and behave as published writers do? (4) Were students able to structure their writing projects and organize their time effectively so that they met deadlines and produced quality material throughout what amounted to a year-long independent study? (5) Did students' thinking skills appear to expand as a result of the emphasis placed on editing and rewriting? (6) Did writing styles broaden and mechanical skills improve?

Productivity. The answer to the first question about whether writing activity increased was an unqualified yes on two counts.

First, the amount of writing increased for more than half the students in both groups studied. Second, large numbers of students, even those whose rate of productivity remained fairly even, reported that in all their years of school they had never written as much as they did in this class. Such feedback revealed more than just how little writing is normally expected of students; often students went on to explain that even when they were told to write for their other classes they chose not to. Chad said:

> I think I really never knew the boundary of my writing skills until this year. I was not a mature, developed writer; I had never edited a paper or even written a paper that I thought was half-way decent until this year. During elementary and junior high school years, [I always felt] yeah, I have to write another paper for English class, bummer!

Andy explained:

> English class this year has been somewhat different. Unlike most of my earlier teachers [sic] we don't diagram sentences or work with nouns and verbs, etc. [Our work] is really based the whole year on [our] own writing. I think this is the most I have written in one class ever.

Evidence of increased productivity was found in a number of places. First, the number of students adding "extra pieces" to their folders increased with each quarter. During the first quarter no students submitted extra work for review. By second quarter around twenty students produced at least one more piece than was required, even though they knew there was no policy to reward them with extra credit. Several other students were deeply involved in lengthy works—e.g. novels, research papers, a "create-your-own adventure" series—that they continued to work on into the following quarter. By the beginning of the final quarter of each year, the number of students producing extra material had nearly doubled and an equal number were working extra hours editing and revising, getting ready to submit their work for publication.

Other evidence of increased productivity came from parents. Fourteen parents came to the midyear parent conference day to talk with the teacher; all but one parent came to school that day to discuss their students' problems in other classes. It seemed that these students who were generally doing poorly in school were doing their best work in English class. In fact, six of the students were doing their *only* work in English, and their parents were curious about what was causing the difference. "My son closes himself off in his room nearly every night and writes. Why?" Ian's father asked. "He won't do any homework for any other class." Since Ian was also one of the most difficult students the teacher had had to manage, she was not totally prepared to answer the parent. She acknowledged, however, that although Ian often caused disruption in her class (as he apparently did in others), he had actually been writing a good deal more than he would have had to to pass the course.

The parent who had not come to discuss her child's school problems, but rather had just wanted to meet her daughter's teachers, also reported her daughter's unusual enthusiasm for her writing. June used this opportunity to express her concern that Nicole, a very quiet, sophisticated young woman, who at the time was working on her second novel, was bored in class and unstimulated by classmates who could not match her writing ability. "On the contrary," her mother said, "Nicole has never been happier. She has always been good at writing reports, but this is the first opportunity she's had to create her own stories. She spends hours every week researching material for settings for her work so her stories have credibility."

Parent feedback also came during "staffings" which were held whenever a student was considered to be in crisis. During staffings, parents, teachers, guidance counselors, the school psychologist, and/or various community social agency personnel attempted to identify the reasons a particular student was failing. In five of the six staffings June attended during the first three quarters of the first year of the study, it was revealed that the student under discussion had given up on everything but his or her writing for English class. In Kristi's case, the contrast between her success in English class and her failure in virtually every other class was striking. Her writing folder, which contained multiple drafts of extra as well as required work, was proof of her efforts in class. Her carefully typed final drafts also revealed a possible explanation for her lack of motivation in other classes: three of her stories told how desperately she missed a cousin and grandmother who had recently died and a father she felt she had lost through her parents' divorce. In a survey conducted approximately six weeks before her staffing, Kristi wrote:

I took Freshman English last year and failed, but I probably would have passed if I had been in this class. I have learned to feel comfortable in what I'm writing. I can now trust people when I have my writing on paper. When I write I feel so proud of myself, I don't care who reads it.

Additional evidence that students began writing more was based on informal observation. It became obvious by the end of the first quarter that an informal network of critiquers had been established by several students from each of the five classes. Groups of students often congregated outside the classroom between periods or at the end of the day to share and critique each other's work. Once in a while students would rush into the room for quick feedback from the teacher, and occasionally a student from one class would request that a piece from another class be shared during his or her period. Primarily, though, they were writing only for themselves.

The most powerful evidence that students began to write more, however, comes from the longitudinal data about the writing behavior of students. Two particularly dramatic examples of how the writing habit had "stuck" are provided by David and Becky. David nearly left school during his second try at getting through several sophomore courses. When he began writing powerful essays in English on topics like drug abuse and suicide, however, he got the attention of most of the class. The recognition was enough to keep him in school, and the more he wrote, the better his material became. By the end of the year he had decided he wanted to become a journalist. In a parent-teacher conference, his mother lamented the fact that she could not afford to send him to college, and David apparently left school the following year without a diploma. When June returned to the school after the year spent in New Zealand, David began sending her the writing he had been doing since he had dropped out of school. "David left school after that year he was in this class," the student who delivered his material said. "He still writes though, everyday. He's been getting good at poetry and he wanted your opinion of these pieces now that you're back." David had never attempted poetry in class, but his new efforts were as impressive as his essays had been.

Becky came to Westerville South in the middle of her freshman year. She was an angry, rebellious adolescent from rural West Virginia. She frequently cut class and had a drug problem. She was very bright, however, and her writing was good, in spite of its unpolished style and weak mechanics. Eventually students began reading Becky's work and giving her enthusiastic, positive feedback. She started coming to class regularly and worked constantly on her writing, experimenting with a variety of types of pieces. After four months, the teacher recommended she sign up for the journalism course the following year and begin writing for the school newspaper. (She was failing her other classes so special arrangements had to be made to get her on the newspaper staff.) Today Becky is a junior and she is making plans to go to college. The journalism advisor considers her a super-talent. She wants to be a journalist, and when she spoke to freshmen students this year, she already sounded like one. She has had numerous articles published in the school paper, and last year she produced a beautifully written, detailed account of her drug rehabilitation experience. It was published in two local newspapers and a national newsletter.

Personal Ownership.   The questions of whether students begin to write for themselves and whether they regard themselves as professional writers are related, and the answers are partially revealed above. Obviously, students who wrote more than before, or more than required, did so for greater rewards than a single grade could provide. The fact that individual pieces were never actually graded further supports this point. Increased self-esteem, strengthened confidence in ability, and emotional release were the reasons most often cited by students (including those who did not do extra work) for writing. Richel said, "I think it is important to be able to write your feelings down on paper because a lot of the times, if you're confused or upset, when you write it down and read it back to yourself everything makes more sense." Sherry, a student who was so terrified about her first oral presentation in September she literally whispered it, gained enough confidence through her writing to say, by the end of January, "I think learning to write is really satisfying, because now if I have to prepare a speech or something else I can do it without any doubt in my mind." (Sherry produced only a short essay first quarter; by the end of third quarter she had completed her seventh chapter on a novel she is writing.)

By second quarter, students had also begun incorporating their writing in their lives outside of school. Four students wrote letters to stores requesting compensation for faulty products, one student wrote to the President to express his concerns about nuclear war, and three students prepared job applications. Sam sent a story based on "Eleanor Rigby" to Paul McCartney along with a letter expressing his concern that a cartoon that is planned to be released soon could destroy the dignity of the Beatle's song. Meghan sent a long-distance dedication to an international radio show hoping to reestablish contact with a friend she missed from her cancer rehabilitation camp.

Evidence also exists to show that students regarded themselves as writers and began to behave in many of the ways writers do. Students often became stubborn about their work, refusing to allow it to be edited in any major way for publication. One sophomore from the study's first year, Robert, actually decided not to submit his poems to one contest that would not accept illustrations along with written entries. Robert was failing all of his other classes, but he had worked hard in English and was very proud of his writing. Just the suggestion that his poetry was good enough to enter a national contest nearly overwhelmed him. It took him four days to decide not to seek more recognition by entering the contest, to uphold his belief that his words could not be separated from his drawings. Indeed, his pride must have been even greater than the teacher first realized, because, two years later, Robert came back to the teacher to ask if she had any extra copies of his work. He had just lost his portfolio in a move.

Professional Characteristics. In addition to taking intense personal pride in their writing and developing professional attitudes about ownership of their work, students also displayed work habits that are typical of professional writers. During conferences they reported writing best in the middle of the night, and they explained their strategies for dealing with writer's block. Many students described the odd experience of having characters they created begin "running away with the story" as if they had lives of their own, or of feeling so involved in their writing they felt themselves becoming one of the characters. They freely expressed the pain of having work sent in for publication rejected, or the frustration of dealing with a piece that "just isn't working." Students talked of writing just for themselves and of writing for publication. Their vocabulary was filled with words like "draft," "critique," "piece," "copy," "edit," "lead," "polish," "proof," and "persona," and when they worked on each other's material they marked up drafts using professional editing symbols.

Students kept files of their finished work, and usually by the end of the year they also had an idea page as well as a collection of several works in progress. A survey done at the end of first quarter showed that only three or four students per class kept lists of ideas for pieces, in spite of the fact that this practice was strongly recommended. (It is a common habit among writers to list *every* idea that is generated.) By midyear, the number of students keeping idea pages had doubled and students reported *needing* to do this to keep track of all the new ideas that kept surfacing. Four out of five former students who presented a panel discussion to new freshmen classes explained that their original resistence to keeping idea pages had vanished. Each of these senior and junior writers indicated that they had file drawers full of ideas. "Once you start writing *a lot,* like I do," Carla, a senior this year, said, "you see stories *everywhere* and you have to jot your ideas down and save them. Otherwise you lose them, because there isn't always enough time to write all the stories out completely."

Organizational Skills. For every student, the idea of being constantly responsible for long-range deadlines and for generating projects entirely on their own was new. Even so, a systematic review of students' folders revealed that approximately two-thirds of the students (eighteen or nineteen per class) were very successful at organizing their time and structuring their work to function effectively on an individual basis and profit from working independently. Most impressive were students who set up computer files either at home or at school to keep track of particularly complex and extensive writing projects. At least ten students worked this way. Five or six students in each class struggled all year with deadlines and continued to seem incapable of handing drafts in on time, in spite of goals they set each quarter to "get a hold of themselves." Another five or six students fluctuated in their performance.

Cognitive Effects. The question about the program's impact on students' thinking skills is the most difficult to answer definitively. This project was not designed to be a quasi-experimental study. (Indeed, it is difficult to conceive of a quasi-experimental study in which the dependent variable can approximate the cognitive complexity associated with writings.) If one accepts the generalization emerging from time-on-task research—that students tend to learn what they have an opportunity to do—there is certainly evidence to support the notion that many students' thinking skills improved during the course of the year.

Evidence of how students' thinking grows through writing was found in numerous portfolios. Students often did more than simply refine language and correct mechanics when they worked through multiple drafts. They used the processes of editing and revising to completely rework ideas from new perspectives. They also used their writing to grapple with philosophical issues or to express opinions about things they studied in other classes.

Bryan's first draft of a poem described life as "having ups and downs." After a discussion about cliches and the need for poetry to make precise use of descriptive language, he completely rewrote his piece. He kept the original theme, but this time he compared going through life with being on various rides in an amusement park.

Jen wrote a long, tender story about a girl's first sexual experience and the trauma she felt in telling her mother about it. After sensing the class's fascination with the piece, Jen decided to write the same story over again—this time as it would have been told by the boy.

Barb tried to write a story about her real-life experiences of meeting a boy at summer camp who had later been seriously injured in a sports accident. The boy died unexpectedly while Barb was polishing the story she had hoped to send him. Instead of abandoning the piece, however, which had originally rambled on too long about every detail of camp life, she completely rewrote it. Her final draft, which was written in the first person rather than the third, was one-fifth of the length of the original piece and effectively focused on what she had really wanted to say in the first place—that losing a friend is intensely painful.

When Lisa couldn't effectively say what she wanted to in a story about the same topic, she found the poem genre worked better. Soon after writing her poem, Lisa explained how struggling with writing affects her thinking:

> I've basically learned how to find mistakes [in my writing], but a lot of the time I don't know how to fix them. I don't mean spelling mistakes or things like that. I'll explain it to you like this. A story is like a pie. It's got a lot of parts to it. Sometimes after

you're done with a story, you read it and something is wrong. It doesn't sound right. It's like a piece of the pie is missing. I can't fix things like that. That's one of my goals—to be able to find the missing piece.

Other students were also reflective about their work. Jenny said:

Looking back on the first couple of things I wrote, I noticed there wasn't much feeling, or originality . . . . They looked like a writing assignment. Now, however, I feel my writing skills have improved.

Kyle believed that by looking at his work critically he would actually gain some important insights into his own thinking. "I've always been writing," he said, "but not like I am now. This year, from [listening to] all the discussions and guests, I have learned to put my thoughts on paper . . . . My goals for this year are to finish understanding why I write the way I do."

Mike's story about an imaginary kingdom called Cuaraperide is an example of how students take ideas from other classes and expand on them in their portfolio work. The story, which describes how Cuaraperide lost an important war after eliminating its defense budget in favor of building its domestic programs, was Mike's attempt to explain how peace, war, and economic issues are interrelated. He was introduced to this concept in history class.

Improvement. The final question, has students' writing improved?, is the "bottom line" for many educational researchers and teachers of writing. While it is not possible within the constraints of this kind of study to demonstrate exactly how much growth in terms of writing style or mechanical skill took place among all the students in these two years, it is possible to provide examples of the kind of knowledge and skills many students acquired.

Formal records were not kept during the first year of students' progress through individual areas of difficulty. In talking with some of these students two years later, however, it was discovered that most believed they had mastered skills primarily by writing. For example, one junior recalled not knowing how to set up dialogue at first, and then learning it all at once when she needed it for a story which she eventually published. Another student, currently a senior, remarked that she is no longer threatened by having to write research papers for other classes. She had done a research paper as part of her portfolio work two years ago and she felt she had, as a result, mastered both the form and the techniques of this type of writing.

During the second year, June borrowed and adapted Atwell's (1987) method of focusing students' attention on two or three problem areas at a time and documenting progress as attempts are made to eliminate stylistic, grammatical, and spelling errors. A review of the portfolios revealed that simple mechanical errors such as homonym confusion and misuse of punctuation marks were eradicated rather quickly. (It should be kept in mind that these "simple" errors had not been eradicated during the ten or eleven previous years of schooling.) Learning the technical aspects of writing dialogue was also mastered quickly by most students. Other problem areas, such as subject/verb agreement, parallel construction, verb tense consistency, pronoun agreement, and run-on sentences and fragments were more difficult to eradicate, but in most cases students were at least aware of their problem even if they didn't always know how to fix it. Chad wrote, "My biggest problem, I think, is that I'm not good at parallelism. In most of my portfolio I have used it in one form or another. I'm learning how to use it now after many mistakes . . . . It seems now that I'm developing an ear for bad grammar, and also an eye for it."

Students also learned some tricks of the trade as they became increasingly involved in their work. Stephanie discovered, for instance, that fluidity is important in writing and sometimes writers need to "write past" problem spots. She said, "I can tell I've learned from writing because, before, I would set limitations on my writing. Now I just seem to let the words flow out onto the paper." Jill also found that good writing takes multiple drafts and writers need to begin by simply getting as much on paper as possible. "What I have learned . . . is that when I write, I should just let myself go. What I mean by this is that I should just write and write. I shouldn't worry about the mistakes I've made. I also have learned that nobody can write a perfect paper the first time, and for some reason I thought I should."

Rich and Missy perfected some of their literary techniques after becoming more experienced with writing short stories. Rich claims he learned how to end a chapter. "By ending a chapter in suspense," he says, "it will make the reader curious and he or she will read on." Missy discovered a seldom-disclosed practice of fiction writers: When writing a story, she says "it's easier to start out with an idea and expand on it. Put some lies in it—well, not really lies, but stretch the truth. Stories don't just pop into your mind. Maybe ideas do, but you have to make the ideas bigger."

Classroom Characteristics Contributing to Success

The data suggest that at least six factors contributed to the creation of a culture of writers in this particular classroom: (1) using, almost exclusively, reactive, improvisational teaching and modeling as modes for the "teaching" of writing; (2) dramatizing the notion that writing is important; (3) dramatizing the notion that the student's writing was important; (4) deemphasizing grading while emphasizing critiquing; (5) focusing on the positive; and (6) altering tactics and criteria to accommodate individual differences. As is often the case in qualitative work, the general conclusions listed above are hardly surprising; the significance of this and much other qualitative work can be found in the specific descriptions of how general principles were operationalized in particular settings. What follows is a look at how the six factors listed above worked in this classroom.

Improvisational Teaching and Modeling.   June's reliance on improvisational teaching became apparent during a debriefing session during the first year of the program. June commented that when she was teaching writing, she was almost always "flying by the seat of my pants. I know all teachers take advantage of the moment and sometimes digress from the lesson," she said, "but when I teach writing, that's the norm."

June was somewhat defensive about this practice. She noted, for example, that she did not normally approach the teaching of literature in such an improvisational way. Close examination, however, revealed that the teacher did, indeed, engage in reactive rather than proactive teaching. This generalization held for both the teaching of mechanics and grammar and the teaching of other content related to writing. For example, an editing session in which the student and the teacher were puzzling over why a line of the student's poetry didn't quite work led to the conclusion that the conjunction should be "but" rather than "and." This, in turn, led to a brief explanation of the meaning of the term *conjunction*, a term which the student undoubtedly had been exposed to throughout her school career but which she had still not quite understood.

Similarly, Penny's frustrations with reworking a draft on the death of her father was an impetus for a mini-lesson—this time directed to the class as a whole, which had been asked to stop their own writing for a moment to help Penny—on the personal essay genre and the characteristics that make work in this genre successful.

The only thing resembling direct instruction was the use of modeling and teaching through example. June was, herself, a model. She had worked for years as a writer and editor, continued to write while teaching, and shared her frustrations, problems, and solutions with class members.

One technique she used was sharing events from her own life and explaining how these events could be shaped into different types of writing. Once, her youngest son came home from school very upset because his science-project mealworms had died over the weekend, and he wanted to give them a funeral. In relating Marc's story to the class, June demonstrated how she could have used the episode to create a humorous story about the growing pains of little boys and mealworm funerals, a mother's personal essay on how parents yearn to protect their children from sadness, or a poem on the loveliness of childhood innocence.

June also commonly shared student work that was either superb or superbly illustrated as a particular point for aspiring writers to note. Frequently scheduled roundtable discussions permitted close examination of students' works in progress. The ostensible purpose of these discussions was to help the writer, but the critiquers' writing skills were also undoubtedly expanded as they helped a particular student work through a problem.

Finally, literature was consciously used as a model in the teaching of writing. Indeed, the teaching of writing and the teaching of literature were mutually reinforcing. For some students establishing a professional kinship between themselves and authors such as James Thurber, Edgar Allen Poe, John Steinbeck and Carson McCullers, whom they had studied in class, was the only way to interest them in the study of literature. When Richel began producing short stories that explored family relationships during adolescence, for example, many of her characters were reminiscent of those created by Carson McCullers. The teacher discussed Mc-

Cullers's work with Richel, showing her the parallels, and Richel decided to read a collection of this well-known author's short stories for her book report.

Despite June's initial defensiveness about her somewhat improvisational style while teaching writing, we have concluded that this style is a significant factor in the creation of a culture of writers. The style allowed students and their interests to be at the center of the curriculum, for them to feel ownership over what was going on (a feeling which, in fact, was not an illusion), and for the curriculum to be relevant. It seems significant that skills which were not learned through the nine or ten prior years of schooling were learned rather quickly in this classroom culture.

Importance of Writing.   Most teachers realize their subject is important; what they may not recognize is that their students do not necessarily share in this realization. Teaching requires, in part, a public relations campaign to sell the subject. Such a campaign was consciously constructed in this classroom, and we believe it contributed to the creation of a culture of writers.

To be sure, June was herself a walking advertisement for the importance of writing. For years she had made a living as a writer, she cared deeply about writing, and she undoubtedly communicated her interest and passion in many unconscious and subtle ways. She also did very conscious and unsubtle things which all teachers of writing—whether they have been professional writers or not—can do to sell their subject.

Probably the most successful selling tactic was bringing writers into the classroom to talk about their work. Because she had many contacts in the profession, June was able to arrange for professional writers to speak and read their work to her classes. Some of the most successful speakers were not professionals at all, however. For instance, one of the school's guidance counselors, a popular figure among students, was invited to speak to the class after she told the teacher of her attempts to write an article for her statewide professional association. The process she described paralleled both the experiences described by professional writers and the experiences of students in the class who had begun to approach writing as a professional endeavor.

By far the most successful speakers—the best salespersons for the importance of writing—were upper-class students. The practice of inviting older students into the classroom was actually initiated by students. Students in one class decided they wanted to meet the authors of their favorite pieces in the school literacy magazine which, at that point, only included work from students in the gifted and talented program. John was one of these students. This skilled writer—and champion wrestler—was invited to talk about his work as a writer. His message that he wrote primarily for personal satisfaction seemed to influence many students. The teacher now has a cadre of juniors and seniors who are willing to share their writing experiences with other students. No more effective salespersons have ever existed.

Importance of Students' Writing.   June signaled to her students not only that writing is important; she also consciously and unconsciously communicated that their writing was important. She did this in several ways.

First, she allowed, in fact she required, students to generate their own topics and choose the genre in which they would work. (Students who had limited themselves to a single genre were often encouraged to expand their repertoire by trying other forms, but ultimately the choices and the responsibilities were the students'.) The teacher encouraged students to make their portfolio work meaningful to themselves. In the case of John, a boy who had been transferred to the school after having assaulted his former principal, meaningful writing took the form of a statement to his attorney of what had happened. For other students, work took the form of letters to the editor, reports for other classes, job applications and other material described earlier. (See Evidence of Success section.) While getting students to write for themselves rather than simply to meet course requirements was listed earlier as a goal of the writing curriculum, having students write for real purposes can also be viewed as a means to the end of creating a culture of writers.

Related to the issue of meaningfulness was the emphasis placed on publication. The teacher not only helped students enter writing contests, she also actively created markets for their work. The school literary magazine, which previously contained work only from students from gifted and talented program, now had submissions from a whole other group of students. When the teacher discussed her classroom practices at the local university or before a group of teachers from another district, she read selections of students' work. Whenever possible, she also arranged to bring some of her students along to help with the presentation. Whenever work was presented publicly or printed in some form, it was listed on the "Publications Record" chart which hung on a bulletin board in the back of the room.

Students also published their own literary magazine, which contained at least one piece of writing from each student, and each class produced an evening theatrical presentation of excerpts from the collection. These presentations, which were different for each class, were done in an oversized classroom with limited scenery (risers, stools, ladders) and simple staging. Professional lighting was rented to create a theatrical atmosphere which, for some students, was itself a magical experience.

Scripts for the production were created totally from students' writing: pieces were sometimes read chorally, in small groups or individually; sometimes dramatized; and sometimes put to music. As might be expected, parents were usually extremely enthusiastic about the evening and students often described it as their best experience of the year. Even the handful of students who didn't get involved in the performance, because participation was voluntary, noted the significance of the event once it was over. Todd compared the value of the readers' theater project with other curriculum activities:

> I think the readers' theater was a very nice and constructive project. You might not think I was that involved and I wasn't, but what I saw was a bunch of kids and a teacher get together as a group and work very hard on what was important to them. My personal opinion is that readers' theater could take over [the study of] Shakespeare for the years to come.

While the theatrical production was literally and metaphorically the most dramatic way of selling the notion that students writing is important, this message was also communicated in less dramatic but equally significant ways. Most tests on literature required that students write essay answers. While this may seem like an obvious way of signaling to students that their writing is integral to all aspects of their learning, surprisingly few teachers, in either the English or other departments, used anything but objective, short answer tests in their classrooms. Reasons for this practice ranged from needing objective measures of progress that would satisfy parents to needing efficient methods of coping with heavy teaching loads.

Other ways were also used to emphasize the importance of students' writing. Unlike one teacher in the building who had kept a former student's work for years, but never told her, this teacher expressed her appreciation for students' writing at every opportunity. She filled bulletin boards with their stories and poems. One bulletin board posted comments class members had made during roundtables or conferences about their writing experiences, alongside similar sounding comments famous writers have made about their work. In addition, she joked—but half seriously—about how all writing folders needed to be kept in the metal filing cabinet in the front of the room, "In case the building should burn down!"

Deemphasis on Grades and Emphasis on Critiquing   Grades were deliberately deemphasized in evaluating students' writing. Rather, the emphasis was on analyzing and critiquing work. The way the teacher accomplished this was by writing comments on drafts and showing how mechanics should be fixed, but not assigning a numerical grade to the writing. Drafts were also often edited in this way by other students. Students were expected to make necessary revisions in order to produce perfect final copies of each piece. Then, at the end of the quarter, the teacher held a conference with each student and together they placed a value on the complete portfolio. This grade was as much a valuation of students' progress and effort as it was a measure of ability.

The notion of evaluating work through critiquing was established early in the year when students were preparing presentations for the speech unit. Rotating juries of five or six students were set up to judge other students' presentations. Evaluation sheets were used to guide jury members through the critiquing process and at the end of each speech results of the evaluation were presented and discussed.

Students were also given practice critiquing written material. A mini-lesson based on some of Atwell's (1987) techniques explained how critiquers can help authors view their work more objectively. Another lesson provided students with the symbols that are universally used by professional editors. (Students and teacher then agreed to use these symbols in all of their editing.)

Deemphasizing grades while emphasizing critiquing gave students both a realistic appraisal of their work and a hopeful attitude about their abilities. Students quickly become comfortable with the idea that writing is never really finished. Amy explained it this way: "Knowing that my writing improves everytime I write is important [to me]. I know not to give up on a piece that doesn't seem to work. Just give it time and someday it will all come together." Another student, Barb, explained her understanding of how work develops, and in doing so she revealed how never having a final grade put an end to a piece encourages students to rework material no matter how many quarters it overlaps.

> In the beginning I wrote poems with a style that was a little too cutesy and catchy. I realized this and decided to try another form of writing: stories and essays. I learned that, in a way, every piece of writing reveals a little bit of the writer. In the next quarter, I would like to take the stories I have previously written and make them very special, if you know what I mean. And when I decide to write poems again, the style will be more tender.

Emphasis on the Positive. A great deal has already been said about the positive attitudes that dominate this classroom. Clearly, the teacher operates from the belief that the more students feel positive about their work, the more they will write, and consequently, the more their work will improve. During individual conferences and roundtable discussions, June makes a point of describing what is effective about a piece or what technical skills are used correctly, before suggesting any changes. This does not mean that false praise is showered on students. Positive comments are sincere, and they accurately describe students' work. At the same time, standards are high, and June does not hesitate to tell a student what still needs work. Nor do students hold back honest comments. Crystal explains: "I do like how we all learned that it is okay for us to express what is awkward in other students' writings. It is great that we don't get hurt by that. It took a little while, but it happened."

Students' comments frequently revealed the effect positive feedback has on their desire to work. Jamie, who does not consider himself a particularly successful student, did not turn in any writing the first quarter of this year. He said he had always done poorly in English, he could not write, and, besides, his handwriting was so poor no one would be able to read it anyway. After reminding

Jamie that he could fail for the quarter if he didn't begin writing soon, June encouraged Jamie to start one small piece. She assured him that he could probably write better than he thought since he was an avid reader. Eventually, Jamie produced some of the most insightful and sophisticated essays the teacher had ever received from a student. At a presentation to university students, a member of the audience compared his work to John Carver, a well-known minimalist writer. Encouraged by this and other positive feedback from the teacher, Jamie began doing extra writing. In January, he explained his feelings about writing:

> I have learned a lot about writing. I learned that I can write well and I never knew that before. It is a big thrill for me when I write and people enjoy hearing it. . . . I want to write a novel. I lost the one I was working on, but I won't let that stop me. I've already started on another one and I have hopes this one will be my best. . . . I know deep down inside I can write anything and write it well. I couldn't do that before.

Other students shared Jamie's new-found enthusiasm. "The most important thing [to remember]," Christie said, "is that if you keep pushing yourself and keep rewriting, taking out and adding to a piece, it's going to get better each time." Rich said "During the past four and half months, my personal writing has developed a great deal. I know now how to express my feelings on paper. My sentences make sense, instead of sounding dumb. In the past I worried about people making fun of my writing, but not anymore."

Individual Differences.   Closely related to a deemphasis placed on grades and a positive approach to students' work was the importance placed on individual differences among students. Individual differences were given special consideration when portfolio work was being evaluated. Certain students have exceptional ability and June placed high standards on their work. When Jenny submits three or four chapters of her novel, which was set during the Civil War and which had been painstakingly researched (Jenny once spent three days trying to verify the color of Jackson's horse!) June did not automatically give her portfolio an A because it was more extensive and more competent than most other students. Rather, she explained to Jenny that she has extraordinary talent and her levels of perfection must be higher than most. Jenny accepted this and eagerly accepted the challenge of broadening her skills even further.

Other students required different sorts of consideration. Sam could technically be classified as gifted. He was not in the gifted program, however, because of personal problems that affected his grades in eighth grade. His creativity was extraordinary and his rate of productivity was equally amazing. His writing was rich with symbolism and a challenge even for adults to read. He did not function well with deadlines, however, and he worked sporadically, requiring large amounts of time, all at once, from the teacher. He was exceedingly hard on himself, as well, and bright enough to know when feedback was too generous. In short, he was a very demanding student: he needed a setting in which he had enough freedom to work on his own, but was not so indulged he would never play the school game well enough to actually succeed as a student. He also needed to be rewarded fairly for his excellent work.

Students like Jamie and Lisa required still other compensations at first. They were so reluctant to get started writing that June had to reward mediocre first attempts sufficiently to keep them writing. As work improved from these and other students like them, she increased demands for perfection, explaining this policy to the students as she did so. Students readily accepted their treatment and considered it to be basically fair.

Respect for individual differences was also fundamental to the initial procedures set up for portfolio work described earlier. Students worked on their own ideas in their own ways. The belief that good writing can only begin with a student's own ideas and initiative dictated that students would have both the freedom and the responsibility for developing themselves along with their work. Separation of personality (the writer's persona) and writing was inconceivable. As a result, no idea was squelched before it is tried, and no plan for publication was viewed as impossible. With each new piece, students were encouraged to reach beyond what they had already accomplished, in spite of the mistakes they would inevitably make in their efforts. Before long students accepted these mistakes in their own and others' work and recognized them for what they were: areas of growth, not ignorance or lack of skill.

When this happened, students lost whatever sense of limits they may have once felt, and they became empowered to produce their best possible work.

CONCLUSION

Researchers have traditionally been suspicious of the generalizability of single case studies, and practitioners have always known that what works for one teacher will not necessarily work for another. Undoubtedly what happened in this classroom was as much a product of who this teacher is as it is a product of what she did. Even if another teacher of writing should employ the strategies and techniques described in this paper, he or she will not necessarily get the same results.

Still, the findings employed in this study can be used heuristically by teachers, administrators, and policy makers. Teachers are challenged to consider the utility of responsive, improvisational teaching. They are also reminded of the possible need to "sell" the utility of their subject to students; of the need to expressively communicate that they value students' work; of the limits of using grades as an incentive, at least in certain subjects and with certain students; of the dividends reaped from being positive yet avoiding false, sugarcoated praise; and of the need to accommodate individual differences.

Administrators are challenged to consider how secondary schools might be reorganized to make it more likely teachers can teach in the manner described in this chapter. Robert at one point commented that June teaches the way good elementary school teachers teach. For example, she attempts to personalize the writing curriculum, and know each of her 140 students personally. She even fills bulletin boards with displays of students' work. It is very difficult to personalize a curriculum for 140 students, however, and to sustain the energy level that is required to do this year after year. Maybe it is even impossible. If cultures of writers are to be created and sustained in our schools, new organizational structures and the reallocation of resources may be required.

Finally, this study challenges policy makers to be a bit more open-minded with respect to how they conceive of curriculum design and teacher evaluation. This teacher's writing curriculum was the antithesis of the curriculum structured around carefully sequenced behavioral objectives. Similarly it is unlikely that this teacher—while teaching writing—would be rated highly in an evaluation system built around teacher effectiveness research. It is unlikely, however, that anyone would dispute that this teacher was successful in the teaching of writing.

CHAPTER 21

A Teacher Reflects on his Urban Classroom

Art Isennagle, Columbus City Schools, Ohio

The theme of this chapter is similar to that of the previous one. The author once again is a classroom teacher. The classroom this time is in an urban elementary school. The teacher describes how he socializes his students to believe that they can learn and that learning is important. He also indicates that, once this socialization process has taken hold, his students have more discretion over their own learning than would be found in classrooms organized around rules and regulations, rewards and punishments, and teacher-assigned seatwork.

I've been asked to write about my experiences in the classroom because I have received recognition for a supposedly unique teaching style. In this chapter I will define my philosophy of teaching, describe the structure of my classroom, and then share with you the outcomes of this environment and why these outcomes occur. I think it will become obvious that indeed things are not that much different.

PHILOSOPHY

Like the poet and educator Robert Frost, I regard myself as an awakener, not a teacher. John Milton Gregory regards the teacher's mission as one "to excite the mind of the pupils, to stimulate their thoughts" (cited in Hendrick, 1987, p. 54). Gregory states that "the true function of the teacher is to create the most favorable conditions for self-learning." Self-learning comes from a love of lifelong learning and a knowledge of how to learn. Young children know they come to school to learn but do they know they *can* learn? I have found students who arrive at school with fragile identities, many times questioning their self-esteem. Many seem to have a low frustration tolerance. Easily discouraged, they seem sometimes to suspend the reality of their own successfulness. "I can't" becomes a disgusted moan as seven-year-old Bryan is given paper on which to write an open-ended response to a story he just heard read aloud. When offered assistance, Bryan deliberately bangs his elbow on the desk and turns away, not wanting to try. With similar frustration, eleven-year-old Sherry throws a reader to the floor exclaiming, "I'm gonna be bad! I can't read anyway."

As a teacher in an urban school with an approximately 90 percent minority population, I have found children like Bryan and Sherry to be the norm. I have worked with children who attempt to masquerade their ability to succeed by deliberately presenting facades of failure. In my experience I have had students say to me, "It's a game. We can fool parents and teachers if they think we don't know. We just get an attitude." How many children learn to regard successful learning as something beyond their reach? All children can learn. Yet how many students realize that for themselves and act upon it? Before children can learn how to learn they must know and believe they can learn.

It seems necessary then for teachers to draw up definite plans of action as well as alternative approaches to allow children the chance to own high expectations, to achieve success, and to develop a desire to meet their potential. Preparing this sense of academic identity is as crucial as preparing an inviting environment and exciting lesson plans. In my classroom I work to promote both a desire to learn and a knowledge of how to learn by developing a sense of personal and academic self-esteem and identity. This is achieved through active student involvement, student ownership of learning, and a strong network of teacher, student, parent, and community support.

An academic identity, also thought of as a learner's positive self-esteem, empowers and awakens a student's desire to try, to learn, and to discover. When children enter a classroom with injured or under developed senses of self-esteem, they must be taught first to know they can learn and that all students are expected to do so. I think of the second grader who, when faced with the first A in his academic career, burst out shouting, "I never thought I could do THIS!" This academic identity is enveloped in the idea that before one can become one must be. A sense of personal and academic mission must be built into every classroom structure. What we perceive, we can believe. One new second grader recently confided to me that when he walked into my room he thought he "was going to flunk." I asked him why. "Because I couldn't read. So I got an attitude." When asked what made the difference, the boy replied, "You wouldn't put up with the attitude. You called my parents in the first week of school and gave us a tape recorded book. I can read that whole book and I like to read."

I teach to awaken children to the reality of their own potential. My philosophy of teaching is based on two objectives I set for all students:

1. To learn that they can learn anything and everything.
2. To learn how to develop the love and skills of lifelong learning.

To accomplish these goals I incorporate the following elements in my teaching:

- a stimulating environment immersed in print
- active student involvement
- high expectations for students
- student ownership and choices of learning
- strong enthusiastic support from the teacher, students, and parents that uphold the classroom as a community of learning.

STRUCTURE

Plato once noted that "What is honored in a country is cultivated there" (cited in Huck, 1976). This is also true for the classroom. I made the decision that the goals and elements of my teaching philosophy were to be reflected and incorporated into my daily classroom structure, routine, and climate. Long before the first day of school, I make the classroom and its climate ready to capture the hearts and minds of all who enter. Quality children's literature, including picture books, poetry books, biography, nonfiction, and chapter books, fills my room. I tempt children into books by displaying them front cover out. I also spend much time the first few weeks introducing and sharing some of the displayed books, especially some high-interest books with repetitive, cumulative building verse and catchy rhythms such as Nancy Van Laan's *Possum Come A-Knockin'* (1990).

> Possum come a-knockin'
> at the door, at the door.
> Possum come a-knockin'
> at the door.

Used in conjunction with the knocking-like rhythms that open Beethoven's Fifth Symphony, my students acquired an appreciation for the story and developed confidence in their own ability to read the book. One of my second-grade classes was so impressed with this book that they created their own musical version of this book and entitled it, "Learnin' Come A-Knockin." These students had certainly developed an enjoyment for learning, especially when writing such words as: "when learnin' come a-knockin' at our brains, at our brains, when learnin' come a-knockin' at our brains."

Proudly displayed wall charts of such class-generated work share equal billing with the poems and pieces of published authors, both classic and contemporary. These pieces are all used as part of my daily reading curriculum, giving children confidence in their own ability to read and learn and stretching their appreciation and appetite for learning. By actively and emotionally involving students in books and learning, I work to ensure the capture of every learner's heart before I reach his or her mind.

Another rhythmic favorite used in my classroom is the delightful collection of verse by Eloise Greenfield called *Nathaniel Talking* (1988). A crowd-pleasing favorite, at least in my experience, this book's delightful rap poem "Nathaniel's Rap" was a daily must read for two straight weeks in my classroom. I wrote the poem out so each child could have a copy to read from. We would read the poem daily. There seems to be something in the mind of a child, in my observations at least, that considers the reading of a poem a simpler reading experience than that of a story, but just as complete. One morning three or four weeks later, the class came in together with a surprise for me. In unison they performed "Nathaniel's Rap" in complete rap fashion, with bobbing heads and undulating arms and shoulders, completely from memory. What caught my attention most with this incident was the pride, enthusiasm, and ownership of learning that these second graders demonstrated. Many observers have noticed and commented upon the same features when they have visited my classes over the years.

A glance around the room reveals books in plastic tubs, crates, and many displayed on shelves throughout the classroom. Picture books, fiction of all kinds, poetry, as well as informative nonfiction are included. A sampling of titles includes such books as *The Napping House, Mufaro's Beautiful Daughters, Flossie and the Fox, Mirandy and Brother Wind, Crow Boy, Madeline, Brown Bear, Brown Bear, The Jolly Postman, Blueberries for Sal,* and *Sing a Song of Popcorn.* A print-immersed environment with many books, magazines, and a variety of other materials helps cultivate an attitude that honors and pursues learning.

In setting up a structure for my class, I work to establish both an intangible framework of mindset and spirit as well as a tangible structure of set routines, customs, and classroom practices. A print-immersed classroom helps to convey a sense of purpose and mission, but I take this learning-lover's attitude that I want to establish several steps further. Each student's heart must be caught up in the passion and enjoyment of learning and reading. This attitude is a mindset that must be nurtured daily. Time for this cultivating of spirit is set into every day's lesson plans. It is imperative that I teach each student that they can learn, regardless of whatever they believe hinders them. Moreover, if they can realize that they want to learn and that they can enjoy learning, then suddenly the old barriers of failure and inadequacy don't exist anymore. A love for learning has taken top priority.

Teaching students to know they can learn requires that I couple an academic sense of identity with a sense of mission. This begins the first moment I meet my pupils.

> Welcome, graduating class of the year 2001. Yes, you are all learners, discoverers, and future high school and college graduates. In June, 2001, you will no longer be in second grade but you will be going to college. Why? Because I have some of Ameri-

ca's finest, some of the brightest students in the nation. Not one of you cannot learn. Don't play games with me, your parents, or yourselves and pretend you can't because I know and you know that you can. You will graduate from college and do something special for the world. Each of you will make me famous. Why? Because of the great things that each and every one of you will do, starting today.

How many children get this kind of talk on a daily basis? Like daily medicine I see that my students receive this everyday until it becomes a mindset. This is part of what they come to school for, to have their spirits challenged to dream and reach for the stars.

For the reluctant few that resist my rhetoric, I continue by using the lure of materialism.

How many of you want to drive a fancy car? How many want a nice house and fancy clothes? Here's how to get them. Breaking into the rich man's world means you have to use your mind. In this class we'll use our minds because we are here to learn. Learning is the most wonderful thing in the world and together we will learn. We're a team, a learning team, and we're going to rely on each other as a learning family to survive. We're going to teach each other because everyone has something to teach everyone else. Everyone has something special to contribute.

By verbally as well as visually inviting my students, I become a pied piper of learning, an awakener, as Robert Frost would say.

A sense of academic mission is now placed within the framework of acting and cooperating as a team. The first few weeks are ones of teaching and practicing cooperation, learning how to aid mutual self-discovery, and establishing team spirit within a learning context. I have seen that children need many opportunities to restructure or modify their individual working models of the world. These first few weeks of school are crucial then for the restructuring and the assimilation that I guide my students through. Many of them need to work through individual differences with others as they begin to place a high priority on their mutual purpose for being at school.

Learning teams are established through flexible grouping, and a strong sense of class unity is built as I work to establish a mutuality of purpose and spirit between me and my students. Stories, poems, songs, games, dramatic play, writings, comments, and non-verbal cues such as smiles, applause, hugs, thumbs up, winks, and handshakes and high fives underscore both a team spirit and a oneness of purpose. All of these methods are used throughout the day in large doses to establish that intangible mindset, that invisible but strongly felt spirit that will help structure my routines, procedures, and practices.

I often take familiar tunes and create a new set of lyrics that I use both for reading practice and for self-esteem building as I build that academic identity within each child. It is ridiculous to assume that children don't need this building of spirit. They do, and, if first established, then the entire class has a framework or mindset that can be called upon throughout the year. To help cement their sense of academic identity, I created the following words to the tune "I'm Going to Wash that Man Right Out of My Hair":

> I'm going to read, write, study, and learn all I can
> I'm going to read, write, study, and learn all I can
> I'm going to read, write, study, and learn all I can
> and I'll go to the top.
>
> Don't interrupt me now.
>
> Concentrate! Concentrate!
> Do your best. Be your best.
> Dare to be different. Shine like stars.
> Go to the top. Yea! Sister/Brother.
>
> If the work becomes a challenge
> If you find the stuff gets hard
> You can if you think you can
> Stick to the job till it's done
> And you will find that you win! Oh yes! Oh yes!

To the tune "Fame" the children learn to sing:

> We're going to learn forever.
> Were going to go to the top.
> We're going to learn forever.
> Learning never will stop.

Daily read and sung, verses such as these become part of the soul, spirit, and heart of each child, and gradually, the old sense of failure and inadequacy begins to fade.

Ownership of learning and a sense of mission become fused together as children unite as one. When one member of the team decides to test the others, that person is met with words from the entire group such as, "Would you please get it together? You're interrupting our learning time and we're here to learn." Disruptions begin to cease or at least decline as students realize the seriousness of their peers. What once began as only the intense purpose of my own idealism becomes part of the classroom structure that guides day-to-day learning.

My intangible structure now begins to support and give shape to a tangible framework of routines, procedures, and customs that give the classroom a relaxed yet well orchestrated atmosphere. Mornings are devoted to reading and writing activities while the afternoon is primarily spent on math, social studies, science, health, and the arts. Yet even with the afternoon subjects, a strong literature, reading, and language arts emphasis underlies and supports these subjects. A strong sense of purpose and enthusiastic joy are cultivated daily within a structure that allows for movement and alternating periods of talk and quiet work time. A sample schedule follows:

9:00–9:30	Peer or partner reading
	Group reading or singing—creeds, mottos, poems, songs
	R-E-A-D
9:30–10:30	Whole-class reading/language arts instruction/pre-writing
10:30–10:55	Flexible groups/individual conferences
	Classroom reading/writing time
10:55–11:00	Exercise/calisthenics to music
11:00–11:30	Read aloud by either teacher or student to whole class
11:30–12:30	Lunch and recess
12:30–1:00	Flexible groups/individual conferences
	Classroom reading and writing time
	Finish morning projects
1:00–2:00	Math (whole class and groups)
2:00–2:45	Social studies/science/health
	(within language-based and arts context)
2:45–3:30	Arts/library/physical education

After a scheduled reading time, I lead the class in group readings or singing, sometimes focusing on their written work, sometimes on "older authors," and sometimes on a mixture of both. Occasionally, I may brandish a plastic sword or some other prop as I lead my class in character during this activity. Afterwards, the children play R-E-A-D by walking to a piece of writing somewhere in the room and reading until they hear the signal "R-E-A-D" at which time they move to a new piece of writing. I sometimes substitute some other literary game such as "Poet's Moment," when we may rhyme words or quote favorite pieces or listen to a quick verse. The rest of the morning is spent in a variety of reading and writing activities, all of which are necessary for empowering the children to become a community of readers and writers. Group and peer support is critical and is made a part of the daily structure as children aid each other in reading, editing, writing, and publishing.

What is obviously missing from this schedule is any reference to traditional seatwork. This does not mean that skills are not addressed; however, these are dealt with during flexible-group sessions and individual conferences. If a child needs remediation on a particular skill, then worksheets may be used as the situation requires.

Empowering students becomes my major focus in the classroom. The following are some of the methods I use in order to do this:

- enthusiastic teacher and peer support with high expectations and goals
- immersion in print
- hands on, activity-oriented learning
- student ownership with choices and celebrations of student- and class-generated work
- integration of reading and writing with all content and arts classes
- daily social reading and opportunities to team learn and assist peers
- enriched curriculum for all students with classic and contemporary authors
- enriched vocabulary, and concepts within context that allow for mental stretching and academic pride
- follow-up activities such as listening to tapes, making models, puppet retellings, scroll television retellings, drawing the story in cartoon form, and creative writing
- parent support through constant contact, parent reading and writing breakfasts with students, F.R.E.D. (Family Reading Ev-

ery Day), and parent volunteers in the classroom on a daily basis

- community support through newsletters to and from other schools; literacy, reading, writing, and math clubs; and support from local bookstores and other businesses.

Everything done in the classroom, all the tangible and intangible parts of the structure, and all teacher- and student-generated activities have a hidden agenda—to empower, enthuse, and excite each child's passion for lifelong learning. Even cheers done at the end of the day echo the theme that "we're going to read, study, learn, and get BETTER!"

OUTCOMES

What are the results of these attempts to empower? What are the outcomes of establishing an environment, support systems, and a sense of academic identity in each student? Is it a cure-all?

No. I still have students who resist and require constant effort to keep them in line and on task. Yet, overall the development of academic pride and identity, enthusiasm, and confidence in their own abilities are some of the major strong points in the growth of my students. Quality literature, an enrichment approach for all students, and high expectations foster the growth of their "successful learner" images. High achievement feeds self-esteem. While working with the art teacher, second-grade Gordon asked her if there were any words she'd like to have spelled. "Just ask me anything," Gordon said. "Like ask me to spell choreography, chlorophyll, or botany. Want to know how I know? Because my teacher wants us to learn bad! We are serious about learning in my room!"

One parent reported to me that her son came running home one day shouting, "Mommy, I learned a college poem." He then proceeded to recite the following Tennyson poem:

How dull it is to pause, to make an end,
To rust unburnished, not to shine in use!
        Come my friends,
'Tis not to late to seek a newer world.
        That which we are, we are.
One equal temper of heroic hearts,
Made weak by time and fate but strong in will
To strive, to seek, to find, and not to yield.

I recently came across that same student who is now in fourth grade. He ran up to me as I was on my way home, calling out that he still remembered those poems. "I can still do that college stuff!" he exclaimed. When asked which poems, he answered, "All of them." He then quoted Tennyson, Dickinson, and a couple of contemporary poets, beaming with pride. Learning had become something that was no longer intimidating.

When learning becomes nonthreatening, children's creativity soars. Even their interests widen to include subjects sometimes thought above them. One group of second-grade students surprised me when they chose Beethoven's "Ode to Joy" as their favorite tune to use for a class song and composed the following:

> Join our march for reading and writing,
> Helping others read today.
> Brothers, sisters, friends, and cousins,
> Reading with each other.
> To be smart and go on to college
> You have to read and write your best.
> Share a book with someone special.
> Make it happen everyday.

These results happen because the learning became student owned.

Sometimes the outcomes seem somewhat astounding. Daily, as students are preparing to go home, there is often a increased rush of activity as children try to get one more thing accomplished. Visitors frequently hear remarks such as:

> I want to finish my journal entry. I told myself I wanted to write twenty-five pages and I only have five more to go.
>
> I've memorized the whole Emily Dickinson poem. You know, the one that starts, "I'm nobody. Who are you? Are you nobody too?"
>
> I'm going to write a poem tonight.

Then there are always two or three who find themselves the last to leave because they are still reading lines of a Shakespeare poem from a chart posted on a back wall. Or there is often one student who can't decide between *Little Red Riding Hood* or a Beverly Cleary chapter book to take home for family reading. Jason summed up many of the children's feelings one day when he exclaimed, "Do I gotta go? I wanna read. I'm burnin' to learn!"

These things happen because a real identity has been established in these students. They will proudly tell people when they will graduate and that they like to read and learn. This is their identity. They are learners. They have a goal.

Long after I am out of the picture, I believe these children will still be learning. Why? Because they are awake and they are "burnin' to learn."

CHAPTER 22

The Risk of Writing Outside the Margins: A Reexamination of the Notion of Access

Bonnie Meath-Lang, National Technical Institute for the Deaf, Rochester Institute of Technology

The themes and ideas developed in the previous two chapters are revisited here. The focus here, however, is on a teacher of deaf college students engaging in the dialectical process of (1) teaching writing by building a supportive community and (2) building a supportive community by engaging students with their own and their fellow students' writing.

30 September 1990

It is 8:52. For the last few minutes, I have been discussing transitions and showing students where they have made connections naturally in their own free writing at the beginning of class. We all agreed that connections are quite important. That's pretty funny when the clock nudges fifty minutes after the hour at our place. Immediately, I stop; the business majors jump up, throw on backpacks with the grim look of Alpine rescuers, and run to get to the strategically placed building that some of us surmise to be in a suburb of Buffalo. The others scramble to find their lab work, finish a last math problem, ask me to clarify the assignment I gave in the rush. Cheryl rolls her eyes: "Doesn't this make us look like puppies in a kennel, falling all over each other?" Almost simultaneously, Paolo approaches me: "Forgot to ask—is this composition a first or final draft, which?"

"This one's a final, Paolo . . ."

He sighs. In the air, he shapes a circle with his hands, mirroring and paralleling his head. With a swift slice of the right hand across his neck, he severs the "head" and puts it, delicately, on an imaginary platter. Then he grins.

"OK, you two—Cheri and Paolo—I want you to both think about what you just said tomorrow when we do metaphors. Those were terrific!"

"What was?"

"What you just said . . . If you don't remember, I do. Have a good day."

My eye has wandered over to Rita. Two young men are patting her on the shoulder, and she looks near tears. Damn, it's 8:59. I intrude on the moment, because it's now or lost for the day.

"I didn't pass the writing portfolio again. It's my third time. Sometimes, I think the school just wants our money."

The 9:00 class is filing in.

"Could you come by my office, Rita? We could have a cup of coffee and talk there."

"My schedule is full . . ."

"Will you look at the calendar and set up another time?"

"Sure . . ." she brightens. "Here's my journal. I have an important question in it for you, OK?"

We duck behind my slightly annoyed-looking colleague. It is, after all, 9:01. But he follows me out hurriedly and shoves a memo in my hand.

"It's a proposal from Program Review. We think we need a new name to reflect our role—someone thought of Transitional English Program."

I tell him I think that's a particularly inappropriate name.

I have never heard Cheryl's voice. Nor Paolo's. Nor Rita's.

Their physiological voices, that is. The voice and style and cadences that flow from their hands are distinctive and vivid. When signing and writing, they are conversant, challenging, reflective. They are also "marginal" in many senses and in the same sense. All are deaf. All are enrolled in a class called essay writing because they are "marginally qualified," a descriptor used by our program to indicate students with ability who are not yet considered ready for a college composition course. All had hearing parents who were variously unable to communicate with their deaf child. All use American Sign Language (ASL) and natural Sign English, have a strong sense of membership in the deaf community, and express varying degrees of unease about their relationship with hearing communities. Additionally, Paolo's home culture is Hispanic, and Cheryl faces powerful, gender-based oppression of her educational goals.

We write together. In our various stages of marginalization, we have decided to cross the figurative and literal margins of English 101 discourse and teacher-student wariness. The purpose here—and the purpose of this chapter—is to come to a more intersubjective, dynamic version of the question of access.

Since 1975, and the impact of Public Law 94-142, access has been put forth as the major goal of equal education. Unfortunately, the interpretation of access which has dominated in the last fifteen years has been a singularly one-sided notion. Access was considered in wholly institutional, architectural terms: put up a few ramps, hire an interpreter or two, discuss the economic plusses and minuses of bilingualism. The institutions were thus cast as hospitable benefactors. Access was rarely viewed as a reciprocal issue or a pedagogical possibility. What faculty development and in-service work occurred after the passage of 94-142 and ancillary legislation exhorted teachers to "show compliance" and "provide reasonable accommodation." The moral neutrality of these directives is striking. A passion for justice paled in the eighties, an era bent on repudiating a preceding time of work for social change. So "access" became a mere meeting of requirements, if not going to court against them. As a result, Cheryl, Paolo, and Rita have spent the last twelve years in mainstream schools mandated to aspire to the minimum.

And yet, to what do these beneficiaries have access?

CULTURAL AND LINGUISTIC CONSIDERATIONS

When speaking of access and deaf students, we might be mindful of a broader array of educational possibilities. The first, most educators would agree, is access to the English language in a dynamic form, an area which has proven most troubling for deaf learners and educators (Moores 1982). The second form of access is access to the teacher, if not free from, at least not dominated by, linguistic and cultural barriers. The third type of access comes from my need, and other teachers' needs. We must find ways to have access to students' experiences, not to appropriate them, but to learn from them; not in the vain hope of finding a "common ground" that is contrived and dominated—and defined—by majority culture, but in an effort to communicate human experience actively and vividly.

Ted Aoki (1985) speaks of all marginalized persons "dwelling in the in-between." Maxine Green (1978) speaks of educators coming to "the verge." Paulo Freire (1970) refers to "limit acts." While each of these curricularists have distinctive meanings attached to these phrases, all are referring to the act of pushing against the limits of our own experience as well as that of others, within various political and social constraints. For those of us who work with students on the margins, students "at risk" in institutions which may be unfamiliar with those students' ways of knowing, "the verge" is a narrow space in which to balance our hopes and fears. We may push—against bureaucracy, against apathy, against self-defeat—but the shove had better be considered, or the students pay the price. We may topple into a ravine of collegial resentment, parental misunderstanding, and personal domination if we aggressively charge the boundaries of the school system's or the individual student's lives. So we engage in a choreographed curriculum, a dance of encounter allowing us to move cautiously on the edge of those other worlds that "access" is supposed to unfold to us.

Again, I say to "us." One of the great disappointments in the discussions of policies and laws ensuring the education of differently abled students has been the lack of focus on reciprocity. There is an assumption that it is these children and young adults who are being permitted to pursue a finer education, shoulder to shoulder with "more complete" peers. This deficit model operates one way; transmission of information from the majority culture, represented by the mainstream school, to those who will assimilate its norms—albeit with difficulty. The model views the education of these students as an act of largess, a charitable burden. To be sure, the implementation does not always reek of sanctity: in a national committee, an administrator turned to my husband, who is profoundly deaf, and sighed, "We're spending dollars on nickel kids." In a rather repugnant way, this man touched on the real problem. Because the discourse of educational policy surrounding students put at risk has been centered on legislative and administrative concerns rather than as a *curricular* matter, these children are viewed as a poor investment. Were the discussion to be reframed around curriculum, the emphasis might be radically different.

Deaf students, and other disabled and minority students, have often been termed "experientially deprived." The sheer silliness of the term is staggering. Everyone has experiences; a deaf person growing up in the twentieth century certainly has had a few. And everybody is experientially deprived. For example, at age forty-one, I have not yet had the opportunity to live in an Asian culture. This unreflected labeling proceeds from both a deficit model and a transmission view of curriculum. Such vocabulary does not admit to two basic facts: (1) Children and young adults learn from one another as much as from the formal teaching to which they are exposed. The presence of peers who view the world differently in our classrooms is a powerful curricular and pedagogical opportunity—for both students and teachers; and (2) Some students put at risk in schools see themselves as members of a distinctive, different culture. Many Deaf students are in this situation, and even more identify with a more inclusive Deaf community (Padden and Humphries 1988). In this light, then, curriculum needs to be reconsidered. Remediation and augmentation are not the only goals. A view of the presence of these students as one way to foster genuine multicultural education must be worked toward and articulated. And here, the teacher's need for access is pronounced. Unless that teacher is deaf, or a member of the cultural or differently abled group to which her students belong, she will need to find ways of seeing the world and the words through the student's lens. She will need to put *herself* "at risk."

RISK AND DIALOGUE

A certain amount of danger is communicated in that very inade-quate term "at risk," is it not? That is to be expected. I am talking about dialogue, and dialogue is dangerous. It causes worry. It is approached, very often, with trepidation. One never knows what to expect when other people have the chance to talk. I have put myself at risk; in T. S. Eliot's terms, my universe could well be disrupted, my preconceptions shattered.

The students—bless their hearts—figure this out quickly enough. When John Albertini and I were participants in a dialogue journal study (Albertini and Meath-Lang 1986), the students wasted little time in moving from polite, school-related discourse to searching questions. That pattern has been replicated (Reynolds in press), pointing to the essential vulnerability that accompanies access. Just as access puts students at risk of assimilating the best and worst of majority culture and others' insensitivity, teachers in dialogue with students are risking. They risk having a knowledge they would not otherwise possess. That knowledge can pit them against authorities, who assess their students quite differently, and against the students themselves, who challenge their teachers in the course of authentic communication.

At the beginning of this chapter, I spoke of three types of access: access to a dynamic literacy, access to genuine communica-tion with a teacher, and access to students' experiences to inform teaching. I also introduced Cheryl, Paolo, and Rita. Through their words and mine, in the writing and conversation we have had with one another, I would like to examine the ways we are constructing a text in the margins of academic life.

RITA'S STORY: ACCESS TO DYNAMIC LITERACY

Rita came by the office the day after her disappointment. She has now been in college for five years—she has taken three leaves of absence. She has completed almost all of the courses in her major, but cannot have access to the necessary liberal arts courses at this mainstream college because of her English. She tests at the eighth-grade level on the California Achievement Test. She scores below chance on the Michigan Test of English Language, a test developed for second-language learners. There are few tests developed for, or by, or normed on deaf persons. So such tests provide a very partial view. Thus, our program encourages the use of portfolios of student work for assessment as well.

Rita is much more cheerful today. She is stylishly dressed, on her way to a co-op interview. She tells me that she and her mother talked on the teletypewriter for a long time the night before.

"Mom says, 'Take a vocational certificate and get out of there. You can't fight the system. You can get a good job and an apartment here in Michigan—see your deaf friends, be close to Dad and me.'"

"It sounds like your mom is fed up."

"Me, too . . ."

"You wouldn't consider trying a fourth time?"

She looks at me as though I am crazy. She's probably right. I look at a few of the papers scattered from her portfolio of six essays. They are not great, stilted and empty, riddled with surface errors.

"I'm changing the topic a little, Rita, but I'll get back to the point. You really seem to like the journal; you put a lot of work into it. Your entry yesterday was fascinating." That is an understatement.

Rita becomes animated again. She agrees that the journal is a place where she can experiment. She likes the dialogue. She rather wishes I would "correct" the whole journal, but understands why I don't interrupt the flow of ideas and knows that I "model" correct English back to her often in response. She likes the letter-like type of writing. Signing emphatically, she says, "My writing *feels* better in my journal."

It looks better as well. Here is what she had written the day before:

Hi Bonnie—

I have another interesting topic about death related to the last page that I wrote it to you. Yeah, I know what you mean about God, religions and history of this earth. Where did you study this religion and what kind are you in?

I know, I don't like to hear or talk about death but it is a good way to be prepare for it because we can't live forever. I'm curious of your opinion. Do you believe of being ashes or buries? My believe is in being ashes someday. Then, therefore someone or my future husband will put me in the expensive bottle, to threw out in the ocean with a rose. So, my soul will go enter to the heaven and being happy in my rest of life. Another reason, why I want to do that because I don't want to be under the ground in disgusting leftovers. I rather to be clean.

My good friend is against my believe because she rather to be bury so her body can give to the earth as recycle for surviving people. She don't believe in ashes which it could be waste and being a hundred percent that no one can find my body in millions of year. Also, thereafter she believes that she will be reborn from the leftovers to become someone's part of the cell as cat or dog or different person.

That is very hard to make the decision and which one is proof the better choice for the individual people. What do you believe and any ideas about this? My interests are coming from thru my own thoughtfuls since I was young. . .

There are some surface errors here, but by no means as many as in the essays. The content is vivid, the language inventive. Of course, "inventiveness" does not always charm review committees, especially when nontraditional students do the inventing. There is much distrust in nonstandard language ("I mean, do they really know what they are doing?"). Yet, Rita's "disgusting leftovers" will stay with me long after many conventional, correct compositions.

More to the point, Rita's reflection was well structured, rhetorical, and rich in content. I pointed this out to her, both in our talk and in my written response. She agreed. Her eyes drifted back to the essay on top of the pile. She winced a bit.

"What do you think went wrong there?"

"Oh, it was a comparison-contrast essay on NTID [National Technical Institute for the Deaf] vs. Gallaudet. That was hard. I don't know how to do comparison-contrast; you know I don't understand that . . ."

I couldn't believe my eyes, and asked her to repeat.

"Rita, you did a fantastic comparison-contrast essay in the journal. You compared cremation and burial. You argued your case. You acknowledged your friend's point of view."

She looked stunned. Then she took the journal and flipped to the previous entry.

"Did I do anything right in this one? Anything like a formal essay?"

THE RISKS IN STUDENT-GENERATED CURRICULUM

Rita's story is fraught with ambiguity. Certainly, she has experienced some success in her writing, specifically in her journals. The audience is rather limited there, however. She, and her teachers, need time to connect what she already knows to more public writing; to perhaps use the writing in the journals as material for compositions. That is, if topical control is allowed. Rita is interested in reincarnation, evolution, and the economy. Being asked to write about NTID versus Gallaudet is not all that interesting to her, although she has attended both colleges. The assumptions made in assigning topics versus generating them with students from life, literature, and work should also be compared and contrasted, particularly when writing is being assessed. In the back of the text, too, is Rita's mother, muttering on the keyboard, "You can't fight the system." Rita knows she could—or at least challenge it once more. But is it worth her energy? I do not yet know her decision on fighting for access to liberal arts with her journal writings.

I do know that students demonstrate an array of linguistic functions in dynamically oriented language classrooms and writing communities (Albertini and Meath-Lang 1986; Meath-Lang 1990). I have argued for the use of dialogue journals as curriculum (Meath-Lang 1990), and others have demonstrated access and dynamism in ASL/English classes taught bilingually. Such efforts frequently put the students in curricular control and that is a risk. Some schools prefer not to think about that. Moreover, teachers must be careful listeners, and fast on their feet, to attend to the pedagogical content produced by students. Rita had not experienced access to her own texts through a reader's response. Her *techniques,* in addition to her flaws, had never been pointed out to her in dialogue. She is now beginning a process of accessing her own writing—reading it critically, thinking of herself as an editor/writer, not simply a victim.

CHERYL'S STORY: ACCESS TO COMMUNICATION WITH A TEACHER

I am confident that Cheri will get into liberal arts soon. Anyone who can inject sentences like "She glided into the white room in a diaphanous white dress, lay on the white bed and stared at the white curtains floating in the breeze" into an essay on what she did over the weekend is not long for remedial English. Unlike Rita, Cheri had stated the rationale for journal writing by the fourth week of the course, in terms superior to my own:

> Men and women equal. Hmm. Right now I prefer having a guy for just boyfriend rather than marry. I could and will wait until my Mr. Right comes to me. I wonder when and how long that will be?! (to meet Mr. Right)
>
> My mother is okay, which I'm glad of it.
>
> I just got back here from home, today is Sunday, but went to check on my mother, and seeing that she is fine, I left to come back to school.
>
> I can't wait until Thanksgiving break vacation. But the worst part that I'm not looking forward to is the exams. Gee, them makes me nervous.
>
> I like reading what you write to me. Not because of what you write about. It just that I'm learning how, like when I read how you write, language, grammar. I learn and want to write like that. I hope you understand what I mean? I can't explain it. It's the writing of yours, not what you write about. Now, how, don't think what you write about is a bore, that's not it.
>
> Well, my sweetheart is suppose to call me at 1:00 in the morning. He haven't yet. I guess you can say he is not very punctual. Don't ask me why I want that creep. Sometimes I feel that I'm crazy. Not crazy in love AHH! I don't mean that. HA HA.
>
> Sometimes guys are not nice to girls, no respect. Don't you ever have an ex-boyfriend who don't treat you well?
>
> My weakness is that I couldn't let go of him until I find the guy who that treats me well and the one I like. I don't like the guys in N.T.I.D. so far.
>
> I better go, have other homework to finish.
>
> Bye for now!
>
> Your Pal

Cheryl's reflective language amazes. Her issues are not academic. She is hard working, bright, and a writer all her life. While subject to the vagaries of measurement most deaf students experience, she has generally performed well. She had always been mainstreamed—and found it lonely in a "wild" school—but lived in a city with a large deaf community, and had good deaf friends.

Her academic goals are clouded by two dark forces, however, and she reaches out to teachers in response. First, she struggles with relationships aimed to please. Second, and perhaps more fundamental to the first, her parents denigrate her writing in particular and her education in general.

I am uncomfortably aware that I mean something to Cheryl. I do not mean that that in itself is a problem—she means something to me—but I'm wary of the idea of "role models." No one life can be a carbon copy for another. But I can see when my clothes are being checked out and approved, when the young women in class ask, "How do you become *professional?*", when I hear about my life from other people they have asked. Cheryl writes: "It's interesting why you like kids but don't have kids. You and your husband would never have time together. Maybe I won't have kids and a husband to control me . . ." It's somewhat disconcerting to imagine Cheryl's father leafing through this journal, reading that passage and hitting the roof.

Not that I should worry. Cheryl comes in for her final writing conference, exhausted from studying and getting rid of an unhealthy relationship. We talk about her writing, over which she expresses deep insecurity. Without looking up, she says, "Before your parents died, did they read your writing?"

"Well . . . a little, I guess, Cheryl. Not much, because they died before I had written much."

"My parents refuse to read my writing. . . Well, actually, my dad refuses. He says I'm wasting my time; I should be a secretary and stop dreaming. Mom says my writing scares her. I use big words, and she doesn't understand them. She and Dad never finished high school."

"Maybe they feel a little sad that you and your sister are learning so much. Maybe they're afraid of losing you."

"I think they don't have enough to think about, Bonnie. On break, one night, I said to Mom: 'Quick! Exactly what are you thinking about right now?' She looked at me blank. And I said, 'Oh, forget it . . .' I wonder if she has dreams or thinks about other things than housework. I don't know."

She goes on to inform me that she has signed up for next quarter, and that she will take another course with me. She has decided to look seriously at an accounting degree. Her parents will not support her, but she has made an appointment with Vocational

Rehabilitation. She is confident that she will be funded. Could I please write a letter to attest that she is a conscientious student?

Cheryl is gradually moving to take control of her life. Her confidence has not been helped by peer indifference in her high school and parental indifference to the dreams she speaks of so often, although she understands more readily her parents' pain. The affirmations she has received—and the genuinely critical reading of her work as well—has come from the teachers who could understand and make themselves understood to her.

One cannot emphasize enough the importance of teachers' attending to the communication necessary for access. In the case of deaf students, obviously, this means a commitment to learning another language and studying another culture rigorously. These considerations may also operate for teachers of English as a second language and minority students. Further, students like Cheri—and all students—deserve teachers who will take the time to discuss matters of importance. The "personal" flows into and from the academic and professional, and we need to be prepared for that. When students are "different," this can be challenging. It is hard to know with Cheri, for example, when deafness enters into the interactions she reports with her parents. Issues of gender and class seem important here, too; and teachers need to be alert to our membership in multiple communities. We may need to be resistant to an idea of causality in our dialogue with students like Cheri.

PAOLO'S STORY: ACCESS TO STUDENT EXPERIENCE

Paolo is a teddy bear. Warm and engaging, he is always the cheerful respondent, the work group leader. He is very self-conscious about his English, and has written a rather "name, rank, and serial number" journal. In a writing conference with him, I am tempted toward causality once again:

"You're not writing much, Pedro. Do you prefer, perhaps, to write to a man or a deaf person?" (I am thinking of some graduate students in education who work with us.)

"No, no—I am not old-fashioned. My sister and I are liberated. And I want to know what a hearing person thinks. I just have a hard time writing."

"Is there anything you *like* to write?"

He thinks for a moment. Slowly he shakes his head.

"Is there anything you *like,* period?"

He tells me that his hobby is reading history.

"Well, how about using your journal to talk about historical ideas, to summarize your reading, to express your opinions about world events?"

"I can do that?"

Indeed he did. The next entry was a four-page discussion of a book on the Third Reich. At the end of an excitedly written, hard-to-follow summary, Paolo wrote, "Now Saddam Hussein is just like Hitler, 'cuz the President say so!!! We must stop him!"

In my response, I asked him to compare Hitler and Saddam Hussein, but to show the differences, too. And how should we stop him?

Paolo's next entry came a week later: "You are a tough! Hitler and Saddam are different, I think now. When you ask me, I think I can't write, that is why. Really, I can write. But the compare is not good . . ." On the next page he wrote, "I think more careful to write . . ."

I worried that he might be discouraged by the question. Fortunately, the Civil War series on PBS was on the next week, and he wrote on every installment. At the end of each episode, he expressed an opinion. In one week, I learned that Paolo was deeply religious but hated religious bigotry, came to America illegally but was now safe, had joined a class action suit against a shady insurance firm, despised Mexican food, and thought every country in the world should have nuclear capability in order to keep everyone quiet. He also asked why I would marry a deaf person and if I knew any other languages.

It would be mind boggling to explain how all of this connected to Gettysburg and the Ford Theatre. The point here is that, through writing, I learned a great deal about Paolo and his thinking.

The learning also had to take place indirectly. The margins are an area where we are most wary, literally and figuratively. The margins of our papers contain, more frequently than not, unwanted comments. The margins of societies contain, more often than not, people unwanted in some way. So my discourse with Pedro takes place within text—outside of the margins—and is often cautious and circumspect. What I learn should not be invasive, especially in the areas where I sit as a member of the dominant culture. Even where I share a common marginalization, however—gender, for example—I must be careful not to assert that my marginalization is the same as the young women in my classes. We are of another time, another generation.

My access to Paolo is firmly bracketed in academic work. The complaint that teachers who use journals, conferences, and peer feedback—especially for evaluation—are masquerading as counselors does not stand up to the enormous amount of reflection in reading, academic life, disciplines, and careers found in these strategies. Learning is increasingly seen to be a dialogical event, and I learn from and have access to students as deeply in these academic discourses as in those conversations with more personally oriented students. Paolo exemplified this for me.

CONCLUSION

It is imperative that we begin to work in our institutions to broaden the notion of access and make access an inclusive term—inclusive of the pedagogical access students on the margins need, and access to experience of the type students can offer us. In the act, we may all, as Dorothea Brooke asserted in the novel *Middlemarch* (Eliot 1871–1872 ch. 10), "make life less difficult to each other."

15 November 1990

Rita walked in for her final evaluation. As we settled in, I asked her if she wanted some coffee or tea from the office. She giggled, "A teacher never asked me that before. It's like you think we're grown up." I tell her I do think she is an adult. Not everyone does, she counters. I agree. We have a lot to do in this field before students and their teachers will be taken seriously.

I suspect that that is prerequisite to dialogue and access.

CHAPTER 23

A Policy Perspective: Overcoming Gridlock Beyond Schools

Brad Mitchell, The Ohio State University

Throughout this book we have looked within schools to find the sources of and the solutions to the problems of at-risk students. We have largely ignored the problems generated by inequities in the larger society and the macro policy solutions which will be required to resolve current difficulties. Our strategy was intentional. We assumed that radical social revolution is unlikely and that, even in the absence of dramatic societal restructuring, schools could do much to better educate students who are at risk. At the very least, we assumed that we should alter current ways of thinking and contemporary policies, programs, and practices which hurt such students in the guise of helping them. We do not wish to totally ignore macro questions, however, or to suggest that larger policy questions are irrelevant to resolving the problems being addressed in this book. In this final chapter, Brad Mitchell shifts the attention outward to the larger society and to macro policy questions which must be answered if schools are to ever adequately educate students who are at risk.

This book is full of wonderful and important stories and strategies about improving academic success for at-risk students as they live and work *inside* schools. All these ideas and efforts are crucial. This brief chapter, however, attempts to look beyond the school and focuses on broader societal forces which influence attempts to aid at-risk youth. The social, political and economic conditions of children, youth, and families must be recognized and addressed if we are to truly confront the issue of at-risk students.

We are, after all, a nation where more blacks occupy prison cells than rooms in college dormitories. We have a school system that expels and suspends black students at four to five times the rate of white students and is two to three times more likely to label black students as learning disabled. We are a society where financially well-off students with weak academic records are far more likely to attend college than low-income students with strong academic credentials. We work in an economy where a white high school dropout has a 20 percent better chance of getting a decent job than a black high school graduate and where nearly 25 percent of children under the age of five live below the poverty level.

Our national government reports that the median family income of white children is twice that of black children and more than one and three-quarters times that of Hispanic children. It also reports that approximately 40 percent of early-adolescent blacks and Hispanics are behind the modal grade for their chronological age as compared with 26 percent of whites (U.S. House Select Committee on Children, Youth and Families 1989).

This short, closing chapter suggests four public policy recommendations. First, public policy must authorize new, wide-ranging interventions to protect children from market forces. The public regulation of the amount of commercial time during Saturday morning cartoons is a partial but largely symbolic action. The drug market constitutes a far more dangerous and debilitating force. The victimization of vulnerable teenage mothers by drug dealers needs to be confronted directly. Drug dealers freely admit they target young mothers because it ensures a subsequent generation of drug dependency. Perhaps state and federal legislators need to consider enacting stiffer penalties for the selling or distribution of drugs such as cocaine to pregnant women.

In another sense, at-risk students have become a lucrative market for intervention strategists and reform entrepreneurs. Teachers and principals are inundated with the "latest" services and programs to resolve the varied problems of at-risk students. From dropout prevention programs to study-skills videotapes, the at-risk student market is alive and booming. Federal and state governments need to better monitor and disseminate reliable information on policies, programs, and practices designed to help at-risk students. The marketing of daycare programs, preschools, and other "early intervention" programs is another area that needs consistent attention, especially by state and local policy makers. The entry of commercial television into the schools, such as the Channel One experiment, deserves special scrutiny as well.

Second, more females and minorities must secure positions of policy leadership. The noted child development theorist Urie Brofenbrenner once made the self-proclaimed "preposterous" educational reform proposal to hire only females as school principals. His argument was that the ethic of caring embodied by so many females helped enhance the prospect that all students would experience a sense of belonging and respect in the school. Whether one accepts Brofenbrenner's logic or not, the number of females and minorities in policy leadership positions is woefully limited. There were more female principals across America in 1920 in terms of percentages than there are today. Other policy leadership positions such as governor, education aide, legislative subcommittee chair, superintendent, and teacher association president make decisions which impact at-risk students. The voices of more females and minorities in these policy deliberations can only help the prospects of at-risk students because many of these new leaders would know what it is like to be marginalized and segregated.

Third, we must restructure how we govern and finance public education. We must more justly address the school finance question of who pays, how much, for what. Rich communities will have to reassess their obligations to poor communities. School finance plans based on local property tax assessments perpetuate the myth that rich communities do not have much responsibility for poor communities. High numbers of at-risk students concentrated in the nation's poorest neighborhoods will not solicit much support from wealthy communities because they are not considered a treasured resource. Robert Reich concludes his book *The Work of Nations* with a call for a new sense of American community where

> . . . each garden tender may feel competitive with every other, [but] each also understands that the success of the total harvest requires cooperation. While each has a primary responsibility to tend his own garden, each has a secondary responsibility to ensure—and a genuine interest in seeing—that all gardens flourish. (1991, p. 312)

Robert Reich's book also builds a very persuasive case for how profit-crazed businesses around the globe are partially to blame for the growing numbers of at-risk students in America. Reich writes:

> . . . states, cities and even countries have found themselves bidding against one another for the same global jobs. Who successfully lures the jobs becomes a matter of state and local pride, as well as employment; it may also bear significantly upon the future careers of state and local politicians who have pledged to win them. The possibility of a new factory in the region sets off a furious auction; a casual threat to move one already situated initiates equally impassioned rounds of negotiation . . . . Such subsidies and tax breaks obviously reduce the amount of public money available to support primary and secondary schools, local highways and bridges, recreation, waste treatment facilities, and other local amenities. Ironically, . . . these are just the sorts of public investments that are necessary for building the good jobs of the future. (1991, 298–97)

A twist off Reich's logic places the at-risk student and his or her family as a worthy but invisible victim of aggressive business leaders who display little civic responsibility and/or corporate citizenship. Recently released governmental statistics provide even further evidence that the gap between the combined wealth of the top 10 percent of households and bottom 40 percent increased dramatically in the last decade. One is hard pressed to ignore the parallel relationship between the inability of Ronald Reagan's tax breaks in the early 1980s to trickle down to the middle and lower classes and the growth in the number of at-risk students over the decade. Yet, corporate America remains the populist crusader for educational reform with the former CEO of Xerox, David Kearns, firmly at the side of U.S. Department of Education Secretary Lamar Alexander.

The federal government and the nation's business leaders can help state and local policy makers design more just and more productive ways to finance and govern public education. Instead of hiding behind tax abatements and the silver bullet allure of parental choice plans, America's business leaders can help American communities determine questions of fair share and mutual responsibility. The president's historic education summit in September 1989 should have dealt with these tough issues rather than the pronouncement of six national goals which do not necessarily demand any new federal dollars or new intergovernmental and private sector collaborations and commitments.

Fourth, we must avoid making the same mistake we made with the Great Society programs, where we presumed a link between political empowerment and individual economic advancement. Community development efforts in poor ethnic and black ghettos have not worked. Giving "locals" political voice has increased the number of black and Hispanic elected officials. But these new political leaders inherit a decayed urban infrastructure within a political economy where public investment dollars are scarce and highly sought from a variety of dependent groups such as the elderly and failed savings and loans. Becoming a black mayor or councilperson in an era of dwindling resources and infrastructure decay is not a political victory. Saving or rebuilding the ghetto is a political nightmare and an economic impossibility. Nicholas Lemann discusses in great detail this problem in his book *The Promised Land: The Great Black Migration and How It Changed America*. Lemann writes:

> . . . poor ethnic ghettos are usually temporary communities rising in population during times of migration and falling when the residents begin to move up the ladder. Black ghettos have emptied out especially dramatically over the last generation. Most of them have essentially no employment base and, because they have such high crime rates and poor schools, they aren't likely to attract new residents. The impressive record of black success in America's cities since the 1960s has been almost entirely bound up with leaving the ghettos rather than improving them; with finding work in big organizations, not the inner-city start-ups; with participating in the wider system of electoral politics, not community organizing . . . . Without ending any efforts to improve the ghettos that are now under way, we should change our reigning idea about what will help most: we should be trying to bring the ghetto poor closer to the social and economic mainstream of American society, not encouraging them to develop a self-contained community apart from the mainstream. (1991, 347–48)

Jack Kemp, U.S. Secretary of Housing and Urban Development, is calling for client empowerment where residents take over the ownership and operation of federal housing projects. This form of empowerment serves politically symbolic purposes but it essentially keeps the poor economically imprisoned. False forms of political empowerment should not be accepted as substitutes for economic empowerment. Real economic empowerment involves a coherent public policy to improve the chances that every at-risk child is born healthy, learns to read and write, graduates from high school, puts off parenthood until it can be effectively managed, secures employable skills, and has a job waiting at the end of the line. Empowerment schemes such as site-based management in schools, resident ownership of federal housing projects, and neighborhood crimewatch patrols are valid but incomplete responses to the problems of at-risk students and at-risk families. Corporate leaders and employers in President Bush's new generation of America 2000 communities must work with policy makers to ensure that economic well-being becomes a vital part of the at-risk student jigsaw puzzle. High paying and meaningful employment for all must accompany any serious educational reform effort. Perhaps governors and mayors should bring together their economic development and education staffs to help chart out a more just and productive road for all students and the communities they inhabit.

I have proposed four public policy recommendations to break the state of gridlock for at-risk students—protect children from pernicious market forces, liberate women and minorities to policy leadership positions, restructure school governance and finance, and seek economic empowerment as well as political empowerment for all. Essentially this four-point proposal recognizes the need for coordinated public policy actions involving educational and economic conditions of children and their families. Educational reforms aimed toward at-risk students are necessary but not at all sufficient. We must begin the business of viewing at-risk students in a broader political and economic perspective.

POSTSCRIPT:

IN SEARCH OF

A BOTTOM LINE

Raylene Kos, The Ohio State University
at Lima
Robert Donmoyer, The Ohio State
University

Colleagues who reviewed this book recommended we add a final chapter to pull together the disparate elements of the book and make clear, for the reader, the book's bottom line. This seemingly simple request is not really simple after all. For us, the only bottom line that can be legitimately inferred from this book is that there are no bottom lines in the business of educating at-risk students.

Research certainly cannot provide a bottom line. No amount of research—whether we are talking about traditional social science or the sort of research-based portraits presented in the first part of this book—can provide prescriptions for practice; all research conclusions must be seen as tentative and all must be used heuristically.

To state the matter another way: Research provides windows through which to view at-risk students and their problems, but the building of windows inevitably requires the building of walls. We must always remember that research provides an obstructed view of reality, and we must act accordingly. Our actions, in short, must reflect the absence of a bottom line about educating at-risk youth.

They must reflect the fact that no matter how effective a policy, program, or practice may be, it will not be effective for everyone. Even if we attempt to target our educational interventions to specific populations, not all individuals in the population will benefit, even if the vast majority do. We must develop policies, programs, and practices, therefore, which provide sufficient discretion at the local level to accommodate these individuals who do not quite fit into the structures we have fashioned.

These are rather obvious conclusions, of course, but, as we indicated at the outset of this book, people have often been oblivious to the obvious in the past. Even today, we seem to have a penchant for neat and tidy conclusions and clear and unambiguous recommendations. In short, we still seem desperately to want a bottom line.

Rather than thinking in terms of a bottom line, however, it may be more helpful to think and talk about a line that must constantly be walked. To walk this line successfully we must constantly balance between our need for structure and the need to not be blinded and overly constrained by the intellectual and organizational structures we create. Only if we balance these needs successfully do we have a chance to help rather than hurt at-risk students. Only if we maintain our balance can we even hope to catch a glimpse of who these at-risk students really are.

REFERENCES

CHAPTER 1

Abt Associates. 1977. *Education as experimentation: A planned variation model* (Vol. IV A–D). Boston: Abt Associates.

Allen, J. B., and E. Carr. 1989. Collaborative learning among kindergarten writers: James learns how to learn at school. In *Risk makers, risk takers, risk breakers: Reducing the risks for young literacy learners,* edited by J. B. Allen and J. M. Mason, pp. 30–47. Portsmouth, N.H.: Heinemann.

Archambault, F. X. 1989. Instructional setting and other design features of compensatory education programs. In *Effective Programs for Students At Risk,* edited by R. E. Slavin, N. L. Darweit, and N. A. Madden, pp. 220–63. Needham Heights, Mass.: Allyn and Bacon.

Au, K. H. 1980. Participation structures in a reading lesson with Hawaiian children: Analysis of a culturally appropriate instructional event. *Anthropology and Education Quarterly* 11: 91–115.

Au, K. H., and C. Jordan. 1981. Teaching reading to Hawaiian children: Finding a culturally appropriate solution. In *Culture in the bilingual classroom: Studies in classroom ethnography,* edited by H. T. Trueba, G. P. Guthrie, and K. H. Au, pp. 139–52. Rowley, Mass.: Newbury House.

Baker, J., and J. Sansone. 1990. Interventions with students at risk for dropping out of school: A high school responds. *Journal of Educational Research* 83: 181–86.

Birman, B. F., M. E. Orland, R. K. Jung, R. J. Anson, G. N. Garcia, M. T. Moore, J. E. Funkhouse, D. R. Morrison, B. J. Turnbull, and E. R. Reisner. 1987. *The current operation of the Chapter 1 program.* Washington, D.C.: Office of Educational Research and Improvement, U.S. Department of Education.

Blumer, H. 1969. *Symbolic interactionism: Perspective and method.* Englewood Cliffs, N.J.: Prentice-Hall.

Bobbitt, J. F. 1924. *How to make a curriculum.* Boston: Houghton Mifflin.

Cahoon, P. 1989. Ambassadors: Models for at-risk students. *Educational Leadership* 46 (5): 64.

Callahan, R. E. 1964. *The cult of efficiency: A study of the social forces that have shaped the administration of public schools.* Chicago: University of Chicago Press.

Campbell, D., and J. Stanley. 1963. *Experimental and quasi-experimental designs for research.* Boston: Houghton Mifflin.

Carnine, D. W., and E. J. Kameenui. 1990. The general education initiative and children with special needs: A false dilemma in the face of true problems. *The Journal of Learning Disabilities* 23: 141–44.

Carter, L. F. 1984. The sustaining effects study of compensatory and elementary education. *Educational Researcher* 21: 4–13.

Chenoweth, T. October 1991. *Emerging models of schooling for at-risk students: Promises, limitations, and recommendations.* Paper presented at the University Council for Educational Administration Convention, Baltimore, Maryland.

Clark, C., and R. Yinger. 1977. Research on teacher thinking. *Curriculum Inquiry* 7: 279–309.

Comer, J. P. 1980. School Power. New York: The Free Press.

Conley, S. C. and S. B. Bacharach. 1990. From school-site management to participatory school-site management. *Phi Delta Kappan* 71: 539–44.

Cronbach, L. 1957. The two disciplines of scientific psychology. *American Psychologist* 12: 671–84.

―――. 1975. Beyond the two disciplines of scientific psychology. *American Psychologist* 30: 116–27.

Cuban, L. 1989. At-risk students: What teachers and principals can do. *Educational Leadership,* 46 (5): 29–32.

Cubberly, E. P. 1909. *Changing conceptions of education.* Boston: Houghton Mifflin.

Dawson, J. 1987. Helping at-risk students in middle schools. *NASSP Bulletin* 71 (501): 84–88.

Donmoyer, R. 1985. The rescue from relativism: Two failed attempts and an alternative strategy. *Educational researcher* 14: 13–20.

―――. 1990. Curriculum evaluation and the negotiation of meaning. *Language Arts* 67: 274–86.

―――. 1991a. Administration and evaluation in post-postivist times. *The Review Journal of Philosophy and Social Science* 16: 1, 2.

―――. 1991b. Postpositivist evaluation: Give me a for instance. *Educational Administration Quarterly* 27: 265–96.

Eisner, E. 1985. *The educational imagination.* New York: Macmillan.

Fetterman, D. 1981. Blaming the victim: The problem of evaluation design and federal involvement, and reinforcing world views of education. *Human Organization* 40: 67–77.

Fernandez, R. R., and G. Shu. 1988. School dropouts: New approaches to enduring problems. *Education and Urban Society* 20: 363–86.

Gage, N. L. 1978. *The scientific basis of the art of teaching.* N.Y.: Teachers College Press.

Garfinkle, H. 1967. *Studies in ethnomethodology.* Englewood Cliffs, N.J.: Prentice-Hall.

Glaser, B. 1978. *Theoretical sensitivity: Advances in the methodology of grounded theory.* Mill Valley, Calif.: Sociology Press.

Good, T., B. J. Biddle, and J. E. Brophy. 1975. *Teachers make a difference.* New York: Holt, Rinehart and Winston.

Greene, B., and S. Uroff. 1989. Apollo High School: Achievement through self-esteem. *Educational Leadership* 46 (5): 80–81.

Haberman, M. 1991. The pedagogy of poverty versus good teaching. *Phi Delta Kappan* 73 (4): 290–94.

Hahn, A. 1987. Reaching out to America's dropouts: What to do? *Phi Delta Kappan* 69 (4): 256–63.

Haney, W., and J. Villaume. August 1977. *The Follow Through planned variation experiment.* Department of Health, Education, and Welfare (Education Division), Office of Education, Office of Planning, Budgeting, and Evaluation, Washington, D.C. (OEC-0=74-0394)

Hansen, J. 1989. Anna evaluates herself. In *Risk makers, risk takers, risk breakers: Reducing the risks for young literacy learners,* edited by J. B. Allen and J. M. Mason, pp. 19–29, Portsmouth, N.H.: Heinneman.

House, E. R., G. V. Glass, L. D. McLean, and D. F. Walker. 1978. No simple answer: Critique of the Follow-Through evaluation. *Educational Leadership* 35: 462.

Jones, H. L., B. Pollock, and H. Marockie. 1988. Full-day kindergarten as a treatment for at-risk students: Ohio County Schools. *Spectrum* 6 (1): 3–7.

Kos, R. 1991. Persistence of reading disabilities: The cases of four adolescent disabled readers. *American Educational Research Journal 28,* 875–896.

Kozol, J. 1967. *Death at an early age.* N.Y.: New American Library.

Kuder, S. J. 1990. Effectiveness of the DISTAR reading program for children with learning disabilities. *Journal of Learning Disabilities* 23: 69–71.

Lawrence-Lightfoot, S. 1983. *The good high school.* New York: Basic Books.

Levin, H. M. 1989a. Accelerated Schools: A new strategy for at-risk students. Policy Bulletin No. 6. Bloomington, Ind.: Consortium on Educational Policy Studies, School of Education, Indiana University.

———. 1989b. Financing the education of at-risk students. *Educational Evaluation and Policy Analysis* 11: 47–60.

Lincoln, Y., and E. Guba. 1985. *Naturalistic inquiry.* Beverly Hills, Calif.: Sage.

Mackenzie, D. 1983. Research for school improvement: An appraisal of some recent trends. *Educational Researcher* 12 (4): 5–16.

Maslow, A. H. 1954. *Motivation and personality.* N.Y.: Harper and Row.

Means, B., and M. Knapp. 1991. Cognitive approaches to teaching advanced skills to educationally disadvantaged students. *Phi Delta Kappan* 73 (4): 282–89.

Mikulecky, L. J. 1990. Stopping summer learning loss among at-risk youth. *Journal of Reading* 33: 516–21.

Miles, M., and M. Huberman. 1984. Drawing valid meaning from qualitative data. *Educational Researcher* 13: 20-30.

Miller, S. E., G. Leinhardt, and N. Zigmond. 1988. Influencing engagement through accommodation: An ethnographic study of at-risk students. *American Educational Research Journal* 25: 465–87.

Pallas, A. M., G. Natriello, and E. L. McDill. 1989. The changing nature of the disadvantaged population: Current dimensions and future trends. *Educational Researcher* 18: 16–22.

Richardson, V., U. Casanova, P. Placier, and K. Guilfoyle. 1989. *School children at-risk.* Philadelphia: Falmer Press.

Rist, R. C. 1970. Student social class and teacher expectation: The self-fulfilling prophecy in ghetto education. *Harvard Educational Review* 40: 411–51.

Rivlin, A., and M. Timpane, eds. 1975. *Planned variation studies.* Washington, D.C.: Brookings Institution.

Rogers, C. R. 1983. *Freedom to learn for the 80s.* Columbus, Ohio: Merrill.

Rutter, M., B. Maughan, P. Mortimore, J. Ouston, and A. Smith. 1979. *Fifteen thousand hours: Secondary schools and their effects on children.* Cambridge, Mass.: Harvard University Press.

Shulman, L., and J. Lanier. 1977. The Institute for Research in Teaching: An overview. *Journal of Teacher Education* 28 (4): 44–49.

Slavin, R. E., and N. A. Madden. 1989b. Effective classroom programs for students at risk. In *Effective programs for students at risk,* edited by R. E. Slavin, N. L. Karweit, and N. A. Madden, pp. 23–51. Boston: Allyn and Bacon.

Slavin, R. E., and N. A. Madden. 1990b. What works for students at risk: research synthesis. *Educational Leadership* 47: 4–13.

Slavin, R. E., N. A. Madden, and N. L. Karweit. 1989a. Effective programs for students at risk: Conclusions for practice and policy. In *Effective programs for students at risk,* edited by R. E. Slavin, N. L. Karweit, and N. A. Madden, pp. 355–372. Boston: Allyn and Bacon.

Slavin, R. E., N. A. Madden, and R. J. Stevens. 1990a. Cooperative learning models for the 3 R's. *Educational leadership* 47: 22–28.

Thorndike, E. L. 1910. The contribution of psychology to education. *The Journal of Educational Psychology*, 1: 5–12.

Trueba, H. T. 1988. Culturally based explanations of minority students' academic achievement. Anthropology and Education Quarterly, 19: 270–287.

Tyack, D. 1972. *The one best system.* Cambridge: Harvard University Press.

Vogt, L. A., C. Jordan, and R. G. Tharp. 1987. Explaining school failure, producing school success: Two cases. *Anthropology and Education Quarterly* 18: 276–86.

Wehlage, G. G. 1987. A program model for at-risk high school students. *Educational Leadership* 44 (6): 70–73.

Wehlage, G. G., and R. A. Rutter. 1986. Dropping out: How much do schools contribute to the problem? *Teachers College Record* 87: 364–92.

Wehlage, G. G., R. A. Rutter, G. A. Smith, N. Lesko, and R. R. Fernandez. 1989. *Reducing the risk: Schools as communities of support.* London: Falmer Press.

Weiss, C. 1981. Policy research in the context of diffuse decision making. *Journal of Higher Education* 53: 619–39.

Willis, P. 1977. Learning to labor: How working class kids get working class jobs. New York: Columbia University Press.

Wise, A. 1979. Legislated learning: The bureaucratization of the American classroom. Berkeley: University of California.

CHAPTER 2

Berlin, I. 1966. The concept of scientific history. In *Philosophical analysis and history*, edited by W. Dray, pp. 5–53. New York: Harper and Row.

Campbell, D., and J. Stanley. 1963. *Experimental and quasi-experimental designs for research.* Boston: Houghton Mifflin.

Cronbach, L. 1975. Beyond the two disciplines of scientific psychology. *American Psychologist* 30: 116–27.

Donmoyer, R. 1990. The rescue from relativism: Two failed attempts and an alternative strategy. *Educational Researcher* 14: 13–20.

Dray, W. 1957. *Laws and explanation in history.* London: Oxford University Press.

Eisner, E. 1985. *The educational imagination.* New York: Macmillan.
———. 1991. *The enlightened eye: Qualitative inquiry and the enhancement of educational practice.* New York: Macmillan.

Eisner, E., and A. Peshkin. 1990. *Qualitative inquiry in education: The continuing debate.* New York: Teachers College Press.

Geertz, C. 1973. *The interpretation of culture.* New York: Basic Books.
_____. 1983. *Local knowledge.* New York: Basic Books.
Glaser, B. 1978. *Theoretical sensitivity: Advances in the methodology of grounded theory.* Mill Valley, Calif.: Sociology Press.
Lawrence-Lightfoot, S. 1983. *The good high school.* New York: Basic Books.
Lincoln, Y., and E. Guba. 1985. *Naturalistic inquiry.* Beverly Hills, Calif.: Sage.
Neisser, U. 1976. *Cognition and reality: Principles and implications of cognitive psychology.* San Francisco: W. H. Freeman.
Piaget, J. 1971. *Biology and knowledge.* Translated by B. Walsh. Chicago: University of Chicago Press.
Turner, T. 1973. Piaget's structuralism. *American Anthropologist* 75: 351–73.

CHAPTER 3

Bruner, J. 1986. *Actual minds, possible worlds.* Cambridge, Mass.: Harvard University Press.
Carrier, J. G. 1986. *Learning disability: Social class and the construction of inequality in American education.* Westport, Conn.: Greenwood Press.
Cazden, C. B. 1988. *Classroom discourse.* Portsmouth, N.H.: Heinemann.
Clay, M. M. 1979. *Reading: The patterning of complex behavior.* Exeter, N.H.: Heinemann.
Cooper, H. M. 1979. Pygmalian grows up: A model for teacher expectations, communication and performance influence. *Review of Educational Research* 49: 389–410.
DeStefano, J. 1978. *Language, the learner and the school.* New York: John Wiley and Sons.
Erickson, F. 1987. Transformation and school success: The politics and culture of educational achievement. *Anthropology and Education Quarterly* 18: 335–56.
Glasser, W. 1986. *Control theory in the classroom.* New York: Harper and Row.
McDermott, R. 1987. Achieving school failure: An anthropological approach to illiteracy and social stratification. In *Education and cultural process* (2nd ed.), edited by G. D. Spindler, pp. 173–209. Prospect Heights, Ill.: Waveland Press.
Rist, R. C. 1970. Student social class and teacher expectations: The self-fulfilling prophecy in ghetto education. *Harvard Educational Review* 83: 411–50.

Shumaker, M. P., and R. C. Shumaker. 1988. 3,000 paper cranes: Children's literature for remedial readers. *The Reading Teacher* 41 (6): 544–49.

Sigman, S. B. 1987. *A radical analysis of special education.* London: Falmer Press.

Smith, W. 1980. Language awareness and reading comprehension. In *Discovering language with children,* edited by G. S. Pinnell, pp. 92–95. Urbana, Ill.: National Council of Teachers of English.

Willis, P. 1977. *Learning to labor: How working class kids get working class jobs.* New York: Columbia University Press.

CHAPTER 5

Clay, M. M. 1985. *Early detection of reading difficulties* (3rd ed.). Portsmouth, N.H.: Heinemann.

Dahl, K. L., V. Purcell-Gates, and E. McIntyre. 1989. *Ways that inner-city children make sense of traditional reading and writing instruction in the early grades.* Grant # G008720229. Final report to the U.S. Department of Education, Office of Educational Research and Improvement.

Purcell-Gates, V., and K. Dahl. 1991. Low-SES children's success and failure at early literacy learning in skills-based classrooms. *Journal of Reading Behavior* 23 (1): 1–34.

CHAPTER 6

National Center for Educational Statistics (NCES). 1990. *A profile of the American eighth grader.* Publication #065-000-00404-6. Washington, D.C.: U.S. Government Printing Office.

CHAPTER 7

Bem, S. L. 1974. The measurement of psychological androgyny. *Journal of Consulting and Clinical Psychology* 42: 156.

Benz, C. R., I. Pfeiffer, and I. Newman. 1981. Sex role expectations of classroom teachers, grades 1–12. *American Educational Research Journal* 18: 289–302.

Dusek, J. B., and G. Joseph. 1983. The bases of teacher expectancies: A meta-analysis. *Journal of Educational Psychology,* 75: 327–46.

Entwisle, D. R., K. L. Alexander, A. M. Pallas, and D. Cadigan. 1987. The emergent academic self-image of first graders: Its response to social structure. *Child Development* 58: 1190–1206.

Gilligan, C. 1982. *In a different voice.* Cambridge, Mass.: Harvard University Press.

Kos, R. 1989. The role of affective, social, and educational factors in the maintenance of reading disabilities: A qualitative multi-case study of four reading disabled adolescents. *Dissertation Abstracts International,* 51 (1) 124-A.

Prawat, R. S., and R. Jarvis. 1980. Gender difference as a factor in teachers' perceptions of students. *Journal of Educational Psychology* 72: 743–49.

Rueda, R., and H. Mehan. 1986. Metacognition and passing: Strategic interactions in the lives of students with learning disabilities. *Anthropology and Education Quarterly* 17: 145–65.

Shaywitz, S. E., B. A. Shaywitz, J. M. Fletcher, and M. D. Excobar. 1990. Prevalence of reading disability in boys and girls. *Journal of the American Medical Association* 264: 998–1002.

Wechsler, D. 1974. *The Wechsler Intelligence Scale for Children—Revised.* New York: Psychological Corporation.

Woodcock, R. W., and M. B. Johnson. 1978. *Woodcock-Johnson Tests of Achievement.* Allen, Tex.: DLM Teaching Resources.

CHAPTER 8

Alan Guttmacher Institute. 1981. *Teenage pregnancy: The problem that hasn't gone away.* New York: The Alan Guttmacher Institute.

Bolton, F. G. 1980. *The pregnant adolescent: Problems of premature parenthood.* Beverly Hills, Calif.: Sage.

Children's Defense Fund. 1987. *Adolescent pregnancy: An anatomy of a social problem in search of comprehensive solutions.* Washington, D.C.: Adolescent Pregnancy Prevention Clearinghouse.

———. 1986. *Adolescent pregnancy: Whose problem is it?* Washington, D.C.: Adolescent Pregnancy Prevention Clearinghouse.

Chilman, C. S. 1985. Feminist issues in teenage parenting. *Child Welfare* 64: 225–34.

Furstenburg, F. F. 1976. *Unplanned parenthood: The social consequences of teenage childbearing.* New York: Free Press.

Harris, L. 1986. *Sex, myths, and birth control: The Planned Parenthood poll.* New York: Planned Parenthood Federation of America.

Luker, K. 1975. *Taking chances: Abortion and the decision not to contracept.* Berkeley, Calif.: University of California Press.

O'Connell, M., and M. J. Moore. 1981. The legitimacy status of first births to United States women aged 15–24, 1939–1978. In *Teenage sexuality, pregnancy and childbearing,* edited by F. F. Furstenberg, R.

Lincoln, and J. Menken, pp. 52–67. Philadelphia: University of Pennsylvania Press.

Rapp, R. 1982. Family and class in contemporary America. In *Rethinking the family: Some feminist questions* edited by B. Thorne and M. Yalom, pp. 168–87. New York: Longman.

Real, M. 1987. *A high price to pay: Teenage pregnancy in Ohio.* Washington D.C.: Children's Defense Fund.

Stewart, M. W. 1981. Adolescent pregnancy: Status convergence for the well-socialized adolescent female. *Youth and Society* 12 (4): 443–64.

Zelnik, M., J. F. Kantner, and K. Ford. 1981. *Sex and pregnancy in adolescence.* Beverly Hills: Sage.

CHAPTER 10

ASCD 1990. *Resolutions 1990.* Alexandria, Vir.: Author.

Coleman, M. 1986. Nontraditional boys: A minority in need of reassessment. *Child Welfare* 65 (3): 252–59.

Farrow, J., and E. Schroeder. 1984. Sexuality education groups in juvenile detention. *Adolescence* 19 (76): 817–26.

Green, R. 1987. *The "sissy boy syndrome" and the development of homosexuality.* New Haven, Conn.: Yale University press.

Greene, M. 1988. The Dialectic of Freedom. New York: Teachers College Press.

Harry, J. 1985. Defeminization and social class. *Archives of Sexual Behavior* 14: 1-12.

Hyde, H. Montgomery. 1973. The Trials of Oscar Wilde. New York: Dover Publications.

McCuller, C. 1940. New York Cafe, *The heart is a lonely hunter.* Boston, Houghton Mifflin.

Mass, L. 1986. Insight into gender and roles: (Some) boys will be boys. *Advocate* 473: 54, 56.

Mead, M. 1935. *Sex and temperament in three different societies.* New York: Morrow.

Melchert, T., and K. Burnett. 1990. Attitudes, knowledge, and sexual behavior of high-risk adolescents: Implications for counseling and sexuality education. *Journal of Counseling and Development* 48 (3): 243–45.

Mizell, H. 1986. Considerations preliminary to the development of dropout prevention policies and programs. *Spectrum* 4 (4): 21–27.

Money, J., and A. Russo. 1979. Homosexual outcome of discordant gender activity. Role in childhood: Longitudinal follow-up. *Journal of Pediatric Psychology* 4 (1): 29–49.

Ross, M. 1983. Homosexuality and social sex roles: A re-evaluation. *Journal of Homosexuality* 9 (1): 1–6.

Saghir, M., and E. Robbins. 1973. *Male and female homosexuality*. Baltimore, Md.: Williams and Watkins.

Sears, J. 1989. The impact of gender and race on growing up lesbian and gay in the South. *NWSA Journal* 1 (3): 422–57.

———. 1991. *Growing up gay in the South: Race, gender, and journeys of the spirit*. New York: Haworth Press.

———. 1992. Educators, homosexuality, and homosexual students: Are personal feelings related to professional beliefs? *Journal of Homosexuality* 22 (3/4): 29–79.

Shively, M., and J. DeCecco. 1977. Components of sexual identity. *Journal of Homosexuality* 3 (1): 41–48.

White, L., and D. Brinkerhoff. 1981. The sexual division of labor: Evidence from childhood. *Social Forces* 60 (1): 170–81.

Williams, W. 1986. *The spirit and the flesh*. Boston, Mass.: Beacon.

CHAPTER 11

Gleason, J. J. 1984. "Social and cultural patterns in behavior of the multiply handicapped mentally retarded." Unpublished thesis, Graduate School of Education, Harvard University, Cambridge, Mass.

———. 1989. *Special education in context: An ethnographic study of persons with developmental disabilities*. Cambridge, Mass.: Cambridge University Press.

CHAPTER 12

Brandt, R. S. 1990. Changing schools—but how? *Educational Leadership* 47 (8): 3.

Bruner, J. 1975. The ontogenesis of speech acts. *Journal of Child Language* 2: 1–19.

Cazden, C. 1972. *Child language and education*. New York: Holt, Rinehart and Winston.

Daft, R. L. 1986. *Organization theory and design* (2nd ed.). St. Paul, Minn.: West.

Deal, T. E. 1990. Reframing reform. *Educational Leadership* 47 (8): 6–12.

Deal, T. E., and A. A. Kennedy. 1983. Culture and school performance. *Educational Leadership* 40 (5): 14–15.

Donmoyer, R. 1983. Pedagogical improvisation. *Educational Leadership* 40: 39–43.

Greene, L. E. 1991. Call it culture. *Principal* 70 (4): 4.

Halliday, M. A. K. 1975. *Learning how to mean: Explorations in the functions of language.* London: Edward Arnold, Ltd.

Morgan, G. 1986. *Images of organization.* Beverly Hills: Sage.

Piaget, J. 1971. *Biology and knowledge* Translated by B. Walsh. Chicago: University of Chicago Press.

Rossman, G. B., H. D. Corbett, and W. A. Firestone. 1988. *Change and effectiveness in schools: A cultural perspective.* Albany, N.Y.: State University of New York Press.

Spolin, V. 1963. *Improvisation for the theatre.* Evanston, Ill.: Northwestern University Press.

Wells, G. 1981. *Learning through interaction: The study of language development.* Cambridge, England: Cambridge University Press.

CHAPTER 13

Allington, R. L. 1991. The legacy of "Slow it down and make it more concrete." In *Learner factors/teacher factors: Issues in literacy research and instruction,* fortieth yearbook of the National Reading Conference, edited by J. Zutell and S. McCormick, pp. 19–30. Chicago: National Reading Conference.

Allington, R. L., and P. A. Johnston. 1989. Coordination, collaboration, and consistency: The redesign of compensatory and special education interventions. In *Effective programs for students at risk,* edited by R. Slavin, N. Karweit, and N. Madden, pp. 320–54. Boston: Allyn-Bacon.

Allington, R. L., and A. McGill-Franzen. 1991. *Unexamined impacts of educational reform.* Unpublished paper. State University of New York at Albany.

_____. 1989a. Different programs, indifferent instruction. In *Beyond separate education: Quality education for all,* edited by A. Gartner and D. Lipsky, pp. 75–98. Baltimore: Brookes.

_____. 1989b. School response to reading failure: Chapter 1 and special education students in grades 2, 4, & 8. *Elementary School Journal* 89: 529–42.

Ashton, P. T., and Webb, R. B. 1986. *Making a difference: Teachers' sense of efficacy and student achievement.* New York: Longman.

Birman, B. F. 1988. How to improve a successful program. *American Educator* 12: 22–29.

Clay, M. M. 1985. *The early detection of reading difficulties: A diagnostic survey with recovering procedures* (3rd ed.). Exeter, N.H.: Heinemann.

Comer, J. P. 1988. Educating poor minority children. *Scientific American* 259: 42–48.

Edelmann, M. W. 1988. Forward. In *Children's Defense Budget*. Washington, D.C.: Children's Defense Fund.

Fraatz, J. M. B. 1987. *The politics of reading: Power, opportunity, and prospects for change in America's public schools*. New York: Teachers College Press.

Gartner, A., D. K. Lipsky. 1987. Beyond special education: Toward a quality system for all students. *Harvard Educational Review* 57: 367–95.

Gastright, J. F. April 1985. *Time on any task? The relationship between instructional pacing and standardized achievement test gains*. Paper presented at the annual meeting of the American Educational Research Association, Chicago.

Gottfredson, G. D. 1986. *You get what you measure, you get what you don't: Higher standards, higher test scores, more retention in grade*. Report no. 2a. Center for Research on Elementary and Middle Schools, Johns Hopkins University.

Haynes, M. C., and J. R. Jenkins. 1986. Reading instruction in special education resource rooms. *American Educational Research Journal* 23: 161–90.

Juel, C. 1988. Learning to read and write: A longitudinal study of 54 children from first through fourth grade. *Journal of Educational Psychology* 80: 437–47.

Leinhardt, G. 1980. Transition rooms: Promoting motivation or reducing education. *Journal of Educational Psychology* 72: 55–61.

Levin, H. M. 1987. Accelerated schools for disadvantaged students. *Educational Leadership* 44: 19–21.

McGill-Franzen, A. M. 1987. Failure to learn to read: Formulating a policy problem. *Reading Research Quarterly* 22: 475–90.

_____. 1993. *Shaping the preschool agenda: Early literacy, pubic policy and professional beliefs*. Albany: State University of New York Press.

McGill-Franzen, A. M., and R. L. Allington. Comprehension and coherence: Neglected elements of literacy instruction in remedial and resource room services. *Journal of Reading, Writing, and Learning Disabilities* 6: 149–82.

_____. 1991. The gridlock of low-achievement: Perspectives on policy and practice. *Remedial and Special Education* 12: 20–30.

May, D. C., and E. Welch. 1984. Developmental placement: Does it prevent future learning difficulties? *Journal of Learning Disabilities* 17: 338–41.

Mehan, H., A. Hartweck, and J. L. Meihls. 1986. *Handicapping the handicapped*. Stanford, Calif.: Stanford University Press.

Mergendoller, J., Y. Bellisimo, and C. Horan. 1990. *Kindergarten hold-

ing out: The role of school characteristics, family background and parental perception. Novato, Calif.: Beryl Buck Institute for Education.

Pinnell, G. S. 1989. Reading Recovery: Helping at-risk children learn to read. *Elementary School Journal* 90: 161–83.

Pinnell, G. S., D. E. Deford, and Lyons, C. A. 1988. *Reading Recovery*. Arlington, Vir.: Educational Research Service.

Rowan, B., and L. F. Guthrie. The quality of Chapter I instruction: Results from a study of twenty-four schools. In *Effective programs for students at risk* edited by R. E. Slavin, N. Karweit, and N. Madden, pp. 195–219. Boston: Allyn-Bacon.

Schwager, M., and I. H. Balow. April 1990. "An analysis of retention policies and their possible effects on retention rates." Paper presented at the American Educational Research Association, Boston.

Shannon, P. 1989. *Broken promises*. Granby, Mass: Bergin & Gavey.

Shepard, L. A., and M. L. Smith. eds. 1989. *Flunking grades: Research and policies on retention*. Philadelphia: Falmer.

Singer, J. D., and J. A. Butler. 1987. The Education for All Handicapped Children Act: Schools as agents of social reform. *Harvard Educational Review* 57: 125–52.

Slavin, R. E. 1987. Making Chapter I make a difference. *Phi Delta Kappan* 69: 110–19.

Slavin, R. E., N. A. Madden, N. L. Karweit, B. J. Livermon, and L. Dolan. 1990. Success for All: First-year outcomes of a comprehensive plan for reforming urban education. *American Educational Research Journal* 27: 255–78.

Walmsley, S. A., and T. P. Walp. 1990. Integrating literature and composing into the language arts curriculum: Philosophy and practice. *Elementary School Journal* 90: 251–74.

Winfield, L. F. 1986. Teachers' beliefs toward academically at-risk students in inner urban schools. *Urban Review* 18: 253–68.

Ysseldyke, J. E., M. L. Thurlow, C. Mecklenburg, and J. Graden. 1984. Opportunity to learn for regular and special education students during reading instruction. *Remedial and Special Education* 5: 29–37.

CHAPTER 14

Bredekamp, S. Ed. 1987. *Developmentally appropriate practice in early childhood programs serving children from birth through age 8*. Washington, D.C.: National Association for the Education of Young Children.

Charlesworth, R. 1985. Readiness: Should we make them ready or let them bloom? *Day Care and Early Education* 12 (3): 25–27.

Fleege, P. O. 1991. Stress begins in kindergarten: A look at behavior during standardized testing. (Doctoral dissertation, Louisiana State University, 1990). *Dissertation Abstracts International* 51-11A, 9104130.

Fleege, P. O., R. Charlesworth, D. C. Burts, and C. H. Hart, 1991. "Stress begins in kindergarten: A look at behavior during standardized testing." Manuscript submitted for publication.

Johnson, L. 19 October 1990. Testimony presented at the Texas Education Agency Hearings on Transition Classes, Austin, Texas.

National Center for Fair and Open Testing 1990. Performanced-based assessment spread nationally. *FairTest Examiner* 4 (3): 12.

National Commission on Excellence in Education 1983. *A Nation at risk: The imperative for educational reform.* Washington, D.C.: U.S. Government Printing Office.

Perrone, V. 1990. How did we get here? In *Achievement testing in the early grades: The games grown-ups play* edited by C. Kamii, pp. 1–13. Washington, D.C.: National Association for the Education of Young Children.

Smith, M. L. 1991a. Meanings of test preparation. *American Educational Research Journal* 28 (3): 521–42.

_____. 1991b. Put to the test: The effects of external testing on teachers. *Educational Researcher* 20 (5): 8–11.

Wodtke, K. H., F. Harper, M. Schommer, and P. Brunelli. 1989. How standardized is school testing? An exploratory observational study of standardized group testing in kindergarten. *Educational Evaluation and Policy Analysis* 2 (3): 223–35.

Wortham, S. C. 1990. *Tests and Measurement in early childhood Education.* Columbus, Ohio: Merrill.

CHAPTER 15

Adelman, C. 1983. "Devaluation, diffusion, and the college connection: A study of high school transcripts." Paper presented at the meeting of the National Commission on Excellence, Washington, D.C.

Davis, S. A., and E. J. Haller. 1981. Tracking, ability, and SES: Further evidence on the "revisionist-meritocratic debate." *American Journal of Education,* 89: 283–304.

Damico, S. B., J. Roth, S. Fradd, and A. D. Hankins. 1990. *The route to graduation: Perceptions of general curriculum students.* Final Report. STAR Grant #89-41, Florida Institute of Government.

_____. 1991. Understanding Florida's graduation rate. *Journal of STAR Research* 2: 1–15.

Damico, S. B., and J. Roth. April 1991. "The neglected dropout: General track students." Paper presented at the annual meeting of the American Educational Research Association, Chicago.

Echternacht, G. 1976. The characteristics distinguishing vocational education students from general and academic students. *Multivariate Behavioral Research* 11: 477–90.

Ekstrom, R. B., M. E. Goertz, J. M. Pollack, and D. A. Rock. 1986. Who drops out of high school and why? Findings from a national study. *Teachers College Record* 87: 356–73.

Farrell, E. 1990. *Hanging in and dropping out: Voices of at-risk high school students.* New York: Teachers College Press.

Farrell, E., G. Peguero, R. Lindsey, and R. White. 1988. Giving voice to high school students: Pressure and boredom "Ya Know What I'm Sayin?" *American Educational Research Journal* 25: 489–502.

Fine, M. 1985. Dropping out of high school: An inside look. *Social Policy* 16: 43–50.

———. 1986. Why urban adolescents drop into and out of public high school. *Teachers College Record* 87: 393–409.

Finn, J. D. 1989. Withdrawing from school. *Review of Educational Research* 59: 117–42.

Hess, G. A., Jr., E. Wells, C. Prindle, P. Liffman, and B. Kaplan. 1987. Where's room 185? How schools can reduce their dropout problem. *Education and Urban Society* 19: 330–55.

Miller, S. E., G. Leinhardt, and N. Zigmond. 1988. Influencing engagement through accommodation: An ethnographic study of at-risk students. *American Educational Research Journal* 25: 465–87.

Natriello, G., A. M. Pallas, and K. Alexander. 1989. On the right track? Curriculum and academic achievement. *Sociology of Education,* 62: 109–118.

Newmann, F. M. 1981. Reducing student alienation in high schools: Implications of theory. *Harvard Educational Review* 51: 546–64.

———. 1989. Student engagement and high school reform. *Educational Leadership* 46 (5): 34–36.

Pokay, P. A., L. Jernigan, and D. Michael. April 1990. "Students' perceptions of why they skip class and what can be done about it." Paper presented at the annual meeting of the American Educational Research Association, Boston.

Rumberger, R. W. 1987. High school dropouts: A review of issues and evidence. *Review of Educational Research* 57: 101–21.

Vanfossen, B. E., J. D. Jones, and J. Z. Spade. 1987. Curriculum tracking and status maintenance. *Sociology of Education* 60: 104–22.

Wehlage, G. G. 1989. Engagement, not remediation or higher standards. In *Children at risk,* edited by J. M. Lakebrink, pp. 57–73. Springfield, Ill.: Charles C. Thomas.

Wehlage, G. G., and R. A. Rutter. 1986. Dropping out: How much do schools contribute to the problem? *Teachers College Record* 87: 374–92.

Wehlage, G. G., R. A. Rutter, G. A. Smith, N. Lesko, and R. R. Fernandez. 1989. *Reducing the risk: Schools as communities of support.* London: Falmer Press.

CHAPTER 16

Allington, R. L. 1991. "The legacy of 'Slow it down and make it more concrete'." In *Learner factors/teacher factors: Issues in literacy research and instruction,* edited by J. Zutell and S. McCormick, pp. 19–29. Chicago, Ill: National Reading Conference.

Boyd, W. L. 1987. Public education's last hurrah: Schizophrenia, amnesia, and ignorance in school politics. *Educational Evaluation and Policy Analysis* 9 (2): 85–100.

Clay, M. 1979a. *The early detection of reading difficulties.* Portsmouth, N.H.: Heinemann.

———. 1979b. *Reading: The Patterning of Complex Behavior.* Portsmouth, N.H.: Heinemann.

———. 1990. "Reading Recovery in the United States: Its successes and challenges." Address to the American Educational Research Association, Boston, Mass.

———. 1991. *Becoming literate: The construction of inner control.* Portsmouth, N.H.: Heinemann.

Cohen, D., and D. L. Ball. 1990. Policy and practice: An overview. *Educational Evaluation and Policy Analysis* 12 (3): 347–53.

Conley, S. C. 1988. Reforming paper pushers and avoiding free agents: The teacher as constrained decision-maker. *Educational Administration Quarterly* 23 (4): 393–404.

Cowley, J. 1986. *My puppy.* San Diego, Calif.: Wright Group.

Darling-Hammond, L. 1988. The futures of teaching. *Educational Leadership* 46 (3): 4–10.

———. 1990. Instructional policy into practice: "The power of the bottom over the top." *Educational Evaluation and Policy Analysis* 12 (3): 233–41.

Duffy, G. G., and L. D. McIntyre. 1982. A naturalistic study of instruction assistance in primary-grade reading. *The Elementary School Journal* 83: 15–23.

Durkin, D. 1979. What classroom observations reveal about reading comprehension instruction. *Reading Research Quarterly* 14: 481–533.

Elmore, R. F. 1987. Reform and the culture of authority in schools. *Educational Administration Quarterly* 23 (4): 60–78.

Elmore, R. F., and M. W. McLaughlin. 1988. *Steady work: Policy, practice and the reform of American education.* Santa Monica, Calif.: Rand Corporation.

Glickman, C. D. 1989. Has Sam and Samantha's time come at last? *Educational Leadership* 46 (8): 4–9.

Goodlad, J. I. 1984. *A place called school.* New York: McGraw-Hill.

Goodman, K. S., P. Shannon, Y. S. Freeman, and S. Murphy. 1988. *Report card on basal readers.* Katonah, N.Y.: Richard C. Owens.

Hoffman, J. V., and S. F. O'Neal. 1984. Curriculum decision making and the beginning teacher of reading in the elementary school classroom. In *Changing perspectives on research in reading/language processing and instruction,* edited by J. A. Niles and L. A. Harris, pp. 137–45. Rochester, N.Y.: National Reading Conference.

Joyce, B., and B. Showers. 1980. Improving in-service training: The messages of research. *Educational Leadership* 37: 379–85.

Larrick, N. 1987. Illiteracy starts too soon. *Phi Delta Kappan* 69: 184–89.

McCallum, R. D. 1988. Don't throw the basals out with the bath water. *The Reading Teacher* 42: 204–8.

McLaughlin, M. W. 1987. Learning from experience: Lessons from policy implementation. *Educational Evaluation and Policy Analysis* 9 (2): 171–78.

———. 1990. The Rand change agent study revisited: Macro perspectives and micro realties. *Educational Researcher* 19 (9): 11–16.

McNeil, L. M. 1988. Contradictions of control, part 2: Teachers, students, and curriculum. *Phi Delta Kappan* 69 (7): 432–38.

Malcolm, M. 1983. *I can read.* New Zealand: Reading to Read.

Murphy, J. 1988. Equity as student opportunity to learn. *Theory into Practice* 27 (2): 145–51.

Murphy, J., P. Hallinger, and L. S. Lotto. 1986. Inequitable allocations of alterable learning variables in schools and classrooms: Findings and suggestions for improvement. *Journal of Teacher Education* 37 (6): 21–26.

Odden, A. 1987. Education reform and services to poor children: Can the two policies be compatible? *Educational Evaluation and Policy Analysis* 9 (3): 231–43.

Peterson, B. (1991). Selecting books for beginning readers. In *Bridges to Literacy,* edited by D. E. DeFord, G. S. Pinnell, and C. Lyons, pp. 119–147. Portsmouth, N.H.: Heinemann.

Peterson, P. L. 1990. Doing more in the same amount of time: Cathy Swift. *Educational Evaluation and Policy Analysis* 12 (3): 277–96.

Pinnell, G. S. 1990. Success for low achievers through Reading Recovery. *Educational Leadership* 48: 17–21.

Pinnell, G. S., D. E. DeFord, and C. A. Lyons. 1988. *Reading Recovery: Early intervention for at risk first grade readers.* Arlington, Vir.: Educational Research Service.

Powell, A. G., E. Farrar, and D. K. Cohen. 1985. *The shopping mall high school: Winners and losers in the educational marketplace.* Boston: Houghton-Mifflin.

Rentel, V. M., and G. S. Pinnell. December 1987. "A study of practical reasoning in Reading Recovery instruction." Paper presented at the National Reading Conference, St. Petersburg Beach, Florida.

Richardson, V. 1990. Significant and worthwhile change in teaching practice. *Educational Researcher* 19 (7): 10–18.

Rinehart, J. S., and P. M. Short. October 1990. "Viewing Reading Recovery as a restructuring phenomenon." Paper presented at the annual meeting of the University Council of Educational Administration, Pittsburgh, Pennsylvania.

Sadker, D., and M. Sadker. 1984. *Year 3 final report, promoting effectiveness in classroom instruction.* Washington, D.C.: National Institute of Education (Contract No. 400-80-0033).

Shannon, P. 1989. *Broken promises.* South Hedley, Mass.: Bergin and Gavey.

Soltis, J. F. 1988. Reform or reformation? *Educational Administration Quarterly* 24 (3): 241–45.

Stanovich, K. E. 1986. Matthew effects in reading: Some consequences of individual differences in the acquisition of literacy. *Reading Research Quarterly* 21: 360–407.

Wildsmith, B. 1984. *Toot, Toot.* Walton Street. Oxford University Press.

Wise, A. 1979. *Legislated learning.* Berkeley, Calif.: University of California Press.

CHAPTER 17

Apple, M. 1979. *Ideology and curriculum.* Boston: Routledge and Kegan Paul.

_____. 1982. *Education and power.* Boston: Routledge and Kegan Paul.

Bellah, R., R. Madsen, W. Sullivan, A. Swindler, and S. Tipton. 1985. *Habits of the heart.* New York: Harper and Row.

Committee for Economic Development. 1987. *Children in need: Investment strategies for the educationally disadvantaged.* New York: Committee for Economic Development.

Conley, S., T. Schmidle, and J. Shedd. 1988. Teacher participation in the management of school systems. *Teachers College Record* 90: 259–80.

Connell, R. W., et al. 1982. *Making the difference: Schools, families and social division.* Boston: Allen and Unwin.

Darling-Hammond, L. 1985. Valuing teachers: The making of a profession. *Teachers College Record* 87: 205–17.

Deyhle, D. 1991. Empowerment and cultural conflict. Navajo parents and the schooling of their children. *Qualitative Studies in Education* 4: 277–97.

――――. In press. Constructing student failure and maintaining cultural identity. *Journal of American Indian Education.*

Edwards, R. 1979. *Contested terrain: The transformation of the workplace in the 20th century.* New York: Basic.

Ehrenreich, B. 1989. *Fear of falling.* New York: Pantheon.

Fine, M. 1989. Silencing and nurturing voice in an improbable context: Urban adolescents in public school. In *Critical pedagogy, the state and cultural struggle,* edited by H. Giroux and P. McClaren, pp. 152–73. New York: SUNY Press.

――――. 1991. *Framing dropouts: Notes on the politics of an urban public high school.* New York: SUNY Press.

Finn, C., and Ravitch, D. 1984. Conclusions and recommendations. In *Against mediocrity: The humanities in American high schools,* edited by C. Finn, D. Ravitch, and R. Fancher. New York: Holmes and Meier.

Foucault, M. 1982. The subject and power. In *Beyond structuralism and hermeneutics* by H. Dreyfus and P. Rabinow, pp. 208–26. Chicago: Chicago University.

Frymier, J., and B. Gansneder. 1989. The Phi Delta Kappan study of students at risk, *Phi Delta Kappan* 71: 140–46.

Gitlin, A. 1983. School structure, teachers' work and reproduction. In *Ideology and practice in education,* edited by M. W. Apple and L. Weis, pp. 193–212. Philadelphia: Temple University.

Greene, M. 1984. "Excellence," meanings and multiplicity. *Teachers College Record,* 86: 283–97.

Heath, S. B. 1983. *Ways with words.* Cambridge: Cambridge University.

Hirsch, E. D. 1987. *Cultural literacy.* New York: Random.

Hudson Institute. 1987. *Workforce 2000: Work and workers for the twenty-first century.* Washington: Dept. of Labor.

Levin, H. 1990. At risk students in a yuppie age. *Educational Policy* 4: 283–95.

McLaughlin, D. 1991. Placing script and voice at a Navajo chapterhouse. *International Journal of Qualitative Studies in Education* 4: 299–312.

McNeil, L. 1988. *Contradictions of control.* Boston: Routledge and Kegan Paul.

National Coalition of Advocates for Children. 1985. *Barriers to excellence: Our children at risk.* Boston: NCAS.

National Commission on Children. 1991. *Beyond rhetoric: A new American agenda for children and families*. Washington: U.S. Government Printing Office.

National Commission on Excellence in Education. 1983. *A Nation at Risk*. Washington: Dept. of Education.

National Governors' Association. 1986. *Time for results*. Washington: National Governors' Association.

———. 1987. *Bringing down the barriers*. Washington: National Governors' Association.

Odden, A., and D. Marsh. 1988. How comprehensive reform legislation can improve secondary schools. *Phi Delta Kappan, 596–98.*

Ogbu, J. 1978. *Minority education and caste*. New York: Academic.

———. 1987. Variability in minority school performance. *Anthropology and Education Quarterly* 18: 312–34.

Painter, R. 1991. Outcome-based education program. *Utah's educational reform programs*. Salt Lake City: Board of Education.

Poulantzas, N., 1978. *State, power, socialism*. Translated by P. Camiller. London: New Left Books.

Shor, I. 1986. *Culture Wars: School and Society in the Conservative Restoration 1969–1984*. London: Routledge and Kegan Paul.

Slavin, R. 1990. *Cooperative learning: Theory, research, and practice*. Englewood Cliffs: Prentice Hall.

Swanson, A. 1989. Restructuring educational governance: A challenge of the 1990s. *Educational Administration Quarterly* 25: 263–93.

Timar, T. 1989. The politics of school restructuring. *Phi Delta Kappan* 71: 265–75.

Twentieth Century Fund Task Force on Federal Elementary and Secondary Education Policy. 1983. *Making the grade*. New York: The Twentieth Century Fund.

United States Department of Education. 1987. *Schools that work: Educating disadvantaged children*. Washington: U.S. Government Printing Office.

Uzzell, L. 1984. Robin Hood goes to school. In *A blueprint for education reform*, edited by C. A. Marshner. Washington: Genery/Gateway.

Weis, L. 1985. *Between two worlds: Black students in an urban community college*. New York: Routledge and Kegan Paul.

CHAPTER 18

Barrera, R. 1983. Bilingual reading in the primary grades: Some questions about questionable views and practices. In *Early childhood bilingual education: A Hispanic perspective*, edited by T. Escobedo, pp. 164–84. New York: Teachers College Press.

Bissex, G. 1980. *GNYS AT WORK: A child learns to write and read.* Cambridge, Mass.: Harvard University Press.

Calkins, L. M. 1986. *The art of teaching writing.* Portsmouth, N.H.: Heinemann.

Chomsky, C. 1979. Approaching reading and writing through invented spelling. In *Theory and practice of early reading,* edited by L. Resnick and P. Weaver. Hillsdale, N.J.: Erlbaum.

Dyson, A. H. 1983. The role of oral language in early writing processes. *Research in the Teaching of English* 17 (1): 1–30.

———. 1986. Transitions and tensions: Interrelationships between the drawing, talking, and dictating of young children. *Research in the Teaching of English* 20: 379–409.

Edelsky, C. 1986. *Writing in a bilingual program: Habia una vez.* Norwood, N.J.: Ablex.

Flores, B., E. Garcia, S. Gonzalez, G. Hidalgo, K. Kaczmarek, and T. Romero. 1985. *Bilingual holistic instructional strategies.* Chandler, Ariz.: Exito Press.

Freeman, Y. 1988. Do Spanish methods and materials reflect current understandings of the reading process? *The Reading Teacher* 47 (7): 654–62.

Goldenberg, C. 1990. Research Directions: Beginning literacy instruction for Spanish-speaking children. *Language Arts* 67: 590–98.

Graves, D. H. 1983. *Writing: Teachers and children at work.* Exeter, N.H.: Heinemann.

Harste, J., and K. Short, with Burke, C. 1989. *Creating classrooms for authors.* Portsmouth, N.H.: Heinemann.

Hudelson, S. 1987. The role of native language literacy in the education of language minority children. *Language Arts* 64 (8): 827–41.

Peterson, R., and M. Eeds. 1990. *Grand conversations: Literacy study groups in action.* New York: Scholastic.

Children's Books Cited:

Ada, A. F. 1990. *Rimas y risas: Manzano, manzano* (Rhymes and laughter: Apple tree, apple tree). Carmel, Calif.: Hampton-Brown Books.

Carle, E. 1989. *La oruga hambriente* (*The very hungry caterpillar*). New York: Scholastic.

Cowley, J. *El pastel de cumpleanos* (*The birthday cake*). Translated by Miriam Libman and Berta Hollis. San Diego, Calif.: The Wright Group.

Eastman, P. D. 1967. *Eres tu mi mama?* (*Are you my mother?*) Translated by Carlos River. New York: Random House.

Fernandez, L. 1983. *Pajaros en la cabeza* (*Birds on the head*). Mexico City, Mexico: Editorial Trillas.

Kraus, R. 1974. *Jose el gran ayudante (Herman the helper)*. Translated by Rita Guibert. New York: Windmill Books, Inc. and E. P. Dutton.

Lobel, A. 1980. *Sapo y Sepo, inseparables (Frog and Toad, Are Friends)*. Translated by Pablo Lizcan. Madrid, Spain: Alfaguara.

Lionni, L. 1963. *Frederick, K*. Translated by Ana Maria Matute. Barcelona, Spain: Lumen.

Sendak, M. 1984. *Donde viven los monstruos (Where the wild things are)*. Translated by Agustin Gervas. Madrid, Spain: Alfaguara.

Sonneborn, R. A. 1974. *Alguien se exta comiendo al sol. (Someone is eating the sun)*. Translated by Maria Laura Serrano. Buenos Aires, Argentina: Editorial Sigma.

Wylie, J., and D. Wylie. *Un cuento curioso de colores (A fishy color story)*. Translated by Lada Kratky. San Diego, Calif.: The Wright Group.

CHAPTER 19

Bandura, A., and D. Schunk. 1981. Cultivating competence, self-efficacy, and intrinsic interest through proximal self-motivation. *Journal of Personality and Social Psychology* 41: 586–98.

Meier, Deborah. 1987. "We Know Why We're Here AND WE KNOW WHERE WE'RE GOING." Unpublished Memo.

———. 1988. "Thinking About 'The Peopling of the Americas.'" Unpublished Memo.

Perlez, Jane. 1987. "A Harlem school stresses the basics." *New York Times*. 24 May, sec. 1: 42.

———. 1987a. "A Year of Honor in East Harlem Schools." *New York Times*. 27 June, sec. 1: 29.

Sizer, Theodore. 1984. *Horace's Compromise: The Dilemma of the American High School*. Boston: Houghton Mifflin.

Teltsch, Kathleen. 1987. "An East Harlem Learning Citadel Where Openness Rules." *New York Times*. 16 June, sec. 2: 8.

CHAPTER 20

Atwell, N. 1987. *In the middle: writing reading and learning with adolescents*. Portsmouth, N.H.: Heinemann.

Calkins, L. 1986. *The art of teaching writing*. Portsmouth, N.H.: Heinemann.

Graves, D. 1983. *Writing: Teachers and children at work*. Portsmouth, N.H.: Heinemann.

———. 1984. *A researcher learns to write*. Portsmouth, N.H.: Heinemann.

CHAPTER 21

Greenfield, E. 1988. *Nathaniel talking.* New York: Butterfly Children's Books.

Hendrick, H. 1987. *Teaching to change lives.* Portland, OR: Multnomah Press.

Huck, C. 1976. *Childrens literature in the elementary school.* New York: Holt, Rinehart, and Winston.

Van Laan, N. 1990. *Possum come a-knockin.* New York: Knopf.

CHAPTER 22

Albertini, J., and B. Meath-Lang. 1986. An analysis of student-teacher exchanges in dialogue journal writing. *Journal of Curriculum Theorizing* 7 (1): 153–201.

Aoki, T. 1985. Ave atque vale. *Curriculum, Media, and Instruction News and Notes* 8 (19): 1–4.

Eliot, G. 1984. *Middlemarch.* New York: Modern Library.

Freire, P. 1970. *Pedagogy of the Oppressed.* New York: Herder and Herder.

Greene, M. 1978. *Landscapes of learning.* New York: Teachers College Press.

Meath-Lang, B. 1990. The dialogue journal: Reconceiving curriculum and teaching. In *Students and Teachers Writing Together,* edited by J. Kreeft-Peyton. Alexandria, Vir.: TESOL Publications.

Moores, D. 1982. *Educating the Deaf: Psychology, Principles, and Practices.* (2nd ed.) Boston: Houghton Mifflin.

Padden, C., and T. Humphries. 1988. *Deaf in America: Voices from a Culture.* Cambridge, Mass.: Harvard University Press.

Reynolds, W. In press. Critical pedagogy within the walls of a technological institution: Toward a reconceptualization of classroom practice. *Curriculum Inquiry.*

CHAPTER 23

Lemann, N. 1991. *The promised land: The great black migration and how it changed America.* New York: Alfred A. Knopf.

Reich, R. 1991. *The work of nations.*

U.S. House Select Committee on Children, Youth and Families. 1989. *U.S. children and their families: Current conditions and recent trends.* Washington, D.C.: U.S. Government Printing Office.

INDEX